NATHANIEL TAYLOR, NEW HAVEN THEOLOGY, AND
THE LEGACY OF JONATHAN EDWARDS

Recent titles in
RELIGION IN AMERICA SERIES
Harry S. Stout, General Editor

Nathaniel Taylor, New Haven Theology, and the Legacy of Jonathan Edwards

DOUGLAS A. SWEENEY

OXFORD
UNIVERSITY PRESS

2003

OXFORD
UNIVERSITY PRESS

Oxford   New York
Auckland   Bangkok   Buenos Aires   Cape Town   Chennai
Dar es Salaam   Delhi   Hong Kong   Istanbul   Karachi   Kolkata
Kuala Lumpur   Madrid   Melbourne   Mexico City   Mumbai   Nairobi
São Paulo   Shanghai   Taipei   Tokyo   Toronto

Copyright © 2003 by Oxford University Press, Inc.

Published by Oxford University Press, Inc.
198 Madison Avenue, New York, New York 10016

www.oup.com

Oxford is a registered trademark of Oxford University Press

Library of Congress Cataloging-in-Publication Data
Sweeney, Douglas A.
Nathaniel Taylor, New Haven theology, and
the legacy of Jonathan Edwards / Douglas A. Sweeney.
   p. cm—(Religion in America series)
Includes bibliographical references and index.
ISBN 0-19-515428-2
1. Taylor, Nathaniel W. (Nathaniel William), 1786–1858.   2. Edwards, Jonathan,
1703–1758.   3. New Haven theology.   4. New England theology.
I. Title.   II. Religion in America series (Oxford University Press)
BX7260.T32 S94   2002
230'.58'092—dc21   2002022037

I NJG: 186

9 8 7 6 5 4 3 2 1

Printed in the United States of America
on acid-free paper

to

Ken and Lori Fast Minkema,
and Ethan and Adam too,

dear friends

Acknowledgments

I count it a great privilege to have studied Taylor and the Edwardsian tradition with so many fine scholars and teachers. At Vanderbilt University, where this project was conceived, Jack Fitzmier provided sage counsel, substantial moral and financial support, and insightful readings of early drafts, along with Gene TeSelle, Dale Johnson, Lewis Perry, and Ed Farley. At Yale, where the project continued, Skip Sout and Ken Minkema provided expert advice and warm encouragement, and a host of others helped as well with collegial aid of various kinds (most important, Wilson Kimnach and Kyle Farley). At Trinity, where the project was finished, John Woodbridge, Scott Manetsch, Brad Gundlach, and Steve Alter pitched in with judicious conversation, and several student assistants performed crucial bibliographical and editorial tasks (thanks to Rob Caldwell, Matt Harmon, Jonathan Loopstra, David Michelson, Joe Thomas, Brandon Withrow, and John Mark Yeats, outstanding scholars all).

Many others have also read drafts of these chapters and offered beneficial commentary. I am most thankful in this regard to Joe Conforti, Allen Guelzo, and David Kling, the scholars on whose work this project leans most heavily. But numerous other friends and colleagues have helped in this way as well, including Catherine Albanese, Jim Bratt, Jared Burkholder, Paul Conkin, John Dawson, Richard Goode, Howard Harrod, Brooks Holifield, George Marsden, Gerry McDermott, Mark Noll, Randy Page, Larry Rast, Steve Stein, and Alan Watt. As usual, Cynthia Read and Theo Calderara have lived up to their reputations as outstanding editors at Oxford.

Numerous librarians and archivists have contributed both time and talent to this project. With unfailing efficiency and kindness, Jim Toplon and the interlibrary loan staff at Vanderbilt's Heard Library acquired literally hundreds of hard-to-find publications for me. Anne Womack and the circulation staff at the Vanderbilt Divinity Library, as well as Paul Stuehrenberg and his staff at Yale's Divinity Library, eased the burden of my labors in a wide variety of ways. And Robert Krapohl and the staff of Trinity's Rolfing Memorial Library proved extremely helpful toward the end of my research. The staffs of the following manuscript repositories have also made this book much richer than it ever could have been without them: the Beinecke Rare Book and Manuscript Library (especially Ellen Cordes), the Department of Manuscripts and Archives at the

Sterling Memorial Library, and the Divinity School Archives (especially Martha Lund Smalley), all at Yale University; the archives of the Center Church, New Haven (especially Rosemary Platz); the New Haven Colony Historical Society; the New Milford (Conn.) Historical Society (especially Joy Gaiser); the Connecticut Historical Society, Hartford (especially Ruth Blair); the archives of the Schaffer Library, Union College, Schenectady, New York (especially Dorothy Barnes); the Stowe-Day Foundation, Hartford (especially Suzanne Zack); the Case Memorial Library, Hartford Seminary (especially Edna Madden); the Forbes Library, Northampton (especially Elise Feeley); the American Antiquarian Society, Worcester; the Congregational Library, Boston; the Boston Public Library; the Massachusetts Historical Society, Boston; the Houghton Library and the Harry Elkins Widener Memorial Library, Harvard; the Arthur and Elizabeth Schlesinger Library on the History of Women in America, Radcliffe College; the Boston Atheneum; the Franklin Trask Library, Andover-Newton Theological School (especially Diana Yount); the Essex Institute, Salem; the Phillips Academy Archives, Andover (especially Ruth Quattelbaum); the Historical Society of Pennsylvania, Philadelphia; the Presbyterian Historical Society, Philadelphia; the Department of Rare Books and Special Collections (especially William Stoneman) and the Seeley Mudd Library (especially Nanci A. Young) at Princeton University; the Princeton Seminary Archives (especially William O. Harris); the Amistad Research Center, Tulane University (especially Andrew Simons); and the Department of Special Collections, Vanderbilt University.

Special thanks go to Mrs. John H. Conard of West Hartford, Connecticut, and Taylor H. Conard of Greenfield Center, New York, for help in reproducing their portrait of the young Nathaniel Taylor (1807), appearing on p. 2; to "Rollo" Park (grandson of Edwards Amasa Park) and his family for opening up their home in Nashville and inviting me to explore the manuscript treasures in their attic; and to Charles Beach Barlow, owner of the Taylor home in New Milford, the Rev. Michael J. Moran, senior pastor of New Milford's First Church, and Mrs. Delores Dunn, curator of the New Milford Historical Society, for local wisdom and hospitality in Taylor's hometown.

I would also like to express my gratitude to those who have supported this work financially: to the Graduate Department of Religion at Vanderbilt for a University Tuition Scholarship and the George N. Mayhew Fellowship; to the Vanderbilt University Research Council for a Dissertation Enhancement Award; to the Vanderbilt University Graduate School for a Travel Award; to Dean Joe Hough of Vanderbilt Divinity School (now of Union Theological Seminary in New York) for gainful employment and needed diversions at the Cal Turner Program in Ethics and Moral Leadership; to the Friends of the Princeton University Library for a Visiting Fellowship in Princeton; and to the administration of Trinity Evangelical Divinity School (especially Associate Dean Jim Moore) for a generous sabbatical program and funding for research assistance.

As always, Wilma and David have provided the greatest support of all, filling my life with joy and keeping my scholarship in perspective. But this book is dedicated to our friends Ken, Lori, Ethan, and Adam, in thanks for the kind of love and benevolence that would have made the Edwardsians proud.

Contents

Abbreviations

AAP	William B. Sprague, ed., *Annals of the American Pulpit*, 9 vols. (New York: Robert Carter and Brothers, 1857–69).
Beinecke	Beinecke Rare Book and Manuscript Library, Yale University
BR	*The Biblical Repertory and Theological Review* and its successor, *The Biblical Repertory and Princeton Review* (later the *Princeton Review*)
BS	*Bibliotheca Sacra*
CHS	Connecticut Historical Society, Hartford, Conn.
CL	Congregational Library, Boston, Mass.
CML	Case Memorial Library, Hartford Seminary, Hartford, Conn.
CS	*Christian Spectator* (later the *Quarterly Christian Spectator*)
CSL	Connecticut State Library, Hartford
EI	Essex Institute, Salem, Mass.
EM	*Evangelical Magazine*
HM	*Hopkinsian Magazine*
MQR	*Methodist Quarterly Review*
NE	*New Englander*
PHS	Presbyterian Historical Society, Philadelphia, Penn.
PR	*Princeton Review*
PSA	Princeton Seminary Archives, Princeton, N.J.
PUL	Princeton University Library, Princeton, N.J.
QCS	*Quarterly Christian Spectator* (formerly the *Christian Spectator*)
RI	*Religious Intelligencer*
SML	Sterling Memorial Library, Yale University, New Haven, Conn.
SP	*Spirit of the Pilgrims*
Trask	Franklin Trask Library, Andover-Newton Theological School
WJE (BTT)	*The Works of Jonathan Edwards*, ed. Edward Hickman, 2 vols. (Carlisle, Penn.: The Banner of Truth Trust, 1974; 1834).
WJE (Yale)	The Works of Jonathan Edwards (New Haven: Yale University Press, 1957–).

NATHANIEL TAYLOR, NEW HAVEN THEOLOGY, AND
THE LEGACY OF JONATHAN EDWARDS

Introduction

A very great injustice has been done to Dr. Taylor by those who have represented him to the public as a slippery and cautious disputant, whom it was impossible to hold to a definite and intelligible statement. That many of his opponents have failed to understand him correctly, and that it has not always been easy to reach a clear and precise idea of his meaning, is certainly true. . . . It is not easy to appreciate all the distinctions of a mind of unusual accuracy of thought, or to follow a profound reasoner through all the mazes of an abstruse argument. Men are apt to ignore his distinctions, and then think *him* confused or obscure. They overlook or misconceive the qualifications which limit his language, attribute to him a meaning widely different from his real one, and then feel wronged when he unceremoniously disavows the scheme which they have constructed for him. No one who has any acquaintance with the controversies in which Dr. Taylor bore so large a share, can here become familiar with his works . . . without feeling that he, of all the writers of his time, is most wronged when represented as designedly obscure, or evasive. . . . The only writer whom we recall, in our philosophical literature, who even approaches him in this combination of philosophical exactness of discrimination, with profound earnestness of conviction, is Edwards; and it is somewhat remarkable that Edwards is, to this hour, subjected to the most opposite interpretations—is, of course, the most extensively misconceived—and is, of all writers, most liable to the charge of inconsistency and self-contradiction.

B. N. Martin, "Dr. Taylor on Moral Government"

Nathaniel William Taylor (1786–1858), the Timothy Dwight Professor of Didactic Theology at Yale from 1822 to 1858, was arguably the most influential and the most frequently misrepresented American theologian of his generation. As for his influence, Taylor changed the face forever of New England Calvinism. He created a schism in Connecticut's General Association of Congregational clergy. He contributed more than anyone else to the rise of "New School" Presbyterianism—and thus to the Presbyterian schism of 1837–38. He played a formative role in the lives of many of his era's religious leaders, from Charles G. Finney and John Humphrey Noyes to Horace Bushnell and Theodore Munger. He graduated 815 students to positions of prominence in American culture, sending one-fourth of these students out west to lead the churches, colleges, and benevolent societies of the Western Reserve, the Mississippi Valley, even California and the Sandwich Islands. And he played a crucial role in shaping the postbellum development of evangelicalism.[1]

Despite (yet partly because of) Taylor's tremendous national influence, his views were often misunderstood and misrepresented in the media. Although he published some sermons, doctrinal treatises, and polemical essays during his lifetime, he never released a comprehensive exposition of his views. He probably had little right, then, to complain that his opponents had misconstrued him. But complain he did. And truth be told, he was largely correct. His friends published his lectures on the moral government of God and several more of his essays and sermons soon after he died. But by then it was too late. Taylor's foes had made up their minds and his reputation had been muddied for good.

Taylor and his associates always claimed to be Edwardsian Calvinists, or scholars working in the train of Jonathan Edwards (1703–58). Unfortunately for their image in posterity, however, very few people, then or since, have believed them. This fact has made for a very interesting literature, not just on Taylor, but more significantly on the history of the Edwardsian tradition. My interest in Taylor took its rise from a fascination and a certain dissatisfaction with this literature. Scholars have interpreted Taylor's religious identity in a variety of ways, but very few have interpreted Taylor in a manner close to that in which he interpreted himself. This fact strikes me as curious. There is some validity to the maxim that historians ought to try to understand their subjects, at least in certain respects, better than they understood themselves. But after reading Taylor's attempts to define himself, which came in response to the ways in which more "objective" observers had defined his views, I became convinced that Taylor did indeed know his own mind best. I also became intrigued that so many commentators, then and since, have felt otherwise.

This book represents an effort to understand how it is that Taylor and his associates could have counted themselves Edwardsians. More important, this is a book about what it meant to *be* an Edwardsian minister and intellectual in the nineteenth century— about the evolution of the Edwardsian tradition after the death of its esteemed eponym, about the ways in which Taylor promoted and eventually fragmented this tradition, and about the significance of these developments for the future of evangelical America. Though it contains a great deal of biographical material, it is not a standard biography, nor even an intellectual biography. Taylor's life is already well-known and, though I have made an exhaustive study of the papers (both published and unpublished) available for such a work, they do not provide enough detail regarding Taylor's quotidian rounds to justify a significant biographical revision.

They do, however, justify—in fact, *require*—a revision of Taylor's thought and its significance for American intellectual and cultural history. I will argue in what follows that Taylor's theology has been misconstrued by the vast majority of previous scholars.[2] These scholars have interpreted Taylor variously as a Connecticut "liberal," a Jacksonian "Arminian," or a moderate "Old Calvinist." But nearly all have agreed in depicting him as a powerful symbol of the decline of Edwardsian Calvinism and the triumph of democratic liberalism in early national American religion. Giving credence to Taylor's claim to a major part of the Edwardsian inheritance, I will depict him, rather, as a symbol of the vitality of Edwardsian Calvinism throughout the first half of the nineteenth century, a vitality that calls into question some regnant assumptions about this era and the pace of its religious culture's democratization. Moreover, by charting Taylor's role in the modification, diversification, and ultimate dissolution of the Edwardsian tradition, I will demonstrate his significance in the translation of Edwardsian ideals to the ever-expanding evangelical world that would succeed him. In short, the Edwardsian tradition did not die out in the early nineteenth century. Rather, it grew by leaps and bounds until at least the 1840s. And Nathaniel W. Taylor, more than any other single person, laid the theoretical groundwork for this growth—contributing, to be sure, to the demise of the New England Theology, but also making it accessible to an unprecedented number of people.

The pages of this book fall into three parts, each of which is framed anthropologically (or missiologically, to use a more evangelical term). Part 1, "Enculturation" (chapters 1, 2, and 3), includes a narrative history of Taylor's early life and a discussion of his entrance into what I term the theological culture of the Edwardsians.[3] It provides a fuller and more accurate portrayal of Taylor's intellectual formation than ever before, making sense of his scholarly pedigree in relation to this theological-cultural system.

Part 2, "Recontextualization" (chapters 4, 5, and 6), offers a description and historical analysis of the three main features of Taylor's thought—his definition of original sin, his use of the motif of God's "moral government," and his understanding of spiritual regeneration—as well as the ways in which these features both emerged from and perpetuated the Edwardsian culture in his own day and age. I have labored in part 2 to interpret Taylor on his own terms, to do justice to his theology, as well as to show how it was shaped in the main by Edwardsian cultural forces, and not (as is often suggested) by forces external to that culture (though these clearly played a part as well). As I will explain more fully below, this demonstration requires some methodological flexibility on the part of the reader, for much of part 2 is written in a very theological-historical mode. But this kind of internal, theological analysis is crucial to a proper assessment of Taylor's significance and to the effectiveness of this assessment among historians of religious thought.

Part 3, "Implications" (chapters 7 and 8), unpacks the significance of Taylor's recontextualization of the Edwardsian tradition for American religious history, both in New England and beyond. After describing Taylor's life in the wake of the waves his thought produced, I offer a new interpretation of the waning of the New England Theology[4] and end with an assessment of Taylor's importance for post-Edwardsian Protestantism—an importance largely underestimated in other studies of American religion, but one felt deeply as far away as San Francisco and Hawaii; among constituencies as diverse as the Presbyterian Church, the Holiness movement, the Liberty Party, and the Social Gospel (to name but a few, and not to mention many more centrist evangelical leaders and groups); and among the shapers of cultural trends as great in scope as the institutionalization of Anglo-American revivalism and the so-called evangelical great reversal.

Before getting under way, it might be useful to comment further on the challenge of writing a book like this. In the remainder of this introduction, then, I offer a few words about Taylor's status in America's historical memory, and finish with a methodological rationale.

The Taylor of Historical Memory

Though tremendously influential in the religious and social life of the antebellum North, Taylor has been surprisingly understudied. His name has cropped up in myriad works on religion, theology, social reform, and education in New England and on the western frontier. But he has had only one biography, now almost two-thirds of a century old. While virtually all students of antebellum America know something about Taylor, very few know much about him. That which is "known" about him, moreover, usually derives from oral tradition (grounded in secondary sources) rather than independent study. Many have read Taylor's famous sermon on the doctrine of original sin, *Concio ad Clerum* (1828).[5] But few have read any further in Taylor's sizable and quite lively corpus. Students tend to view his work, which was primarily theological, as dry and esoteric. Many of us have heard (or taught) in survey courses on American religion, or on the social and intellectual history of antebellum America, that Taylor symbolizes the decline of New England Calvinism into a grasping and manipulative moralism. Though quite popular, to be sure, Taylor's Arminianizing, revivalistic, evangelical thought has epitomized, at best, a more humane (if somewhat platitudinous) dilution of the strong-willed Calvinism of a bygone era—and, at worst, a controlling demagoguery that played on the worst instincts of the Jacksonian "common man."

As I aspire to prove in the pages that follow, such "knowledge" about Taylor is nothing if not tenuous. The Taylor of historical memory is the creation of a time-honored tradition of literature on America's religious and cultural history. Dating back to before the Civil War, indeed before Taylor's death, this literature has been shaped by the ongoing struggle to locate (or to develop) a kind of spirituality, a religious sensibility or awareness, that can breathe new life into American culture. Quite often this literature has oriented itself in relation to the life and influence of Jonathan Edwards, thought by many to have been either the greatest or the most significant religious figure in American history. Edwards's career spawned the first theological school indigenous to America, a school known as "the New England Theology." The quest to understand Edwards and the New England Theology, then, has proved very significant, not only for those interested in Protestant thought but for those who have sought to interpret and to contribute to American culture as well.[6]

Understandably, because so few scholars have focused their attention on Taylor's own life and thought and because Taylor became most famous in his own day for his controversial relationship to the New England Theology, Taylor's place in this literature has been established primarily by those engaged for one reason or another with the legacy of Jonathan Edwards. The historical Taylor has at times been lost or neglected in this vast literature on Edwards and American culture. But the importance of this literature to America's spiritual life has meant that, when it has treated Taylor, it has usually given him a mythic stature and rendered him larger than life. While failing at times to deal with him in a manner that is reliable or even truly historical, the historiography of the New England Theology, for better and for worse, has granted legendary significance to Taylor's life and thought that has prepared the way for more careful analyses.

While securing Taylor a place in America's cultural memory, the literature on New England religion has certainly not guaranteed him an honorable niche in the pantheon of our nation's spiritual icons. To be sure, a few of Taylor's interpreters have hailed his doctrinal innovations as positive steps in the direction of a more modern, or liberal, religious sensibility. But most have castigated Taylor for what has often been referred to as his deceptive compliance in the degradation of New England theology and, by implication, American religion. The Taylor of historical memory has achieved his significance primarily for the ways in which he symbolizes religious declension, that ever-present danger in the myth of America. Fortunately for his place in posterity, however, Taylor's historiographical stature is disproportionate in relation to the amount of scholarship devoted to him. Our knowledge of Taylor the myth considerably outweighs our knowledge of Taylor the man. His ubiquitous presence in the literature on New England's intellectual and cultural history belies the fact that very few scholars have actually done much work on him. Ironically, Taylor's very historiographical stature complicates the task of those who would seek to address his thought in the context of his own time and his own concerns.

The few scholars who have attempted to interpret Taylor's thought since World War II have done so largely in the shadow of Taylor's biographer, Sidney Mead. As alluded to above, Mead contended in *Nathaniel William Taylor, 1786–1858: A Connecticut Liberal* (1942) that Taylor's essentially liberal religious sensibility placed him among New England's moderate Old Calvinists and beyond the pale of the dogmatic and sectarian Edwardsians.[7] Not only was Taylor reared in the moderate Calvinism of New Milford, Connecticut, whose Congregational church was shepherded by his paternal grandfather and namesake, an ardent Old Calvinist, but Taylor's education at Yale proceeded under the watchful eye of the college's moderate president, Timothy Dwight, whom Mead also claims for Old Calvinism. Reacting against historians who he thought exaggerated the influence of Edwardsians and their revivalism, Mead argued that the "general temperament" of Old Calvinism even "provided a more likely foundation" for the socially and politically oriented revivals of New England's Second Great Awakening than did the purportedly quietistic and apolitical temperament of Edwardsianism. Mead portrayed the Edwardsians as a fringe group and suggested a revision in American religious historiography that would draw the line of succession for New England's religious thought from the Puritans to the Old Calvinists to Taylor's New Haven Theology. "It is possible," he wrote, "that Edwardeanism or Consistent Calvinism was never *the* New England theology."[8]

Mead's interpretation was not without precedent[9] but, in the wake of such broadranging encomiums to the power of "the New England Theology" as George Nye Boardman's *History of New England Theology* (1899) and Frank Hugh Foster's *Genetic History of the New England Theology* (1907), it has made quite a revisionary and lasting impression.[10] Indeed, especially in recent years Mead's interpretation of Taylor has won the minds of most specialists. Mark Noll, Allen Guelzo, David Kling, and, most recently, William Sutton have all portrayed Taylor—for better or for worse, but usually for worse—departing from Edwards and reclaiming the Old Calvinist tradition.[11] Many, however, and especially nonspecialists, continue to characterize Taylor in the manner of his original opponents—as the inveterate Arminianizer of New England Calvinism. Dating back to the epithets against which Taylor fought constantly during the controversy over his New Haven Theology, the notion of Taylor the "Arminian" or "Pelagian" has maintained a strong currency among both friends and foes ever since. William McLoughlin was only the most prominent recent scholar to depict Taylor as either an outright Arminian, a soft Calvinist with strong Arminian tendencies, or a deceptive Arminian wolf in Calvinist sheep's clothing.[12]

Not all scholars interpret Taylor as an Old Calvinist or an Arminianizer, but the vast majority does.[13] In fact, Mead's view of Taylor has combined with Joseph Haroutunian's *Piety Versus Moralism: The Passing of the New England Theology* (1932)—a widely influential neo-orthodox jeremiad against New England's alleged declension after Edwards—to yield a historiography in which Edwardsianism is rarely discussed after 1820, and Taylor can be seen as nothing but the most powerful symbol of its demise. As early critics such as the Old Calvinist clergyman and college president Ezra Stiles (1727-95) have succeeded in defining the New Divinity for most historians since Haroutunian, so have Taylor's Edwardsian opponents—the Tylerites, named after Taylor's arch-rival Bennet Tyler (1783-1858)—succeeded in defining the New Haven Theology. They have set it apart from their own, ostensibly more authentic Edwardsian beliefs, repudiating Taylor's claims of allegiance to New England's Edwardsian tradition. Not all subsequent commentators have shared the Tylerites' animus against Taylor and his followers, but virtually all have shared their notion that Taylor must be distinguished from the Edwardsians as a man of an essentially different spirit.[14]

This has not been entirely infelicitous. There are important differences between Taylor and some of Edwards's more obeisant disciples that must be pointed out in any attempt to assess Taylor and his significance. But there are also some major weaknesses in the traditional interpretations of Taylor, not the least of which is that they fail to account adequately for the Taylorites' self-perceptions. As we shall see, Taylor and his friends consistently claimed fidelity to Edwardsianism, taking pains to distinguish themselves from both Old Calvinism and Arminianism. Traditional interpreters of Taylor have no way of accounting for this, except to assert condescendingly that the Taylorites were either deceiving themselves or being intentionally deceptive about their intellectual loyalties in order to shield themselves from criticism.

Likewise, recent historians have failed to account for the long duration of "the New England Theology," the "New Divinity" or, as I prefer to call it, simply the Edwardsian theological tradition. Insiders and outsiders alike acknowledged the imposing presence of Edwardsianism throughout the first half of the nineteenth century. Scholars and clergy would continue to discuss it matter-of-factly for decades to come. More recently, however, the assumption seems to have been that "the New England Theology" too was a ruse, a conceit invented to legitimate illicit departures from Edwards's teaching. One might well make the case, as some have done in recent years, that Andover's Edwards A. Park (1808-1900), the so-called last of the consistent Calvinists, invented that great monolith or seamless garment that *he* first called the New England Theology in an effort to defend himself against Presbyterian heresy hunters in the early 1850s.[15] But this would be a far cry from the now common notion that the Edwardsian tradition dissolved shortly after the Revolution and, by implication, that Park invented the New England Theology de novo.

In short, our historical memory of Taylor and his times needs filling out. A misleadingly powerful hermeneutics of suspicion, employed first by Taylor's rivals and carried forward throughout the mainstream of American religious historiography, has impoverished our understanding of Taylor and the writings of the New Haven theologians. There is no way around this. But there may be a way through it. By posing new questions about the nature and study of Edwardsian history, we may well find a way to take seriously the Taylorites' self-identity without dismissing the concerns of their critics. In the process, we may also find a way to come to terms with the New England Theology without swallowing all its adherents' claims whole.

Methodological Concerns

Histories of religious thought are not exactly in vogue these days, let alone histories of Protestant theology in New England. As social and cultural history have come to dominate even the study of American religion, and a "new religious history" has risen to prominence in the guild, the avant garde have tended to bypass dead WASP elites from the Ivy League in favor of previously marginalized representatives of the "lived religion" of ordinary folk.[16] Further, as Charles L. Cohen has noted, a "post-Puritan paradigm" has begun to emerge for the study of American religious history, constituting the most important recent development in the field. And "despite—or because of—the attention previously lavished on them, Puritanism, Edwardseanism, and revivalism fare problematically in the new design."[17]

For the most part, these recent trends have proved a boon to those of us interested in developing a fuller and richer portrayal of American religion. Even for those like me who remain most interested in religious thought, the new history can help in the development of more complete interpretations of the roots and fruits of religious ideas in everyday life. Few would contest the compliment of sociologist Rodney Stark that, "in contrast with times past, historians today are more than willing to discuss how social factors shaped religious doctrines." But "unfortunately," continues Stark, "at the same time they have become somewhat reluctant to discuss how doctrines may have shaped social factors." And as historian David Shields has added, "[N]o one reading the manuscripts submitted to the academic presses and journals during the [1990s] can escape the conviction that theological literacy among early Americanists has declined. . . . Now, the controversies that fired the greatest intellects of the Reformed movement seem scarcely fathomable to many."[18]

Sadly, Shields is right. Most American historians are now virtually illiterate theologically. And it is no wonder that the best recent work in the burgeoning field of American religion offers little first-rate analysis of religious thought. What is more, while the new historians have abandoned theologians as subjects of study, theological historians, for their part, have largely ignored the new history. Consequently, a division of labor governs the study of American religion wherein religious thought is usually left to denominational partisans, while most scholars slight the important connections between religious thought and religious practice.

In what follows, I do not pretend to offer a comprehensive social or cultural history of the New England Theology, or even of the New Haven Theology. In order to do justice to the self-perceptions of Taylor and his colleagues, especially with regard to the disputed significance of their thought, I have focused more on Taylor and his role in the evolving *Edwardsian* theological culture than on Taylor's relationship to American culture at large. From a methodological point of view, this is a somewhat unusual approach, and may require a word of explanation.

Cultural history, as many have noted, is rather tricky business. A frustratingly plastic genre of literature, it has come to include almost any kind of historiographical analysis in which one's subjects are interpreted in relation to one or more historical contexts. But as the new religious historians have pursued this genre in recent years, it is fair to say that their primary goal has usually been to broaden our view of American culture (and religion's role within it), not to deepen our knowledge of America's religious traditions. Indeed, most of what passes today as the cultural history of American religion could be described as "religion and" historiography—studies of *religion and* American politics, *religion and* American education, *religion and* race, ethnicity, class, gender, and region. The list goes on. Much of this work has been outstanding and certainly has enlarged our narratives of American cultural history. But implicit within it is the assumption that such grander narratives are most important, that religion should be studied mainly in the service of other kinds of history. In the pages that follow, I do not claim to have bucked this trend altogether. I would not want to. Master narratives are very important, and I hope to contribute to them here. But for reasons that will become clear, I have focused more intently on the theological culture *of* the Edwardsians than on American culture in general *and* the Edwardsians' relationship to it.

When interpreted only in thin, doctrinal terms, or in terms of "religion and" historiography, the Edwardsian tradition remains susceptible to the power of the declension model of religious history. Theologians like Taylor and the secular culture in which he worked can be shown to differ in important respects from Jonathan Edwards and his milieu, and the New England Theology can be assumed to have disappeared by about 1830. When defined in thicker, "culture of" terms, however, it becomes clear that the Edwardsian tradition actually gained momentum during the Second Great Awakening. It included not only those deemed sufficiently orthodox by self-appointed Edwardsian gatekeepers but all those who participated in and took their identity from the expanding social and institutional network that had been sinking roots to support and promote Edwardsian thought. While it certainly evolved with the secular culture, the Edwardsian culture adapted and survived not only the American Revolution but also the radical transformations of America's early national period, supporting Taylor's doctrinal adjustments much as it had supported those of his forebears—and the Edwardsian movement thrived well into the antebellum period.

Unfortunately, it is the thin, genetic, approach and the "religion and" approach to Edwardsian history that have dominated the literature. Edwards's own doctrine and his orientation to American culture have typically been set up as a standard against which the doctrine and cultural posture of his followers have been measured for fidelity. Only those whose doctrinal articulations evinced a sufficient reverence for and a seemingly literal continuity with Edwards's own phraseology—or who proved so culturally conservative that they refused to adapt to the changing times—have been deemed authentically Edwardsian. While these methods of charting the development of the New England Theology do have their advantages (particularly for those most interested in demonstrating the singular brilliance of Edwards's thought or the dangers of Edwardsian "moralism" and "democratic" forms of religion), on the whole it has not proved conducive to the study of nineteenth-century Edwardsian thought, especially that of Taylor.

As Edward Shils has written, "[T]he givenness of a tradition is more problematic than it looks. Every tradition, however broad or narrow, offers a possibility of a variety of responses. Every tradition, given though it is, opens potentialities for a diversity of responses."[19] This is especially true of the Edwardsian tradition, whose eponymous predecessor was such an eclectic. Edwards was an occasional rather than a systematic thinker. He did not present his theology in a well-wrapped package, with all its loose ends neatly tied up. His thought emerged from his pastoral labors, from his love affair with the Bible, and from the heat of controversy. Edwards attracted followers not only with his genius and his defense of Calvinist orthodoxy but also with his passion for things divine and with the elusiveness of his theological system. It was only natural that his followers, as living, breathing thinkers in their own right, should pursue his thought to diverse conclusions. In short, Edwards had never pretended to provide canned answers to life's greatest spiritual questions. And even the most scholastic and dogmatic theologians have always claimed that their theology seeks to give contemporary expression to divine revelation rather than merely to perpetuate the expressions of their predecessors. "Traditions change," argues Shils, "because the circumstances to which they refer change. Traditions, to survive, must be fitting to the circumstances in which they operate and to which they are directed."[20]

For too long now we have tended to portray Edwards's ideas as though they transcended or at least gained the upper hand on the surrounding culture, while we have portrayed the Edwardsians—and especially Taylor—as gradually losing that upper hand, succumbing to their cultural milieu and thus forfeiting their ability to uphold the purer ideals of Edwards. Although it is interesting to debate the ways in which Edwards's ideas could have or should have unfolded in the rarefied air of logical possibility, it is also very important to understand the ways in which Edwardsianism actually did develop on the ground. If we are going to make sense of the claims of dispossessed Edwardsians like Taylor to continuity with the Edwardsian tradition, we will have to resist facile generalizations about the resonance between Taylor's writings and the spirit of his age, and look more closely at what it meant to be an Edwardsian in the nineteenth century. Joseph Conforti and David Kling have laid the groundwork for this project with their careful work on the New Divinity movement and the creation of the Edwardsian tradition. Scholars such as Mark Valeri, as well, have offered culturally sensitive portrayals of early Edwardsian leaders like Joseph Bellamy. But very little of this sensitivity has been applied to the thought of Taylor.[21]

Thus, rather than begin treating Taylor's relationship to the Edwardsian tradition by isolating his best known doctrinal statements and comparing them ahistorically to the statements of his forebears, I will show that Taylor's thought emerged from and was shaped by a uniquely Edwardsian theological culture. I will explain how this intellectual culture gradually surrounded and grounded New England's Edwardsian tradition and suggest the many significant ways in which Taylor stood in continuity with it. Clearly, this will require a measure of methodological dexterity. For in order to demonstrate the power of Edwardsian culture in New England and to do justice to Taylor's theological place within it, I will have to offer, among other things, a thick description of that culture, a theological-historical analysis of Taylor's role in its development, as well as less complicated narratives of Taylor's life and historical significance. But the risk of being labeled a methodological misfit is worth the taking.

In the end, whatever Edwards may have meant by his doctrinal propositions, Edwardsian language gave birth to a rich and relatively diverse theological world. Rather than continue the debate over whether Taylor grasped the true meaning of Edwards's thought, I hope in what follows to elucidate the ways in which Edwardsian language shaped Taylor's religious horizons and the ways in which, for better and for worse, Taylor carried forward the logic of the Edwardsian tradition, contributing mightily to the intellectual culture of evangelical America.

I

ENCULTURATION

1

Birth of a Theologian

The Early Life of Nathaniel Taylor

[He] liked to sit on his mother's lap and be called "Natty."
Rebecca Taylor Hatch, *Personal Reminiscences and Memorials*

Nathaniel W. Taylor was reared in small-town New England—New Milford, Connecticut, to be precise—in Litchfield County, along the east bank of the storied Housatonic River. A town of roughly 3,000 people in the year of Taylor's birth (1786), New Milford supported a largely rural way of life. It boasted more sheep than people, most of the latter working on farms and living a long day's journey by horse from the nearest city. About 35 miles northwest of New Haven (soon to be Connecticut's co-capital), New Milford lay less than 10 miles from the state's wooded border with New York. And though it had hosted a number of Quakers, Episcopalians, Baptists, and Separates, most of its citizens favored the Congregationalism of the standing order. New Milford epitomized Connecticut's "land of steady habits."

But while, like most of the rest of New England before the middle of the nineteenth century, New Milford's economy was largely agrarian and its citizens largely conservative, Taylor's hometown was not as isolated as this might suggest. By 1790, New Milford sustained no fewer than eight tavern keepers (it straddled one of Connecticut's post roads), as well as eight merchants, four blacksmiths, four cobblers, four joiners, three lawyers, two doctors, two silversmiths, two millers, one saddler, one hatter and—last but not least in this era of increased geographical mobility—one wheelwright.[1] Indeed, New Milford proved an integral part of the economic and cultural life of western New England and eastern New York, or the land that lay between the Connecticut and Hudson River valleys. Moreover, its web of connections to the rest of this region guided Taylor's early development, opening his mind to the world around him and making him as much a son of New England as he was of New Milford's farms.

A Sturdy Heritage among the Puritans in the Land of Steady Habits

The Taylor family first settled in Connecticut among the colony's earliest Puritans. In 1639, the family patriarch, John Taylor, migrated from England with the Puritan minister Ephraim Hewitt. He bought land in Windsor the following year and established a successful business there. Beyond this, we know practically nothing about his life.[2]

We do know a bit about his death, however, which was memorialized in Cotton Mather's *Magnalia Christi Americana* (1702). Apparently, Taylor sailed back to England with goods for sale on a poorly built ship, recently constructed in the fledgling colony of Rhode Island. The ship set sail from New Haven's harbor in January of 1647 (O.S.). No one knows for sure what happened, but Taylor was never seen again. According to the Rev. James Pierpont (whose daughter Sarah would later marry Jonathan Edwards) in a letter printed in Mather's *Magnalia*, many of the colonists feared that the ship might not prove seaworthy. Prayers were offered:

"Lord, if it be thy pleasure to bury these our friends in the bottom of the sea, they are thine: save them." The spring following, no tidings of these friends arrived with the ships from England: New-Haven's heart began to fail her: this put the godly people on much prayer, both publick and private, "that the Lord would (if it was his pleasure) let them hear what he had done with their dear friends, and prepare them with a suitable submission to his Holy Will." In June next ensuing, a great thunder-storm arose out of the north-west after which (the hemisphere being serene) about an hour before sun-set, a SHIP of like dimensions with the aforesaid, with her canvas and colours abroad . . . appeared in the air coming up from our harbour's mouth, which lyes southward from the town, seemingly with her sails filled under a fresh gale, holding her course north, and continuing under observation, sailing against the wind for the space of half an hour. . . . her main-top seemed to be blown off, but left hanging in the shrouds; then her mizzen-top; then all her masting seemed blown away by the board: quickly after the hulk brought unto a careen, she overset, and so vanished into a smoaky cloud. . . . The admiring spectators could distinguish the several colours of each part, the principal rigging, and such proportions, as caused . . . the generality of persons to say, "This was the mould of their ship, and thus was her tragick end."[3]

As put to verse in a Longfellow poem that has furthered the memory of this "Phantom Ship" (1850), the story concludes, as it began, with a word of prayer:

> And the pastor of the village
> Gave thanks to God in prayer,
> That, to quiet their troubled spirits,
> He had sent this Ship of Air.[4]

Thus began the colonial ancestry of Nathaniel William Taylor, with the sort of "special providence" that would anchor him firmly in the depths of the New England mind.

To make a long story short, the remainder of Taylor's family history, though full of Puritans and their descendants, proved much more mundane. John Taylor's widow, Rhoda, remarried, this time to a man named Hart.[5] She removed to Norwalk and took her two sons, John and Thomas Taylor, with her. For his part, young John grew up to thrive as a prominent citizen of Northampton, Massachusetts, most famous then for the Congregational ministry of Solomon Stoddard. He served as a Captain of Troop or Horse in the Hampshire County militia, dying in pursuit of a group of Indians on May 13, 1704. Thomas (1643–1734) grew up in Norwalk, eventually married and had 10 children, helping to settle the town of Danbury in 1685. According to Orcutt, he lived as "a prominent and useful man for many years," dying at the ripe old age of 92. Thomas's fourth son, Daniel (1676–1770), who lived to be 94 himself, remained in Danbury his entire life and worked as a farmer. He was said to have been a man of "unblemished character, and much esteemed for his integrity and piety." But most importantly for our story, he fathered the Rev. Nathanael Taylor (1722–1800), the first of the clan to live in New Milford and the venerable grandfather of our central character, the Rev. Dr. Nathaniel William Taylor.[6]

Nathanael Taylor exerted great influence in Connecticut. While but a farm boy he enrolled at Yale, graduating in 1745—though he was best known then as the only student who could kick a football over the college. Upon leaving Yale, he taught in a grammar school for a couple of years in Hampshire County. He received a license to preach on October 7, 1747, and began to supply local pulpits whenever he could. By January of 1748, he was preaching regularly in New Milford and getting to know some of the townspeople rather well. On February 23, in fact, he married none other than Tamar Boardman, daughter of the First Church's founding pastor, the late Rev. Daniel Boardman. It came as little surprise, then, that this church called Taylor unanimously to succeed his father-in-law, ordaining him on June 29 of that very year.[7]

By all accounts, Nathanael Taylor served his congregation diligently and was beloved of the vast majority of New Milford's citizens. As described by the son of one of his friends, "Mr. Taylor, in person, was tall and erect, possessing an uncommonly vigorous constitution, and was active and graceful in all his movements, while his countenance was expressive of great good nature and cheerfulness, and his general manner in society was altogether engaging." As echoed by his own successor in New Milford's pulpit, Stanley Griswold, Taylor "possessed one of the best constitutions of body, vigorous, alert, healthy, endued with great activity and much gracefulness in youth, many marks of which were visible in old age. At nearly four score his frame was bowed but very little, the lustre of his eye was not quenched, and though 'the almond-tree flourished' in his locks, few of his hairs had fallen. His voice was manly and commanding. His presence was venerable."[8]

Taylor's parish, geographically speaking, was the largest in the state, and he kept very busy preaching the gospel and supporting his family. He and Tamar set up house in a sizable parsonage next to the church, raising five children there, three boys and two girls.[9] In addition to his salary, the town gave the Taylors a generous settlement worth a thousand pounds, most of which came in the form of land that Taylor farmed for additional income. As a further supplement to his salary, he opened a grammar school in his home, preparing a goodly number of boys for their entrance exams at Yale. Eventually, all this work led Taylor to the accumulation of substantial wealth, and he became one of the richest ministers in all of Connecticut.[10]

Taylor was best known theologically for his advocacy of Old Calvinism, a fact put to extensive use by Sidney Mead.[11] As stated gingerly by Thomas Robbins, "Mr. Taylor's theology was not after the strictest form of Calvinism, though it was undoubtedly in the main Calvinistic. I suppose he sympathized much more with President Stiles than with Dr. Bellamy." Much more indeed. Taylor sided with Ezra Stiles throughout his controversy with the Edwardsians, serving as a faithful member of the Yale Corporation (1774–1800) during Stiles's tenure as president (1778–95), visiting him frequently in New Haven, and preaching to the students there. In his own congregation, Taylor went so far as to admit unconverted parishioners to communion, a practice that scandalized the evangelicals of New England. And as Edwardsians such as Bellamy took over Taylor's Litchfield County ministerial association (founded in July of 1752), he remained a dissenter, quietly opposing their church reforms (more on these later).[12]

Despite his reputation for Old Calvinism, however, Taylor was best known in New Milford, and almost everywhere else as well, for his practical skills in pastoral ministry and his patriotism during wartime. Beginning in 1759 he served as chaplain of the Connecticut regiment commanded by Colonel Nathan Whiting that fought the French and Indians at Ticonderoga and Crown Point. He preached a famous farewell sermon at the close of this campaign and the soldiers liked it so much that it was published. Too old to serve in the Revolution, Taylor proved his valor once again in April of 1779 by remitting a year's salary to his war-torn congregation—this in the very year that he had persuaded leading parishioners to donate ninety-four pounds and sixteen shillings "for the relief of the distressed inhabitants of the towns of New Haven, Fairfield, and Norwalk." Taylor's most famous parishioner, the patriot lawyer Roger Sherman, lived in New Milford before moving to New Haven in 1761, serving in the Continental Congress and signing the Declaration of Independence. And two of Taylor's sons (Augustine and William) took up arms in the Revolution, Augustine ascending to the rank of general and fighting in the War of 1812.[13]

Such heroism would doubtless have made a much deeper impression upon his grandson than Taylor's Old Calvinism, which by century's end was quickly growing obsolete. Besides, by the time young "Natty" turned four his grandfather had stepped down from New Milford's pulpit, so Nathaniel William Taylor seldom heard the Old Calvinist preach. In 1787, at the age of 65 and after 39 years of ministry to the people of New Milford, the senior Taylor finally asked for an associate pastor. Less than three years later, on January 20, 1790, New Milford's First Church ordained another recent graduate of Yale College, Stanley Griswold of the class of '86. Subsequently, though Taylor preached from time to time in other towns, he rarely filled his former pulpit in New Milford. Now independently wealthy, he surrendered his salary to the church and received only a nominal remuneration until his death in 1800.[14]

Thus, while Mead and others have argued that young Natty Taylor's mind was incubated in a thoroughly Old Calvinist climate, it will become clear upon inspection that the boy's thought and religious identity hatched and matured in a larger world than the one whose roost was ruled by his grandfather. Up and down the Housatonic, and especially in Litchfield County, the religious winds were shifting as Old Calvinists like Nathanael Taylor lay dying. The Edwardsians had begun to ignite the revivals of the Second Great Awakening, fanning the flames of church renewal throughout New England. Even in New Milford, Stanley Griswold harbored doubts concerning his colleague's Old Calvinism. And before long, the First Church itself finally succumbed to the winds of change. Under the influence of a new minister, the Rev. Andrew Eliot, the church did away with the Half-Way Covenant in 1808, a move that led to the closure of New Milford's Separate Church in 1812.[15]

Young Natty in New Milford

Of the Rev. Nathanael Taylor's three sons, only two went off to college—Augustine, who graduated from Yale with the class of 1777; and William, who graduated in 1785. His oldest son, Nathaniel (1753–1818), chose to go into business instead, and soon became a wealthy farmer and apothecary (the townspeople often called him "Doctor

Taylor"). He married a girl from another prominent family in New Milford, Ann Northrup (1751–1810), on August 31, 1774. The two settled down in a stately home that his father built them, next to the church and facing the center of New Milford's scenic town green.[16] Nathaniel and Ann had four children, three of whom survived to adulthood: John (b. September 20, 1777), Charlotte (b. March 20, 1782) and the baby, Nathaniel William (b. June 23, 1786), named after both his father and his uncle.[17]

Unfortunately, little is known about Nathaniel William's boyhood. Orcutt describes him as a "precocious boy" with profound affection for his mother. His daughter Rebecca remembered that he "liked to sit on his mother's lap and be called 'Natty.'" Ann Taylor apparently "idolized him," dressing him up and showing him off, no doubt contributing to the strength of the later theologian's ego. The family had African "servants" as well who surely doted on little Natty, though it is uncertain whether these servants were free or enslaved. In either case, we know that their bonds to the Taylor family proved quite strong, for they were "descendants" of the "people" of the Rev. Nathanael Taylor for whom Nathaniel William Taylor "retained an affectionate interest till their death."[18]

More than anything, Nathaniel William impressed those who knew him with his mind. He was very bright, "an apt scholar," who "always" stood "at the head of his class." But like his grandfather, he also impressed them with his body. As will be seen below, he enjoyed a reputation for virility and good looks, attracting listeners with more than theology alone. He "delight[ed] in sports of every kind," but particularly in the fox hunt. His horsemanship was said to be excellent and he had a "fondness for domestic animals." He loved to hunt and fish. He took great pleasure in the outdoor world. And, as he grew up, he was also known as an avid gardener.[19]

Preparation for Yale College

Taylor prepared for college under the tutelage of Azel Backus (1765–1817), the man who first introduced him to the world of Edwardsian theology. Fatherless since the age of five, Backus converted to Christianity under the ministrations of his New Divinity uncle, the Rev. Charles Backus, a Congregational minister in Somers, Connecticut. Azel went on to Yale, where he graduated in 1789, moving north to become a grammar school teacher in Wethersfield. He read theology with his uncle Charles, was licensed to preach right away (1789), and soon found himself filling the prominent pulpit in Bethlehem, Connecticut occupied formerly by the recently deceased New Divinity leader Joseph Bellamy. Backus settled permanently as Bellamy's successor in April of 1791, continuing Bellamy's practice of preparing boys for college.[20]

Backus was known throughout Connecticut not only as a leading Congregational churchman but also for his unique, backwoodsy and highly emotional preaching style. As Bennet Tyler would remember in a letter to pulpit historian William Sprague,

> His manner and style of speaking in the pulpit were . . . unlike those of any other man. He made no display, and had none of what would be called the graces of oratory. Yet few men have had greater command over an audience than he. He never failed to secure attention, and not unfrequently the whole congregation were melted into tears. . . . He, rarely, if ever, delivered a sermon without weeping. . . . As a pastor, Dr. Backus was greatly beloved.[21]

Backus served as moderator of the General Association of Connecticut in 1808, spear-heading a drive to revive the churches by shoring them up against the "graceless," and barring those who were "Christians only in name" from the Lord's Supper. In a pub-lished address to Connecticut's Congregationalists signed by Backus on behalf of the association, a clear call was made to "come out and be separate" from the unregenerate world. The address denounced both half-way membership and the "formal, slumbering Christians" that comprised it. In classically Edwardsian form, it reasoned that "when churches are composed of members who have only the form, without the power, of godliness, it must needs be, not only that offences will come, but that the discipline, which the gospel requires to be exercised toward the offenders, will be wholly neglected." In honor of his leadership in strengthening America's churches, Princeton awarded Backus a D.D. (Doctor of Divinity) in 1810. He ended his ministry in upstate New York as the founding president of Hamilton College (beginning in 1812), helping to spread his cherished Edwardsian ideals into the west.[22]

Despite such achievements later in life, however, it was Backus's grammar school that proved most important to the history of the New England Theology. An "intimate" friend of President Dwight, Backus sent most of his students on to New Haven, fueling Edwardsian efforts at Yale with his ability to shape young hearts and minds. In the words of his anonymous biographer, "most of his students boarded in his house, ate at his table, and knelt at his altar, and were treated as his children." Such proximity inten-sified both the personal and theological influence that Backus exerted over the boys. It also contributed to his reputation as a committed and caring teacher. In fact, Backus's methods were so highly regarded that he attracted students "from the remotest states" and he "was obliged to refuse many applications for admission." In short, Backus proved an outstanding pedagogue, inspiring similar skills in many of his charges—he enjoyed "the uniform and cordial affection of his pupils."[23]

Most important to our story, Backus "was peculiarly fond of young Taylor." He not only taught Taylor Latin and Greek and sent him packing off to Yale. He also molded his mind—as well as his piety and even his preaching style—after the manner of the Edwardsians. He kept close tabs on the 14-year-old who left his parsonage in 1800 to spend virtually all his remaining years down in New Haven. And he lived long enough to see the fruit of his labors in Taylor's life, dying in the knowledge that his favorite student had become a successful minister. As relayed by one of Taylor's own admiring students, one who seems to have recognized Backus's powerful influence not only on Taylor but (vicariously) at Yale as well: "Dr. Taylor's pupils have often heard him, in that familiar intercourse with them which was so pleasant to him, and both pleasant and instructive to them, give an account of his meeting with Dr. Backus soon after he began to preach. His old instructor pressed towards him, with tears of joy streaming down his face, exclaiming, 'I've heard about you! I've heard about you!'"[24]

2

Coming of Age among the Edwardsians

Taylor's Religious Horizons

> In order to appreciate Dr. Taylor justly, it is necessary to look not merely
> at his theories . . . but at the circumstances and surroundings which evoked
> and largely moulded his thinking. All men, while they have the roots
> of their character and achievements in themselves, are strongly impelled
> and guided in their development and outworking by the external influ-
> ences in which they find themselves immersed. . . . The conditions and
> objects that environ them are the provocatives and objects of their think-
> ing. . . . It is impossible to understand the genesis of Dr. Taylor's theo-
> ries irrespective of the atmosphere he breathed, the training he enjoyed,
> the forms of doctrinal and practical opinion which in his view most ur-
> gently required an antidote, and the evils, real or supposed, which he aimed
> to remedy.
>
> *The Biblical Repertory and Princeton Review*

As might have been expected, the Princetonian who penned these lines did not really
intend for his readers "to appreciate Dr. Taylor justly" as a result of his cultural analysis
of New Haven Theology. He advocated this approach rather to undermine Taylor's thought
by relativizing, indeed trivializing it against the backdrop of "the peculiar chaotic state of
New England theology" which existed "when Dr. Taylor came upon the theatre." He wanted
his readers to know (or at least to believe) that "as [Taylor's] reading and theological culture scarcely extended beyond the astute metaphysical theologians of New England, he
knew little of standard Augustinian and Reformed theology, beyond the fragmentary representations and misrepresentations of it, found in these second-hand, and in many respects, hostile authorities." Consequently, "to the day of his death he never comprehended
this theology in its import, spirit, logic, power. He confounds it with certain dogmas which
it disowns, mere New England provincialisms, and quite as often with the caricatures of
its adversaries."[1] For this writer, as for others who apply the methods of cultural history
to the study of alien or disliked people or ideas, the intent was to pull his subject down a
notch or two, to reveal Taylor's feet of clay, to circumscribe his significance and to make
Princeton theology shine by comparison.

To discuss Taylor's thought as a product of the Edwardsian theological culture,
however, is not necessarily to undermine or trivialize it. While all historical analysis
involves a certain measure of circumscription and delimitation, of contextualization and
thus of relativization, in what follows I am not interested in discrediting Taylor's thought

or belittling his significance. I am interested in the ways his theological heritage shaped and limited his thought world. But I do not believe that these limits per se necessarily undermine his beliefs. While neither a Taylorite, a Tylerite, nor a Princetonian myself, I want to guard against the assumption that by definition the cultural history of ideas denies any enduring value or truth in those ideas.[2] To say that Taylor's theology was shaped and limited by his cultural context is not to say that it has meaning and value only within that context. Whether Taylor was right or wrong about original sin, the moral government of God, or the regeneration of the soul (and surely he was both right and wrong), what is interesting for the purposes of this book is the relationship between his arguments and the development of American Protestantism, especially New England's Edwardsian Protestant tradition. In this chapter, then, after a brief examination of Taylor's college years and immersion into the culture of the Edwardsians, I want to reach back to the era in which that culture first emerged, the era of New England's "Great Awakening," and trace the roots of Taylor's rich Edwardsian heritage.

Trekking the Derby Road

While Taylor was nurtured as a young boy among the agrarians of New Milford and attended grammar school in the rustic parsonage of the little town of Bethlehem, he spent his teenage years and early adulthood in the much wider world of Yale College under the forceful influence of its high-profile president, Timothy Dwight. Dwight was a grandson of Jonathan Edwards, a great promoter of Edwards's legacy and, ironically, an annoyance to leading Old Calvinists in Connecticut. He was the very man that Taylor's grandfather had voted against in 1793 when the Yale Corporation sought a successor to divinity professor Samuel Wales. Two years later, however, he succeeded Ezra Stiles (another opponent) to Yale's presidency—a transition that signaled a minor but significant shift in the school's religious orientation. Almost immediately, he led the college through an old-fashioned Edwardsian revival. And over the course of the next two decades he won Yale over to a moderate, New Light evangelicalism, powerfully perpetuating Edwardsian culture by training a generation of New England's leaders.[3]

The Dwight student who would do the most to further his teacher's theological mantle proved to be Taylor, who matriculated at Yale in the fall of 1800. Barely 14 years old at the time, Taylor trekked the Derby Road that descended from New Milford to New Haven, riding horseback on his grandfather's favorite pacer. He trotted eagerly into New Haven with a maturity far beyond his years. Little did he know then that he would stay for most of the rest of his life, dying nearly 60 years later in that very place.[4]

According to the U.S. census, New Haven had 5,157 residents in 1800, a number that increased by 800 percent during Taylor's tenure there. Already the third largest city in New England (after Boston and Providence), New Haven would grow during Taylor's lifetime into one of the largest industrial towns in one of the world's great industrial regions.[5] By 1800, nearby Hamden boasted a mass-production armory that had been founded two years earlier by the famous inventor Eli Whitney. New Haven, for its part, boasted a lucrative shipping business that facilitated the emergence of the area's mercantile economy. Progress was slow by current standards. Taylor would enter middle age before he enjoyed running water, a sewer system, paved sidewalks, paved streets, or even street lights. He lit his room at college, and later at home, with wax candles and whale-oil lamps, living largely in the dark after dusk. Further, the Embargo Act of 1808, and then the War of 1812, exerted a devastating effect on the local economy. But by 1821 the town green was off-limits to cattle. By 1822 New Haven's first steamboat line began. By 1839 its inhabitants enjoyed railroad service to Hartford, and by 1848 they could ride the rails to New York City. On the eve of the Civil War, no fewer than four railroad companies housed principal offices in New Haven. Three others housed branch offices. And four steamboat companies continued to maintain headquarters in town. With business booming, New Haven remained the largest city in Connecticut. And it was poised for even greater growth in the wake of the Civil War.[6]

Taylor's first semester at Yale took a toll upon his health for, like many of his peers preparing for positions of leadership in society, he taxed his body and his brain without the aid of modern technology. During his first semester at Yale, he suffered both visual impairment and what he called "rheumatism," experiencing so much pain that he had to return home. He enrolled again the next fall. But his eye trouble recurred, and he repaired a second time to the consoling arms of his adoring mother. Now despondent, he stayed in New Milford until the fall of 1805, when he finally returned to graduate with Yale's class of 1807. As Taylor remembered years later, "[W]hen I came [to Yale] the last time, (for I entered three different classes,) it was rather to gratify my parents, than with any expectation or intention of being a scholar; for, though I had previously felt an intense interest in study, I had by that time entirely lost it. Occasionally, however, my emulation was stirred; but it was to little purpose, as I had abandoned the thought of either doing or being much in future life."[7]

It was not until the end of Taylor's junior year at Yale that his attitude had changed with regard to the purpose of his studies. Not coincidentally, it was also at the end of his junior year that Taylor experienced conversion under the ministry of Timothy Dwight. As Taylor's daughter later recalled, "[T]he first ray of hope which came to him in his distress was hearing Dr. Dwight, in one of his prayers at college, repeat the text, 'A bruised reed shall he not break, the smoking flax shall he not quench' [Is. 42:3 and Matt. 12:20]." Soon thereafter, Taylor entered a period of intense introspection that culminated in a meeting with the president. As one of Taylor's students later recounted,

> There was a classmate and particular friend of his, who at the same time, by the working of the Divine Spirit, was concerned for his eternal interests. The two friends communicated their feelings to each other. And one day, while walking together, they raised the question whether they should call on President Dwight, who had invited all persons thoughtful upon religion to call and converse with him. At length, while still talking and doubting on that question, they came to Dr. Dwight's gate. There they stopped and hesitated. Soon, Taylor said, 'Well, I shall go in.' 'Well,' rejoined his companion, 'I think I will not, to-day.' Taylor did go in. And the result of his conversation with that eminent Christian guide, was that he gave himself to Christ, in a covenant never to be broken.

Taylor's anonymous companion never converted. But the relationship then cemented between young Taylor and his mentor Dwight did lead to the conversions of many others. And as Taylor went on to surpass his spiritual guide in the world of theology, he frequently attributed his achievements to Dwight's supervision of his new birth. In the years to come, in fact, the two would often remember Taylor's conversion and would encourage one another with the hope of eternal life. As Taylor remembered, Dwight's "heart melted under" this evangelical hope. "The tears flowed freely" as they discussed the world to come.[8]

During college, Taylor initiated a lifelong friendship with Stephen Van Rensselaer, son of the wealthy General Stephen Van Rensselaer of Albany, New York (one of the last of the Dutch patroons). And though their friendship is said to have cooled a bit after Taylor's evangelical conversion, they remained close and traveled together after they graduated. They journeyed to Montreal in order, they claimed, to study French, planning a tour of Europe together the following spring. Taylor served as the younger boy's "tutor," working with him for several months. Tellingly, though, before too long these friends parted ways. "The gay life became so irksome to my father," remembered Rebecca, "that after a few months he returned to New Haven and entered Dr. Dwight's family." He stayed in touch with his once-born friend, but the two shared little in common. And Taylor devoted the rest of his life to the work of gospel ministry.[9]

By entering "Dwight's family" Taylor became an apprentice in ecclesiastical leadership, taking room and board in Dwight's house in 1808 and 1809, and reading theology with Dwight for another two post-baccalaureate years. During this time, these soul brothers grew even closer to one another—so much so that, as Taylor's friend Leonard Bacon would put it later, "to say that [Taylor] was a favorite pupil of President Dwight, does not adequately express the intimacy of the relation between them." Taylor served as the elder man's secretary, a position coveted by students at Yale. As John R. Fitzmier has explained, the aging president had long suffered from exceptionally poor eyesight. Functionally blind by this point in his life, he was given funds by the Yale trustees to hire a scribe. While Taylor served in this capacity he helped Dwight to draft his systematic theology, which was comprised of a round of sermons he had preached for years in the college chapel. Taylor cut his scholarly teeth on Dwight's *Theology: Explained and Defended* (1818-19), eating it up and strengthening his resolve to become a theologian himself.[10]

Most important for the New England Theology, this apprenticeship represents the period in Taylor's life when he was baptized by immersion into the culture of the Edwardsians. True, Dwight's Edwardsian credentials have been contested by more scholars than Sidney Mead. He was, after all, a privileged member of Connecticut's standing order and not a sharped-edged critic (like the most radical Edwardsians) of New England's religious establishment. Nevertheless, he remained strongly devoted throughout his life to the theology of his grandfather Edwards, as well as to that of his uncle—and New Divinity mentor—Jonathan Edwards, Jr. And he did as much as anyone else in America's Revolutionary generation to take the concerns of the Edwardsians into the corridors of New England's cultural power.

Indeed, Dwight declared two years before his death that "the two Edwardses, father and son, have exhibited as high metaphysical powers, as Europe can boast; and have thrown more light on several abstruse subjects, of the highest importance, than all the Philosophers of that continent and [Great Britain], united." In his well-known *Travels in New England and New York*, Dwight claimed that he had "not a question" concerning the "truth" of his grandfather's theology, asserting that "the late President Edwards has more enlarged the science of theology than any divine of whom either England or Scotland can boast; and the loss of his works would occasion more regret than . . . the whole literary world, would feel for the loss . . . of the whole works of half the ancient authors now extant." In a letter to an English correspondent in 1805 Dwight had clarified that he objected to Hopkinsian extremes (discussed later) precisely because he thought Edwards had "gone as far" theologically "as the Bible warrants." Dwight had shown himself a faithful Edwardsian upon his ordination and installation at Greenfield, Connecticut (1783), by eradicating the Half-Way Covenant there. And Dwight's ministerial students at Yale took in a diet consisting almost entirely of Edwardsian theology.[11]

But what did this diet look like? And how had it become so popular? In short, what exactly did it mean for Taylor to enter the culture of the Edwardsians? To answer such questions well I must go back to the era of the Great Awakening and trace the emergence of the Edwardsian theological tradition. To do so will require a departure from the story of Taylor's life, as we flash back to an era that pre-dates his time at Yale. But, in the end, such an exercise will enrich the primary narrative by deepening our understanding of Taylor's place among the Edwardsians.

The Sociology of New England's Great Awakening

At least since 1948 when Perry Miller published "Jonathan Edwards' Sociology of the Great Awakening," students of colonial America have taken a keen interest in the social and political aftermath of the pan-colonial revivals of the 1740s. Miller confessed that Edwards himself was primarily a "Pietist" who lacked a sophisticated social theory and for whom the only problem that really mattered "seemed to be the 'distinguishing marks' of a work of grace." But he insisted that Edwards's "career in Northampton was every bit as intense a social experience as that of Aristides in Athens." Despite Edwards's intoxication with the divine, he did have social concerns, he led a revival that carried great social implications and, as the extracts from the manuscript sermons printed in Miller's essay demonstrated, he was even known to have engaged in cultural criticism from the pulpit: "Even while he had his eyes fixed on heaven, his feet were on the earth." Because he was a renowned public figure, his teachings could not help but take on a more than strictly spiritual significance.[12]

It was Edwards's international fame as the theologian of revival that ensured for him this broader, cultural significance. While his private notebooks reveal that his theology had begun to crystallize quite early in his career,[13] not until the revivals known for over 150 years now as "the Great Awakening" did Edwards become a major public figure. In recent years historians have questioned the utility of the phrase "the Great Awakening" to describe what some depict as a sporadic, largely unrelated and heterogeneous series of revivals that shared no clear-cut chronological or regional parameters.[14] But whatever the utility of this phrase for delimiting all the revivals of mid-eighteenth-century America, the New England revivals of the 1740s did prove, in historian Edwin Gaustad's words, great and general: "The Great Awakening of New England was not a series of isolated revival meetings, held over a period of several decades—as was the case in the middle and southern colonies. It was a rushing flood that swept over all the land, recognizing no boundaries, whether social, civil, or ecclesiastical, leaving no inhabited area untouched, and receding as suddenly as it had come."[15] While Edwards was not the only leader of the pro-revival New Light party, he and his New Divinity disciples played a powerful role in the restructuring of New England religion. Though a few hotly contested finer points of New Divinity doctrine and the often extreme and embarrassing side effects of their fellow New Lights' coarse and histrionic methods inhibited Edwardsian successes in the pre-Revolutionary period, by the end of the eighteenth century the Edwardsian party had effected a minor transformation of New England society.

The story of New England's Great Awakening and its aftermath has been told often and told well. For our purposes, though, it is important to highlight the consequences of the Awakening for the Edwardsians and their place in New England society. For Edwards and many other New Lights, the revivals came as a godsend. These clergymen had worried for some time that their parishioners were languishing spiritually, suffering from the twin dangers of laxity and self-sufficiency in religion. Theologized then and since as the errors of antinomianism (apathy or opposition to divine law) and Arminianism (self-determinacy in salvation), respectively, these dangers had haunted New England towns since at least the 1630s. To many, however, they seemed especially threatening in the generation or so preceding the Awakening. While the well-worn cyclical interpretation of American religious history—with its continuous, cyclical sequence of religious decline and revival—has come under critical scrutiny in contemporary historiography, and while it is now clear that the Great Awakening did not represent a simple reversal of the alleged decline in religious adherence and theological orthodoxy in the early eighteenth century, it is also clear that many of the participants in New England's Great Awakening deemed the first third of the eighteenth century a period of religious declension. Edwards certainly did. In his famous *Faithful Narrative* (1737) of the Northampton revival of 1734–35, he noted that the 1720s and early 1730s had constituted "a far more degenerate time . . . than ever before."

> The greater part seemed to be at that time very insensible of the things of religion, and engaged in other cares and pursuits. Just after my grandfather's death [1729], it seemed to be a time of extraordinary dullness in religion: licentiousness for some years greatly prevailed among the youth of the town; they were many of them very much addicted to night-walking, and frequenting the tavern, and lewd practices, wherein some, by their example exceedingly corrupted others. . . . and indeed family government did too much fail in the town. . . . There had also long prevailed in the town a spirit of contention between two parties, into which they had for many years been divided, by which was maintained a jealousy one of the other, and they were prepared to oppose one another in all public affairs.[16]

In addition to this rise in religious laxity and apathy, moreover, Edwards also lamented an increase in what he and his colleagues termed Arminianism. Though this term had become something of a "bogy" by this time, employed widely by the orthodox to condemn heresies much broader in scope than those originally opposed by the anti-Arminian Counter-Remonstrants at the Synod of Dordt (1618–19), the increasing appeals of New England's theological liberals to a rational religion of human decency and goodness did pose a genuine, albeit minor, threat to the Calvinists' doctrines of grace.[17] About the year 1734, wrote Edwards, "began the great noise that was in this part of the country about Arminianism, which seemed to appear with a very threatening aspect upon the interest of religion here. The friends of vital piety trembled for fear of the issue." Edwards himself, however, remained calm and dealt with this "noise" by preaching a firmly

Calvinistic sermon series on justification by faith. The Northampton revival of 1734–35 ensued, priming the revivalistic pump for the Great Awakening five years later.[18]

During and after New England's Great Awakening, Edwards and his followers would endeavor to steer a consistent middle course between the poles of antinomianism and Arminianism. As noted well by William Breitenbach, they struggled against difficult odds to maintain a traditional theological balance of both divine sovereignty and human responsibility, grace and law, piety and moralism.[19] The centrifugal forces of spiritual frenzy often associated with the revivals militated against this effort; but the Edwardsians persisted, refusing to prejudge any potential sign of the Spirit (however unusual), though insisting that alleged signs be measured against the teachings of the Bible and the canon of Christian charity. Indeed, distinguishing authentic works of the Spirit from their counterfeits soon became the chief theological task of the Edwardsian revivalists. Their beloved Awakening had unleashed the mighty forces of sectarianism in New England and by the Revolutionary period a variety of sects had mushroomed on the fringes of New England society, exhibiting both antinomian and Arminian tendencies. As Edwards lamented to his Scottish correspondent John Erskine in July of 1750, "the devil's devices in the various counterfeits of vital, experimental religion, have not been sufficiently attended to, and the exact distinctions between the saving operations of the Spirit of God and its false appearances not sufficiently observed." In his effort to rectify this problem, Edwards recommended Joseph Bellamy's *True Religion Delineated* (1750) as that which "has a tendency to give as much light in this matter, as any thing that ever I saw." He asserted in a laudatory preface to Bellamy's work that clerical efforts to guard against undue enthusiasm by delineating true from false religion provided "the greatest possible service to the Church." History had shown that even the greatest revivals could be "nipt in the bud" if their leaders failed to undertake this crucial task.[20] Bellamy's book would eventually approximate, in one historian's words, a "*Pilgrim's Progress* of New England." As Harriet Beecher Stowe's Horace Holyoke remembered of his grandmother's well-worn "blue book" (*True Religion Delineated*) in a moment of exaggeration, "there is not the slightest doubt that it was heedfully and earnestly read in every good family of New England; and its propositions were discussed everywhere and by every body."[21] Whether read as a theological treatise for pastoral study or a bedside manual for pious revival converts, *True Religion Delineated* symbolized for many New Englanders the larger Edwardsian concern to guard against both antinomian and Arminian extremes.

Though unhappy when the revivals got out of hand and when they lost control of the evangelical enthusiasm they had helped to generate, the Edwardsians bore a certain measure of responsibility for the rise of sectarianism in New England. Their heavy emphasis on experimental religion and the purity of the church had encouraged the very separations from polluted mainstream Congregationalism that they lamented. Especially in New England's hill country and the frontier regions of the north, but throughout the more settled regions as well, the revivals divided Congregational parishes over issues such as the necessity of the new birth, the nature of moral purity, the requirements for church membership, and the right use of baptism and the Lord's Supper. As historian James Walsh has demonstrated, "schism was so rampant" after the Awakening "that it seems every church in Connecticut suffered a separation at some time."

Historians of New England's frontier regions have testified that sectarianism and the proliferation of new denominations became even more prevalent there. By the time of the Revolution, for example, one-third of New Hampshire's churches were non-Congregational. While the Great Awakening of the 1740s had not been able to permeate the sparsely settled, fledgling townships of the north to the extent that it had the more established regions of central and southern New England, the north enjoyed tremendous demographic and economic expansion in the years prior to the American Revolution. By the late 1770s and early 1780s its inhabitants would experience yet another powerful revival, known as the New Light Stir on the New England frontier and the New Light revival in Maritime Canada. Mainstream Congregationalists did participate in this later revival but the New Light Stir became particularly important for the spread of sectarianism in these areas. As Stephen Marini has shown, "between 1770 and 1815 the frontier became a stronghold not for traditional New England Congregationalism, but for Radical Evangelical dissent." In short, the Great Awakening had opened the floodgates of religious enthusiasm and pluralism, permitting a wide variety of sects— from the antinomian Sandemanians to the Arminian Freewill Baptists to even more radical groups such as Mother Ann Lee's Shakers—to flourish, and allowing the Edwardsians' worst fears for the revivals to come true.[22]

Such divisive fruits of the Awakening tasted bitter to many New Englanders and, not surprisingly, a formidable opposition arose quite early on to face Edwards and his fellow New Lights. Led by Boston's Charles Chauncy, New England's Old Light party comprised both Enlightenment rationalists such as Ebenezer Gay and Lemuel Briant who deemed New Light religion harmful, and some "catholick" moderates such as Nathaniel Appleton and Edward Holyoke who advocated affectional religion but were suspicious of the revivalists' methods. After an extensive tour of New England, New York, and New Jersey, where he observed revival excesses first-hand and warned the churches against rising enthusiasm, Chauncy composed his now famous tour de force against the Awakening, *Seasonable Thoughts on the State of Religion in New England* (1743). He charged the revivalists with antinomian heresy and called his readers back to a more measured and reasonable Christianity. In response to the morally irresponsible and often slanderous messages of New Light extremists such as James Davenport and Andrew Croswell, the Old Lights also passed legislation restricting itinerant preaching. While often labeled liberal for their loose theological demeanor and their influence in the later rise of American Unitarianism, the Old Lights in this period usually presented themselves as conservative defenders of the status quo. They advocated a renewed respect for and maintenance of New England's parish boundaries and clerical establishment, a traditional attendance on the means of grace, and a conservative piety that avoided emotional extremes.[23]

Edwards and his supporters winced at Old Light criticisms. Despite the undeniable novelty in New Light practices, New England's mainstream revivalists held traditional or conservative evangelical hopes for the Awakening.[24] They, too, worried when fellow New Lights became divisive and threatened to subvert the New England Way; and they bore guilt by association with more radical peers. In the wake of the revivals, the Edwardsians' middle course became more and more difficult to steer, and when Edwards himself was ejected from Northampton in 1750 and branded hastily with pure-church extremism, their cause appeared hopeless. A small band of Edwards's students and close followers stuck by him during those first few trying years at the Stockbridge Indian mission. But before Edwards published his major theological treatises on the *Freedom of the Will* (1754) and *Original Sin* (1758), few would have guessed that by century's end the Edwardsians would constitute the most powerful religious party in New England. Even after Edwards's premature death in March 1758, his New Divinity disciples had to struggle to gain respectability. Already tarnished by New Light extremes and Old Light critiques, their reputation suffered even further when a group of former moderate New Light colleagues and theologically conservative Old Lights coalesced expressly to oppose them. While never comprising a very clearly defined movement, these new anti-Edwardsians called themselves "Old Calvinists." They attempted to marginalize Edwardsian theology as "New Divinity" based on pure church fanaticism and they portrayed themselves as the party of traditional New England orthodoxy. They professed to adhere more closely than the Edwardsians to the Calvinism of the Westminster standards and by the late 1760s had coined the moniker "Hopkintonian" or "Hopkinsian" to associate all the Edwardsians with the controversial doctrinal innovations of Edwards's best-known follower, Samuel Hopkins.[25]

Needless to say, New England's Great Awakening did not turn out to be all that Edwards had hoped. The revivals subsided; many parishioners reverted to harmful pre-Awakening habits; others joined new sects; a few (Edwards's uncle Joseph Hawley included) even committed suicide. Further, by midcentury the Awakening had produced at least four major factions on the region's religious landscape—the Edwardsian-led New Lights, the Separates/sectarians, the Old Lights, and the Old Calvinists—only one of which continued to pursue Edwards's own agenda.[26] The Edwardsians were now clearly but one party among several competing for New England's religious allegiances. Ironically, however, while this fact compromised the Edwardsians' commitment to evangelical unity, it also enabled them to secure a unique and lasting place for themselves at New England's ecclesial table. Their struggle to maintain a consistent course in the face of sectarian defections and the invectives of both Old Lights and Old Calvinists fostered an amalgamation of their energies and yielded an impressive amount of solidarity. Throughout the second half of the eighteenth century the New Divinity clergy would take advantage of their newfound esprit de corps to infiltrate New England culture with a more specified, uniquely Edwardsian religious and theological agenda than would have been imaginable a few years earlier. By the Revolutionary era the New Divinity movement constituted the most clearly defined religious movement in the region.

The Rise of an Edwardsian Theological Culture

Reared in a Puritan culture that was superficially unitary and coherent,[27] in the wake of the Great Awakening the Edwardsians found themselves entrenched in religious combat with many whom they might have deemed consorts just a few years earlier. While the New Divinity movement arose originally to promote a cautious via media between the religious extremes augmented by the revivals, the Edwardsians' ongoing effort to defend their ministries from the charges of these new foes led them to erect theological boundaries around their movement that revealed minor but significant departures from traditional Puritan orthodoxy. Ironically, their attempts to formulate a theology of revival that mediated between antinomianism and Arminianism provoked charges that the Edwardsians themselves harbored both antinomian and Arminian tendencies and New Divinity theology became famous for its innovations rather than for its traditionalism. Edwards A. Park, the Edwardsians' greatest defender, once explained that their theology proved "original and novel, because it combines the one-sided truth which the Antinomian had distorted, with the one-sided truth which the Arminian had distorted; separates the two truths from the errors with which the Antinomian and the Arminian had intertwined them, and harmonizes the two into one capacious system."[28] But whether or not the Edwardsians had succeeded in reaping the wheat from both fields—the antinomian insistence on divine sovereignty and the Arminian emphasis on human responsibility—without also taking any of the chaff, by the Revolutionary period the novelty of the New Divinity was seldom questioned.

Gaustad has claimed that the New England Theology "was the monument of the Awakening."[29] No one would contend that it constituted the only such monument; but the New England Theology did leave an enduring memorial to the theological imagination of New England's evangelical Calvinists. Indeed, it comprised colonial America's first indigenous theological tradition. Theologically conservative Old Lights and Old Calvinists clung to the traditional formulas of the Westminster Assembly (1647–48); theologically liberal Old Lights echoed religious concerns first voiced by dissenters and Latitudinarians in Great Britain; and sectarian New Lights patterned their religious commitments after Britain's radical dissenters, though usually leaving formal theology to their elitist counterparts in the established churches. But the Edwardsians sought to infuse traditional Calvinist doctrines with freshness, immediacy, and contemporaneity, recontextualizing their Puritan heritage for eighteenth-century New England. As we have seen, critics of the Enlightenment have denigrated their attempts to do so as anthropocentric and moralistic. Others have deemed traditional Calvinism incompatible with the age of Enlightenment and thus portrayed Edwardsian theology as inconsistent. In the words of one recent historian, "to declare oneself for the experimental method while determining to preserve one's faith is like inviting venomous snakes into one's home while determining never to be bitten."[30] But some scholars have begun to move beyond the now standard criticisms of Perry Miller's hyperbolic claims for Edwards's modernity and reexamine the ways in which the Edwardsians and other eighteenth-century evangelicals engaged the leading intellectual concerns of their era without fully embracing them. While it is clear that not all the results of this engagement derived directly from Edwards's own appropriation of Calvinism, the innovations of the New England Theology did stem largely from Edwards's creative attempts to reanimate his Puritan legacy with the spirit of his age.[31]

Though often equated with the doctrinal particularities of its best-known spokesman, Samuel Hopkins, New Divinity theology was always more multifarious than this identification suggests. Critics often lumped all Edwardsians together as Hopkintonians or Hopkinsians, and Hopkins's *System of Doctrines* (1793) did serve to codify the New Divinity for many outsiders,[32] but Edwardsians disagreed frequently over doctrinal details and Hopkins himself resisted the use of his name as a party label. As he once wrote to the Princetonian Samuel Miller, "[N]o scheme of doctrines have got the name of *Hopkintonian* by my consent or [the] invention or desire of any of my friends. This was the invention of the late Rev. William Hart of Saybrook, a reputed Arminian."[33]

Even Hopkins's closest friends and disciples could prove critical of his theology. Soon after the publication of his *System*, Jonathan Edwards, Jr., wrote him with a list of 24 criticisms of the work. While Hopkins had solicited Edwards's comments and while Edwards expressed great admiration for his mentor's work overall, Edwards's critique was not atypical among Edwardsians. Likewise, Hopkins disapproved of the ways in which many younger New Divinity colleagues promulgated Edwardsian dogma. In a conversation with the future Princeton president Ashbel Green in 1791, he complained that "they were rash and imprudent, and made unjustifiable expressions; and that they proclaimed their peculiar sentiments too much on all occasions, where they had not time fully to explain them and to guard them against abuse." Historians have consistently distinguished at least two identifiable subtraditions within the Edwardsian movement—one stemming from the often sharp-edged polemics of Hopkins and Emmons and the other emanating from the more evangelical and ecumenical strains of Bellamy and Dwight. And while it is important not to exaggerate the differences between the fraternal ranks of Edwardsian theology, it is also important not to dismiss Edwardsian thought as monolithic or hegemonic.[34]

Despite the relative diversity of New Divinity thought, however, the Edwardsians did enjoy a great deal of theological unity and comradery, agreeing almost unanimously on the basic outlines of a few core concerns. These concerns centered, moreover, around two distinctive foci from which all other Edwardsian commitments radiated: the emblematically Edwardsian distinction between the natural and moral ability to obey God, and the Edwardsians' thoroughgoing insistence on immediate repentance. William Breitenbach has referred to the distinction between natural and moral ability as "undoubtedly the most important mark of the New Divinity," the "shibboleth of their tribe." Sidney Mead once described it, tongue in cheek, as "that most subtle tool of all the New England theology . . . which enabled [Edwards's] followers to perform marvels of dialectical ingenuity, even to hold apparently diametrically opposite ideas as entirely consistent."[35]

Edwardsians had been wielding the distinction since its definitive American articulation in Edwards's *Freedom of the Will* (1754), using it to combat liberal foes who questioned why the God of the Calvinists held sinners damnable for an inborn, natural depravity that did not lie within their power to change. If we entered the world dead in trespasses and sins, asked these critics, what right would God have to hold us accountable to the moral law? The Edwardsians responded by first chiding the liberals for questioning the goodness and sovereignty of God, and then arguing that God does not hold us accountable for that which we are powerless to do. Original sin had not eradicated our natural capacity to obey the divine commands, but had only disoriented the human will and affections so that sinners no longer desire what is right. As Edwards himself contended, "sin destroys spiritual principles, but not the natural faculties. . . . There seems to be nothing in the nature of sin, or moral corruption, that has any tendency to destroy the natural capacity, or even to diminish it, properly speaking."[36]

Edwards had explained this by analogy. He told of two prisoners, one a repentant prisoner bound by chains and prison bars but teased with an offer of pardon if only he would rise up and beg for it at the feet of his king, the other a "haughty, ungrateful, willful" prisoner who had been given the same offer, but whose chains had been removed and whose prison door had been opened. Though naturally or physically able to comply with the terms of his release, the second prisoner proved "so stout and stomachful, and full of haughty malignity, that he can't be willing to accept the offer: his rooted strong pride and malice have perfect power over him, and as it were bind him, by binding his heart." For Edwards, these prisoners exemplified the difference between natural and moral necessity and, concomitantly, between natural and moral ability. The first prisoner suffered under a natural necessity to remain in prison, a natural inability to do what he wanted, and thus could not be blamed for his condition. The second prisoner, however, could be blamed. He remained in prison only by a moral necessity. Though naturally able to experience release, he was morally unable (because unwilling) to do so. Driving this distinction home, Edwards asked rhetorically: "[W]ho can't see, that when a man, in the latter case, is said to be 'unable' to obey the command, the expression is used improperly, and not in the same sense it has originally and in common speech? And that it may properly be said to be in the rebel's power to come out of the prison, seeing he can easily do it if he pleases; though by reason of his vile temper of heart which is fixed and rooted, 'tis impossible that it should please him?" Edwards's followers would make great use of this logic. In a move that distanced them somewhat from most traditional Calvinists, they based their doctine of human depravity strictly on voluntary or moral inability rather than on any kind of physical or natural necessity, insisting that the sinner "can" obey God if only "he will."[37]

Most of the New Divinity's defining doctrines derived from this creative and controversial distinction. Such key Edwardsian notions as the moral government theory of the atonement, the doctrines of disinterested benevolence, and the willingness to be damned for God's glory each emanated from their emphasis on the human freedom to do as we will and concomitant denial that human nature itself necessitates against our willing true virtue. The traditional Calvinistic understanding of the atonement seemed to subject sinners to a predetermined lottery of salvation wherein those who had not been elected to receive Christ's imputed righteousness shared none of the benefits of his atoning sacrifice and had no choice but to wallow eternally in their sins. While the Edwardsians maintained the doctrine of election and some of the traditional forensic language as well, they insisted that Christ's atonement applied to all and that the only thing keeping sinners from reaping its benefits was their refusal to convert. Likewise, the Edwardsian commitment to natural ability encouraged a more optimistic understanding of human potential. The one whose will and affections had truly been renovated by God's Spirit need not become demoralized by traditional Calvinist lamentations about the "old Adam" that remained in the regenerate heart to inhibit its sanctified strivings. Though none of the early Edwardsians held out the ideal of Christian perfection, they did claim that the saints could and should love disinterestedly. The divine command "Be ye holy; for I am holy" was not made in vain. Unlike the sinner, the truly regenerate Christian need not languish psychologically under what Luther termed the *incurvatus in se*, or the inescapable curvature of seemingly good intentions back in upon our own self-interest. God's grace frees us from inordinate and debilitating self-interest and enables us to love both God and neighbor with truly virtuous intent. Indeed, for ardent Hopkinsians, it frees the saints to such an extent that they would be willing to be damned, if necessary, for God's greater glory. While not all Edwardsians approved of the Hopkinsian doctrine of "unconditional submission," or "resignation," it too derived logically from the Edwardsians' religious voluntarism.[38]

The second main focus of the Edwardsian ellipse, the doctrine of immediate repentance, also accorded with the notion of natural ability. Indeed, these doctrines grew up together in the fertile soil of revival. Dissatisfied with what they deemed the tranquilizing effects of the now conventional Puritan program of preparation for salvation, with its increasingly perfunctory use of the means of grace and its complacence with half-way church membership, the Edwardsians called parishioners out of their spiritual ruts and into a direct encounter with God. Because no natural inability held them back from becoming wholehearted Christians, sinners had no excuse but to repent, convert, and obey the whole counsel of God. In fact, if churchgoing sinners failed to repent immediately, and continued to crawl lamely through what had become the long-drawn-out preparatory stages of the Puritan morphology of conversion, they fared worse by divine standards than the reprobate who stood outside God's covenant community entirely. "Unregenerate doings," for the Edwardsians, or the halfhearted use of the means of grace, were terribly sinful. They represented the worst in lax and insincere piety. While the New Divinity clergy maintained the Calvinist doctrine that regeneration came only by divine grace, and believed, too, that traditional means of grace such as church attendance, Bible reading, and prayer typically preceded the new birth, they feared that all too many parishioners used the means as a crutch and evinced a worrisome lack of soteriological earnestness, fortitude, and resolve. The Edwardsians thus abbreviated the traditional and rather lengthy Puritan conversion morphology and encouraged their flocks to quit wandering the barnyard and enter the sheepfold at once. They admitted that no one would enter but by grace; but they claimed that God was a good shepherd and was calling them in.[39]

New Divinity opposition to Stoddardeanism and the Half-Way Covenant arose as an obvious corollary to and the most powerful symbol of the Edwardsian commitment to immediate repentance. While startling to many of his contemporaries, Edwards's reversal of his grandfather Solomon Stoddard's liberal and long-standing policy of admitting all of Northampton's upstanding churchgoers to the ordinances of baptism and the Lord's Supper does not surprise us in retrospect. Neither does his rejection of the more moderate terms of the Half-Way Covenant. As the American historian and statesman George Bancroft once claimed, "there was nothing half-way about Edwards." Furthermore, as Allen Guelzo has aptly remarked, "[T]he New Divinity desired nothing so much as to repudiate the notion of a church-in-society . . . which embraced all members of a community as a covenantal entity." They believed that the community of the converted constituted a radically new kind of society, standing apart from the ways of the world and witnessing faithfully thereby to the transformative powers of the gospel. While the Edwardsians did not dismiss the traditional Puritan notion that God covenants with entire parishes, communities, and even nations, they contended that only God's covenant of grace, made with individual, wholehearted converts, proved salvific. Unregenerate "seekers" fooled only themselves with their ceremonious acts of contrition and their mundane piety. God demanded true virtue, and true virtue flowed only from the regenerate heart. Edwards did have a keenly analogical imagination and viewed the world, replete with what he called "images or shadows of divine things," through powerfully sacramental lenses. But the Edwardsians' insistence on limiting access to their two most special *ordinances* (a term they preferred to *sacraments* in that they denied that water, bread, and wine were instruments of grace) to twice-born saints undermined the more "sacramental," incarnational, or means-oriented spirituality of pre-Awakening New England. In New Divinity opposition to the Half-Way Covenant we find a recapitulation of the themes of natural ability and immediate repentance that symbolized for many the Edwardsians' opposition to the conventional reliance on earthly means of grace and refusal to rely for salvation on anything short of God's own providence. As depicted by New England's Harriet Beecher Stowe in her novel *The Minister's Wooing* (1859), the Edwardsians offered sinners a ladder to heaven but knocked out all the rungs.[40]

If these core theological concerns defined the boundaries of the New Divinity, delineating the Edwardsians' understanding of true religion from the alleged counterfeits of their adversaries, New Divinity social ties and institutional initiatives propelled their movement.[41] Beginning gradually in the decades following Edwards's death and growing rapidly by the end of the eighteenth century, a uniquely Edwardsian theological culture emerged, surrounding and grounding the development of New Divinity doctrine. An example of what historian Thomas Bender has called "cultures of intellectual life,"[42] this theological culture provided an increasingly strong and complex infrastructure that would support the Edwardsians' theological activities for years to come. Knit closely together by a common, largely rural demographic background, a connection to Yale College, an intricate kinship network, and regular correspondence and social contact, the members of this theological culture combined efforts to promote Edwardsian theology by means of education, ecclesiastical reform, publication, and cooperative revivalism.

The success of New Divinity "schools of the prophets" is well known. By taking post-baccalaureate ministerial hopefuls into their homes as pastoral apprentices, New Divinity theologians such as Joseph Bellamy, Charles Backus, and Nathanael Emmons trained the lion's share of New England's future pastors. After receiving his own theological education in the Edwards home, Bellamy trained such influential Edwardsians as Jonathan Edwards, Jr., Levi Hart, John Smalley, and Samuel Spring, approximately 60 clergymen in all. As Mark Valeri has noted, "between 1765 and 1783" these and other "followers took fully half of New England's pulpit appointments." Emmons, the popularity of whose school contributed to the need for a regular transport from his town of Franklin, Massachusetts, to the main road between Providence and Boston, trained more than 90. During the second half of the eighteenth century, dozens of these schools sprang up throughout New England, breeding strong genetic links with successive generations of Edwardsian ministers. By the time of New England's Second Great Awakening, literally hundreds of New England ministers could trace their pedagogical genealogy back to Edwards himself.[43]

New Divinity inbreeding was not strictly pedagogical. Edwardsian educational ties also contributed to an expansive kinship network as many young Edwardsians met their spouses in these intimate scholastic settings or in the homes of other New Divinity colleagues. Levi Hart, for example, married his mentor's daughter, Rebecca (or Betsy) Bellamy. Samuel Hopkins, who ran his younger brother Daniel (of Salem) through the theological paces, became a brother-in-law to the Edwardsian David Sanford (they married sisters), a father-in-law to Samuel Spring, and a stepfather-in-law to Nathanael Emmons (whose second wife was Hopkins' stepdaughter). Emmons himself had four Edwardsian brothers-in-law. The list goes on. Peter Starr, who studied theology under Bellamy, married the sister of New Divinity minister Ammi Robbins. Josiah Andrews, who studied under Abel Flint, married Flint's sister-in-law. The Edwardsian Asahel

Hooker married Edwards's granddaughter Phoebe Edwards. Bloodlines continued to hold Edwardsians together well into the nineteenth century. The Edwardsian Jacob Ide, for example, married Mary Emmons and became the first editor of her father Nathanael's works. Edwards A. Park married Edwards's great-granddaughter Anna Maria Edwards. Leonard Woods's biographer, Edward A. Lawrence, was his son-in-law as well. And Yale's Noah Porter married Nathaniel Taylor's first daughter, Mary.

This Edwardsian kinship network, the spirit of collegiality engendered by the schools of the prophets, and the many lifelong friendships begun in them facilitated what Joseph Conforti has termed a "group consciousness" among the New Divinity clergy. Most Edwardsians had arrived at these schools already sharing common social and geographical backgrounds. They hailed primarily from modest, rural Connecticut families (often from Litchfield County) but also from such backwoods regions as Berkshire County, Massachusetts. Their opponents often depicted them as country bumpkins and labeled their theology accordingly as "Berkshire Divinity," but most New Divinity men also held bachelor's degrees from Yale College and exhibited a high degree of theological sophistication. Indeed, the Edwardsians were cutting-edge scholars who worked together to publish hundreds of sermons and treatises—often discussing their themes with one another before sharing them with the public—and who undertook the publication of many of Edwards's unpublished manuscripts as well. Jonathan Edwards, Jr., and Samuel Hopkins led the way in this latter effort. In fact, Edwards, Jr., who did the most to disseminate his father's works, accumulated a great deal of money and land (in Tioga County, New York) by receiving half the profits from their sale. The voluminous pattern of fraternal and often intimate New Divinity correspondence remaining extant attests to the Edwardsians' advanced theological literacy and to a powerful collective consciousness developing out of their shared experiences. As Park has written, "the epistles of the early Hopkinsians to each other were in the main, theological treatises." They were often quite personal as well, however, and served to facilitate ongoing social and professional ties. Edwardsian friends worked side by side in support of the gospel ministry, exchanging pulpits, traveling and working together to promote revival, and holding joint, evangelistic conference meetings and conferences of prayer. The activities of this expansive brotherhood provided the adhesives necessary to sustain a coherent Edwardsian social network well into the nineteenth century.[44]

Ecclesiastical reforms provided further institutional support for this growing social network. By the end of the eighteenth century New Divinity partisans had gained control of many of New England's ministerial associations and thereby played a major role in examining, licensing, and dismissing the region's pastors. As clerical counterparts to the Congregational consociations, which had handled routine religious business and church-state conflicts in Connecticut's counties since the adoption of the Saybrook Platform in 1708, these quasi-presbyterian ministerial associations helped to organize the work of the pastors. Several of Connecticut's leading associations, such as Hartford North, Litchfield, and, later, Litchfield South, bore a marked Edwardsian stamp. Joseph Bellamy, for example, was said to have ruled the Litchfield Association "with an iron hand." Though usually more staunchly independent and antipresbyterian than their colleagues to the south, Massachusetts ministers also formed associations. In western Massachusetts Edwards and Hopkins played leading roles in the Hampshire Association and, after its founding in 1763, Edwardsians infiltrated the Berkshire Association as well.

To the east, when theologically liberal clergy began to dominate the Salem Association, its Edwardsians pulled out and formed their own "Salem Ministerial Conference." Edwardsians became dominant in the Essex Middle Association as well and Nathanael Emmons presided as senior member of the powerful Mendon Association for nearly 25 years. Originally embracing three parishes near Emmons's Franklin, the heavily Edwardsian Mendon Association eventually extended "from Worcester to Dighton, and from Abington to Seekonk, enclosing the pastors of thirty-three different churches, in twenty-nine different towns."[45]

These successes enabled New Divinity clergy to venture what James Walsh has termed "an all-out assault on the Half-Way Covenant in the latter part of the eighteenth century." Led in large measure by the writings and example of Joseph Bellamy, the Edwardsians managed to overturn Stoddardean and Half-Way practices with such success that, in Connecticut, "by 1800 the ratio of pure to open churches was four to one." As this Edwardsian victory secured a belated vindication of Edwards's clerical reputation, it also eased the transition of many Separates back into the Congregational churches and thus strengthened the Edwardsians' hand even further against Old Lights and Old Calvinists. By 1842, Congregationalist Joseph Tracy would note that "every Congregational church in New England, probably, has either adopted that doctrine [i.e. the Edwardsian doctrine of the pure church], or become Unitarian." And New Haven's Rev. Samuel W. S. Dutton confirmed that "now among the orthodox Congregational churches of New England, there is not one, which does not require experience of the renewing grace of God, as the qualification for admission to . . . any of the priviledges of its members."[46]

The rise and expansion of the Edwardsian theological culture did not proceed uncontested. As Perry Miller intuited in his benchmark essay on Edwards's sociology of the Great Awakening, the Edwardsian struggle to revive and reform New England's religious life entailed a noteworthy and at times bold critique of New England's sociocultural status quo that frequently proved offensive to more conventional Christians.[47] Understandably, New Divinity pastors generated a great deal of anxiety with their ceaseless, revivalistic calls for immediate repentance and their persistent appeals to natural ability. They sometimes split churches with their demands for purity and their disdain for Half-Way measures. The Edwardsians' all-or-nothing piety and quixotic ideal of a converted community of visible, agapic saints contained implicit countercultural challenges to many of New England's most cherished assumptions and customs. Theirs was an attempt to gain control of the Congregational standing order rather than to separate from it. But in defining their cultural boundaries over against Old Lights, Old Calvinists, and Separates, the Edwardsians could sound rather radical and even sectarian.[48]

Edwards expressed his own radical, revivalistic agenda of evangelical purity in several places, but in few so vividly as entry #205 of his typological manuscript notebook, "Images of Divine Things."

> The time for weeding a garden is when it has newly rained upon it. Otherwise, if you go to pull up the weeds, you will pull up the good herbs and plants with them. So the time for purging the church of God is a time of revival of religion. It can't be so well done at another time; the state of the church of God will not so well bear it. It will neither so well bear the searching, trying doctrines of religion in their close application, nor a thorough ecclesiastical administration and discipline; nor will it bear at another time to be purged from its old corrupt customs, ceremonies, etc.[49]

For Edwards, the importance of revivals lay not only in spiritual transformation but in converted behavior and social life as well. While numerous scholars have pointed to Edwards's aristocratic and authoritarian proclivities as a likely source of his concern for "thorough ecclesiastical administration and discipline,"[50] Edwards also held deeply rooted concerns for justice and social welfare. In the days before America's industrial revolution, the rise of sociology, and the subsequent concern on the part of many reformers to address systemic social problems, Edwards opposed the individualism and acquisitive self-interest of both Enlightenment (proto-capitalist) social theory and New England business practices, encouraged Christian charity toward the poor and oppressed, repudiated the exploitation of the Housatonic Indians by his own relatives, the Williamses, and by other frontier traders, and heralded a radically theocentric benevolence as the only true virtue. He was certainly no modern moral hero. He had strong patriarchal tendencies that exhibited themselves in such vices as a frequently condescending demeanor and a long-lasting practice of slaveholding. But he did believe that regeneration and conversion went hand in hand, that new life in Christ necessarily entailed a commitment to justice and love. As he insisted in the new church covenant he established during the Great Awakening in Northampton:

> In all our conversation, concerns, and dealings with our neighbor, we will have a strict regard to rules of honesty, justice, and uprightness; that we don't overreach or defraud our neighbor in any matter, and either willfully or through want of care, injure him in any of his honest possessions or rights; and in all our communication, will have a tender respect, not only to our own interest, but also to the interest of our neighbor; and will carefully endeavor in everything to do to others as we should expect, or think reasonable, that they should do to us.[51]

Edwards battled New England's sins throughout his career, and not always in a prudish or holier-than-thou manner. He concerned himself not only with maintaining traditional sexual taboos and sabbatarian restrictions but with nearly the entire gamut of New England's social ills. As he explained in his seventh sermon (in a poignant series of 15) on the nature of Christian charity (1738), "[C]onsidering the profession we make of Christianity, we are too selfish. . . . We in this land are trained up from generation to generation in a too niggardly, selfish spirit and practice; and notwithstanding all our professions of religion, . . . without doubt we do in general come vastly short of what is required of Christians in the New Testament."[52]

Edwards's worries about New England social life were not unfounded. Throughout the eighteenth century, and especially during and after the Great Awakening, New England underwent a tumultuous period of demographic and economic expansion, not to mention political revolution. Land became scarce, land speculation skyrocketed as tens of thousands of young people moved out to the frontier, subsistence farming began to give way to mercantilism and a market economy, and the legal system became less neighborly, more complex and impersonal. New England's towns, for so long the hub of the region's social and economic life, became larger, more diverse, and less isolated as new roads and bridges were built to facilitate trade. Even family life changed, as more affectionate and egalitarian parenting styles replaced old-fashioned patriarchal authority. In short, New England's social structures became more complex than ever before.[53]

These changes did not bode well for the cultural authority of New England clergy or the traditional moral values they espoused. The increasing complexity of New England society meant that the established clergy no longer stood alone as the dominant force in the development of New England mores. Business, law, medicine, and politics attracted a growing number of the region's best and brightest, crowding the stage of New England's cultural leadership. Nathan Hatch has noted that in Massachusetts, "clergymen had constituted 70 percent of all learned professionals in 1740; by 1800 they were only 45 percent, despite the fact that their number had doubled." The expansion and increased accessibility of print media in post-Revolutionary, rural New England contributed further to this decline in ministerial power. No longer the undisputed local sources of knowledge, the clergy had to accept more narrowly defined roles within the intellectual life of their parishes. Thus, as teenage pregnancies, unfair business practices, and community acrimony rose all around them, they felt increasingly impotent to effect any wide-scale change. Even their salaries failed to keep pace with those of other professionals and a growing number of clergy took up medicine as well to maintain their customary standards of living. As the Revolution approached, talk of liberty, republicanism, and civic humanism replaced the language of theology as the predominant discourse of New England public life. Tellingly, fewer and fewer parents gave their children biblical names. In time it became clear that religion would be left to play only a supporting role in the rise of the new nation. And as its founding fathers codified the legal principles of the United States in its federal and state constitutions, the clergy's diminished role was increasingly sanctioned by force of law.[54]

The religious voluntarism inculcated by Edwardsians and other New Lights was partly to blame for this decline in clerical authority. As conversion and consent to evangelical principles replaced religious birthright and station within New England's godly commonwealths as the basis of religious authority, one no longer had to be a leader in the Congregationalist standing order to guarantee oneself a credible voice in the many normative and inherently ethical debates over New England's future. Harry Stout has argued that the decade of the Great Awakening proved "the most critical period in colonial New England's intellectual and religious history." Nothing else "came close to wreaking the internal havoc created by the ministers themselves in the midst of their raging debates. Nor would any event tip the balance of Congregational authority so firmly and decisively in the laity's direction. Suddenly it was the people—guided by their self-made leaders—who had to take responsibility for their religious lives to retain God's special favor for New England."[55] As the Revolution approached, some pastors became preachers of politics to maintain their voice in New England's public square. While generally sticking to standard gospel preaching on Sundays, they used election day, fast day, thanksgiving day, and militia day services to provide moral guidance, inspiration, and religious sanctions for an increasingly political people. These occasional fusions of religion and patriotism did not last long among the Edwardsians, however, for as the war ended, old fears resurfaced concerning America's rising secularity and immorality. In many respects, the war had only intensified earlier socioeconomic trends. Furthermore, it had led to an alliance with the French, whose mores had always been held suspect by the scions of the Puritans. Often sharply critical of their new nation's emergent values, the Edwardsians gradually abdicated their traditional roles as guardians of New England's public square and began hurling gospel criticisms at the new, more secular captains of American civic life.[56]

As W. R. Ward has emphasized, the evangelical revivals of the eighteenth century "almost everywhere . . . began in resistance to a real or perceived threat of assimilation by the state in its modern shape."[57] Though eclipsed for a time during the fervor of the Revolution, the cultural criticism that accompanied the Edwardsian revivals largely supports this generalization. Distressed by the acquisitive and often egocentric behavior legitimated by the successes of an ascendant market economy, and concerned over the rise of secular social values validated by the Revolution, Edwardsians frequently responded with radical criticisms of their neighbors' social and economic practices or with blanket denunciations of what many termed religious "infidelity." Heralding the notion of disinterested benevolence, Edwardsians such as Joseph Bellamy, Samuel Hopkins, and Nathanael Emmons stood squarely against the enlightened self-interest of market capitalism. Many Edwardsians also repudiated both religious and economic justifications of slavery. Indeed, Hopkins has been nominated by one historian as "the father of the antislavery movement in America." After moving to Newport, Rhode Island, in 1770 and observing the slave trade first-hand, this former slaveholder dedicated much of his life to antislavery reforms and the colonization of ex-slaves back in Africa. Several other Edwardsians, most notably Levi Hart, Jonathan Edwards, Jr., and Nathaniel Niles, joined Hopkins in the early antislavery movement. Edwards, Jr., supported immediate manumission and he and Hart played leading roles in the founding of the Connecticut Society for the Promotion of Freedom and for the Relief of Persons Unlawfully Holden in Bondage in 1790. The African American Edwardsian Lemuel Haynes, who served white parishes in Granville, Massachusetts, and Rutland, Vermont, became the first black pastor in America ordained by a white denomination. Other Edwardsians protested the rise of Deism, skepticism, Jacobinism, and Freemasonry in America—all manifestations of infidelity. Some became so wary of American infidelity that paranoia set in. Timothy Dwight, for example, gave credence to rumors of a secret order of Masons—the Bavarian Illuminati—conspiring to undermine religion, morality, and government wherever it went. In every case, the Edwardsians found much to resist in the rise of independent America. Certainly, they too could condone and even exploit the secular values of the new nation when such activity furthered their own agenda. But as the Edwardsian theological culture gained increasing momentum, Edwardsian clergy spent less time trying to manipulate New England's public life and more time building their own institutions and converting individual souls. By the end of New England's Second Great Awakening, they would demonstrate that voluntaristic and even disestablished religion could exert as much cultural force as the politicized faith of the colonial New England Way.[58]

The Edwardsian Enculturation of Calvinist New England

By the end of the eighteenth century, the Edwardsian or New Divinity Movement had achieved a considerable following. Bounded by strong doctrinal and social commitments and sustained by a vital theological culture, by 1800 the Edwardsians constituted the fastest growing religious movement in the region. Already in 1787 Jonathan Edwards, Jr., had claimed that "a majority" of the Connecticut clergy and a strong majority of the "young" ministers "mean to embrace the system of my father and Dr. Bellamy." Edwards A. Park estimated in 1852 "that about the year 1756, there were, in our land [New England], four or five Edwardean clergymen; in 1773, there were forty or fifty; and in

1796, there were more than a hundred," adding that by century's end "the spirit of the New Divinity was in the hearts of thousands, who did not favor it in all its forms."[59] But Edwardsian advances in the eighteenth century would not even begin to compare to the movement's tremendous growth in the nineteenth century. Historians have usually misrepresented New Divinity preaching as dry and esoteric, asserting that New Divinity pastors drove their flocks away with irksome presentations of metaphysical polemics. But in fact, many Edwardsians proved quite winsome preachers and, overall, the New Divinity gained more adherents than it lost with its strident socio-theological agenda. Indeed, the Edwardsian theological culture underwent its most significant expansion beginning in the first decade of the nineteenth century (ca. 1798–1808) as a result of the New Divinity–led revivals of New England's "Second Great Awakening."[60]

Having prepared for a special outpouring of divine grace by organizing extensive "concerts of prayer" and leading common or "circular fasts," the Edwardsians nurtured New England's Second Great Awakening with pulpit-swapping itinerancy and special evangelistic conference meetings.[61] Before they knew it, thousands of New Englanders were flooding their churches with applications for membership. This may seem strange to those of us reared to believe that New Divinity sermonizing was arid and irrelevant. Edwardsians have seldom received their due as the dynamic leaders of New England's massive turn-of-the-century revivals. In all actuality, however, the Edwardsians did prove avid and effective revivalists. As David Kling has noted, "[N]ot every New Divinity minister fostered a revival during the Second Great Awakening, but nearly every revival that did occur took place within the parish of a New Divinity pastor."[62]

The result was that, beginning in the late 1790s, Edwardsian preaching, polity, institutions, and theology infiltrated the region to such an extent that it would not be inappropriate to speak of an Edwardsian enculturation of Calvinist New England during the first third of the nineteenth century. Contemporary accounts from observers all across the religious spectrum suggest that friends and foes alike recognized the extent to which Edwardsianism had captivated New England's Calvinist imagination. The liberal William Bentley admitted with regret in 1813 that Hopkins's theology stood as "the basis of the popular theology of New England." Berkshire clergyman Sylvester Burt wrote in 1829 that the main contours of Hopkinsianism, "waiving a few points," had become standards for "the orthodox and evangelical clergy of N. England at the present day." Princetonian Archibald Alexander testified in 1831 that "Edwards has done more to give complexion to the theological system of Calvinists in America, than all other persons together. This is more especially true of New-England; but it is also true, to a great extent, in regard to a large number of the present ministers of the Presbyterian church." His colleague Samuel Miller affirmed in 1837 that "for the last half century, it may be safely affirmed, that no other American writer on the subject of theology has been so frequently quoted, or had anything like such deference manifested to his opinions, as President Edwards." Bennet Tyler claimed in 1844 that the Edwardsians comprised the "standard theological writers of New England." And as Samuel M. Worcester noted in 1852, "within fifty years past," Edwardsian theology had "so pervaded the orthodoxy of New England, and that too, so silently and imperceptibly, that there are hundreds of very good Hopkinsian ministers, who may never have given any more particular attention to Hopkins's 'System of Divinity,' than to the 'Aphorisms' of Confucius." By 1853, the Edwardsian

Mortimer Blake could boast that Edwardsian theology had "modified the current theology of all New England, and given to it its harmony, consistency, and beauty, as it now appears in the creeds of the churches and the teaching of the ministry."[63]

Edwardsians took advantage of their high profile throughout the nineteenth century to reprint Edwards's works dozens of times in runs that would total in the hundreds of thousands. Edwards's bibliographer has demonstrated that the American Tract Society alone "published fifteen Edwards items . . . between 1827 and 1845, and reprinted them innumerable times. The Society must have distributed approximately a million Edwards items before it ceased, in 1892, to list them among its publications." Further, as New Haven's *Christian Spectator* noted in 1821, the first American collection of Edwards's works, published in 1808, had "[placed] a useful body of divinity in the library of almost every young clergyman, in this part of the country." Edwards's *Life of David Brainerd* (1749) and *History of the Work of Redemption* (1774) proved the most popular of his works and exerted a major, formative influence on American popular culture. The *Life of Brainerd* went through more reprints than any other Edwards work. The spiritual chronicle of a melancholy and short-lived Edwardsian missionary to the Indians, this redaction of Brainerd's diary made the name of its subject "better known to the average churchgoer of the next generation" than the name of Edwards himself. As for the *History of Redemption*, a sermon series first published in Scotland a full 16 years after Edwards's death, John Wilson has suggested that by the nineteenth century it became "as influential as any other single book in fixing the cultural parameters of . . . American Protestant culture." Rooting American life in the transcendent history of salvation, Edwards's *History of Redemption* imbued American history with divine purpose and significance. Briefly put, the success of Edwardsian revivals generated a substantial market for the theology that undergirded them and the Edwardsian clergy stepped in happily to meet the need they had created.[64]

Edwardsian successes in publishing signaled the burgeoning of their achievements in missions, benevolent reform, and education as well. David Brainerd became a virtual patron saint for America's (as well as Great Britain's) emergent Protestant missions movement. His grave became a shrine visited by evangelistic admirers from both sides of the Atlantic. His spirit pervaded the Connecticut and Massachusetts Missionary Societies, which arose with the Edwardsian revivals and whose magazines disseminated news of such revivals and conversions throughout the region. As one historian of Yale's missionary endeavors noted in 1901, "[T]hough his flaming life burned itself out before Brainerd was thirty, no other missionary, perhaps, has proven such a stimulus to seekers after holiness; nor has any other biography led so many in every land to enter upon mission work . . . as Brainerd's memoir." Edwardsians stood at the vanguard of both frontier evangelism—which culminated in the organization of the American Home Missionary Society in 1826—and foreign missions. As N. L. L. Beman recalled in a letter to Edwards A. Park in 1860, their theology "laid the foundation" for the American Board of Commissioners for Foreign Missions, founded in 1810 as the country's first foreign missions organization. Their roles at Williams College (home of the famous Haystack Prayer Meeting of 1806 that helped give birth to America's foreign missions movement) and Andover Seminary ("the missionary seminary"), moreover, led to an unprecedented swelling of New England's missionary ranks. During the American Board's first 30 years, more of its missionaries hailed from Williams than from any other college; during its first 50 years, 40 percent of its missionaries had studied at Andover.[65]

Edwardsians also took major strides in the increasingly popular realm of benevolent reform during the first half of the nineteenth century. While there is doubtless some truth to the once-predominant view that their reform efforts proved largely conservative in this period, doing as much to repress or control behavior and to maintain the status quo as they did to alleviate human suffering, it is important not to underestimate the ongoing Edwardsian commitment to disinterested benevolence and agapic neighbor love.[66] Edwardsians played leading roles in the founding of several Christian educational societies, from the American Education Society, the Doctrinal Tract Society, and the American Tract Society, to the Congregational Board of Publication. They maintained a strong witness against slavery and provided substantial support to the American Colonization Society. Some of them also opposed the federal government's Indian removal policies and supported temperance reforms.[67] Their cultural criticism did become less radical in this period of tremendous Edwardsian growth. Colonizationism, for example, offered a rather moderate course of action in an era that saw the rise of immediate abolitionism and, after its founding in 1833, the Edwardsians consistently opposed the Garrisonian tactics of the American Anti-Slavery Society.[68] But by this time Edwardsians no longer saw themselves as shapers of public policy. The decline of ministerial authority in the Revolutionary era, combined with the demise of the Federalist party and the disestablishment of Congregationalism in the early national period, led to a change in tactics among many reform-minded clergy of New England's former standing order. Rather than reform society from the top down, by walking the corridors of power and Christianizing the social order, Edwardsians sought increasingly to effect change from the bottom up, by converting individual souls and channeling the energies of the regenerate into local church work and voluntary societies.[69] While at its worst this new strategy dulled the prophetic edge of earlier Edwardsian theology and encouraged an abdication of Christian responsibility for the welfare of society at large, at its best it confronted hundreds of thousands with the challenge of disinterested love and enlisted unprecedented numbers in local churches and other reform societies.[70]

Edwardsians ensconced themselves at many of New England's leading schools in this period—not just the obvious ones like Yale and Andover Seminary, but Amherst, Dartmouth, Mount Holyoke, Williams, Bangor Seminary, and even the Baptist College of Rhode Island (later Brown University, which was led at the turn of the century by the young Edwardsian Jonathan Maxcy)—thereby acquiring the means to enculturate future generations of the region's leaders. The first four theology professors at Bangor Seminary were all students of Nathanael Emmons. Similarly, Amherst, Dartmouth, and Mount Holyoke shared strong Edwardsian roots. Williams's benefactor—Colonel Ephraim Williams of the notorious, anti-Edwardsian Williams clan—had no religious agenda at all for the school he endowed. He intended it as a "Free School" for the sons of the military. But soon after its founding in the early 1790s Williams took on a clearly Edwardsian character. Throughout the first half of the nineteenth century, and particularly during the presidency of the famous Edwardsian revivalist Edward Dorr Griffin (1821–36), Williams served as a bastion of the Edwardsian theological culture.[71]

The notion of an Edwardsian enculturation of Calvinist New England during the first third of the nineteenth century calls into question what has become a near-standard argument in recent years, the argument for Edwardsian decline in this period in the face of a resurgent Old Calvinism. As the New Divinity gained an ever-widening currency, its boundaries did expand and its theology became more diffuse. Long-standing disagreements between radical Hopkinsians and more moderate Edwardsians hardened as distinct "Exerciser" and "Taster" parties emerged within the ranks.[72] Unprecedented numbers claimed Edwardsian discourse as their own, and it was only natural that a variety of differences would emerge over how best to appropriate the language and customs of such a powerful theological culture.

This broader and more diffuse Edwardsianism, however, should not be confused with Old Calvinism. The fact is that, in the face of tremendous Edwardsian successes in the heyday of New England's Second Great Awakening, the region's Joseph Lathrops, David Tappans, and Jedidiah Morses became a dying breed. As one historian has noted of Morse, his liberal opponents increasingly considered him an Edwardsian and, upon retiring from public life, Morse in fact "relinquished the leadership of the orthodox to his Hopkinsian friends." Bangor Seminary's Enoch Pond explained in his *Sketches of the Theological History of New England* (1880) that as Edwardsians and Old Calvinists joined forces early in the nineteenth century to combat both social and religious infidelity, the Edwardsians proved more energetic. Their union "retain[ed] the better, the more essential parts of both" parties. "It embrace[d] all the leading features of the soundest Calvinism" and "it adopt[ed], to a considerable extent, the improvements of Edwards and his followers." But there was the rub. The Edwardsians themselves had never repudiated "the soundest Calvinism." Thus, to adopt Edwardsian improvements was to unite largely on Edwardsian terms. The theology of New England's united orthodox front became the "theology which was taught by such men as Bellamy, Hopkins, and the younger Edwards, and West, of Stockbridge, and Smalley, Spring, Emmons, Austin, Griffin, Worcester, and Dwight. This is the theology which has been preached in nearly all our revivals during the last sixty or seventy years, which has filled up our churches with young and active members, which has aroused and sustained the spirit of missions, which has fostered and directed nearly all the charitable enterprises of the day." As George Park Fisher confirmed in his history of Yale's College Church,

> the election of Dr. Dwight to the Presidency of Yale College [in 1795] marked the triumph in New England of the Edwardean theology. . . . From that time the old Calvinism, as something distinct from the Edwardean Divinity, disappears from view. . . . By a variety of agencies, the party professing the ancient Calvinism and eschewing "the improvements" of the New Divinity, has been quite obliterated in New England. Eighty years ago, the followers of President Edwards among the Calvinistic clergy, were said by his son, the younger President, to be few in number. At present, there are some who are scarcely aware that there ever was a time, since his death, when the Calvinists of New England did not regard President Edwards as the most authoritative expounder of their principles.[73]

In this light, it makes better sense to speak of an Edwardsian absorption of Old Calvinism than to argue for an Old Calvinist co-optation of Edwardsianism. Andover Seminary provides a further case in point. Allen Guelzo cites the famous Edwardsian/ Old Calvinist compromise in the founding of Andover as a major stage in the Old Calvinist co-optation of Edwardsianism. However, there is plenty of evidence to suggest yet another Edwardsian triumph at America's first modern seminary. While a few of the most stringent followers of the radical Hopkinsian Nathanael Emmons began complaining by the late 1810s that the seminary was going to the Old Calvinist dogs, there were others who complained that the school had become too Edwardsian. There were outsiders, for example, who deemed this institutional legitimation of Hopkinsianism ridiculous. After perusing a "Review of the Constitution & Associate Statutes of the Theological Seminary in Andover" printed in the liberal *Anthology* for December 1808, William Bentley concluded that Andover's "Calvinists have been made to play into the hands of the Hopkinsians."[74]

Insiders, as well, resented the Edwardsian domination of the seminary. It is said that founding Old Calvinist theologian Eliphalet Pearson resigned the Bartlet chair of natural theology after only a year because he felt disappointed that Hopkinsianism had become so dominant at Andover. Pearson's disappointment was not unfounded. The vast majority of Andover's leading faculty members—from Leonard Woods to Edward Dorr Griffin, Moses Stuart, Ebenezer Porter (the seminary's first president), and Edwards A. Park—shared Edwardsian sentiments. All were required to subscribe to the school's Hopkinsian "Associate Creed," a doctrinal standard for the seminary insisted upon by Edwardsian founders not content to repose on Westminster's Shorter Catechism alone. Furthermore, Andover's board of visitors ensured that the Edwardsians would maintain a consistently strong presence at Andover for years to come. Established at the seminary's founding to placate Hopkinsians fearful of co-optation by Old Calvinists, the board of visitors was a self-perpetuating committee of two clergy and one layperson, each of whom had to subscribe to Andover's Associate Creed. As Andover historian Henry Rowe explained, the visitors were "given power to review the acts of the Trustees, to interpret the Creed and the Associate Statutes, as occasion might arise, and to preserve the orthodoxy of the Seminary. . . . The Visitors were intended to be censors of the school as long as the sun and moon endure." In short, while the fears of Emmonsists may not have been groundless (Hopkinsianism did give way to a broader Edwardsianism in the theology of Woods and at Andover generally as time wore on), their claim that the seminary had gone over to the Old Calvinists was alarmist. As Leonard Bacon would summarize at Andover's semicentennial commemoration, "[I]n a little while the Old Divinity leaven was quietly purged out, and Andover theology had become (quite to the discontent of a few extremists on both sides) a moderate Hopkinsianism."[75]

While the rustic origins and evangelical bearing of the Edwardsians, then, might lead later highbrow pundits such as Oliver Wendell Holmes to lampoon their theological culture as a rude and rickety "one-hoss-shay" (one-horse chaise), it is clear that this shay carried the day among nineteenth-century New England's traditional Protestants.[76] And if the historical novels of Harriet Beecher Stowe and her brother Henry Ward Beecher provide any indication, Edwardsian theology belonged not merely to ministerial elites, but was internalized and appropriated at all levels of New England society. Edwardsian sermons were

> discussed by every farmer, in intervals of plough and hoe, by every woman and girl, at loom, spinning wheel, or wash-tub. New England was one vast sea, surging from depths to heights with thought and discussion on the most insoluble of mysteries. And it is to be added, that no man or woman accepted any theory or speculation simply *as* theory or speculation; all was profoundly real and vital,—a foundation on which actual life was based with intensest earnestness.[77]

As Daniel Walker Howe has argued, contemporary distinctions between "high" and "popular" culture create confusion when employed in antebellum contexts: "No alienated intelligentsia then existed in America except for the Concord Transcendentalists. . . . It was an age when partisan politics and organized religion dominated the culture far more than they do today, and when political and religious loyalties were fierce." This argument holds especially true in New England, where literacy rates were higher perhaps than anywhere else in the western world. Henry Boynton Smith once remarked that "the most abstruse and metaphysical dogmas have there been worked into the heart and life, as nowhere else in the world. . . . No other people ever passed through such a process." In an early *Atlantic Monthly* review of William B. Sprague's *Annals of the American Pulpit*, Stowe echoed this theme: "[N]owhere in the world, unless perhaps in Scotland, have merely speculative questions excited the strong and engrossing interest among the common people that they have in New England. Every man, woman, and child was more or less a theologian."[78]

Within the Edwardsian ranks, women especially served as the lay theologians, as well as the religious activists and the standards of evangelical piety. From the exemplary piety of Abigail Hutchinson, Phebe Bartlet, and Edwards's own wife, Sarah, in his *Faithful Narrative* and *Some Thoughts Concerning the Revival*;[79] to the formative roles played by women such as Sarah Edwards, her daughter Mary, Newport's Susanna Anthony, and the elderly Phebe Bartlet in the theology of Edwardsian clergymen such as Samuel Hopkins, Timothy Dwight, Elias Cornelius, and Justin Edwards;[80] to the religious leadership provided by numerous women in revival conference meetings, benevolent societies, missions, and Sunday schools [81]—Edwardsian women led the charge in the Edwardsian enculturation of Calvinist New England. Sarah Osborn and Susanna Anthony led the women's praying society that anchored Newport's First Church. Osborn spearheaded the town's revival of 1766-67 out of her home and pioneered in providing spiritual ministry to the town's African American community. Together with Anthony, she became the key player in her congregation's decision to call Hopkins as pastor (1770) and served as his advisor and confidant after his settlement.[82] Nathanael Emmons's second wife, Martha Williams Emmons, performed most of her reclusive husband's pastoral calls.[83] Mary Lyon founded Mount Holyoke Seminary in 1837, overseeing 11 revivals and training scores of Edwardsian women as missionaries and social reformers before her death in 1849.[84] The list could go on. But in brief, many more women than men converted during and contributed to the Edwardsian revivals of the Second Great Awakening. Significantly, their role in the tremendous expansion of the Edwardsian theological culture contributed markedly to the broader "feminization" of New England religion in this period, a fact that is usually overlooked by scholars in the tradition of Ann Douglas, who tie the feminization of religion to the decline of Calvinism and the rise of romantic or sentimental liberalism.[85]

This was the rich culture of Nathaniel Taylor's theological life—the one to which Azel Backus introduced him and into which Timothy Dwight immersed him. These were the historical forces that shaped young Taylor's intellectual horizons. And this was the world that Taylor would lead into the antebellum period.

3

Taylor at the Reins of the "One-Hoss Shay"

New Haven and the Edwardsian Theological Culture

Taylor . . . exercises a positive power upon you. He is a genius in theology—an enthusiast, and he makes you feel. Somehow he plants a truth within a man and it becomes life and power. You will think for weeks on some thought or view that he throws out. In short he is a Teacher, and a true Teacher is rarer than a true Poet. Should you hear him you would probably at first revolt from him. You would be disgusted with his dogmatism and wonder where his power lies. But wait and yield yourself to his influence and soon you will see and feel it. The chief effects of his teaching, I think, are these. He makes you feel a few important truths strongly. He makes you think for yourself; and no man can be effective without some degree of these.

Theodore T. Munger

It did not take long for Taylor to feel at home in the Edwardsian culture.[1] Always an ardent supporter of New England's Second Great Awakening, he had known of this culture for years before he roomed and boarded with it in New Haven. He had entered his twenties before he moved into the Dwight manse as an apprentice, already a mature thinker with a voracious intellectual appetite—more than ready, that is, to sink deep roots into the fertile soil of New England divinity. And while there, he formed a couple of lifelong friendships with individuals who, in very different ways, would keep him grounded in Edwardsian soil for the rest of his days.

"Twixt Smiles and Tears"

The first of these important friendships was struck with none other than Lyman Beecher, Taylor's most intimate male companion and ecclesial soul mate for half a century. It was while serving as Dwight's secretary that Taylor first met the elder Beecher (his senior by over 10 years), who was then a Presbyterian pastor on Long Island. As recounted by Taylor's daughter, "[G]oing into the study one afternoon to write for [Dr. Dwight], my father found waiting there a rather small, plain-looking man." Supposing him to be a local farmer who had "come to arrange with the doctor for his winter supply of potatoes," Taylor offered the man a chair and sat down to work. To Taylor's surprise, when Dwight arrived he "greeted the man with great cordiality, and introduced him as Mr. Beecher of East Hampton, Long Island." Taylor's daughter continued: "Many years after Dr. Taylor reminded Dr. Beecher of this interview. 'Ah, yes,' he replied, 'we took hold of hands in Dr. Dwight's study, and we never let go!'"[2]

Never, indeed. As one of Taylor's students would later testify, "the two men loved each other like brothers." Stories abound of Beecher's presence in the Taylor family home, frequently unannounced and testing the patience of the Taylor women. A common friend remembered of Beecher, "[H]e seemed unwilling to be elsewhere than at Dr. Taylor's. I remember meeting him, at an early morning hour, with a string of black-fish, with which he was returning from Long Wharf to the doctor's, in sufficient season to enjoy them at breakfast." The two competed with one another in the raising of early cucumbers. They exchanged pulpits with one another while Beecher pastored in Litchfield (1810–26). Most important, they confided in one another about the things that mattered most, laboring endlessly on behalf of New England's churches. Rebecca Taylor Hatch spoke of this vividly in her memoirs. "I do remember," she wrote, "when I was a little girl, how [the Rev. Beecher] would rush into the house, speak to no one, rush out and promenade back and forth over the wide garden walk, then in, and up the back stairs to my father's study."[3]

Beecher moved to Cincinnati in 1832 to accept the presidency of Lane Seminary, leaving New England, as Hatch noted, "to the great sorrow of my father." On Beecher's first visit back east, she continued, "he came to our house. We were at dinner. My father, hearing his voice at the door, rushed out. We followed, and there were the two D.D.'s hugging and kissing each other." Sadly for Beecher, Taylor died first, leaving the older half of this pair bereaved. Beecher agonized over the loss of his closest companion. Two years later, he mustered the courage to approach Taylor's widow with a request. The poignant story of their encounter as told by Hatch is worth quoting at length:

> He asked my mother if she was willing that he should be buried at the side of my father, who died in 1858. Professor Goodrich, the lifelong friend of both, being present, fearing that the question should startle and worry my mother, replied: "Brother Beecher, there is room in *my* lot in the cemetery, if you wish to be laid in New Haven." "I wish to lie beside Brother Taylor and in *his* lot," was Dr. Beecher's reply. My mother gave him every assurance and he was satisfied. The summer before he died another visit was made. Before the good-bye came at the front door, he pointed toward the cemetery but did not speak. Mrs. Beecher said: "Mrs. Taylor, he wishes to know if you are still willing that he should lie beside your husband." My mother reassured him and he went down the steps ""Twixt smiles and tears."[4]

Beecher's body was later buried within the Taylor family plot, marked prominently near the front of New Haven's Grove Street Cemetery. But it had to be carried there from Brooklyn, where Beecher died at the age of 87 after spending hours in the New York home of Taylor's daughter. She remembered his visits this way. The Rev. and Mrs. Beecher

> often called at our home in Clark Street, and he would invariably talk of my father. Seating himself before his portrait, Dr. Beecher would exclaim: "Ah, why did Taylor die, and why do I live?" Again he would sit before it and weep, without a word. And when his mind was weakened by age, and other friends were forgotten, one would say: "Surely you remember Dr. Taylor," and he quickly replied: "Oh, yes, yes, Taylor, Taylor, a part of me, a part of me." Once when looking at his photograph he exclaimed: "Oh, Lord God,

bring my soul to see the man with whom I walked in sweet counsel in this world." Again, his daughter, striving to cheer him, said: "You remember Dr. Taylor," he replied: "Don't tell me of him now. I cannot bear it."[5]

"Nat Taylor, Fair Beyond Compare"

The other important friendship Taylor cemented during this time was with Rebecca Marie Hine, his childhood sweetheart and second cousin. Rebecca was the only daughter of Major Beebe Hine and Lois Northrop Hine, who kept an inn on New Milford's green next door to the Taylors. Though "Becky" was three years younger than "Nat," the two were play-mates in New Milford whose relationship turned romantic during their teens.[6]

Not long after Taylor entered Yale, the Hines sent Rebecca to New Haven as well to attend "Miss Hall's school" for girls, one of the best in the state of Connecticut. She boarded in the home of Rector Hubbard of Trinity Church, New Haven's only Episco-palian congregation. While there, she developed several lifelong friendships of her own, including one with Henrietta Edwards, Jonathan Edwards's great-granddaughter and the future wife of Eli Whitney. Her best friends of all were the daughters of Noah Webster, by then one of New Haven's most prominent citizens: Julia, the oldest daughter, who would later marry Chauncey Goodrich (Taylor's good friend and colleague at Yale) and set up house across the street from the Taylors on the corner of Temple and Wall; Harriet, whose second husband was the Rev. William Chauncey Fowler, an Amherst professor and politician who would publish reminiscences of Taylor's ministry; and Emily, Rebecca's best friend, who took a liking to Taylor herself (she once referred to him as "Adonis"), and between Rebecca and whom young Natty would often carry childish notes.[7]

Apparently, Becky's friends all thought that Nat was simply gorgeous. In fact, a re-markable number of descriptions of his physical attractiveness survive, nearly all of which remark upon his height, muscular build, and enchanting black eyes. His classmate Richard Storrs once said that "he never could forget the impression that [Taylor's] beauty made upon him," alleging that "it was more than he could describe." Not quite so awestruck, William Fowler found the words with which to describe it. But he, too, was impressed with Taylor's manly mien: "In stature he was taller than the middle height, with a frame rather squarely built but well knit, a full muscular development, but without any ten-dency to leanness on the one hand or obesity on the other. He had a clear complexion, a bright beaming black eye, black or dark brown hair, and clear cut features." Fowler also remembered an occasion on which Taylor demonstrated his virility, proving that even after his ordination he had not become effete. "About the year 1816, a tall, active, strong man, said to him, 'Were it not for your coat I would give you a whipping.'" Clearly impressed, Fowler went on to report that "Mr. Taylor calmly replied, 'I can take it off.'" As Taylor matured, his friends continued to speak of his "superior physical qualities . . . a lofty and symmetrical forehead, suggestive of profound and original thought, a beautiful, melting, and speaking eye, benignity and dignity in his whole countenance, and a strong, deep, varied and sonorous voice." Even well into his old age, Taylor was known as a handsome man. Theodore Munger, who knew him then, extolled his "per-sonal attractiveness," which he claimed was "beyond that of any man I had ever met":

He was already sixty years old, but the splendor of the man was not dimmed. A massive head, hair brushed back and falling to his shoulders in heavy locks, with a tendency to curl, a chin strong enough for fight but not too heavy for vigorous thought, a forehead broad and high, rising in a full domed head, and eyes no word describes so well as beautiful—black, deep without fire, soft and pensive—a singular combination, and indicating heredity from beautiful women.

A commemorative set of verses on Taylor's Yale class of 1807 sums up his charming reputation among those who knew him:

> Nat Taylor, fair beyond compare,
>   The pride of all Yale College O—
> He wins each heart and makes it smart,
>   And glories in his conquest O![8]

From all accounts, Rebecca Hine was quite an attractive woman herself. Her parents had groomed her since birth for a graceful role in high society. And while not nearly so many accounts survive of her physical appearance, her portrait attests to the physical beauty that Taylor saw. As her daughter related, "[M]y mother, being an only daughter, her father was very particular in all things relating to her appearance and manners. Her saddle-horse was never ridden by anyone but herself; her clothes and shoes were usually purchased in New York. I have one chair which stood in the house; the back of it is very straight. Since it came into my possession I have never wondered at the erect carriage of my mother." And as Nat boasted in a little love poem to his "Nancy" while a sophomore at Yale,

> There is something in her air
>   That greatly hits my fancy;
> 'Tis not her face, her shape, her hair,
>   But 'tis the whole of Nancy.[9]

Taylor once said that "they were never engaged, for there was never any need of it." So the two got married without much ado on October 15, 1810. Rebecca's parents hosted the ceremony in their large New Milford home, which as an inn was especially well-suited for such an affair. With a "wide hall running through the centre, and a ball-room on the third floor," the house must have echoed the sounds of laughter and celebration into the night. The newlyweds stayed a few days in New Milford so that Taylor could preach to his home congregation. They then moved back to New Haven to establish a home of their own.[10]

In 1812, they moved into the house in which they would live for the rest of their lives, raise their children, and entertain a host of friends and visiting dignitaries. A clapboard colonial, it sat on the southwest corner of New Haven's Temple and Wall Streets, just north (by about a block) of the town green. The descendant of generations of successful farmers, Taylor had horticulture in his blood. To no one's surprise, then, he settled in by planting a garden. Though, unlike his grandfather, he had no need to supplement his income by selling produce, he spent countless hours during the next 46 years cultivating his unusually verdant back yard.[11]

The Taylors counted among their neighbors some of the nation's leading citizens, from longtime friends such as the Websters to new acquaintances like Jedidiah Morse who, after retiring from his Charlestown pulpit in the spring of 1820, bought a house next door to the Taylors and moved his famous family there. Jedidiah's son, Samuel F. B. Morse, was already grown by the time this happened. But he, too, spent time in the house,[12] took care of it after his father's death (in June of 1826), and sold it in 1828 to the evangelical philanthropist Arthur Tappan. Across the street lived the Goodrich family, father Chauncey a friend of Nathaniel and faithful ally in ministry at Yale, and mother Julia Webster Goodrich a friend of Rebecca for many years. Taken together, these families (and others, like the Hillhouses and Whitneys farther away) comprised a remarkable little community. It is no wonder that Taylor's home was known as "the scene of a very bright intellectual and social life."[13]

The Taylor's had six children, five of whom lived to adulthood. Their oldest, Mary (b. 1811), who "inherited something of her father's mental power," married a clergy-man-scholar, Noah Porter, later the president of Yale College (1871–86). The second daughter, Harriet, also married a man of the cloth, Dr. Samuel G. Buckingham of Leba-non, Connecticut. Buckingham served for 50 years as the pastor of Springfield's South Congregational Church, succeeding Mary's husband, Noah Porter, to the pulpit there. Next came Susan (b. 1816), who married a doctor, Abel Bellows Robeson of Walpole, New Hampshire, and set up house near her husband's practice in New York City. When Robeson died tragically at the age of 36, Susan moved back in with her parents and died of tuberculosis a few years later (1856). Rebecca (b. 1818), the youngest daugh-ter, married Walter T. Hatch, a wealthy merchant, banker and broker in New York City. In 1902 she endowed the Nathaniel William Taylor Lectureship at Yale, and in 1905 published her *Personal Reminiscences*. The family baby and only boy, Nathaniel William Taylor, Jr. (b. 1823), lived an intriguing life as a doctor, farmer, world traveler, and Union soldier. He graduated from Yale College (1844) and Yale Medical School (1846), did not marry until 1865 (when he wed Elizabeth Hubbard of Bloomfield, Con-necticut), and had no children—and apparently not much religion either.[14]

According to one of his students, "Taylor's life at home was beautiful. He was a com-panion to his children as truly as to his wife. Amid all his labors, he was always ready to turn aside to gratify the slightest wish of any of them. . . . And they were always satisfied with his company; for no one could interest and please them so well." Another noted the popularity of the Taylor home in the Yale community, suggesting that the Professor was not his household's sole attraction. "In the fine old university town there was always so-ciety of the best, and the house where 'the Taylor girls' were as great an attraction as their brilliant father, was visited by a host of guests, many of them marked by social elegance as well as intellectual culture. To the sisters came suitors in plenty." Accounts like this, while hyperbolic, reveal that Taylor enjoyed a stable, supportive, and very traditional family life—one that enabled him to devote a great deal of energy to his work.[15]

"A Mahogany Preacher in Our House"

That work intensified significantly several weeks before Taylor's wedding when, on August 21, he received his license to preach. Issued by the New Haven West Association, the ministerial body toward which the town's Edwardsians gravitated,[16] the license granted him permission to preach in any of Connecticut's Congregational churches. He did so willingly, though somewhat nervously, gaining confidence as a public speaker and making known his allegiance to the Edwardsian ways of his mentor, President Dwight. As Orcutt stated symbolically of one of his first preaching occasions, "[W]hen called to address his youthful associates in New Milford [right after his wedding], many of whom did not sympathize with his Christian faith and fervor, he selected for his text the words, 'If I say the truth, why do ye not believe me?' and preached the gospel then, as always afterwards, as though he believed it to be true." Taylor's late grandfather might well have resented such strident enthusiasm in his pulpit.[17]

Taylor continued to preach supply in several different Connecticut churches, studying with Dwight in preparation for a permanent call. And then early in 1811, he preached on probation for six Sundays to one of the most prominent congregations in all of Connecticut. New Haven's First Church—known as the "Center Church" for its position on the town green between Trinity Episcopal Church and what is now called the United Church—had muddled along without a pastor since the departure of Moses Stuart, who had left in 1810 to accept an appointment at Andover Seminary. Taylor had preached there a few months before, on November 1, 1810, receiving a stipend of $10 and impressing the leadership with his potential. Invited back now "with a view to his future Settlement in the Gospel ministry," he inspired them once again with his pastoral skills. The church voted on July 16 to extend him a permanent call. But apprehensive about his ability at just 25 years of age to serve this prestigious congregation in the manner to which it had become accustomed, Taylor blenched when he learned that the vote had been less than unanimous. It took a second, more urgent call, as well as some prodding from President Dwight, to convince him that his settlement was indeed the will of God. As he recounted years later in a letter to William Sprague,

> When I received a call to the church in this city, which I, in every suitable way, tried to avoid accepting, Dr. Dwight was very anxious that I should accept it. I told him frankly my principal objection. You know the great popularity of my predecessor in that pulpit; and I told Dr. Dwight that, if I were settled there, I could expect nothing else than that I should be dismissed within a year. "Why so?" said he. "Because," replied I, "I cannot satisfy the demands of the people as a preacher." He thought I could. I said, "I think not without a miracle." He answered with emphasis, "You do not know what you can do. No young man of even respectable talents knows what he can do, and hence, in many cases, they do so little. Believe me," said he, "I have no fears of the issue, and I know much better what *you* can do, than you know yourself."[18]

That settled it. Taylor was ordained and installed at the Center Church on April 8, 1812. Dwight preached the ordination sermon on "The Dignity and Excellence of the Gospel," a ringing defense of theological orthodoxy against the rise of "infidelity" that set the pace for Taylor's ministry in New Haven. Before long, Taylor himself was speaking out against infidelity, opposing the plans of the Universalists to plant a congregation in town. He also proved an unusually ardent advocate of church discipline—even for an Edwardsian—a trait that led to the withdrawal of some who chafed under Taylor's youthful rule and a slight increase on the membership rolls at Trinity Episcopal. Shortly after his ordination he did consider leaving the church to pursue further studies at Andover Seminary. But success in ministry changed his mind. The congregation treated him well, going so far as to give him a $500 bonus in 1815. Soon Taylor was lauded as one of the finest pastors in all New England, a perfect fit in his high-profile, tall-steeple congregation.[19]

It was Taylor's success in reviving the church that secured this reputation and earned him the love and respect of all who now honored the memory of Edwards. Taylor's ministry, moreover, followed the pattern of Moses Stuart, the first Edwardsian pastor in the Center Church's history. Only six years earlier, on February 8, 1806, the church had begun to make a remarkable turn toward Edwardsianism when Stuart accepted the call to serve as the congregation's senior pastor after its people dismissed the ailing and embittered Old Calvinist James Dana. Almost immediately, Stuart initiated what Taylor's successor, Leonard Bacon (among many others), would call a revivalistic "revolution" at the church, winning it over for the "New Divinity." By January 26, 1809, when the congregation adopted a new "Confession, Covenant, & Articles of Practice," Stuart succeeded in abrogating the Half-Way Covenant there, reserving membership for professing Christians and barring the children of nonmembers from baptism. Despite these restrictions, his ministry thrived. And when he left after only four years, church leaders worried about the future. They held high hopes for their new minister, and Taylor did not disappoint them. He carried on the revolution, riding Stuart's Edwardsian wave, preaching revivals there in 1815, 1816, and 1820–21, and adding nearly four hundred members to the rolls in only a decade. As Newman Smyth would later characterize the Stuart-Taylor era at the Center Church's 250th anniversary celebration,

> [T]he coming of Moses Stuart to this church had been like the springing up of the fresh breeze, and the inflowing of a great tide of power. It was the beginning of the revival era of the church. His ministry of hardly four years' duration was an innovation, and when he exchanged his reviving pastorate for his fearless professorship at Andover, Moses Stuart left the heart of this church full of the impulse of the new divinity. But if Moses Stuart's ministry was like the coming in of the tide over the parched sands of an arid theology, Dr. Taylor's preaching was that tide in its full flood and resistlessness of power.[20]

Unlike Stuart, Taylor even managed to get James Dana back to the church, a feat that signaled the growing appeal of Edwardsian efforts at church renewal. One of the movement's most deeply entrenched opponents, the Old Calvinist Dana had been at odds with the Edwardsians for years—first with Bellamy during the infamous Wallingford Controversy of the late 1750s; then with Edwards, Jr. when Dana was settled in New Haven (1789); and finally during the conflict over Stuart. After his firing, Dana left the church he had served for many years and began to attend the College Church, in whose pulpit Dwight presided. While there, for reasons unknown, Dana's Old Calvinist biases "were overcome" and he was encouraged to resume his attendance at the Center Church. After an initial Sunday visit, his former flock was overjoyed. They voted to invite their former pastor to reunite with them more permanently, as well as to "furnish him with a suitable & proper seat for his accommodation." Not long thereafter, Taylor encouraged Dana to sit with him in the pulpit. Dana obliged, and remained there in a visible display of support for Taylor until his final sickness and death a few months later (August 1812).[21]

Before long, the Center Church meetinghouse was bursting at the seams and discussions were underway about the construction of a new building. On November 12, 1812, the church approved the proposal of a local entrepreneurial syndicate to finance and build a new meetinghouse in return for "the avails" of the current structure, as well as the sole right to the sale of pews for the new sanctuary. The "old brick meetinghouse" then in use had stood since 1757, but still had materials fit for reuse in other projects. And in an era when Connecticut's citizens still paid a tax in support of the churches (the Congregationalists were not disestablished there until 1818), the idea of raising a building without an additional capital campaign proved quite attractive. Late in December of 1812 the city granted the church a permit. Architect Ithiel Town was hired to design the new facility. He drew up plans based on London's church of St. Martin-in-the-Fields and soon the green was full of the sights and sounds of manual labor. Some local resistance emerged when it was learned that the new construction would disturb the burial ground that had lain behind the church since the days of the Puritans. A petition to block the project subscribed by 178 people was presented in March of 1813 at a public meeting of concerned residents. And when workers started to dig, a group of townspeople arrived with shovels "and began to throw back the earth as fast as it was thrown out." But the building project continued, this opposition soon faded away and, 21 months and $35,000 later, the congregation moved into its new home. A dedication ceremony was held on December 27, 1814, at which President Dwight graced the assembly in a closing prayer. Still only 28 years of age, Pastor Taylor now preached the gospel in one of the grandest Federal churches in all of America.[22]

Mitigating the fears of many residents regarding the disturbance of the graveyard was the rapid development in recent years of New Haven's Grove Street Cemetery. Heralded as the world's first public cemetery to be laid out in family plots, Grove Street began in 1796 when James Hillhouse led a group of 30 New Haven residents in buying land and developing what they described as "a new burial ground, larger, better arranged for the accommodation of families, and by its retired situation better calculated to impress the mind with a solemnity becoming the repository of the dead." The cemetery opened the following year with the burial of Martha Townsend, after which funerals on the green soon tapered off. In 1812, they ceased entirely with the interment of Martha Whittlesey. And nine years later the city removed the remaining gravestones from the green (approximately 800 in all) to new plots parceled out for them in the cemetery—leaving behind only the 137 now under the church (in which a crypt was built that houses them to this day), as well as the subterranean remains of an estimated four to five thousand people.[23]

Taylor's success at the Center Church had much to do with his work ethic. He "was laborious in preparing his sermons," as William Fowler remembered fondly. A mutual friend once said to Fowler that he had seen Taylor early one morning writing a sermon in his shirt sleeves. "You are stripped to your work," the man called out with admiration to the pulpiteer. "Sermons, now-a-days, are not written with the coat off." Regretfully, Fowler agreed that Taylor's diligence was rather unusual, adding that "it was pleasant" on his own morning walks to witness his pastor "thus employed."[24]

As Fisher phrased it, Taylor took great pains to communicate "the momentous doctrines which he was commissioned to enforce" with a simple clarity that proved accessible to every member of his congregation. "Since the days of President Edwards," he asserted, "no one has preached with greater plainness and directness of application, what some call the severe truths of religion." Fisher was not alone in his assessment of

Taylor's preaching. Many attested his passion for the laity and his unique ability to engage an audience with otherwise esoteric themes. He "always leaned to the side of the congregation," Theodore Munger once recalled. And when talking to seminary students, he "had little mercy for the dull or indolent preacher. He said: 'I never blame a man for sleeping in church; if he does, it is my fault. Give the people something to think of and they will keep awake.'"[25]

Taylor also kept them awake with impressive oratorical skills and what Charles Hodge once referred to as an alluring "magic power." Another Princetonian, Lyman Atwater, who grew up under Taylor's preaching and studied theology with him at Yale before moving south to double-cross him, honored the memory of what even he could not help but describe in the following terms: "[Taylor's] noble and massive forehead, . . . his wondrous eye, lustrous with intelligence and benevolent earnestness, his voice, so clear, sonorous, and grand—in short, his whole face, attitude, and expression, bespoke a great and extraordinary man. They were a power upon every man, woman, and child in his audience. For any congregation to have a worthy pastor, gifted with such a presence, is itself a benediction." Likewise, more faithful friends bespoke "the deep heavy tones" of Taylor's regal "trumpet voice," and the "impressive flashes of that eye through which the soul looked out from beneath the 'dome of thought.'" In the pulpit, it was said, "his face was bright with intelligence and instinct with emotion. His manner was dignified and self-possessed, as if he was master of the situation." Again, "his voice was deep-toned and impressive. And often his word, like the Word of God, was a hammer which, by successive blows, broke the sinner's heart, and the waters of contrition flowed forth." Of all his admirers, it was a local boy who summed these traits up most succinctly. As recounted by Fowler, "[W]hile the North church and the Center church were in progress of erection, two boys were, at a certain time, discussing the comparative beauty of the two houses. One said, 'We have got a mahogany pulpit in our house (the North church),' and the other boy replied: 'We have a mahogany preacher in our house.'"[26]

Whether or not such eulogistic commendations were entirely true, the evidence of Taylor's charisma and personal magnetism is overwhelming. As one of his colleagues would insist, "the love of his people for him knew no bounds." Another affirmed that "rarely has a pastor been so beloved by his people," explaining that "the reasons for this are plain":

> They knew that he loved their souls, and sincerely desired their spiritual welfare. He endeavored to become acquainted with them individually, and with their state of feeling respecting religion. He assiduously sought opportunities to confer with them on their salvation. . . . with them, as with all men, he was affable, frank, courteous, affectionate, without any assumed dignity or artificial manner, free from all small and mean traits, liberal-minded, open-hearted, and generous.

As yet another observer noted, "Dr. Taylor was more than an eloquent and fervid preacher—he was a devoted and sympathizing pastor, who was a joy to his people, and to whom his people were also a joy."[27]

One of the most visible signs of Taylor's success as a parish pastor and spiritual counselor was the conversion in 1815 of Sereno Dwight, the President's son. When only seven or eight years old, Sereno had contracted scarlet fever. His family had feared the worst and his worried father had vowed to God that, if his boy survived, he would train him up as a gospel minister. Sereno recovered from his physical ailments. But he did not undergo conversion and, breaking his father's heart, he entered the law instead of the ministry. In the summer of 1815, however, things began to change. Sereno attended a revival at New Haven's Center Church and, in response to Taylor's preaching, he finally experienced the new birth. Needless to say, his father was thrilled. Taylor received his mentor's son into church membership the following October. Not long thereafter, Sereno made good on his father's promise. He was licensed to preach in 1816 and gave his first sermon in Taylor's pulpit. Before the year was up he was serving as chaplain to the U.S. Senate. In 1817 he accepted a call to Boston's newly founded, evangelical Park Street Church, where he remained in faithful service the next 10 years. Due to ill health, he had to resign his pulpit in 1826, never to return again to pastoral ministry. But he lived until 1850 and remained a leader of the Edwardsian movement. He wrote a classic biography of Edwards, published a major edition of Edwards's *Works*, and went on to serve as president of Hamilton College—reinforcing his father's and Taylor's Edwardsian commitments in New York.[28]

Despite his reputation for such effective pastoral ministry, however, Taylor's workload tended to wear him rather thin. Even for a young man like himself, such a whirlwind of pastoral activity would eventually take its toll. An ardent preacher, eager revivalist, friend to sinners as well as saints, Taylor even played host to the president of the United States in 1817. In short, like many ministers, he burned his candle at both ends. As Fisher related, moreover, he soon became an insomniac whose active mind—even at bedtime—simply "refused to cease from its work." It is no surprise, then, that an offer to teach at Yale would prove attractive. Nor is it difficult to believe that Taylor would leave the Center Church in November of 1822 with what his successor described as "a physical constitution seriously impaired by the intense and long continued mental excitement which had characterized his ministry." Taylor had served his people well. But he was working himself to death. He was exhausted, and it was time to move on.[29]

"The Idol of His Pupils"

Since the beginning of the nineteenth century, Timothy Dwight had expressed interest in expanding Yale's theological curriculum. A keen supporter of general theological education, not to mention an educated ministry, he had long felt the need for "a more complete and systematic course of theological instruction in Yale College." Even before the opening of Andover Seminary (1808), in fact, he had announced his intention to offer a similar post-baccalaureate program in New Haven. So when Andover founders Jedidiah Morse and Samuel Spring rode into town to seek his blessing on their new venture in graduate-level theological education, Dwight quickly granted his "warm approval" but also publicized his resolve to "embrace the earliest opportunity" to form a seminary at Yale. Furthermore, after the meeting he whispered in confidence to Taylor that his own son Timothy (a prosperous New Haven merchant) had invested money toward this end.[30]

Though President Dwight did not live long enough to see these plans materialize, soon after his death in 1817 the pieces began falling into place. During the recess after commencement in the fall of that very year, two recent graduates approached Eleazar T. Fitch, the college's Livingston Professor of Divinity, with a request. Rather than move on to Andover Seminary, they hoped to remain right there at Yale and prepare for pastoral ministry under his care. Fitch consented and, by 1820, a dozen other Yale alumni had remained in New Haven to prepare for pastorates with him too.[31]

By early in 1822, Fitch's ad hoc seminary was growing large—so large, in fact, that 15 of his students petitioned the faculty requesting formal reception as a graduate school the following year. Fitch supported these students publicly, arguing the need for such a reception on the grounds of his overburdened schedule as well as the desire, now shared by many, to modernize Yale's theological curriculum. His faculty colleagues lent their support and sent a resolution to the Yale Corporation requesting the establishment of a post-baccalaureate theological program. To the delight of all concerned, the corporation approved the idea quickly, opening the "Theological Department in Yale College" (it was only later called Yale Divinity School) right away. Though in its first year of operation (1822–23) the school enrolled only two additional students, by its third year it had enrolled 16. By 1835, the school moved into the newly constructed Divinity Hall. And by the time of Taylor's death (1858), it had prepared 815 people for ministry assignments around the world.[32]

As it turned out, Timothy Dwight, the merchant son of President Dwight, had indeed invested money for such an endeavor. An active lay evangelist, he also led a group of 60 laymen who met in his home every Saturday night, sending out delegates to Connecticut's churches to try and encourage local revivals. Clearly, then, he supported the mission of Yale's new theological department. He also wanted to honor the memory of his late father. So he founded the Timothy Dwight Professorship in Didactic Theology at Yale, hoping to attract his father's protégé to the venture. He liquidated $5,000 in assets, helping to raise further subscriptions as well, endowing the chair with approximately $20,000 in all (including a gift from Professor Fitch in the curious amount of $1,666.66). Taylor was persuaded to assume the chair. (Bacon once said, "I do not speak at random when I say that the Dwight professorship was founded for [Taylor], and that the Theological Department was planned with the expectation of making him a teacher of theology"). He was installed right away. And he received the customary (and honorary) D.D. from the largely Edwardsian Union College the following summer, granting his title an air of academic respectability.[33]

As has been alluded to already, Professor Taylor now became the most prominent intellectual leader in what was by this time a very lively intellectual community. The aged Eli Whitney, who had already invented the cotton gin, was now living north of town and modeling the use of interchangeable parts and mass production at his world-famous armory in Hamden. New Haven resident Noah Webster was in the final stages of compiling his dictionary.[34] Yale's Benjamin Silliman had recently begun to publish the *American Journal of Science and Art*, while Cornelius Tuthill had just undertaken to publish the *Microscope*. Jedidiah Morse was pioneering in the modern study of geographical science. His son Samuel would soon begin work on the electric telegraph and Morse code, painting some of America's best-known portraits in the process. And Yale College continued to attract many of the nation's best and brightest, shedding more light with each passing year on southern New England and beyond.

Even in the midst of all these luminaries, however, Taylor's star soon shone the brightest, and his reputation as a cultural leader continued to grow. Fisher articulated a sentiment expressed by many other observers when he said that Taylor was "unquestionably the central figure in the Seminary." He went on to submit (in words that he must have known would frustrate future historians): "You cannot know him from his printed works. There was vastly more in the man than can be transferred to paper. Everything seemed different when it was warm from his lips. His extemporaneous flashes often surpassed his most elaborate discussions. He had a royal nature; a weight of personality, more easily felt than analyzed; an intellectual fascination that cast a spell over all within the circle of his influence." Indeed, the weight of testimony to Taylor's influence as an intellectual and a teacher burdens the historian trying to offer an objective assessment of the man. As with his appearance and preaching skills, his friends and acquaintances described his teaching with so many superlatives that their accounts seem nearly incredible. All affirmed Taylor's status as "the idol of his pupils," who were consistently "fascinated with the charm of his enthusiasm." As Munger maintained, "[T]here is no contagion so strong as that which passes from teacher to pupils, and Dr. Taylor had the power to convey it beyond any man I have ever known." Others echoed the notion that Taylor possessed an unusual "magnetic power," a singular "gift" or "peculiar power" for inspiring his pupils. Fisher explained that this had much to do with Taylor's love and compassion for students, and his devotion to spending hours with them in extracurricular discussion:

> He loved young men. He loved their warmth, their willingness to look at new truth, their frankness, their bright hopes of the future. . . . Not long ago, he mentioned to me that, the day before, he had reproved one of his class with more severity, perhaps, than the case required; expressing, at the same time, his grief, and adding, that he had been kept awake a great part of the night, by the thought that Christ would not have spoken so. Who will wonder that such a man drew to him the affections of his pupils?

Who indeed? As stated by Anson Stokes in his classic *Memorials of Eminent Yale Men*, "[A]s a stimulating instructor in theology, Taylor . . . has been unexcelled in America."[35]

Taylor's method in the classroom was to lecture boldly for about an hour and then sit back and encourage his students to respond in kind. George S. Merriam relished the experience. "When his lecture was over," he recounted, "[Taylor] would draw out his tobacco-box, refresh himself from the contents, and say, 'Now, young gentlemen, I'll hear *you*,'" noting that "the give-and-take which followed . . . was the best hour of the day.'" Munger remembered much of the same, adding, "[W]e were taught by precept and example to question and argue, and sometimes we tried our hand at it with the master, but always with defeat if we failed to agree. He gave no quarter, and his delight in victory was so great that we rather enjoyed it—waiving our own discomfiture."[36]

Taylor loved a good argument and taught his students to argue with him, all the while instilling respect in them for logic and critical reason. He reminded them often of an old saying that was attributed to Joseph Bellamy: "Do not be afraid of investigation and argument—*there is no poker in the truth*." As Taylor's lecture notes attest, he told his students at the beginning of class,

> In every part of our progress I invite the utmost freedom on your part. I shall be ready to answer all your questions remove all doubts explain what I may have stated not concisely

or imperfectly: and if placed in the wrong myself shall most freely acknowledge the same for we are never too old to learn. At the same time I shall expect to find your object the same as mine not to support any particular views but the acquisition of truth and if sometimes you find yourselves tripped up when very confident of your footing I shall hope . . . you manifest no feelings but those of good nature.

Fisher remembered that "there was something adventurous, almost chivalrous," in Taylor's willingness "to go wherever the truth would lead him," recalling vividly not only Taylor's "sayings . . . to this effect" but also "the gesture and the flash of the eye, which accompanied them." And though this sometimes yielded a cockiness that Taylor worked hard to guard against, and that rubbed off all-too-easily on the more impressionable seminarians ("in the form of inordinate self-confidence and a too liberal disregard of seniors and superiors, and good authorities," as one of them put it), nearly everyone remembered him as a bold and courageous thinker. "Go over Niagara," he told the young men. "Don't flinch, be true, be a man."[37]

Taylor's Extracurricular Labors

As will be seen more fully below, Taylor used his platform at Yale to further his Edwardsian agenda, steeping his students in Edwards's theology and modeling an Edwardsian approach to ministry. Moreover, he did so now as one of the most prominent clergymen in the northeast, attracting attention by force of his office to his uniquely charismatic (and ultimately controversial) leadership style. Even after assuming his post at Yale, Taylor maintained an active commitment to revival preaching that made a clarion Edwardsian call for immediate repentance. To be sure, Old Calvinists had a place for revivalism as well. But the Taylorites' radical commitment to 180-degree conversions and immediate repentance distanced them from the more thoroughly covenantal and means-oriented spirituality of Old Calvinism.

Inasmuch as Taylor retained this commitment to gospel preaching throughout his life, a brief survey of his subsequent career in Connecticut's pulpits will have to suffice. Taylor continued to preach regularly at New Haven's Center Church prior to his successor Leonard Bacon's installation in March of 1825. He then helped to pastor New Haven's Third Church from its founding in 1826 until the settlement of its first permanent pastor, Charles A. Boardman, four years later. He served regularly for nearly a year as the stated preacher of Hartford's North Church. And when his former student, Elisha Cleaveland, turned against him at the Third Church and began to oppose the congregation's historic commitment to New Haven theology, the church split and Taylor returned in November of 1838 to preach supply for over a year to the majority—now renamed New Haven's Chapel Street Church (later the Church of the Redeemer) and led by the Timothy Dwight who had earlier endowed his chair at Yale. In the meantime, Taylor had managed to preach for extended periods of time at New Haven's Plymouth Church, Free Church (later named the College Street Church), and North Church. He had also obliged the congregations that sought him out as a guest preacher during New Haven's major revival of 1831. And he persisted in supplying pulpits, substituting for Fitch in the College Church, and supervising revivals throughout his career. As Leonard Bacon once summarized, "[T]here is no Congregational church in this city, almost none in this neighborhood of churches, which has not, in some vacancy of its pastorate, sought and enjoyed his powerful ministration of the word."[38]

Taylor's daughter remembered that even her father's "Lectures on the Moral Government of God," when delivered twice to Yale's "Academical" students (as distinguished from the "Theological" students), yielded revivals each time. As Fisher added gratefully, "[T]here is a large number of ministers among our graduates, together with many in other professions, who date their conversion from interviews with him." Taylor encouraged his students to emulate his persistency in preaching, even if they too became academics, bragging that when Moses Stuart "gave up preaching and even going to meeting" after moving to Andover Seminary, "he lost his spirituality, but by constant preaching I have kept mine."[39]

Taylor's colleagues in the New Haven Theology, Beecher and Goodrich as well as Fitch, maintained busy revival schedules as well. As one observer would note, Taylor's Yale associates "co-operated most heartily" with him, promulgating his evangelistic agenda and "acknowledging him as the chief among brethren." Together, these men "were almost like brothers of a common household. . . . They knew one another with perfect intimacy. . . . There were no ambitions, or jealousies, or divisive influences, to part them asunder, or in any way to prevent complete harmony in their plans or their efforts." While, unlike the others, Beecher never taught at Yale, he nevertheless defended Taylor and his Edwardsian revivalism from his pulpits in Edwardsian Litchfield and Unitarian Boston, to his Presbyterian hot seat in Cincinnati, to his grave in the Taylor family plot. Goodrich, a former pastor in Middletown, Connecticut, who had turned down the presidency of Williams College at the tender age of 31, stood the next closest to Taylor. He taught a course at Yale on "Revivals of Religion" and, as a co-pastor of Yale's College Church, became the prime mover behind the school's several antebellum revivals. While Fitch was no great orator, he, too, managed to become a prominent Edwardsian revivalist. With Goodrich, he facilitated the revivals at Yale and, as Livingston Professor of Divinity and pastor of the College Church, preached a regular course of Edwardsian and Taylorite theology to hundreds of Yale students.[40]

In the tradition of Timothy Dwight, Taylor, Goodrich, and Fitch made sure that Yale's theological curriculum maintained a heavy Edwardsian flavor. Between the fall of 1834 and the spring of 1840, for example, students withdrew Edwards's *Works* from the school's library nearly twice as often as the next most popular volume.[41] Taylorite involvement in New England's religious periodicals also proceeded along Edwardsian lines. Beecher's guiding hand in New Haven's *Christian Spectator* and Boston's *Spirit of the Pilgrims* ensured that both journals granted space to Taylorite authors while promulgating revivalistic, Edwardsian theology.[42]

New Haven's *Spectator* emerged from the Doctrinal Tract Society founded by Beecher, Taylor, Goodrich, and others in 1818 to combat Episcopalianism and Unitarianism in New England. As one of Taylor's arch-rivals, Joseph Harvey, remembered in 1832, this tract society originated with a meeting held in Taylor's study in 1817. It did publish a few tracts, including Taylor's anti-Arminian *Man, A Free Agent without the Aid of Divine Grace* (1818). But its efforts culminated in the publication of the *Christian Spectator*, edited initially by another Dwight student, the Rev. Thomas Davies, beginning in 1819. In an extremely adulatory "Review of the Works of President Edwards," published in 1821, the journal declared that "the churches of New-England, if they could wish to be named after any man, would choose that it should be after Edwards." Indeed, "we do think that no writer since the days of the apostles, has better understood and taught the word of God, or has more ably defended its doctrines." In 1823 the *Spectator* reiterated this theme, ranking Edwards as the best American theologian ever and then, "leaving a blank space, as is sometimes done in the English Universities, to indicate the compara-tive standing of candidates for academical honours," ranking Edwards, Jr., next. When Goodrich bought the *Spectator* in 1828 to make it the official organ of the New Haven Theology, it maintained its Edwardsian focus, now devoting a great deal of copy to the Taylorites' intra-Edwardsian battles. It published numerous articles covering hundreds of pages on the theology and internal conflicts of the Edwardsian tradition, claiming figures such as Edwards ("this 'prince of divines'"), Bellamy, and Nathan Strong as theological ancestors.[43]

Beecher, along with Edward Dorr Griffin, Benjamin Wisner, Leonard Woods, and Samuel A. Worcester, founded *The Spirit of the Pilgrims* in 1827, not as an explicitly Edwardsian journal, but as an orthodox trinitarian organ that would combat the rise of Unitarianism in the Boston area. They hired the Emmonsist Enoch Pond to be their first editor, however, and throughout its six volumes (1828–33) the journal gave space to Taylorite concerns and promulgated Edwardsian views. Pond, for example, reprinted an old Samuel Hopkins sermon on "The Importance and Necessity of Christians Con-sidering Jesus Christ in the Extent of His High and Glorious Character," and extracts from a Nathanael Emmons sermon entitled "Faithful Ministers Avow Their Religious Sentiments," in his effort to stem the Unitarian tide. And in the introduction to the journal's fourth volume, its underwriters characterized their "views of doctrine" in terms of a commitment to biblical orthodoxy "as explained by Edwards and his coadjutors and followers."[44]

The New Haven theologians carried forward a strong Edwardsian commitment to benevolent reform as well. They remained quite proud of New England's activist heri-tage, characterizing the benevolence boom of the first third of the nineteenth century as the "practical effects" of "the metaphysics of Edwards, Bellamy, and Smalley." The *Quarterly Christian Spectator* boasted in 1831:

> Nine tenths, at least, of all the money that has been raised in the United States for for-eign missions, has been contributed in New-England; and a large share of the remainder by men educated here. The American Tract Society was transferred from New-England, and is indebted for the most of its efficiency to New-England men. The American Sun-day School Union was planned in New-Haven. . . . The system of charitable assistance for pious indigent young men, who are studying for the ministry, is a New-England sys-tem, and the principal funds which have been expended in this cause, have been raised here. In regard to domestic missions, we can point our presbyterian brethren to four hundred of their own churches, planted and sustained by the benevolence of the congre-gationalists of Connecticut alone. And all over our country, and in all denominations of christians, we see those who were educated in New-England, uniformly bearing a leading part in every operation of benevolence.[45]

Taylorites played at least minor roles in a wide variety of social reform efforts, from the temperance and Sunday School movements—Taylor began a Sunday School pro-gram at the Center Church very early in his ministry and served as the first president of the Connecticut Sunday School Union, founded in 1825—to Bible societies, charitable societies, and the movements against Freemasonry and the theater.[46] As one might expect, however, they reserved their best efforts for the cause of evangelism and missions, particularly home missions. By 1872, only 31 of the approximately 850 students trained at Yale Divinity School had served in foreign missions. But as will be made quite clear in part 3, Yale alumni had taken significant strides in the evangelization of the American frontier, especially in Illinois and the Mississippi Valley. Taylor, who was a corporate member of the American Board of Comissioners for Foreign Missions, also served as the founding secretary of the Domestic Missionary Society of Connecticut, an organization established in response to a rousing sermon by Lyman Beecher to the Congregationalists of Wolcott on "Building Up the Waste Places in Connecticut" (1812). Taylor's students, inspired like most other young Edwardsians by the zealous piety of David Brainerd, formed a potent missions association at Yale from which the famous "Illinois Band" emerged to convert the American West for evangelical Protestantism. As the *Spectator* noted in 1831, "[T]he best interests of this country are vitally connected with the character, to be formed by the inhabitants of the Valley of the Mississippi." Beecher's *A Plea for the West* (1832), released upon his own move to Cincinnati, only confirmed this sentiment. America itself had become a vast and expanding mission field.[47]

The Edwardsians of the first half of the nineteenth century lived through an era of social change in New England that proved more extensive and intensive than anything the early Edwardsians had encountered in the decades following the Great Awakening. In 1790, most New Englanders still lived on farms; by 1860, however, most lived in urban areas and worked for wages. In between times, New England underwent what some social historians have referred to as a transportation revolution and a market revolution. New Haven itself changed from a rural town to a minor city during Taylor's tenure at Yale.[48]

Furthering the trend set by earlier generations of Edwardsians, the Taylorites responded to these changes with a heavily spiritual message of individual conversion. Less interested than even their forebears in Christianizing the social order from the top down since Connecticut's disestablishment of Congregationalism in 1818,[49] Taylor and his followers worked to ameliorate American society one soul at a time. While remaining very public figures, and thus undermining later scholarly efforts to dismiss their conversionistic piety as essentially private and socially irrelevant, they believed firmly that social improvement must begin with spiritual renewal, and the kind of spiritual renewal occasioned by fervent, personal faith in Christ. In the words of local historian Mary Hewitt Mitchell, "as the character of politics changed" during the antebellum period, New England's leading churchmen "gradually withdrew until today there is on their part little active participation in politics and the ruling class is of another kind."[50]

The Taylorites did maintain a casual interest in national politics. Lyman Beecher, for example, who was always more political than his colleagues in New Haven, campaigned publicly with William Henry Harrison in 1840, and the Taylorites consistently supported the Whig political agenda. Eleazar Fitch once preached an old-fashioned version of the national covenant to the future civic leaders among Yale's student body: "If you . . . shall, in your various stations, wait on God," he proclaimed, "and fulfill your appointed duties; the God of our fathers will bless you. Jehovah shall dwell in the land, its glory and defence." Even Taylor himself could at times espouse a Christian republicanism, arguing that the health of the nation rested on the level of genuine piety among its citizens. The Taylorites' spiritual agenda did bear significant political implications, then, and was often expressed in language that carried rather heavy political overtones.[51]

But to argue with Daniel Walker Howe that the theological "objective" of the New Haven Theology involved "formulating into a religious ideology the culture associated with Whiggery" is to overstate the case. First and foremost, the Taylorites—Lyman Beecher not excepted—saved souls. Their republican language and support for Whig values, though related closely to their Edwardsian piety, were by-products of their larger effort to convert Americans to lives of uniquely Christian discipleship. Further, as Douglas Strong has demonstrated, while Taylor's views did pan out politically in a wide variety of ways—not least in upstate New York, where they inspired groups as radical as the Liberty Party of the 1840s—they did so indirectly. Taylor himself opposed these developments. And those who led them became exasperated with his apolitical caution.[52]

This point becomes clear in a telling article, "Christian Politics," published in the *Spectator* at the end of 1835, where the author makes what he calls an "important" distinction between "civil liberty" and "the liberty of the gospel." For the Taylorites, "the latter," or gospel liberty, "is an emancipation of the soul, a deliverance from the bondage of sin and Satan." The former, or "civil and political privileges should be estimated and sought after only as they contribute to this deliverance, and to the advancement of the Redeemer's kingdom." In Augustinian and Edwardsian fashion, the Taylorites promoted civil liberty, civic virtue, and social reform not as ends in themselves, but as they supported or manifested true virtue, which was measured only by divine standards and found only among the regenerate inhabitants of the city of God. Without grace, they contended, "the course of our nature is downward":

> All history bears testimony to this truth, and that there is no remedy for the evil but a change of our nature. What the world calls virtue is nothing but a tinsel morality, a fashionable costume, prescribed by public opinion, and not by the law of God. The virtue which qualifies a people for self-government, and which constitutes the life-blood of republics, is obedience to God. This virtue is essential to national prosperity, and the condition on which national blessings are bestowed.

Christian politics and Christian republicanism were pursued in an entirely different realm (or "kingdom") than their secular counterparts—their common adjective made a world of difference.[53]

While this critique of secular morality enabled the Taylorites and other latter-day Edwardsians to effect significant social changes without explicitly politicizing their churches or their message, however, it also led to a very spiritualized understanding of America's increasingly complex social ills and a frustratingly gradualist (and thus implicitly politicized) approach to their cure. Because the Bible told Christians to submit to all lawful authority, the Taylorites held that "forcible opposition to government, and violent revolutions, are not necessary to aid the work of moral or political reform." Indeed, "they usually have a contrary tendency, by the encouragement of vice, of a spirit of insubordination and general licentiousness." Law and order, on the other hand, created conditions conducive to the spread of the gospel and the peaceful transformation of individual hearts.[54] The Taylorites did speak out against the corruptions of wealth and power, the evils of slavery, and the general viciousness of American society, but their persistent focus on personal piety and their virtual silence on the nation's macro-level social problems have led recent commentators to charge them with "sanctifying" the economic aspirations of Yankee entrepreneurs and leaving the needs of the emergent working class to more "plebeian" Christians.[55]

Perhaps nowhere are the shortcomings of the Taylorites' overwhelmingly spiritual approach to social reform more evident than in the realm of antislavery. Like nearly all fellow Edwardsians, the Taylorites proved consistent advocates of colonizationism and opponents of the evils of slavery.[56] When push came to shove, however, their concern to uphold law and order, to ensure the South's peaceful transition away from a slave-based economy, and to promote Christian charity among all concerned undermined their efforts to put an end to the practice. Their opposition to radical abolitionism was common throughout New England. Like many other well-meaning whites, the Taylorites repudiated the acrid tactics of the Garrisonians and believed that the slaves' best interest lay in owning their own land and running their own government. But at times the Taylorites hid behind their rhetoric of realism and moderation, lacking the courage to take steps even they knew were right.

When in 1831, for example, the citizens of New Haven rose up in fierce opposition to Simeon S. Jocelyn (Taylor's former parishioner who since 1829 had been the white Congregationalist pastor of New Haven's African Ecclesiastical Society), Arthur Tappan (the great evangelical philanthropist and Taylor's next-door neighbor), Samuel Cornish (the well-known black Presbyterian pastor and antislavery leader in Philadelphia), and their backers who sought to found an African American labor college in New Haven, the Yale faculty failed to muster enough moral courage to quell the resistance and the project flopped. By this time, approximately 800 black people lived in New Haven, comprising roughly one-ninth of the city's population. Formally disenfranchised since 1818 by Connecticut's state constitution, and facing powerful racial prejudice, deeply entrenched segregation, dismal living conditions, and virtually no economic opportunity, New Haven's black community received little help from even the most courageous of the clergy.[57]

Leonard Bacon provides the best example of the Taylorites' frustratingly moderate, though quite consistent, antislavery reform. The main architect of the Taylorites' colonizationist position and a well-known antislavery activist throughout the antebellum period, Bacon led in the founding of New Haven's African Improvement Society in the summer of 1825 and went on to cofound the city's *Journal of Freedom* in 1834. He preached at the funeral of Jehudi Ashmun, the former governor of Liberia who died in New Haven in 1828 and was the first person of color buried in the Grove Street Cemetery. He served on the committee that raised support for the defense of the Amistad slaves and eventually enabled their long journey back to Africa (accompanied by two missionaries). He helped to found the American Missionary Association, which was inspired by the Amistad case and played a major role in Negro education. He served as senior editor of the *New York Independent*, a Congregationalist free-soil weekly that proved very influential throughout the northeastern United States. None other than Abraham Lincoln, not long before his death, told Bacon that his *Essays on Slavery* (1846) had played a major role in shaping Lincoln's own approach to the subject. Bacon's own brother, David Bacon, toiled for two years as a missionary doctor among the ex-slaves of the troubled colony of Liberia; and his son, Major Edward Bacon, served as a northern officer in the Civil War, leading a battalion of black troops into battle. But, in the end, even Bacon proved weak-kneed and disappointingly ineffective, leading an oppressively moderate colonizationist charge that did almost as little to placate slaveholders as it did to free the slaves.[58]

Indeed, it took the passage of the Kansas-Nebraska Bill and repeal of the Missouri Compromise in 1854 to spur Taylor and most of his associates to any serious civil action. Taylor and Bacon spoke out publicly at anti-Nebraska meetings held in New Haven on March 8 and 10, 1854. The aging Taylor, who had spoken just four years earlier in favor of the Compromise of 1850,[59] contended that "the Nebraska Bill is a mean attempt to violate a fair bargain." If "worst comes to worst," he threatened, "I could lay off the garments of my profession and put on a soldier's coat in the cause of freedom. . . . I will go to the Throne of Grace with prayers and tears for my country, and thence, wiping these tears, if need be, to battle and to death." At New Haven's storied Kansas meeting on March 22, 1856, Taylor's former student Samuel W. S. Dutton (whose house was now a stop on the underground railroad) and Lyman Beecher's son, Henry Ward Beecher, sold Sharpe's rifles (known as "Beecher Bibles") from Dutton's pulpit at the United Church, inspiring the 60 New Haven members of New England's Kansas Company to secure freedom for the black residents of Kansas. In July of 1857 Taylor provided the lead signature on a letter from 43 of Connecticut's leading citizens to President Buchanan opposing the use of the army to enforce the Kansas-Nebraska Act in Kansas. But even in these late efforts he seemed as concerned with fair play and the safety of the Union as with the abolition of slavery. While the Edwardsians' narrowly spiritual understanding of conversion may have symbolized a powerful cultural (and even countercultural) critique in the second half of the eighteenth century, in this era of Edwardsian dominance it also provided a spiritual escape from the gritty work of social change.[60]

For better and for worse, then, Taylor belonged to the Edwardsians and, after his appointment to the Dwight chair, he would help to lead them into the future. Further, his connection and continuity with the Edwardsian theological culture should not prove nearly as surprising as it has ever since his death. For despite their reputation, the Taylorites and those closest to them always deemed the New Haven Theology a vital extension of the Edwardsian tradition. Taylor's daughter Rebecca, for one, identified her father as a proponent of what she called the "New Divinity," and distanced him quite clearly from "old Calvinism." His son-in-law Noah Porter noted that "the works of all the New England divines were the familiar hand-books of his reading." Leonard Bacon called Taylor "the last, as the elder Edwards was the first, of the great masters of the distinctive theology of New England. . . . The names in that succession . . . are few,— Hopkins, the younger Edwards, Smalley, Emmons, Taylor,—and the last, not least in the illustrious dynasty." George Park Fisher referred to Taylor as "the last of our New England schoolmen, . . . the compeer of Emmons and Hopkins, of Smalley and the Edwardses," noting that "probably none of his contemporaries was so well acquainted with the great divines of the New England school of theology, beginning with the elder Edwards. The principal works of President Edwards, Dr. Taylor knew almost by heart." Lyman Beecher defended his own and Taylor's fidelity to Edwardsianism on many occasions, distancing their thought from Old Calvinists and Arminians alike. He spoke glowingly of Edwards. His children pointed to Edwards as their father's "favorite author" or, as Beecher's biographer Stuart Henry has phrased it, his "Protestant surrogate for a patron saint." In a letter to his son George in November of 1830, Beecher advised, "next after the Bible, read and study Edwards, whom to understand in theology, accommodated to use, will be as high praise in theological science as to understand Newton's works in accommodation to modern uses of natural philosophy."[61]

Taylor himself, though less concerned with theological labels than most of his peers, did not fail to confess his own allegiance to the Edwardsian tradition, working almost exclusively with Edwards and the Edwardsians as his authorities at hand, and defending Edwardsianism constantly from the criticisms of Unitarians, Methodists, and other Arminians.[62] In short, Taylor was steeped in the theological culture of the Edwardsians. Since his teenage years they had nurtured him spiritually, excited his intellect, and shaped his world. And now that he held the reins of the Edwardsians' fabled "one-hoss shay," he would try to steer it in the manner he thought best suited to his own day, while working to keep it from collapsing under the weight of its mighty load.

In part 2, then, I examine his arduous work as a clerical teamster, paying special (and unusual) attention to the historical significance of Taylor's thought. I focus closely on his claims to continuity with the Edwardsians, leaving the role that he played in the decline of Edwardsian culture to part 3. I provide, thereby, a corrective to the long tradition of interpretation that largely neglects his self-perception, ignores the details of his thought, and overlooks the Edwardsian identities of hundreds of other antebellum thinkers.

II

RECONTEXTUALIZATION

4

"He Can If He Won't"

The New Haven Doctrine of Original Sin

> You can and you can't,
> You shall and you shan't,
> You will and you won't,
> You'll be damn'd if you do,
> You'll be damn'd if you don't.
> popular New England rhyme

Taylor was a polemical rather than a systematic theologian. The vast majority of his writings arose from the heat of controversy. In fact, posthumous works excepted, all of Taylor's theological work hit the press between 1816 and 1837, most appearing in the late 1820s and early 1830s during the heyday of the Taylorite controversy. Taylor's daughter Rebecca remembered how seldom the family enjoyed her father's presence during this period in their home at 48 Temple Street: "I have often heard my mother say that during the early years of the theological controversy, in which my father was engaged, he was so engrossed that she often had to be satisfied with only a smile from the opposite end of the table at meals."[1]

Despite the polemical or occasional character of his corpus, however, Taylor's thought did hang together. Not only did it take a definite shape and direction from the discourse of the Edwardsian theological culture but it developed according to a coherent pattern that centered on three major loci: the doctrine of original sin, the theme of God's moral government, and the doctrine of regeneration. I will devote the next two chapters to the second and third of these loci. The second, the theme of divine moral government, derived from Taylor's belief in the justice and equity of God's plan of salvation. It overarched his entire theology and provided it with a con-sistently evangelistic (not moralistic) orientation. The third, the doctrine of regenera-tion, stood as the culmination of Taylor's theology, the teaching toward which all others were directed. It built on the evangelistic impulse provided by his understand-ing of the world's moral structure and enabled him to preach boldly for immediate repentance. I want to focus in this chapter, though, on Taylor's most famous (and infamous) teaching, the one most often identified with Taylorism itself—his doctrine of original sin.

In the midst of the buoyant optimism of early national America, New England's Cal-vinists found it increasingly difficult to defend their notion of human depravity. While the Edwardsians continued to resist the many caricatures of their doctrine, finessing a concept of depravity based on voluntary (moral) rather than physical (natural) inability, their foes remained skeptical. New England's liberal Christians, especially, sought to discredit such Edwardsian subtleties by pitting them against high Calvinist orthodoxy and its language of natural or total depravity—a divide-and-conquer strategy intended to undermine Edwardsian successes by buttressing similar criticisms from the now-dwindling Old Calvinists.[2] The revolt against Calvinist views of sin was only magnified in the 1810s by the coming of age of American Unitarianism; by the early 1820s it had culminated in the famous debate between Harvard's Henry Ware and Andover's Leonard Woods over the allegedly deleterious moral effects of the Calvinists' low view of human nature. Ware and other liberals beheld a "pernicious tendency" in the Calvinist belief in "the entire worthlessness of all the works of righteousness and good dispositions" of the unconverted. "For if human virtue be thought of no value, and of no estimation in the sight of God, the motive for its practice is weakened, if not destroyed."[3] Unfortunately for New England's Calvinists, Ware seemed to many observers to have gotten the best of Woods. Taylor and his colleagues certainly thought so. As Bennet Tyler remembered later, Taylor "was heard to say, that . . . Dr. Ware had the better of the argument, and that Dr. Woods had put back the controversy with Unitarians fifty years." The Taylorites soon entered the fray themselves to salvage what they could. Their embarrassment over the seeming impotence of New England Calvinism to defend and promote itself proved tremendously significant for Taylor and for the development of the New Haven Theology. Frank Hugh Foster exaggerated only slightly when he claimed that the Unitarian controversy "determined [Taylor's] whole theological career." It "was his purpose to refute the Unitarian reasoning thoroughly, and for this end to explore completely the whole subject of anthropology, that led him to the theological positions . . . which have received the name of Taylorism."[4]

Goodrich and Fitch spoke out first in lectures to the Yale students. Beginning with a controversial address by Goodrich on Saturday evening, December 15, 1821, they made larger claims than usual that the liberal critique of the Calvinist doctrine of depravity and its purportedly stifling effect on moral endeavor rested largely on a common misapprehension of New England orthodoxy. Contrary to standard opinion, the best of the New England theologians had never presented sin as an innate property of human nature that renders us sinful (and thus helpless to do good) before we sin. They had always portrayed sin, not as a natural or ontological necessity, but as a moral or voluntary activity committed by agents who possessed within themselves *genuine* power to do otherwise. As Fitch defined it in his *Two Discourses on the Nature of Sin* (1826), "sin, in every form and instance, is reducible to the act of a moral agent in which he violates a known rule of duty."[5]

Edwardsians such as Asahel Nettleton and Bennet Tyler balked. For while no self-respecting Edwardsian would ever have said that one stands guilty before God prior to committing sin, few would have portrayed human natural ability so optimistically either. It was one thing to say that sin was in the willing, that the wayfaring sinner "can" turn to God if only "he will," and thus to deny that sinners were compelled to sin by natural force; but it was quite another to suggest that this natural ability to obey God could ever *really* overcome our moral inability to do the same, especially when sin was described as a moral act. Both leading parties within the Edwardsian ranks, the Exercisers and Tasters, had been denying that for years: Exercisers such as Nathanael Emmons and Samuel Spring–whose party label derived from their argument that sin existed, not in any innate psychological faculty or inbred sinful "taste" but only in individual sinful "exercises"–on the grounds that, while humans bear responsibility as the agents (or exercisers) of their sin, no moral act (of any kind) ever occurs without direct divine efficiency; and Tasters such as Asa Burton and Nathaniel Niles–who insisted that all *are* born with an innate (though incorporeal) sinful tendency from which all our individual sins stem–on the grounds that all moral acts spring from motives and that before God renovates the affections in regeneration they are governed ineluctably by our moral taste for sin.[6] Nettleton, who recognized Taylor as the architect of the New Haven innovations, wrote him an angry letter soon after Goodrich began lecturing on original sin:

> You may speculate better than I can; but I know one thing better than you do. I know better what Christians will, and what they will not receive; and I forewarn you that whenever you come out, our best Christians will revolt. . . . [Y]ou are giving the discussion a bad turn, and I have lost all my interest in the subject, and do not wish my fellow sinners to hear it. I do fear it is a trick of the devil to send brother Taylor on a wild goose chase after what he will never find [i.e., a new and better way to defend orthodoxy], and which if found would not be worth one straw.

Others complained as well. The ex-president of Princeton, Ashbel Green, suggested in his journal *The Christian Advocate* that Fitch was a Pelagian who "aim[ed] to overthrow the orthodox doctrine of original sin." He expressed "surprise and grief, that on the very spot, where we had supposed the sound theology of President Edwards had taken deeper root than any where else in the world, there should be promulgated, by men called orthodox, a system subversive of the radical principles of that great and good man!" Closer to home, criticism appeared even in New Haven's *Christian Spectator*, as Fitch's doctrine of sin became part of a minor debate over the nature of Edwards's notion of original sin.[7]

When criticized, however, the Taylorites defended their doctrine of sin by making their own appeal to Edwards, claiming to have applied his distinction between natural and moral ability faithfully. In a letter to Lyman Beecher, Goodrich stated that his and Taylor's understanding of original sin was "the necessary result of the immovable principles established in [Edwards'] treatise on 'Freedom of Will.'" Likewise, in his *Two Discourses on the Nature of Sin*, Fitch explained that he had based his own view of sin on the natural/moral ability distinction and asserted that this Edwardsian distinction should be applied "over the broad field of moral agency." In his published rejoinder to Ashbel Green, Fitch reiterated his continuity with Edwards. While he admitted that, like nearly every other New England theologian, he had departed from a few of the finer points of Edwards's theology, he insisted that the vast majority of the New Haven doctrine of sin "exactly concur[s] with the principles of Edwards."[8]

Despite such claims of allegiance to Edwards and the Edwardsian tradition, the New Haven doctrine of sin continued to cause quite a stir and, for a time, seemed to threaten Yale's fund-raising efforts. Following the publication of Fitch's *Two Discourses*, the college employed a recent graduate, the Rev. Hubbard Winslow, to raise money for the establishment of a professorship in Sacred Literature. Winslow preached a Sunday morning sermon in this capacity at the Congregational church of Fairfield, Connecticut, which was followed in the afternoon by a sermon from the church's former pastor, Nathaniel Hewit. Hewit used his sermon to denounce Taylor as a dangerous Arminian and Pelagian and encouraged the people of Fairfield to withhold their money from Yale. While Hewit did not dissuade the congregation from supporting the new professorship, he did worry the folks in New Haven. Thus, when the Fairfield church invited Taylor to come and defend himself against Hewit's allegations, Taylor knew what he had to do. Hewit's was not an isolated or unrepresentative voice. Taylor accepted the invitation and preached what soon became, not only the definitive articulation of the New Haven doctrine of original sin, but one of the most famous sermons in American history as well.[9]

Taylor's *Concio ad Clerum* (or "charge to the clergy") took its name, not from its debut in Fairfield, but from its better known and eventually published form presented to the annual assembly of Connecticut's Congregational clergy in the Yale chapel on commencement eve, September 10, 1828. Though it did not offer a great deal that was new in the development of the New Haven Theology, it did provide the first major pronouncement of New Haven doctrine by the school's undisputed leader. Taylor, Beecher, Goodrich, Fitch, and others had been discussing and working on their rearticulation of Edwardsian themes for over 10 years by the time Taylor preached the *Concio*, but not until 1828 did Taylorism become a watchword (and a byword) among Calvinists throughout the eastern United States.[10]

In retrospect, the thesis of Taylor's sermon appears surprisingly conservative: humans are depraved "by nature," or "such is their nature, that they will sin and only sin in all the appropriate circumstances of their being." Building his argument upon the work of such orthodox luminaries as John Calvin, the Westminster divines, Joseph Bellamy, Jonathan Edwards, St. Paul, and St. James (in that order), Taylor tried to pacify the fears of traditionalists like Nettleton, Tyler, and Hewit by distancing the New Haven doctrine of sin quite clearly from Arminianism. While his Arminian peers taught that depravity arises largely from the circumstances of temptation, Taylor showed his fidelity to Calvinist anthropology by insisting that depravity derives from human nature itself. "No change of condition, no increase of light nor of motives, no instructions nor warnings, nor any thing, within the appropriate circumstances of [our] being, changes the result. Unless there be some interposition, which is not included in these circumstances, unless something be done which is above nature, the case is hopeless." Our natural condition is such that we are certain to sin and only to sin unless and until God enables us, by grace, to do otherwise.[11]

Nevertheless, Taylor's sermon created a firestorm, inadvertently fanning the sparks of New Haven Theology into the flames of the Taylorite controversy. As we will see later, Taylor's critics objected not so much to what he affirmed in the sermon as to how he affirmed it and to the ways in which his affirmations symbolized New Haven's bypass of some key elements of high Calvinism.[12] By the middle of the 1830s it had become clear that the peculiarities of Taylor's phraseology had launched American Calvinists into one of the most intricate and important debates over the nature and implications of their creed that the western hemisphere has ever seen. The major components of this phraseology provide the structure for the remainder of this chapter.

Certainty without Necessity

The Edwardsians' seemingly ubiquitous distinction between natural and moral ability had a long history, predating even Edwards himself. By the early 1830s, its validity, utility, and desirability seemed so self-evident to Edwardsians such as Lyman Beecher that he asserted in a sermon at Andover Seminary that all the best thinkers in the history of Christian orthodoxy, when at their best and when charitably interpreted, espoused the distinction—even the high Calvinists (though not as forthrightly as many others). Beecher exaggerated. While most of the best thinkers had avoided the pitfall of divine determinism, arguing that God neither compels us to sin nor forces us into righteousness, the language of moral and natural ability was relatively rare. St. Augustine and John Calvin, for example, two of the most authoritative theologians in all of history for Reformed Protestants, distinguished only between "necessity" (*necessitas*) and "compulsion" (*coaction* in Calvin). They contended, in Calvin's words, that "man, while he sins of necessity, yet sins no less voluntarily." But in doing so they posited a "necessary tendency to sin" that derives from "the defects that have entered our nature." They believed that, while human nature was created good, it had been thoroughly corrupted in humanity's Fall. Though originally righteous, humans after the Fall found themselves *naturally* unable to do good. "All parts of the soul were possessed by sin," wrote Calvin. "[T]he whole man is overwhelmed—as by a deluge—from head to foot, so that no part is immune from sin and all that proceeds from him is to be imputed to sin."[13]

Beecher's claim notwithstanding, the language of natural and moral ability did not gain wide currency until it was championed by the Scottish theologian John Cameron (c. 1579-1625) during his stay among the Reformed Protestants of France during the first quarter of the seventeenth century. A general habit of distinguishing theologically between physical and moral causes had originated somewhat earlier, deriving in large measure from the efforts of the great Jesuit theologian Robert Bellarmine (1542-1621) to mediate the heated post-Tridentine debates within the Roman Catholic Church (and between Catholics and Protestants) over the nature of efficacious grace. Bellarmine softened the hard-nosed Augustinianism of the Flemish Catholic Michel Baius and provided a via media in the controversy between Dominicans such as Domingo Banez and fellow Jesuits such as Luis Molina over the proper Thomistic understanding of grace and free will. Attempting to avoid both the charge of determinism heaped on the Dominicans and that of Pelagianism leveled against other Jesuits, he (along with the Spanish Jesuit Francisco Suarez) argued that divine grace operates "congruously," or in a manner consistent with human free will. He admitted with the Dominicans that grace operates *prior* to the movement of the human will, eliciting the desired response infallibly. But with the Jesuits he contended that grace elicits its response morally, not physically—it achieves its ends in a manner congruous with free human consent.[14] It remained for Cameron, however, and for Cameron's followers in the Academy at Saumur, Moise Amyraut (1596-1664) and the "Amyraldians," to place the natural/moral ability distinction per se on the theological map.[15]

The Amyraldians and the doctrine of natural ability proved quite controversial among Calvinists in seventeenth-century Europe. Amyraut and his colleagues claimed to be faithful followers of Calvin. But high Calvinists such as Geneva's Francois Turrettini

(1623–87), a theologian highly regarded by Edwards,[16] viewed them as dangerous com-
promisers, not only in their doctrine of natural ability but in their innovative teachings
on original sin, predestination, and biblical inspiration as well. Charged repeatedly
(though unsuccessfully) with heresy while yet alive, the Amyraldians and their natural/
moral ability distinction finally received posthumous condemnation in the *Helvetic Formula Consensus* of 1675. Referring to the inability of sinners to believe in or obey God's
call of salvation, the Swiss *Formula Consensus* declared: "We hold therefore that they
speak inaccurately and dangerously, who call this inability to believe moral inability,
and do not say that it is natural."[17]

Ironically, however, while the natural/moral ability distinction appeared to many as
a threatening component of Amyraldian heresy when posited as a modification of scholastic Calvinism in seventeenth-century Europe, and though it was perpetuated in Great
Britain most notoriously by Richard Baxter, a Puritan pastor viewed with suspicion by
wary high Calvinists for his tendency toward theological catholicity,[18] it received great
acclaim when wielded as a weapon against Arminianism in eighteenth-century America.
Though Edwards's work on sin, grace, and free will certainly received its own share of
criticism, nearly everyone regarded its author as an orthodox Calvinist. By espousing a
rather unorthodox distinction for conservative ends, and by laying much more emphasis on moral inability than on natural ability, Edwards managed to separate the doctrine of natural ability from its earlier stigma, ensuring it an enduring and respectable
place in American theology. Though criticized by Old Calvinists in New England and
a few Presbyterians to the south, by the nineteenth century it had found grudging acceptance even among the stalwartly Calvinistic Princeton theologians.[19]

For Taylor, as for other Edwardsians, the natural/moral ability distinction played a
very formative role. Not only did Taylor employ the distinction but throughout his career he claimed that Edwards was "the most distinguished orthodox writer on the subject" of sin and moral agency. In response to the suggestion that he had abandoned the
distinction, he retorted, "we fully believe in that distinction," and appended a traditionally strong Edwardsian affirmation of absolute moral inability: "[W]e believe also with
Edwards, that 'moral necessity may be as absolute as natural necessity.'"[20] Indeed, Taylor believed himself more authentically Edwardsian than his opponents, whose articulations of original sin he thought too often lapsed into the non-Edwardsian language of
inborn, physical depravity.[21] But he also recognized that many people would resist New
Haven's claim that its innovations derived by direct logical descent from Edwards on
natural ability. He felt it incumbent to clarify the extent to which he and his colleagues,
in true Edwardsian form, had improved upon the traditional Edwardsian solutions to
the question of original sin and provided "the only" doctrine defensible in their own
day and age "against Pelagian or Arminian objections."[22]

In a letter to Lyman Beecher in January of 1819, Taylor proposed "that something
should and may be done toward settling points which Edwards did not aim to settle."
He felt that, while Edwards had succeeded in demolishing the "absurdities" of the
Arminian notion of "self-determination," the anti-Arminian agenda of his work on free
will had limited his larger extrapolation of human moral agency. By the late 1810s,
Taylor realized that the currency of the time-honored Edwardsian catchphrase "he can
if he will" had depreciated significantly. Arminians and Old Calvinists had been calling the Edwardsians' bluff for some time, pressing them to come clean as to whether

they really held out anything worthy of the name ability at all. The traditional Edwardsian notion of moral inability, founded as it was on the ineluctable inclination toward self-centered sin in the soul destitute of the indwelling Holy Spirit, seemed vastly to out-weigh the merely theoretical promise of natural ability. Thus, it no longer sufficed to respond to the perplexities of troubled seekers with glibly rehearsed stock phrases like "he can if he will." Taylor described this phrase to his students as a "mere truism, nonsense, or absurdity" since, from an Edwardsian point of view, "*willing* is the thing to be done." At an installation sermon for his son-in-law Noah Porter, he insisted that preachers who take human natural ability seriously must assert "he can" even "if he won't."[23]

Clearly, this rhetoric signaled at least a slight departure from the traditional Edwardsian use of the natural/moral ability doctrine. Despite his declared commit-ment to the veracity of this distinction, Taylor came to believe that, over time and *as traditionally articulated*, the Edwardsian promise of natural ability had become empty. It "has no existence," he admitted finally, "and can have none. It is an essential noth-ing." The overemphasis placed by his peers on moral inability had rendered the Edwardsian doctrine of natural ability virtually useless. Consequently, Taylor coined his own soon-to-be-classic catchphrase, "certainty without necessity," sometimes re-ferred to as "certainty with power to the contrary," substituting it whenever possible for the language of natural and moral ability and hoping thereby to breathe new life into the soul of the New England Theology. Conceived as a way to rearticulate the doctrine of moral inability without destroying the sinner's sense of obligation, Taylor's new dis-tinction between the certainty of sin in all pre-regenerate moral endeavor (which he affirmed) and the necessity of such sin (which he denied) enabled him to avoid the now-counterproductive term "inability" altogether. He could now speak about original sin, in other words, without explicit recourse to the older, debilitating notion of human moral impotence. Despite his end run around the language of inability, however, and despite his ongoing dissatisfaction with the predominant use of the natural/moral abil-ity distinction, Taylor employed the two distinctions synonymously, admitting when pressed that his innovation expressed no new doctrine but only enhanced the effective-ness of the original rhetoric.[24] In a letter written in March of 1832 to his skeptical Edwardsian colleague Edward Dorr Griffin, Taylor defended his new distinction by asking, "[W]hat was the doctrine of president and Dr. Edwards, except the simple certainty of action with power to the contrary. Is this a novelty?" As he told his students, "[T]here is great diversity as to the meaning of *inability*. What is meant by this in common lan-guage, when predicated of the will? . . . [I]t means a *simple certainty* resulting from the perverseness of the present state of the will, that the opposite act of will, will not take place. Moral inability always implies natural ability."[25]

Most of Taylor's opponents remained unconvinced by his claims of orthodoxy for New Haven's certainty/necessity distinction. Joseph Harvey of Westchester denounced it as a Pelagian wolf in orthodox sheep's clothing. Princeton's Charles Hodge, who had qualms enough affirming the natural/moral ability distinction, also deemed it too much to bear. Hodge had felt for some time that many Edwardsians distinguished too sharply between natural and moral ability, glossing over the corruptive effect of moral inability on human nature itself. Now his worst fears were confirmed. As he told his students, he viewed the Taylorites' doctrine of sin as a denial of "any inability at all." Similarly,

Lyman Atwater, soon to become a Princetonian himself, repudiated Taylor's distinction, arguing that the "orthodox" use of the natural/moral ability distinction "is utterly inconsistent with that semi-Pelagian scheme which now undertakes to skulk behind this distinction, as its main defence."[26]

Clearly, the doctrine of "certainty without necessity" portrayed human natural ability in a manner new to the history of the New England Theology. The early Edwardsians usually described moral certainty in terms of necessity, for, as Edwards contended throughout *Freedom of the Will*, they believed that "[moral] necessity is not inconsistent with liberty."[27] But despite obvious changes in Taylor's manner of presenting this doctrine, his phraseology represented little more than a new way of expressing an old truth. In fact, Edwards himself may have paved the way for this innovation. Less than a year before his death, he shipped a public letter across the Atlantic to his friend John Erskine, protesting the manner in which the disciples of the Scottish philosopher Lord Kames, Henry Home, had distorted his views in support of Kames's own moral determinism:

> "I have largely declared," stressed Edwards, "that the connection between antecedent things and consequent ones, which takes place with regard to the acts of men's wills, which is called moral necessity, is called by the name of 'necessity' improperly; and that all such terms as 'must,' 'cannot,' 'impossible,' 'unable,' 'irresistible,' 'unavoidable,' 'invincible,' etc. when applied here, are not applied in their proper signification, and are either used nonsensically, and with perfect insignificance, or in a sense quite diverse from their original and proper meaning, and their use in common speech: and that such a necessity as attends the acts of men's wills, *is more properly called 'certainty,' than 'necessity.'*"

Taylor could not have said it better. Nor would he have wished to, for as one anonymous Taylorite explained in 1835, New Haven continued to believe it important to "declare the absoluteness of man's moral impotence, or the entire aversion of his heart to goodness." As good Edwardsians, however, they deemed it "no less important, and no less scriptural, to maintain the natural power, than the moral impotence of man." As another contributor to the *Quarterly Christian Spectator* concluded in 1838, "[W]e cannot see, we have never been able to see, that [the Taylorite doctrine] is anything but a statement, in so many terms, of the old established New England doctrine of man's natural ability to do his duty."[28]

The Fallacy of Physical Depravity

The chief theological concern in Taylor's doctrine of original sin—and one of the main reasons he distinguished so clearly between the certainty and necessity of sin—lay in avoiding the notion that sin resided as a property or component of our natural constitution. It lay, in other words, in avoiding any semblance of what the Taylorites referred to as the doctrine of physical or constitutional depravity.

Though rarely espoused explicitly,[29] the notion of physical depravity appeared to the Taylorites to be a logical implication of the way some high Calvinists interpreted the traditional doctrine of hereditary or propagated depravity. Opponents of Taylorism such as Joseph Harvey, Bennet Tyler, and Leonard Woods, for example, believed that depravity "has descended from the common ancestor of our race to all his posterity," being "transmitted from parent to child." They contended that depravity is transmitted or propagated in the same manner and condition that "human beings are propagated, . . . fallen, corrupt," and that it was "as natural to man, as reason, or speech, or sympathy, or natural affection, or any other property which is said to be natural." They argued further that Taylor misinterpreted the orthodox, Edwardsian doctrine of sin (including the natural/moral ability distinction) insofar as he repudiated this understanding of propagated depravity.[30] In the face of such Tylerite assertions, Taylor insisted that he affirmed the natural/moral ability distinction and the orthodox doctrine of sin only insofar as he repudiated this understanding of hereditary sin. "If there is truth in any thing," he once asserted, "sin—depravity—cannot consist in any created structure or attribute of the human mind, nor in the ill-desert of one being transferred to another." For Taylor, to say that sin is propagated or handed down organically from one generation to the next proved as harmful as saying that God created depravity immediately in the soul. Either way, one implied that sin constituted a necessary, inevitable, and virtually physical part of human nature. While not yet aware of genetic phenomena or DNA, Taylor knew that terms like propagation and heredity connoted biological processes with very natural, indeed unavoidable consequences for the shape, not only of human bodies, but of human personalities and behavior as well. Thus, he believed that for an Edwardsian to speak of propagated or hereditary depravity was to speak heresy, for it was to suggest that depravity was a biological or physical condition and thus to undermine the hallowed doctrine of natural ability. Taylor argued that no version of physical depravity had ever "obtained the sanction of any Orthodox Confession of Faith." While various high and Old Calvinists had employed language that verged on this teaching, they had done so in error.[31]

Taylor opposed the notion of physical or constitutional depravity on more practical grounds as well. He felt, for example, that by depicting sin as an organic component of all human creatures, it rendered the Creator the author of sin. "No demon can be conceived to be so exclusively and so criminally the author of sin in others," he wrote, "as God is represented to be by this theory." As Goodrich once noted in support of this claim, Edwards himself had avoided portraying God as the author of sin by repudiating any adherence to physical depravity. Quoting loosely from an argument Edwards made in *Original Sin* against the English theologian John Taylor, Goodrich recalled: "Edwards says of his opponent, 'he supposes the doctrine of original sin to imply some positive influence—some quality or other not from the choice of our minds, . . . but like a taint, tincture, or infection altering the natural constitution, faculties, and dispositions of the soul. Whereas truly our doctrine neither implies nor infers any such thing.'" Goodrich gloried in the support Edwards provided for New Haven doctrine: "[H]ow explicit is Edwards in saying that sin lies wholly in our choice!" Taylor also thought that the notion of physical depravity rendered God's moral law unjust. To an evangelical Calvinist like Taylor whose career peaked during the rise of forensic psychiatry, guarding against the impression that Calvinist anthropology exculpated unrepentant sinners by depicting them incapable of righteousness seemed paramount. As American lawyers developed the ancient doctrine of *mens rea*, declaring the mentally ill not culpable for their crimes insofar as their insanity had deranged their natural volitional capacities, revivalists like Taylor scrambled to preach Calvinism in a manner that could sustain their listeners' sense of guilt and responsibility for sin. As Taylor once exclaimed, "[S]urely, the Spirit of God is not sent into this world, to bring stones [and] animals to repentance."[32]

Unbeknownst to most New England Congregationalists, this dispute over propagated or physical depravity rested in large measure on the views of the origin of souls implied, though usually not stated, in its contestants' arguments. Like the distinction between natural and moral ability, the issue of hereditary depravity had a long history. Indeed, debates over this doctrine date back nearly as far as Christian theology itself and, among the most refined and scholarly thinkers, have often included discussion of the origin of souls. Though several theories existed in the early centuries of Christian history, after the time of St. Augustine most Western theologians adopted one of two dominant views of the soul's origin: "creationism," which posits that God creates each soul individually and infuses it immediately into its body, or "traducianism," which posits that all souls derive from the soul of Adam, being traduced or handed down via sexual generation. After serious consideration of a neo-Platonic notion of the preexistence of souls early in his life, Augustine himself leaned toward traducianism. Though he never made an unambiguous or definitive pronouncement in favor of traducianism (to the end, he remained repulsed by the materialistic understanding of the soul it seemed to imply), he did seem to favor this position over its alternatives and he firmly opposed the rather muddled creationism of the brash Vincentius Victor in his *Treatise on the Soul and Its Origin* (419). While most Lutherans would also adopt the traducianist position, most Catholic scholastics and most Calvinists affirmed creationism.[33]

Most Edwardsians, however, proved unconcerned about negotiating this speculative theological terrain and frequently seemed unaware of its implications for the doctrine of original sin. Edwards's own doctrine of sin implied a creationist view of the soul, as he argued that *all of reality* is created and thus sustained continuously by God from moment to moment. For Edwards, while all human souls were united ontologically to the soul of Adam by divine fiat or divine constitution, nothing existed or continued in existence apart from God's ongoing creative activity; everything—souls and bodies—depended on God each moment for its being and secondary causes such as sexual reproduction were only *occasions* through which God's efficient causation operated.[34] Most of Edwards's followers either modified or ignored his "occasionalist" doctrine of continuous creation, however, and showed little interest in probing the origin of souls. Some, like Joseph Bellamy, assumed a creationist position tacitly. A few radical Exercisers—who denied any real autonomy to the human soul and attributed all moral activity to direct divine efficiency—defended creationism explicitly. But Timothy Dwight is perhaps typical of most Edwardsians. In sermon 32 of his theological system, "Human Depravity; Derived from Adam," Dwight confessed ignorance on this issue, claiming not to know whence the soul and its depravity came. "Many attempts have been made to explain it," he wrote, "but I freely confess myself to have seen none, which was satisfactory to me; or which did not leave the difficulties as great, and, for aught I know, as numerous, as they were before."[35]

By the time of the Taylorites and Tylerites, this Edwardsian reticence regarding the origin of souls had become problematic. Without recourse to the time-honored scholastic discussion of creationism and traducianism, the Taylorites defended what clearly stands as a creationist position: "[S]ouls . . . are not derived from each other," they contended, "or framed by the instrumentality of ancestors, but are created simple, entire, and unchanging in their essences by the immediate power of God." They tended to describe the notion of propagated depravity in implicitly traducianist language and believed that the biological (or physical) transmission of sin implied in such language undermined their cherished Edwardsian commitment to natural ability. For their part, the Tylerites repudiated the stigma of physical depravity and argued that one could maintain both propagated depravity and natural ability consistently. However, the Tylerites ignored the question of the soul's origin altogether. Though their commitment to natural ability seems to have placed them in the creationist camp, their failure to explicate the doctrine of propagated depravity in creationist terms left the Taylorites scratching their heads. The two camps thus debated the doctrine of physical depravity as ships passing in the night, neither side quite sure where the other went wrong. When the Tylerites would repudiate physical depravity and affirm natural ability, the Taylorites professed near unanimity with these erstwhile opponents and held out the olive branch. But when the Tylerites would insist on the propagation or transmission of sin from parents to children, the Taylorites threw up their hands in frustration. A traditional scholastic framework may not have made this dispute any more profitable. Indeed, it would likely have rendered the Taylorite position as problematic as that of the Tylerites for, in historical perspective, Taylor's position stands as something of a novelty. Most creationists, though a bit more careful than the Tylerites to uphold the goodness of the soul per se, also employed the language of propagated depravity. But a greater awareness of the scholastic struggle with this problem may well have rendered the discussion more coherent.[36]

As things stood, and as we will see more fully below, the Taylorites believed that all souls arrive in mint condition directly from the hand of God. It is certain that they will acquire an inherent tendency to sin as soon as they are able, as soon as they take their first moral steps or perform their first moral "exercise." But it is just as certain that this sinful tendency derives, not from our natural constitution itself, but from the fact that we are born into a fallen world, a world full of scarcity and sin, a world alienated from its Creator. Taylor restricted the certainty of sin to "the appropriate circumstances of our being" in order to emphasize this very point. Given the goodness with which God has created our natures, in theory, or "in some other circumstances" than those ordained for us, human nature might well find a way to persist in holiness. Taylor knew this claim was only hypothetical, that it "affects not the truth nor propriety of ascribing [people's] sinfulness to their nature, since in all the circumstances which belong to their proper place in the system, they all become sinful." Further, as early as the *Concio ad Clerum* he admitted he was "not saying . . . that there is not, what with entire propriety may be called a disposition or tendency to sin, which is the cause of all sin; nor that there is not, as a consequence of this disposition or tendency, what with equal propriety may be called a sinful disposition, which is the true cause of all other sin, itself excepted." But he wanted to insist in true Edwardsian fashion that "that which is the cause of all sin, is not itself sin." He wanted to insist, in other words, on the "absurdity" of physical depravity, the absurdity of claiming "that there is sin, before sin." Humans sin in spite of—and because of—a genuine natural capacity to do otherwise. Their souls are not sinful when received from the hand of God. They only become sinful, or take on a sinful orientation, in response to the world around them. As Chauncey Goodrich claimed in defense of his more famous friend, Taylor's view of human nature and its sinfulness "corresponds to that of Edwards," who knew that a "stone is not heavy when considered in itself, [or] when withdrawn from all connection with the earth. . . . Dr. Taylor rests the certainty [of sin], as Edwards does in the case of the stone, on the connection of the internal constitution . . . with 'the appropriate circumstances of its being,' and not on either of them taken separately."[37]

The Enigma of Native Depravity

Despite his rejection of physical or propagated depravity, Taylor did believe in original sin. Indeed, as Noah Porter remembered at Yale Divinity School's semicentennial celebration, an overwhelming sense of universal human depravity constituted "the prominent element in Dr. Taylor's personal religious history."[38] In a restricted sense, and in a manner that has often baffled more traditional or Westminsterian high Calvinists, Taylor held human sinfulness to be hereditary. Though not transmitted sexually or genetically from parent to child, he considered the human propensity to sin a natural aspect of the human condition derived or inherited from Adam and Eve and passed on throughout all subsequent generations.

Taylor viewed individual sinful acts as positive evils. But like Edwards before him, he described original sin in largely privative terms—as a loss of original righteousness. In keeping with Augustinian tradition, Edwards had attributed the original righteousness of Adam and Eve to what the medieval scholastics termed the *donum superadditum*— the superadded gift of grace granted them prior to the Fall to govern or rightly order their natural appetites and enable their ongoing obedience. Edwards identified this prelapsarian grace with what he called "superior principles," infused into the souls of our "first parents" to control the "inferior principles" that comprised human nature as such. Though created good and intended to equip humanity for survival, hese latter, inferior principles (such as self-love and the instinctual desire to secure freedom, honor, and pleasure), Edwards argued, compared to "fire in a house; which, we say, is a good servant, but a bad master; very useful while kept in its place, but if left to take possession of the whole house, soon brings all to destruction." He contended that God, knowing the great harm such fire could do if left unattended, granted the superior principles as supernatural means through which the founders of our race, with divine help, might contain the flames of human nature. Unfortunately, however, Adam and Eve failed to take full advantage of this grace. Notwithstanding its influence, they fell prey to the Serpent's temptation, rebelled against their Creator, and fell hopelessly into sin. Consequently, and "because it would have been utterly improper . . . and inconsistent with the covenant and constitution God had established, that God should still maintain communion with man, and continue, by his friendly, gracious vital influences, to dwell with him and in him, after he was become a rebel," God withdrew the superior principles and left human nature to its own devices. Its subsequent lack or privation of original righteousness—for Taylor and Edwards as for many other Augustinians—constituted hereditary (or original) sin. All now enter the world bereft of original righteousness and heirs of Adam's sin. "As God withdrew . . . his vital gracious influence from the common head [Adam]," wrote Edwards, "so he withholds the same from all the members" of the race. Thus, while a positively evil choice initiated the Fall, and while the deprivation of original sin leads to the depravation of individual sins, original sin per se is a privative condition rather than a positive entity. As Taylor would phrase it, all people "are born destitute of holiness" (a condition of privative, original, hereditary sin) and thus "are by nature totally depraved" (committing positive, evil acts).[39]

Though Taylor took pains to point out that his privative understanding of original sin accorded with that of Edwards, the Tylerites deemed this effort a ruse put forward to distract the orthodox from what in reality represented a denial of original sin. Despite several attempts to explain otherwise, Taylor quickly acquired a reputation for believing that human nature had escaped the Fall unharmed. Joseph Harvey questioned how he could maintain confidence in the *certainty* of sin when he denied that sin had any underlying, efficient cause. "To ascribe a certain, uniform effect to occasion or contingency," he contended, "is absurd." It "is the same as to ascribe it to no cause. Actual sin . . . , if it be a certain and exclusive effect, must result from a cause which is sinful." Similarly, Bennet Tyler argued that human nature underwent a fundamental change in the Fall and that Taylor failed to account adequately for the subsequent universality of human sin. He suggested that, by claiming that humans now enter the world with the same nature as prelapsarian Adam, Taylor had essentially given up on original sin. Taylor responded by denying that he had claimed any such thing. While he believed human nature to be the same "in kind" now as before the Fall, he also recognized an important difference. Now lacking the aid of God's supernatural grace, human nature had become disoriented, lost in sin, and could no longer maintain "the degree of propensity to natural good" enjoyed in the Garden of Eden. Sin, he explained, can indeed be "traced" causally to human nature, but only in the sense that "the physical or constitutional propensities of man [created] for natural good," and which "constitute a part of his nature whether he be sinful or holy," become "the ground, reason, cause, or occasion of his depravity" in the context of "the appropriate [read fallen] circumstances of his existence." In other words, despite the undeniable difference in the disposition of human nature since the Fall, the Tylerites were wrong to contend for a *fundamental* transformation of human nature as a result of the Fall. In doing so, they risked undermining the doctrine of natural ability. While humans do now sin by nature, this does not mean that we sin due to any fundamental inadequacy of our God-given, natural constitution. For, invoking again the authority of Edwards, "with [the] exception of what was . . . supernatural in Adam; that is, in respect to their human nature, Adam and his posterity, according to Edwards, are alike." Though Adam possessed a superadded gift of grace that unregenerate sinners must now live without, "human nature in Adam, and human nature in his posterity are one and the same thing."[40]

While Taylor held that all humans, even small children, were totally depraved,[41] his privative understanding of original sin led to further controversy by leaving open the question of infant damnation. Because original sin did not mean for him that infants enter the world bearing guilt for a natural constitution that is sinful in itself, they do not become damnable sinners prior to committing actual sins. In the *Concio ad Clerum*, Taylor argued for the possible salvation of infants who die before reaching the age of moral accountability. Since "some knowledge of duty is requisite to sin," he reasoned, and since no one can know for certain the "precise instant" when babies begin to attain this knowledge and violate their duty—only that they sin "as soon as they can" or "as soon as they become moral agents"—it remains impossible to pinpoint the beginning of individual human culpability. The Taylorites had become sensitized quite early to what

Jean Matthews has called the widespread "republicanization of theology" in the nineteenth century and the related "revulsion against" the seemingly tyrannical doctrine of infant damnation. Well before the appearance of Taylor's *Concio*, Lyman Beecher and *The Spirit of the Pilgrims* had begun to fight an extended paper war with the Unitarian *Christian Examiner* in order to defend their fellow Calvinists from the *Examiner*'s charge that, historically, they had encouraged belief in the damnation of infants. In typically hyperbolic fashion, Beecher protested that none of the authors highly regarded by contemporary Calvinists ever taught a positive doctrine of infant damnation. Beecher was right to highlight the fact that many had soft-pedaled this issue, leaving the matter ultimately to inscrutable divine wisdom. But he also misled the public by glossing over the obvious implications of the high Calvinist understanding of native depravity. John Calvin and the Westminster Confession, for example, taught that dying infants who had been elected by God for salvation went to heaven, but clearly implied that non-elect infants did not. While Edwards himself equivocated on the time at which depravity commences in infants (thus leaving the door open for Taylor's postponement of the age of culpability), he too leaned toward the notion that non-elect infants suffered eternal torments (though he suggested that their punishment was not "so aggravated" as that of others). Embarrassed by the vulnerability of New England Calvinism on this issue, by March of 1825 Beecher had recommended to Asahel Hooker that they deemphasize their doctrine of original sin. "As it respects the character and destiny of infants," he confessed, "it gives to the enemy the advantage of the popular side."[42]

Taylorite uneasiness concerning this issue only intensified in 1833 with the publication of Gardiner Spring's *Dissertation on Native Depravity*. The son of Samuel Spring, nephew of Nathanael Emmons, and an alumnus of both Yale College and Andover Seminary, Spring had carried conservative Edwardsian commitments to New York City in 1810 upon his call to the Brick Presbyterian Church. In the *Dissertation on Native Depravity*, which he delivered in person in Yale's chapel, he repudiated the Taylorite postponement of infant depravity as a Pelagian heresy, arguing that all infants knowingly and voluntarily violate divine law as soon as they begin their existence.[43] The Taylorites responded quickly, restating their own position in a less provocative manner and hoping to dispel the idea that Spring had proffered a more authentically Edwardsian view. As Taylor summarized in the *Quarterly Christian Spectator*, "[T]he exact difference . . . between Dr. Spring and the New-Haven divines, is this; while he maintains that infants sin, at the very instant of their creation, we, without denying or affirming the truth of his position, choose to say, that they sin as soon as they are moral agents; even so early that the interval, if there is an interval, between birth and sin, needs, in popular language and ordinary cases, no particular notice." Taylor had confessed in an earlier dispute with Spring that, "on the question respecting *the instant*, in which moral agency and sin commence, we have little controversial ardor." But now Taylorite ardor had been piqued. While Taylor revealed no more interest than before in *pinpointing* the commencement of moral agency (a futile task anyway), he did expend a great deal of energy discussing the timing of infant depravity and expounding on his notion that humans sin, and only sin, as soon as they become able and in all the appropriate circumstances of their being. He stated that "in popular language it may be properly said that [infants] sin from the first" or "from the beginning." But he insisted that to push such language to a simplistic, literal extreme was to commit a grave error. Technically speaking, individual human sin does not begin prior to moral agency. As the New Haven theologians had been contending for several years, moreover, neither Edwards, nor Bellamy, nor Dwight had claimed otherwise. Even the Tylerites stood much closer to New Haven on this issue than they liked to admit.[44]

Of course, the Tylerites failed to see these alleged resemblances and continued to tar New Haven with a Pelagian brush. In their *Evangelical Magazine*, newly founded to help defend the faith against Taylorite innovations, they reasserted their distance from Yale and heralded Spring's continuity with New England orthodoxy. In 1835, Leonard Woods published his own *Essay on Native Depravity*—more irenic than that of Spring, but still aimed closely at the Taylorites. Woods chastised those "who profess to believe the doctrine of native depravity" but who "do not consider real, personal sin as commencing immediately after birth." He reproved these anonymous but clearly wayward preachers for claiming "that sin commences as soon as moral agency" but failing to specify precisely what and when that means. The Tylerites were clearly frustrated with the complexity of the New Haven Theology. They distrusted Taylorite subtlety and despised what they deemed the Taylorite penchant for toying with time-tested truths. Perhaps Joseph Harvey summarized their sentiments most aptly. Speaking of Taylorite theology, he quipped, "[I]ts nature is such, that it produces Arminianism, and only Arminianism, in all the appropriate circumstances of its being."[45]

The Ignominy of Imputation

Tied closely to debates over native depravity was the traditional Augustinian doctrine of the imputation of Adam's sin. Held in one form or another by most confessional Protestants since the Reformation, this doctrine taught that Adam stood before God as the representative of all humanity and that, as a consequence of his Fall, God imputes Adam's sin to all his posterity. God, in other words, regards the entire human race as having sinned "in Adam," reckoning all of us guilty for humanity's Fall from grace.

As one might expect, and like most Edwardsians before him, Taylor forsook this forensic explanation of original sin. He apologized for the many highly respected theologians who had affirmed the doctrine of imputation, declaring, "all that can be said in extenuation of these 'fooleries' is, that great and good men may believe the most palpable absurdities without seeing them to be such, when they suppose themselves obliged to adopt them in defense of revealed truth." When not apologizing, moreover, he lambasted the doctrine in both its classical Augustinian and more recent federalist forms. He attributed the classical Augustinian understanding of imputation—which based the doctrine on a Platonic conception of humanity's seminal, ontological union in Adam and thus Adam's real headship of the human race—to what he called an untenable "Platonico-Aristotelian Realism," contending brashly, as one of his students noted, that "Augustine was a heathen, converted to Christianity from Manicheism. He was a poor interpreter [of Scripture doctrine] & inferior in this respect to *any* N[ew] E[ngland] clergyman of the present day." Taylor attributed the modern conception of imputation, espoused by those latter-day advocates of Calvinistic "federal theology" who had gradually severed its original ties to Augustine's metaphysical realism—thus denying humanity's ontological unity in Adam but viewing Adam, nevertheless, as the divinely appointed federal or "covenanted" representative of the human race whose Fall determined the fate of all his progeny—to a misguided zeal for maintaining the shell of a dogma whose underlying substance had been discarded.[46]

In America, the Princeton theologians stood as the leading proponents of the modern federalist understanding of imputation and the leading critics of the Edwardsian repudiation of this doctrine. In Princeton's *Biblical Repertory* for January of 1830, the seminary's head and founding professor, Archibald Alexander, published an essay charting the early history of the Pelagian heresy and singling out the "denial of original sin" as that "radical" Pelagian error "from which all the rest naturally germinated." In a thinly veiled critique of New England's Calvinists, Alexander concluded his article with a resounding affirmation of "the old doctrine of the ancient church, which traces all the sins and evils in the world to the imputation of the first sin of Adam," claiming the doctrine of imputation as the only effective antidote to an ever-present Pelagian menace. When the New Haven theologians responded by rejecting Princeton's assumed continuity with "the old doctrine of the ancient church" and claiming that their brethren to the south actually stood closer to New England than to Hippo or even Geneva on this issue, they found themselves again in the heat of controversy concerning the doctrine of sin. The Taylorites contended that the question of imputation had become, "in this country at least, chiefly a dispute about words." Much like the Edwardsians, the Princetonians had given up on the Augustinian and early Calvinist notion of humanity's oneness in Adam. According to the bygone defenders of the classical doctrine of imputation, "Adam's sin . . . was *truly* (though not personally) ours; being ours (*communiter*) in *common* with him, as our federal head." But "on the principles of our *existing* [or contemporary] philosophy," shared by the Princetonians as well as the Edwardsians, to say "that a certain sin is not (*personaliter*) *personally* ours, is to say, that it is not '*truly*' ours" and is thus to deny any real connection between ourselves and Adam's sin. The Taylorites recognized Princeton's passion to maintain the notion that God imputes the guilt of Adam's sin to his posterity and they admitted that this concern did continue to separate Princeton from New England. But since the Princetonians denied that such imputed "guilt" derived from our own culpability, the Taylorites concluded that these colleagues had denuded even the term *guilt* of its traditional meaning.[47]

The last thing the Princetonians wanted was to be identified with Taylor. In the person of Charles Hodge, therefore, they firmly denied having departed from orthodox tradition on this matter. It was the Taylorites, said Hodge, who had misrepresented the orthodox doctrine of imputation. Its standard or authoritative Calvinistic defenders knew that "nothing more is meant by the imputation of sin, than to cause one man to bear the iniquity of another." Glossing over the metaphysical realism involved in older articulations of the doctrine, Hodge argued correctly that, like the Princetonians, the orthodox had consistently denied the *personal* or *numerical* oneness of Adam and his posterity (a point with which the Taylorites would have agreed). Moreover, he said, if the differences between New England and Princeton on this issue comprised "a mere dispute about words," it would not have been because Princeton had moved away from, but because Yale could not escape, the veracity of this historic doctrine. All agreed that Adam's descendants suffer evil consequences as a result of his Fall. "The question then is, is this evil of the nature of punishment? If it is, then the doctrine of imputation is admitted; if not, it is denied." Hodge suggested that the Taylorites were struggling too

hard to overcome the legacy of Edwards on this doctrine and thus tended to characterize all its adherents in the terms of his unusual philosophy of human identity. The
Princetonians, however, would not "be burdened with the defence of Edward's [sic]
theory on this subject, which, we think, . . . is not the doctrine commonly received among
Calvinists, but utterly inconsistent with it." While the New Haven theologians opposed
Edwards's doctrine of imputation for the way it implicated all of humanity as willing
participants in Adam's sin, the Princetonians worried that Edwards "had rejected all of
imputation but the name." It was "no matter of surprise," they lamented, "that his followers soon discarded the term itself."[48]

Though Edwards's doctrine of imputation did prove quite Augustinian, Hodge was
right to allude to its peculiar reliance on occasionalist metaphysics. For Edwards, the
imputation of Adam's sin rested on humanity's divinely and continuously constituted
(or created) oneness with Adam. Indeed for Edwards all continuity, all universality, or
"all oneness," like everything else that continues in existence, "depends entirely on a
divine establishment":

> 'Tis this, and this only, that must account for guilt and an evil taint on any individual
> soul, in consequence of a crime commited twenty or forty years ago, remaining still, and
> even to the end of the world and forever. 'Tis this, that must account for the continuance
> of any such thing, anywhere, as *consciousness* of acts that are past; and for the continu-
> ance of all *habits*, either good or bad: and on this depends everything that can belong to
> *personal identity*. And all communications, derivations, or continuation of qualities, prop-
> erties or relations, natural or moral, from what is past, as if the subject were one, depends
> on no other foundation.

Because God creates human being today just as it was created originally in Adam, one
can say truly that all human being, or all humanity, resided and sinned *in Adam*. It is
only just, therefore, that God imputes original sin to our accounts, for original sin is
truly the sin of all.[49]

Since before the time of Hodge, scholars have identified this notion that the justice
of imputation rests, not simply on the wisdom of divine providence, but on humanity's
real, ontological presence in the sin of Adam, as "Stapfer's scheme," after the Swiss
Reformed theologian Johann Friedrich Stapfer (1708-75). Edwards appeared to know
the work of this junior Swiss colleague fairly well. He supported his use of Stapfer's
scheme with quotations from Stapfer's magnum opus, the Institutiones Theologiae
Polemicae Universae (1743-47). He also referred to Stapfer throughout his manuscript
notebooks. For the history of the New England Theology, Stapfer's importance lies in
his refusal to reduce the doctrine of imputation into either of its increasingly popular,
modern forms: mediate imputation (put forth to portray the doctrine in a more equitable light), in which God imputes original sin to us only mediately, or on the basis of
its manifestation in our personal, hereditary depravity; or immediate imputation (put
forth to maintain the divine prerogative), in which God imputes original sin to us immediately, or apart from (or logically prior to) our own hereditary depravity. Before the
modern abandonment of Augustine's metaphysical realism, most theologians found little
need to separate the mediate and immediate aspects of imputation. Their belief in
humanity's real, universal presence in Adam, whether in a seminal or a fully developed
state, meant that personal or hereditary depravity itself had a real basis (rather than a

merely forensic one) in our ontological participation in Adam's sin. Thus, for them, God imputes original sin to us prior to our individual manifestation of hereditary depravity, but does so, not by arbitrary or inscrutable fiat, but equitably—on the basis of our primitive participation in humanity's Fall. As modern Calvinists lost faith in the metaphysical realism of their medieval predecessors, however, it became more and more difficult for them to hold mediate and immediate imputation together. Beginning with Josué de la Place, an Amyraldian at the Academy of Saumur, the more humanistic Reformed schoolmen began repudiating immediate imputation as arbitrary and unfair, heralding the language of mediate imputation as the only appropriate manner in which to convey the doctrine. When high Calvinistic federal theologians such as Francois Turrettini responded by claiming that this change effectively undermined the historic meaning of imputation altogether (insofar as it traced our sins only to inherited depravity and not to Adam himself), and by depicting imputation more and more narrowly in forensic terms, a virtually permanent divide between mediate and immediate imputation was all but certain.[50]

Much like Stapfer, however, Edwards did manage to keep mediate and immediate imputation together. He did so somewhat ambiguously. Indeed, his explication of imputation continues to mystify even the best of scholars. But he did so nonetheless, resisting the temptation to depict the doctrine in purely forensic terms:

> The derivation of the evil disposition to the hearts of Adam's posterity, or rather the *coexistence* of the evil disposition, implied in Adam's first rebellion, in the root and branches, is a consequence of the union, that the wise Author of the world has established between Adam and his posterity: but not properly a consequence of the imputation of his sin; nay, rather *antecedent* to it, as it was in Adam himself. The first depravity of heart, and the imputation of that sin, are both the consequences of that established union: but yet in such order, that the evil disposition is *first*, and the charge of guilt *consequent*; as it was in the case of Adam himself.

Though based on our ontological union with Adam rather than on hereditary depravity, imputation nevertheless *follows upon* and is, in part, mediated by humanity's inherently evil disposition. Though we acquired this disposition in Adam, moreover, and thus prior to our own individual existence, imputation occurs as a *consequence of* and not *as the ground of* that acquisition.[51]

Taylor minced no words in denouncing this scheme. He had no truck for Edwards's occasionalism. Neither did he share Edwards's ontological realism. To him, the notion that all people stood as independent beings and thus could not be one with Adam was a datum of common sense.[52] Taylor was not alone, however, in his rejection of Stapfer's scheme or in his move away from the language of imputation. He knew well that "since the time of Dr. Hopkins and Dr. Edwards" (i.e., Edwards, Jr.), the doctrine of original sin had "undergone considerable modifications in this country, especially in New England." Though these men themselves had retained sporadic references to imputation, they had not perpetuated the metaphysics with which Edwards had undergirded the doctrine. Hopkins, for example, continued to speak of Adam as "the father and head of mankind" whose sin "inferred and implied the disobedience of all." But he attributed humanity's connection to Adam, not so much to any real ontological union (though at times one can find vague references in Hopkins to the possibility of such a union), as to sheer "divine constitution" or "the appointment of God," suggesting in the process that imputation was strictly mediate. By the end of the eighteenth century, as Jay Fliegelman and Joyce Appleby have noted, even mediate imputation became suspect, as the time-honored Calvinistic dictum that in Adam's fall did sin we all "was stigmatized, as it had not been before, as a class doctrine." While increasing numbers of New Englanders adopted Edwardsian theology as a more dynamic and vigorous alternative to Old Calvinism, they simultaneously rejected the notion of imputation as patriarchally oppressive. By the time of Timothy Dwight, then, New England's Edwardsians became quite reticent with regard to imputation, discussing it, if at all, primarily to distance themselves from outmoded views. Dwight himself admitted the great "embarrassment" and "reluctance" that accompanied the doctrine of original sin in his day, confessing "that if I saw any mode of avoiding the evidence by which it is established, I would certainly reject it also." Though he found no evidence for avoiding original sin, moreover, he found plenty for avoiding imputation. In a pointed passage that discussed the biblical use of the verb "impute," he repudiated the notion "that the posterity of Adam are guilty of his transgression," arguing the "obvious" and "irresistible" point "that the sons of Adam" are by no means "punished for the sins of this, their common, parent." By 1852, after tens of thousands of New Englanders had joined the Edwardsian ranks, Edwards A. Park felt free to confess that "Edwards's work on Original Sin is not a perfect exponent of what is now termed the Edwardean faith." He noted correctly that "perhaps no two of our eminent theologians have adopted its theory of our sameness with Adam. . . . It was written amid the constant alarms of an Indian war, under many embarrassing influences of its author's frontier parish, and with a constitution shattered by the fever and ague."[53]

Despite their widely shared concern to escape the stigma attached to imputation, however, the Taylorites' view of original sin did find continuity with Edwards's own resistance to the increasingly forensic language of the ardent federal theologians. Like Edwards before him, Taylor ascribed "the mode of connection between Adam's sin and its consequences to his posterity" to "God's sovereign constitution, in distinction from the mode of strict legal procedure." The perpetuation of sin and guilt was, for Taylor, providential and thus certain. But much as Edwards refused to succumb to the notion that imputation took place apart from any consideration of human blameworthiness, Taylor refused to countenance any view of original sin that portrayed divine providence as arbitrary or that exculpated sinners from their vice. Undeniably, by the early nineteenth century the Edwardsians had departed significantly from Edwards's doctrine of imputation. Moreover, the Taylorites repudiated this doctrine more boldly and forthrightly than most. But as Eleazar Fitch clarified as early as 1826, their chief complaint lay against the notion of *immediate* imputation. They rejected the doctrine, he said, "simply in that sense which involves the literal transfer of the guilt of [Adam's] sin." God *does* hold us guilty for our propensity to sin as soon as it manifests itself in action. Thus, in a very real sense we stand worthy of condemnation as a result of Adam's Fall. In no sense, however, do we stand guilty *for* Adam's Fall. As the New York City Edwardsian Samuel Whelpley contended in a work that made him famous, the latter teaching comprised one of three deadly angles in a deterministic high Calvinist "triangle" (the other two angles being physical depravity and a limited atonement), trapping people within the walls of Adam's sin and exerting grave effects on both evangelism and public morality.[54]

The Significance of Semantics

While Taylor was a proud and independent spirit, he always perceived his modifications of Edwardsian phraseology as faithful enhancements of Edwards's legacy, as changes in orthodox New England's *modus loquendi* and not in the substance of its doctrines. The Taylorites believed that the manner in which one chose to articulate Calvinist doctrine made a great deal of difference. But they almost always claimed that the divisions caused in New England's orthodox community by New Haven views were unnecessary. When understood properly, the differences had everything to do with semantics and very little to do with substance. This was not to say that semantics were unimportant; rather, semantics were worth fighting for. As Goodrich noted during the controversy over original sin, "the use of ambiguous language on this subject, has been a prolific source of obloquy and error." But the Taylorites insisted that their innovations in the manner of expressing orthodoxy should not be mistaken for departures from orthodoxy.[55]

This reasoning pervaded the Taylorites' rearticulation of original sin. Taylor, along with Goodrich, Fitch, Beecher, and others, lamented the unhealthy extremes to which many recent Edwardsians had taken the doctrine. They thought that the ongoing quarrel between Exercisers and Tasters had left New England with an impoverished religious psychology, rendering the discussion of human sin tenuous, frequently incredible, and leaving New Englanders with so low a view of the soul's capacities that evangelistic appeals often seemed perfunctory and even futile. Both the Exercisers and the Tasters had abandoned the unique blend of Neoplatonic, rationalist, and empirical metaphysics that had made the philosophy of Edwards's private notebooks rather esoteric but had reinvigorated evangelical Calvinist theology with a fascinating preachability. The Exercisers had radicalized Edwards's occasionalist approach to causation by neglecting the fullness of what Sang Lee has aptly termed Edwards's "dispositional ontology" and respect for secondary causes. In the process, they offended and even appalled many of their colleagues by making the soul appear to be nothing but the sum of its exercises and thus making God appear to be the only real (or efficient) cause of human sin.[56] The Tasters, on the other hand (including most Tylerites), tried to maintain Edwards's appreciation for the soul's affectional life without sufficient recourse to his doctrine of continuous creation, making the human taste for sin appear as an inborn, propagated faculty plagued with natural inability. As Taster Nathaniel Niles confessed in 1809, natural ability was not all it was cracked up to be. In actuality, sinners "have no more power to renew themselves, than the Ethiopian has to change his colour, or the Leopard his spots— . . . they are without strength—dead in trespasses and sins."[57]

The Taylorites lamented the whole dispute and worked toward what they deemed a less dubious modus loquendi. They approved of the Exercisers' famed notion that sin is in the sinning (i.e., that sin does not exist in the soul prior to or apart from individual sinful exercises), but agreed with most other critics that the Exercisers' impoverished psychology yielded divine determinism. As Beecher once recalled, "Taylor and I used to talk about Emmons, and wonder how he could possibly have room in his system for accountability. To me it seemed an utter impossibility."[58] Rather than return to Edwards's own essentially Augustinian understanding of human nature, however, the Taylorites substituted a conservative, Calvinist version of Scottish faculty psychology, though making clear (unlike the Tasters, who had begun to portray humanity's inborn taste for sin in the terms of faculty psychology) their rejection of propagated depravity. They wound up with what might be called a modified Exercise scheme, heralding the doctrine that sin is in the sinning but depicting humans rather than God as the efficient causes of their own sin. As Beecher would later boast, "I struck hard against Emmons on the one hand, and Dr. Burton on the other. I stood between. . . . The fact is, when I preached free agency, and the Holy Spirit set it home and produced conviction, every body rejoiced."[59] Clearly the Taylorites (Beecher included) leaned closer to the Exercisers than the Tasters. But they sided with neither, claiming continuity with older Edwardsians such as Nathan Strong and Luther Hart. In a posthumous tribute to their colleague Luther Hart, they wrote:

> When he came forward into life, the Exercise and Taste schemes, as they were called, were common topics of discussion. . . . He certainly embraced the former . . . though not in the sense of Dr. Emmons, that all volitions are the product of the efficient, creative, invincible power of God. Why, then, (and the remark is equally applicable to many others,) call his scheme Taylorism? It was his, long before the name was thought of. . . . Twenty years ago, it was sound Calvinism.[60]

Despite their claims to continuity with traditional Edwardsian Calvinism, the Taylorites' Scottish realism did give the doctrine of sin a different flavor than Edwards's Augustinian realism. It is important to recall, however, that almost everyone in New England, including the most ardent Edwardsians, employed the Scottish Philosophy by this time. No one maintained Edwards's own eclectic metaphysics, though all, in one way or another, tried to maintain its powerful homiletical effects.[61]

As the Taylorites stated time and again, they emphasized human ability only to dispel the complacency generated by the Exercisers', Tasters', and Tylerites' emphasis on inability. As Beecher once wrote to Ebenezer Porter, when he began his ministry it seemed to him as though hyper-Calvinism and philosophical necessitarianism ruled the day: "In this condition the people did not need high-toned Calvinism on the point of dependence; they had been crammed with it, and were dying with excessive aliment, and needed a long and vigorous prescription of free agency to produce an alternative, and render the truth salutary by administering the proper portions in due season." Taylor reiterated this pragmatic theme in print three years later: "I believe, that both the doctrines of dependence and moral accountability, must be admitted by the public mind, to secure upon that mind the full power of the Gospel. I also believe, that greater or lesser prominence should be given to one or the other of these doctrines, according to the prevailing state of public opinion." Taylor noted that his forebears focused intently on dependence due to the prevalence of Arminianism: "But the prominence given to the doctrine of dependence in preaching was continued, until . . . it so engrossed the public attention, that many fell into the opposite error of quietly waiting for God's interposition." As might have been expected, this error led to a notable decline in revivals and conversions. For Taylor, however, this historical lesson did not teach simply that ministers ought to abandon "high-toned Calvinism" and Edwards's doctrine of moral inability. He went on: "[N]or would it be strange if the latter kind of preaching [ability/responsibility-oriented preaching] should in its turn prevail so exclusively and so long, that the practical influence of the doctrine of dependence should be greatly impaired, to be followed with another dearth of revivals, and a quiet reliance of sinful men on their own self-sufficiency." There was a delicate balance to be cherished between the doctrines of natural ability and divine dependence that required constant redress. "When both doctrines are wisely and truly presented, the sinner has no resting place. He cannot well avoid a sense of guilt while proposing to remain in his sins . . . [and] he cannot well presume on his resolution of future repentance. . . . He is thus shut up to the faith—the immediate performance of his duty."[62]

In the end, the difference between Taylor's emphasis on the human ability to obey God in spite of the fact that sin was certain to prevail prior to regeneration, and Edwards's emphasis on natural ability in spite of the fact of moral inability, proved largely semantic. But Taylor's option for this semantic road less traveled made all (or at least much) of the difference, both in his relations with fellow Edwardsians and in his identity as a theologian of moral government and of revival.

5

"The Comprehensive Theme of Revealed Theology"

Taylor and the Moral Government of God

> The Moral Government of God was the great thought of Dr. Taylor's intel-
> lect, and the favorite theme of his instructions in theology. It occupied his
> mind more than any and every other subject. . . . This object directed all
> his studies. All his investigations had their starting point from this central
> theme.
>
> Noah Porter, "Introduction" to Taylor's Lectures
on the Moral Government of God

> While lecturing, his voice often trembled, and at times the tears would start,
> especially when speaking of the moral government of God.
>
> Theodore Munger, "Dr. Nathaniel W. Taylor—Master Theologian"

Taylor believed with all his heart that "God is a God of sincerity and truth." To sinners racked with anguish and self-doubt, he declared continually that God's offer of salvation was genuine, reliable, and open to all. Despite what they might have heard from some *hyper*-Calvinist clergymen, the Lord's governance was just and fair. God did not withhold grace from any who earnestly sought it and only those who willfully persisted in the error of their ways would be abandoned ultimately to perdition. At his son-in-law's clerical installation service in Springfield, Massachusetts, Taylor exhorted his fellow ministers to drive this fact home to troubled parishioners, freeing them up from the debilitating psychology of high Calvinism and reassuring them with the infallible promises of the gospel:

> Let . . . the impression be made full, strong, unqualified on every guilty mind, that God
> in his law, and God in the invitations of his mercy, means exactly what he says. Let the
> full-orbed sincerity of a redeeming God, like the sun in mid-heaven, be made to pour its
> melting beams on the dark and guilty mind of the sinner against God. . . . If there is any
> one thing more than another, which would give new power to New England preaching,
> I cannot but think, it is to make a fuller deeper impression of the true-hearted sincerity of
> God in his calls of mercy.[1]

A striking emphasis on God's justice and goodness and on the truly *moral* nature of divine government pervades Taylor's entire corpus. While this emphasis manifested itself perhaps most clearly in the series of doctrines and methodological concerns usually associated with moral government theory per se (and discussed later in this chapter), it also provided a loose infrastructure for his theology as a whole. Taylor did not, as many have claimed, reduce his forebears' rich Calvinist piety to a narrow, do-good moralism. But he did infuse it throughout his career with a powerful and systematic element of dependability, an elixir of sorts to coat the often bitter medicine of divine sovereignty for an increasingly democratic people. He remained to the end a conservative Calvinist and did not go nearly as far as many Baptists, Methodists, Restorationists, and sectarian groups toward democratizing American Christianity. But he did present Edwardsian Calvinism in a manner adapted to his times, applauding divine providence for epitomizing contemporary republican values such as equity and virtue rather than monarchial remnants such as arbitrary power.[2]

"The Providential Purposes of God"

In the *Concio ad Clerum*, Taylor made a statement that would appear frequently throughout the 1830s in the Taylorites' claims to Calvinist orthodoxy: "[T]he writer hopes he shall not be charged . . . with denying what he fully believes—that the providential purposes or decrees of God extend to all actual events, sin not excepted." The Taylorites, in other words, like all good Calvinists, upheld a firm commitment to both predestination and general divine providence, known together as the doctrine of the eternal divine decrees. Taylor would note elsewhere that he preferred to discuss this doctrine under the rubric "the providential purposes of God" rather than perpetuate the more monarchial and deterministic language of divine decrees. He suggested that the terms predestination and decree, being "of heathen origin and of heathen import," tended to cause confusion among the people and that "the use of them, if not unjustifiable, ought on the ground of expediency, at least in many cases, to be relinquished." But he maintained, nevertheless, that "God has from eternity purposed that every event which takes place shall take place." Further, "no event whose actual existence he has purposed will fail to take place." God's providential purposes encompassed even human sin. As one Yale alumnus remembered with thinly veiled regret, Taylor "used to deprecate that any who agreed with him, and especially his students, should say that God does not ordain and decree sin." The Taylorites' commitment to divine fairness did not undermine their traditional Calvinistic regard for God's omnipotent providence. As they summarized in the *Quarterly Christian Spectator*, "God exercises a particular providence in *all* the affairs of the world."[3]

More important than *whether* God exercised such providence, however, was the question *how* God did so and, on this latter question, the Taylorites distanced themselves once again from the deterministic tendencies of high Calvinism. In keeping with their insistence on human natural ability and the significance of secondary causation, they stopped short of characterizing divine providence in terms of immediate divine efficiency, choosing instead to emphasize the infallibility of God's decrees in a manner that left the door open for human free will:

> "That God cannot foresee the actions of his creatures," wrote Taylor, "unless their actions are certain under his government, is indeed undeniable. That God cannot foresee the actions of creatures, without knowing that given antecedents will be followed by given

actions as their consequents, is equally undeniable. But what the connection is between these antecedents and consequent actions,—and how the Omniscient Mind perceives this connection, are questions of more difficult solution."

Taylor went on to suggest that, ultimately, such questions proved *too* difficult for any finite solution. The omniscience of divine foreknowledge and omnipotence of God's predestining will stood beyond question. But so did the viability of human free will. As creatures, he concluded, all we can say for sure (from reason or revelation) is that divine foreknowledge comprehends all of history, making the connections between antecedents and their consequents certain without rendering them necessary.[4]

Arminians such as Wilbur Fisk, a Methodist preacher and educator who had recently become the founding president of Connecticut's Wesleyan University, chafed under this ambiguity, charging the Taylorites with a troubling inconsistency on the issue of predestination. While lauding New Haven for teaching that humans are free moral agents with real ability to do their duty, Fisk claimed that the Taylorites' Calvinistic understanding of predestination compromised this truth, portraying human actions as inevitable derivatives of God's eternal decrees. For Fisk, as for many of New Haven's Calvinist critics, the Taylorites seemed to be confusing both themselves and the public by padding a Calvinist doctrine with Arminian principles. They appeared contradictory and lukewarm, nauseating to those with a taste for more standard (or readily identifiable) fare. On behalf of the Taylorites, however, Eleazar Fitch refuted this charge, arguing that New Haven's repudiation of high or supralapsarian Calvinism did not leave them espousing contradictions or touting Arminian principles. It left them, rather, with a very traditional and coherent infralapsarian Calvinism. Between the Arminians who denied that God foreordains all that occurs and the supralapsarians who depicted the divine decrees as the only significant determinants of human destiny, the Taylorites held to a doctrine of predestination that was neither heterodox nor deterministic. While maintaining human freedom and moral responsibility, they also upheld "the foreordination of all events, and . . . the predestination of men to mercy and to wrath." They believed that God predestines, not arbitrarily, but with human agency, secondary causes, and the good of the entire creation in view.[5]

While the Taylorites' now-universal insistence on history's preordained moral "certainty" without natural, external, or coercive "necessity" did prove rather novel, Fitch was correct to suggest that their infralapsarianism stood in continuity with much of Calvinist orthodoxy. Infralapsarianism, or the notion that God's decree to elect some to salvation and others to damnation *followed* (in logical or natural order) the decree to create humanity and permit its Fall, had become the predominant Calvinist position by the middle of the seventeenth century. As distinguished from supralapsarianism, which taught that election *preceded* the decrees to create and to permit the Fall, infralapsarianism portrayed election as a *response to*, not a *logical prerequisite or determinant of*, foreseen human sin. Everyone acknowledged that the decrees, being eternal and divine, were one and simple (*unicus et simplicissimus*) and thus could not be differentiated temporally. But many attempted nonetheless to discern a rationale or logical order (*ordo*) within divine providence. Employing the precept that "that [decree] which is last in execution, ought to be first in intention," supralapsarians contended that God must have created the world for the purpose of redeeming it. Virtually all agreed that the decision to provide a redeemer and to apply the work of that redeemer to the souls of the elect by the power of the Holy Spirit constituted the last of God's soteriological decrees.[6] It only made sense, then, to infer that God had the salvation of the elect (and, by implication, the reprobation of the non-elect) "in mind" when creating the world or, more appropriately, that God's decree of election must have taken logical precedence over the decrees of creation and the permission of sin. To the infralapsarians, however, this inference made only bad sense. For them, the notion that God intended from the beginning to damn millions to Hell was outrageous. Not only did it cast doubt upon God's benevolent intentions for humanity revealed in the Bible, but it also rendered God responsible for sin. If the decree of election preceded the decree to permit humanity's Fall, then it would seem humanity had no choice but to fall. God's will cannot be thwarted, they reasoned. If God intended redemption as the principal end of creation, then the creation had to become redeemable and the Fall was thus inevitable.[7]

When considered by itself, the issue of predestination or the order of the divine decrees caused little controversy among New England Calvinists. Edwards himself had spoken ambivalently about this problem, frequently employing supralapsarian logic in defense of an explicitly infralapsarian position.[8] His followers, moreover, took comparatively little interest in "clarifying" or "improving" upon this doctrine. Preoccupied with issues such as grace and free will, the marks of authentic conversion, and disinterested benevolence, they had few moments to spare for launching such precarious probes into the hidden depths of the mind of God. Where predestination impinged upon the question of divine justice, however, or upon what Joseph Bellamy referred to as "the wisdom of God in the permission of sin," it took on a tremendous significance. In this era of America's Enlightenment, the Edwardsians, like most other intellectuals, expended a great deal of energy reflecting on the problem of evil. Upset by modern sarcasm and skepticism regarding the traditional Western reliance on God's benevolent providence, they worried over its implications for Christian faith. Did God create the world knowing what great evils would arise? How could a good God allow such pain and suffering to occur? The New Divinity theologians took such questions seriously, often providing bold and uncompromising answers. While seldom defending supralapsarianism *per se*, the most strident of the Hopkinsians offered an account of moral evil that left few wondering whether they believed God had purposed human sin.[9] As we will see below, Taylor's own solution to the question of theodicy, or the question concerning the justice of God in the face of evil, arose in response to such New Divinity answers. After wrestling with the works of his Edwardsian predecessors, Taylor emerged with a new, explicitly infralapsarian response to the problem of evil—a response clearly at odds with the well-known solution of the radical Hopkinsians, but a truly Edwardsian response nonetheless.

The Problem of Theodicy

While Joseph Bellamy's sermons on *The Wisdom of God in the Permission of Sin* (1758) comprised the best known New Divinity defense of divine justice and goodness, Samuel Hopkins's *Sin, Thro' Divine Interposition, an Advantage to the Universe* (1759) was the most notorious. Both works were premised on the ancient Christian notion of *felix* culpa, or the belief in the eschatological benefits and metahistorical felicity of Adam's Fall. Dating back to the Patristic era, this belief in a "fortunate fall" appeared in the *Exultet* written (probably) by St. Ambrose of Milan (c. 339–397) and included eventually in the Roman liturgy for Holy Saturday. It received its classic expression, however, in the work of the Calvinist poet John Milton in *Paradise Lost* (1667). In Milton's epic portrayal of salvation history, a recently fallen and guilt-ridden Adam learns of Christ's eventual triumph over sin and death from the archangel Michael just prior to his expulsion from Eden. "Replete with joy and wonder," Adam exclaims:

> O goodness infinite, goodness immense!
> That all this good of evil shall produce,
> And evil turn to good; more wonderful
> Than that which by creation first brought forth
> Light out of darkness! full of doubt I stand,
> Whether I should repent me now of sin
> By mee done and occasion'd, or rejoice
> Much more, that much more good thereof shall spring,
> To God more glory, more good-will to Men
> From God, and over wrath grace shall abound.[10]

Bellamy employed this time-honored trust in the eschatological triumph of redemption in response to the many personal tragedies of his parishioners during the Seven Years War. In the face of their doubts concerning God's power and goodness, and in reply to an increasing number of Arminians and more secular Enlightenment skeptics who questioned traditional assumptions about divine providence over evil, he assured all who heard him that God remained in control. Building on the renowned (though often ridiculed) cosmic optimism of the Leibnizian theodicy,[11] Bellamy contended that God had foreseen human evil before ever creating the world. Being omniscient and omnipotent, God could have created for us any number of alternative worlds but, in love and wisdom, created this one, the best of all possible worlds. As finite, mutable creatures, our sin was inevitable, but God had always worked good out of evil and would continue to do so until the final day. Over the long term, divine providence guaranteed that vastly more good than evil would result. But in the mean time, the existence of sin made salvation all the more glorious.[12]

Not content to portray God merely permitting sin as an inevitable component of the best possible world, and less concerned than Bellamy about implicating God as the source of sin and evil, Hopkins went further. Whereas Bellamy had suggested in largely infralapsarian fashion that "God's permitting Sin consists merely in not hindering of it," Hopkins contended in supralapsarian fashion that God "*willingly* suffer'd it [sin] to take Place." Indeed, for Hopkins, "God's permitting Sin was as high an Exercise of Holiness, as any we can think of." God knew from eternity that the world *as redeemed* would considerably outshine the world *as created*. By definition, moreover, sin constitutes a necessary prerequisite of salvation. Consequently, God actively foreordained Adam's Fall. In Hopkins's vision of redemptive history, Christ, the second Adam, elevates humanity to a level of existence unattainable by the Adam of Eden. As the eternally appointed savior of the world, Christ "will so bring Things about, that God shall be more glorified, & this shall be, upon the whole, a much better World, than if the Devil had never attempted to dethrone God, and ruin Man: And will make Sin, by which the Devil fought to spoil this World, and rob God of his Honour, the Occasion and Means of bringing this about."[13]

By Taylor's day, this supralapsarian, Hopkinsian theodicy enjoyed wide acceptance among New England's Edwardsians, particularly among those who would comprise the Tylerite faction. Taylor, of course, loathed it, not only for its perfidious implication that "sin is the necessary means of the greatest good" (a phrase he often used in criticism of the doctrine but which none of its proponents actually defended), but also because, to him, it represented yet again the high Calvinist susceptibility to divine determinism. Worried during the 1820s over reports of atheism in New York and over the rise of Universalism throughout the region (both of which forms of "infidelity" held that a God as powerful and benevolent as the Calvinists supposed should or would simply *eliminate* all sin and evil), Taylor reached back behind the Hopkinsians to Bellamy's Leibnizian theodicy, taking care to reappropriate it in more humane, explicitly infralapsarian terms. In an argument fleshed out first in the *Concio ad Clerum*, he criticized what he referred to as the Hopkinsians' "gratuitous assumption" that "God could [both] have adopted a moral system, and prevented all sin, or at least, the present degree of sin." Since God had obviously not prevented sin from entering the world, Taylor believed that it was presumptuous to contend that God could have. He avoided presumption himself by proving careful never to deny absolutely that God could have prevented the rise of sin and evil. But he also proved careful to resist the skeptics' claim that the existence of sin undermined traditional Christian faith in divine goodness. For Taylor, God did not *intend* to permit sin *in order that* salvation might be provided. God has never intended or preferred sin over holiness. Indeed, to employ such supralapsarian logic was to validate the claims of the skeptics, implying that divine benevolence was curtailed or overruled by God's predestining will (at least from the perspective of those predestined to damnation). Rather, God compunctiously allowed for the existence of sin as an inevitable "incidental" in the best possible system of moral government, or in a world that provided for the optimal degree of human freedom. In Taylor's view, God's goodness and power were bounded only by the limits of possibility. God permitted the existence of sin only because it was impossible not to in a finite world of genuinely free creatures.[14]

The Tylerites responded to Taylor's theodicy from several quarters, charging that it placed undue limits and raised irreverent questions concerning God's power and majesty. Leonard Woods spoke for many when he complained that Taylor's understanding of divine justice rendered God impotent, unable to fulfill the alleged divine desire for universal human holiness. Taylor's theory, "as we understand it, implies that there is a vast amount of good which God on the whole desires and chooses to effect, but which he cannot effect." Bennet Tyler came closer to the point at issue: "To say that God prefers, all things considered, that sin should not exist; and at the same time to say that he has purposed or foreordained that it shall exist, is a palpable contradiction. It is the same as to say, that God chooses and does not choose the same thing at the same time." Believing that an omnipotent will cannot be frustrated, these men argued that God could easily have prevented sin without overwhelming our free agency. God had done so with the angels and would do so with the saints in glory. On earth, however, God had chosen freely to do otherwise. Foreseeing that, on the whole, more good would accompany a redeemed world than would accompany a world without sin, God chose to permit sin as a precondition of salvation. In denying this, they contended, Taylor had departed "radically" from traditional New England theology. According to the *Evangelical Magazine*, Taylor had left the orthodox fold "on a question which is fundamental in theology: . . . whether the Lord of heaven and earth is unlimitedly supreme." The Taylorites denied "the supreme independence of God, as it is unequivocally and uniformly revealed in his word."[15]

The Taylorites, of course, repudiated such Tylerite criticisms, contending that their opponents had failed to appreciate the subtlety of the New Haven theodicy. In response to Woods's claim that they had placed irreverent limits on divine power, Taylor asked "whether it does not savor as strongly of presumptuous irreverence to affirm that God could have secured universal holiness in his moral kingdom, but *would not*."[16] The Taylorites also made it quite clear that they deemed the New Haven theodicy a legitimate extension of traditional Edwardsian themes. Edwards, Bellamy, and the best of the Edwardsians, though not as forthrightly infralapsarian as they should have been, nevertheless adumbrated the Taylorite theodicy over that of the Hopkinsians.[17] Moreover, as Taylor stated in several places, New Haven offered its theodicy, not as a dogma carved in stone, but only to demonstrate that New England's Calvinists need not lock themselves into a high Hopkinsian position. It was offered as a suggested alternative to the regnant supralapsarian theodicy and was not meant to provide the final word on the problem of evil. As both parties realized, "to be quite confident of the truth of any theory respecting the existence of moral evil, has been extensively regarded as the mark of a rash and presumptuous mind." Taylor, then, did not declare absolutely that ours is the best of all possible worlds. To him, it seemed quite possible that God has "given existence to some other world or worlds, in which there is more happiness than in this." Surely heaven, for example, comprised such a world. He proposed only that God "could not have made a better world than this in its stead." Given our place in the universal scheme of things, God has created as good a world for us as possible. "Not to have created just such a world, or to have created any other in its stead, might have ruined all other worlds." Further, "the existence of this world may be better than its non-existence, as resulting in a greater amount of happiness to the universe than would exist without it." Conventional arguments concerning his alleged anthropocentrism notwithstanding, when hypothesizing about the problem of evil Taylor typically proved quite theocentric. Though he believed that humans played a key role in God's universal moral government, he urged his hearers away from their groundless assumption that our wants and our needs comprised the be all and end all of creation. God has created a world "which will result in . . . the greatest good which he can secure." But God has also created us with a great deal of personal freedom—clearly our world would enjoy "still greater good" if we would do our part, take our eyes off of ourselves and "employ [our] powers in a perfect manner."[18]

For Taylor, the bottom line on the problem of evil was that no one can "[prove] that God could give existence to free moral agents and prevent all sin." He insisted repeatedly that "it is not limiting to the power of God to say that he cannot accomplish impossibilities." In a truly moral government, "every subject . . . must be a free agent, i.e., he must possess the power to sin, and to continue in sin, in defiance of all that God can do to prevent him." A moral government, then, "is the government of free, uncompelled, voluntary moral agents, and God, if he adopts it, is restricted by its nature and its principles as truly as man is." To argue otherwise, thought Taylor, was to undermine the sincerity of divine revelation regarding the benefits of moral earnestness. If God really had purposed sin and evil as necessary means to the salvation of the elect, then one could never know for sure whether or not one's sin comprised an inevitable part of some predetermined divine plan. God's promise of grace to those who sought it would lose its credibility and our moral system would be subverted. As Eleazar Fitch demanded of the Tylerites in the *Quarterly Christian Spectator*, why—if God really has preferred the existence of sin to a world of pure holiness—would God bother to "conceal the choice of his heart, behind the shadows and pretexts of law and penalty, and take the pain to throw the charge of marring his kingdom upon his *creatures!*" The very suggestion of such duplicity rendered the Hopkinsians' theodicy needlessly anthropomorphic, their God petty, ambivalent, and inconsistent, operating unpredictably from "two hearts." Their supralapsarian scheme portrayed the God of the universe as unreliable, "preferring obedience on the whole here, and preferring sin on the whole there,—nobody can tell where." Even worse, it "sets up an object of adoration, praise and prayer, to whom none can come with the simple confidence of an undivided heart: none, without the chilly suspicion, that the adoration he would fain bring to one heart of God, will be capriciously rejected by the other; . . . the prayer by which he would appeal to one, will be indignantly spurned by the other."[19]

By the end of their dispute, the Taylorites and Tylerites did soften their blows and reach something of an understanding on the problem of evil. Faced with the unpleasant implications of their tacitly supralapsarian position, the Tylerites backed off somewhat from their strident Hopkinsian rhetoric (though they retained their distaste for Taylorite innovation). The Taylorites, in turn (and true to form), held out the olive branch. But even when conciliatory, the New Haven theologians evinced an acerbic antipathy toward any and all supralapsarian logic. "Much as we regret the misunderstanding," they taunted, "we still believe it will be overruled for good; though we cannot see quite so clearly as we suppose some men do, on their own theories, that contention in our churches is better than harmony would be in its stead."[20]

Moral Government and Moral Agency

Though, as we have seen, Taylor's overriding concern to uphold divine justice and equity evolved quite naturally from his immersion in the discourse of the Edwardsian theological culture, it took shape in response to more secular cultural forces as well. While Taylor's own life was defined primarily by the very spiritual affairs of the antebellum evangelical ministry, the effectiveness of that ministry often hinged on its ability to present the claims of the gospel in terms that resonated with a laity accustomed to the everyday world of social and material exchange. As discussed in chapter 2, the rules of this exchange had changed dramatically in America's early national period and would continue to do so throughout Taylor's lifetime. Once a monarchial society loyal to a sovereign king, Americans now lived as self-governing republicans. And once an aggregate of Bible commonwealths governed in accordance with local religio-political covenants, New England now exhibited all the characteristics of a complex modern society. To attract the masses, the region's clergy had to speak relevantly to the needs of their new nation, rearticulating divine truth in a manner that made sense of their parishioners' new situation and that inspired them to carry the faith forward into their brave new world. Moral government theory enabled many ministers to do just that. As William Sutton has summarized, "the demands of republicanism required both a constitutionally limited divine executive . . . and an independent, virtuous citizenry," and Taylor, for one, offered an analysis of the moral government of God that went a long way toward providing both. Though he did not, as many have claimed, give up on the God of premodern Calvinism, he did contemporize that God for an increasingly modern audience. As Taylor knew well, his fellow Americans needed a divine moral governor whose rule encouraged moral effort and upward mobility, not an arbitrary monarch whose potentially despotic sway stifled the democratic virtues of hard work and individual responsibility.[21]

Ever since Perry Miller's classic biography of Edwards in 1949, scholars have paid special attention to the fate of the "covenant theology" among the New Divinity clergy and its relationship to the rise of moral government theory in the early nineteenth century. Miller argued that Edwards's emphasis on divine sovereignty, human dependence, and God's unilateral responsibility for our salvation undermined the more contractual, bilateral, or covenantal soteriology that, to Miller, symbolized declension from authentic Calvinism among the later Puritans. By collapsing the Puritans' preparationist morphology of conversion, heralding the largely unmediated quality of divine grace, and calling for immediate repentance, Edwards and his followers rendered the covenant motif obsolete. In its place, they erected what Bruce Kuklick has called a "constitutional divinity" based, not on a reciprocal relationship between faithful subjects and an obliging king, but on the absolute rule of divine law.[22] Subsequent scholarship has demonstrated that the Puritans' covenant theology was not nearly as contractual or "Arminian" as Miller suggested. Indeed, in seventeenth-century New England, covenant thought usually proceeded quite carefully within the traditional channels of Reformed orthodoxy. It included both bilateral and unilateral soteriological themes, and placed a strong emphasis on the latter. Rather than treating it like Miller, moreover, as a doomed feature of New England's alleged religious declension, recent historians have highlighted the ways in which the covenant motif endured, pointing to the survival of covenant rhetoric—especially regarding America's national covenant with God—well into the Revolutionary period.[23]

Despite these important historiographical corrections, however, nearly all historians remain convinced that the covenant theology departed eighteenth-century New England in a very weakened condition. From its origins in late medieval scholasticism, covenantal thought had always proved quite durable and multifarious. But with the rise of "federal theology" proper (often identified simply, though inaccurately, as orthodox covenant theology) among Calvinists in the late sixteenth century, most covenant theology came to rely on the forensic or imputation-based understanding of salvation so central to Reformed scholasticism. As discussed in chapter 3, though New England experienced no facile decline from a purportedly superior Calvinism to an allegedly harmful Arminianism or liberalism, it did witness a decline in the scholastic language of imputation. Thus, while Miller misconstrued the decline of covenantal themes in eighteenth-century New England (ironically, the Edwardsians' gradual departure from the language of imputation made their divine constitutionalism *less* traditional and *less* high Calvinist than the covenantalism it replaced), in general his thesis has fared quite well. Though frequently retaining a belief in America's divine favor, the Edwardsians, like most other New Englanders, eventually abandoned the Puritans' covenant theology.[24]

Whatever the rate at which the covenant theology ceased to provide New England with its predominant framework for understanding divine/human relations, by Taylor's day the theme of moral government had clearly taken its place. In a manner that paralleled America's political transition from constitutional monarchy to the republican rule of law, New England theology moved away from talk of divinely initiated covenants with an otherwise hapless and helpless people to a discussion of God's just government of potentially virtuous moral agents. While, again, "the transition from covenant to moral government" did not, as more than one writer has suggested, "[mark] the triumph of moralism in New England piety," it did signal the rise of a timely new paradigm for New England theology. It also signaled the triumph of Edwardsianism over the more traditional and covenantal tenets of Old Calvinism. As Allen Guelzo has noted, "[G]overnmental images came easily to the New Divinity, since it was one of the chief philosophic objects of Edwardseanism to prove that God was a moral, not an arbitrary, Governor of creation." Indeed, governmental images enabled Edwardsians to speak to the nation's new republican mentality in a wide variety of ways. Not only had American politics, for example, taken on a new constitutional orientation but American law itself had become more rational, consistent, and less arbitrary. As Lawrence Friedman has summarized, "[I]n the early years of the 19th century, the roles of judge and jury were subtly altered and redefined." American jurisprudence became increasingly nationalized and its arbiters acquired more standardized roles. No longer free to help define or shape the laws, they stuck to the facts of the cases at hand and served as referees of a fixed and reliable judicial system.[25]

As one born just prior to the United States' constitutional convention, Taylor felt keenly the significance of such changes. Convinced that most orthodox Calvinists were speaking past the American people by focusing too intently on the sovereign lordship of God, he complained that "in all the theology of uninspired men, there has been to this hour not even an attempt formally and fully to unfold the comprehensive relation of God to men as their perfect moral governor, in the nature, the essential principles, and actual administration of this government." To one who had come to consider God's moral government "the comprehensive theme of Revealed Theology," this proved nothing less than a travesty. With scarcely concealed bravado, Taylor concluded that "all the attempts made by theologians to systematize the great and substantial truths of both Natural and Revealed Theology, have hitherto proved utter and complete failures." He explained that "all that God does, and all that He says in respect to man, terminates in the grand end of his moral government." Thus, the older, more imperial rhetoric of utter human dependence had clearly outlived its usefulness. God's role as the moral governor of all creatures "is the great, the paramount relation which he sustains to them— a relation to which every other must be subservient."[26]

Despite this pretentious repudiation of all previous theological systems, Taylor himself never published the kind of comprehensive treatment of God's moral government for which he so desperately longed. His relatively unpolished and posthumously published Yale lectures on the topic were as close as he came to such a work. Fortunately, however, these lectures fill two large volumes and provide a detailed picture of the kind of system he envisioned. Though not as refined as his written work, when read in conjunction with that work they do open a large window onto his view of the moral universe.

At the center of Taylor's moral universe stood his oft-stated commitment to the justice of divine government and the corollary that God demanded nothing impossible as requisite to salvation. While admitting that God's law did require sinless perfection, Taylor asserted that "since the fall of man and the promise of the Redeemer," God no longer deemed the law "an actually existing rule of judgment to this sinful world." Rather, in loving response to humanity's Fall, God has inaugurated "an economy of grace" wherein divine law continues to function as "God's rule of action," but in which faith in God's redeeming love now constitutes the only rule of judgment. Since the Fall, argued Taylor, God has governed with both law and grace. Building on St. Paul's teaching in Romans 2:16 ("God shall judge the secrets of men by Jesus Christ according to my gospel"), he insisted that, while sinners do stand condemned to suffer the full penalty of the law, God has responded to our sinful plight with the merciful provisions of the gospel. Knowing that sin was sure to arise in every human heart, God has determined that faith in the good news of divine grace would suffice for admission to eternal life.[27]

As would become clear in Taylor's doctrine of the atonement (discussed below), this distinction between the rule of law and the rule of judgment distanced him somewhat from the teaching of the high Calvinists. In contrast to their notion that God has reserved salvation for the elect alone, or for those to whom God has decided to impute Christ's perfect obedience to the rule of law as a substitute for their own, Taylor claimed that God's rule of judgment has opened salvation to all. Though our failure to meet the demands of divine law is certain in this fallen world, our ability to meet the mitigated expectations of our gracious Judge remains. Even hardened sinners have the ability to trust in the merciful provisions of the gospel. Were this not the case, God's government would prove cruel indeed. In fact, as scholastic theologians had been suggesting for centuries, if human nature stands unable to perform that which God requires without the aid of divine grace, then grace is no longer grace—it is no longer gratuitous, in other words, but is owed to us (in any just moral system) in compensation for the deficiencies of human nature. As argued in the *Quarterly Christian Spectator*, if grace "be such as [God] could not have denied us, and at the same time justly required us to obey him, this aid was as much, and in the same sense, *due* to us, as rational faculties themselves." This claim stood as the basis of one of Taylor's main objections to the Arminian understanding of grace. He argued that the Arminian concept of "prevenient grace" (or, for Arminians, that grace which *always* precedes and enables *any* sinner to respond salvifically to God), though at first glance more equitable than its high Calvinist equivalent, nevertheless seriously undermined the notion of natural ability. By positing a necessary, prevenient rejuvenation of human nature before sinners could perform their duty, it denuded the human soul of any genuine natural capacity for good. "Can it be," asked Taylor, "that before it is possible for God himself to secure right moral action in these creatures of his power, he must make them over again, mending his original work of creation, and by new physical powers constitute them moral and accountable subjects of his government? Was it a task too hard for Omnipotence to make them at first complete moral agents?" Taylor's commitment to the gratuity of divine grace also illumines his assessment of the arch-heretic Pelagius. Contrary to the high Calvinists, declared Taylor,

> the error of Pelagius is, not that he maintained man's ability to obey God without grace, but that man does *actually* obey God without grace. Some, who would seem to think

themselves to be well-read theologians, appear not to know the difference between affirming that man *can* obey without grace, and affirming that he *does* or ever will obey without grace. I affirm the former, and deny the latter. I suppose a *necessity* of grace, not to constitute men moral agents, or able to obey God, but to influence those to obey God who can, but from willfulness in sin never will obey him without grace.[28]

Daniel Walker Howe has claimed that Taylor's concern with "human nature and its potential" was "the central concern of the Whig-Jacksonian era." Whether or not this concern proved central to *all* Americans, it certainly did impinge with comparable force upon their lives as members of a newly democratic society and their roles as believers and citizens in God's moral government. Just as in a democratic republic the health of the nation rested on the freely elicited virtues of its citizens, so in a divine moral government, reasoned Taylor, the viability of the whole rested on the free and virtuous agency of its parts. As he explained in the late 1820s,

[I]t is a truth often overlooked, in theological discussion, that God as a moral governor, can be glorified only by the love and service of beings who are intelligent as well as voluntary. Without such beings, there could be no acts of intelligent communion between God and his creatures, no acts of kindness from him to recipients appreciating his gifts, and no songs of praise to recognize his goodness and his grace. There would be none to distinguish between right and wrong, between God and other objects of affection,—none to admire, to love, to trust, to thank, to serve, to enjoy God, and give a reason for their homage. . . . The moral Governor of moral beings would be unacknowledged and unserved. God, without a creature endowed with reason and qualified to correspond with Him and heaven, would sit upon his throne, the solitary spectator of the laws of matter and the acts of instinct.

Like the United States of America, the moral government of God cannot thrive (and would not even exist) without at least a modicum of genuine human freedom. Thus, the Taylorites fought tirelessly at every turn for the doctrine of natural ability and against coercive or physical conceptions of human depravity and divine grace. As Taylor stated in his Yale lectures, "[T]he influence of moral government being an influence on moral beings and designed to control moral action, is as diverse in its nature from the influence of physical causes, as moral action is from a physical effect; or as a moral cause is from a physical cause." God effects *moral* change by *moral* means—by motivation and persuasion, not by external or physical force. Moral government "leaves the moral liberty of the subject unimpaired." In fact, it "leaves every subject as free to perform the action which it aims to prevent, as to perform that which it aims to secure." As Joseph Bellamy had explained long ago, the decrees by which God governs the world "primarily respect his own conduct." They do not necessitate our actions. They do not even keep us (in theory) from opposing the divine will. Hence the logic of Taylor's fundamental moral distinction: God's government "is designed and fitted to give, not the necessity, but merely the certainty of its effect." Intent on upholding an evangelical Calvinist understanding of divine providence while shielding God from the charge of tyranny, he declared the very idea of "controlling moral beings by physical agency" to be "repulsive" and "degrading."[29]

Clearly, Taylor's concern with human nature and its potential yielded a rather innovative theology of human moral agency. Arminians, Unitarians, and more skeptical theists had long since responded to America's republican optimism by *abandoning* the anthropology of the Calvinists. But Taylor attempted to address this new ethos while *maintaining* a Calvinist anthropology. Most scholars have been conditioned to interpret his emphasis on the moral nature of divine government as a sign of departure from New England Calvinism. But despite his occasionally arrogant and dismissive pronouncements against various orthodox predecessors (usually restricted to classroom lectures), Taylor achieved a creative combination of both contemporaneity and continuity with New England's Edwardsian tradition. Along with his concern to promote moral accountability among the sinners in his charge, Taylor retained a strong, Calvinistic commitment to the rule of divine providence. Thus, while claiming that human beings *could* resist the moral inducements of their freedom-loving God, he remained convinced that this natural ability of ours never *would* thwart God's plans for human history. In the end, his theory proved quite Edwardsian and, in this sense, surprisingly conservative—not nearly as liberal or democratic as the theologies of many of his peers. He emphasized the moral nature of divine-human relations, not to undermine his listeners' belief in divine sovereignty with republican ideology, but to perpetuate an authentic Edwardsian piety, to promote revivals and conversions and to inspire his hearers with the goal of true virtue.

Indeed, true to his Edwardsian heritage, Taylor proved a consistent advocate of affectional Calvinist piety and eschewed any alternative or counterfeit moralism. In the tradition of his New Divinity forebears, he taught that all moral agency stems from either of two radically different "governing principles of action." The once-born world of the unregenerate ("the great bulk of mankind"), he thought, acts on a "principle of selfishness," or what Taylor referred to as "the very substance of moral degradation," the "corroding fire of the eternal pit." The twice-born world of the redeemed, on the other hand, acts on a "principle of benevolence." Its inhabitants demonstrate what Taylor called "an elective preference for God" or, in even more Edwardsian fashion, "an elective preference of the highest well-being of all other sentient beings as [their] supreme object." Between these two worlds lies "a broad and visible line of distinction." As in Edwards's *Faithful Narrative*, moreover, Taylor chose a woman (and a black woman at that), Amy Fowler, to exemplify the kind of elite, theocentric piety practiced on the right side of that line. Addressing his parishioners in an early sermon on "The Habitual Recognition of God," he asked, "Did you ever know a human being in whom it was made more manifest that she set the Lord always before her—that she entered into the reality of those relations in which God discovers himself to his people, and in which the state of mind evinced more decisively its results in peace, and hope, and love, and gratitude, and joy?" Like Abigail Hutchinson and Phebe Bartlet in eighteenth-century Northampton, Fowler modeled a convertive and disjunctive Edwardsian piety for nineteenth-century New Haven.[30]

With Edwards, Taylor believed true religion to be primarily a matter of the affections.[31] He did not pretend that "the sinner does not as well as the saint perform some actions which in their external form are right." But he was sure that even the seemingly good deeds of the sinner stem from a rotten heart. Morally speaking, he felt that the saint simply operates under a different governing or "predominant principle" than the sinner, one that "sways and determines all." In both saints and sinners, he viewed the predominant principle or elective preference as "the grand central power, which takes under its dominion the entire productive energy of a moral being." It constitutes the soul's fundamental affectional orientation and shapes one's entire moral life. Claiming Edwards as his authority, Taylor conceived of one's predominant principle as a very powerful, "practical principle, inasmuch as it is not only a disposition or purpose of heart, but a permanent governing principle, which in its true nature and tendency prompts to, or, etymologically speaking, arranges, or directs all those subordinate volitions . . . which are necessary to the attainment of its object." Each moral agent, he said, "is doomed by a necessity of nature" to act in accordance with either the selfish or the benevolent principle. "It is an ordinance of [our] very being, that [we] cannot serve both these masters, and must serve one." The challenge of the moral life, then, was to break out of one's bondage to the selfish principle and practice disinterested benevolence. This challenge will be discussed at length in chapter 5. But for the present it is important to note that, while Taylor did harbor a few reservations concerning the manner in which Edwards had articulated the doctrine of inability, he fully agreed with Edwards's general understanding of human moral agency. One cannot "act right in subordinate or executive action" with a "morally wrong heart." Sinners need above all else, not simply to do good deeds, but to find a change of heart.[32]

The Nature of the Atonement

The theme of moral government had permeated the "Edwardsian theory" of the atonement since its formulation in the mid-1780s. Though it had strong roots in the theology of Edwards, Bellamy, and Hopkins,[33] that which we call the Edwardsian theory emerged primarily among younger Edwardsian ministers in response to the rise of Universalism in New England during the Revolutionary period. With the successes achieved in the 1770s and 1780s by the Universalist John Murray (an English immigrant who imported his countryman James Relly's notion that the merits of Christ's atoning sacrifice not only allow for, but have actually accomplished, the salvation of all), and with the publication in 1784 of Charles Chauncy's clandestine but home-grown Universalist views in The Benevolence of the Deity and The Mystery Hid, the Edwardsians became alarmed. The spread of Universalism undermined traditional Christian teachings concerning the reality of Hell and the need for conversion. It also seemed to threaten New England's social order. If all were to be saved eventually, it was thought, then soteriological resolve would prove unnecessary. Evangelical humility would no longer govern the reflections of New Englanders on the eternal status of their souls and good works would no longer serve to grant them assurance of their election. The New Divinity's Stephen West, Jonathan Edwards, Jr., and John Smalley responded forcefully to this threat beginning in the spring of 1785. In rapid-fire succession, each one published on the nature and extent of the atonement within the span of a single year. Edwards Jr., who experienced the threat of Universalism first-hand within the walls of his own parish church, preached three sermons on The Necessity of Atonement (1785) that soon became the cornerstone of the Edwardsian position.[34]

Murray's "Rellyan Universalism" posed the greatest early challenge to the Edwardsians. A former Methodist who is often referred to as the immigrant "founder" of American Universalism, Murray employed an evangelical, forensic understanding of salvation to great advantage among New Englanders. As the story usually goes, native liberals such as Chauncy typically propounded an "Arminian" form of Universalism, portraying Hell as a temporary punishment intended to refine or improve people for Heaven. Murray, on the other hand, defended a more popular "Calvinistic" position. Combining forensic logic with a universalized doctrine of what the orthodox referred to narrowly as the believers' union with Christ (*unio cum Christo*), he concluded that Christ suffered on behalf of all humanity, providing a plenary, legal atonement for all human sin. "As all died, and were lost in Adam," wrote his mentor James Relly, "it is evident they were then in him, then unified to him, so that his sin was their sin." Just "as in Adam," moreover, "so in Christ." All humanity is *already* "united in him, in all he did, and suffered: saved in him . . . , risen with him, ascended and seated with him."[35]

Faced with the rising popularity of this new democratic doctrine of the atonement, the Edwardsians struggled to defend their cherished distinction between true religion and its damnable counterfeits. But rather than revert to the more elitist high Calvinist notion that, while in theory Christ died for all he actually united with and thus atoned for the sins of the elect alone, they decided to abandon transactional language for the atonement altogether. Following the lead of Edwards, Jr., they departed from more traditional explanations of the atonement that described its efficacy in terms of Christ's payment of our debt and satisfaction of God's wrath, offering instead a "moral government theory" that portrayed the Savior's passion as a "vindication of the divine law and character." For Edwards, Jr., and his peers, Christ "did not, in the literal sense, pay the debt we owed to God." Practically speaking, this would mean either that he relieved humanity as a whole of any obligation whatsoever (antinomianism) or applied such payment secretly to the accounts of a privileged few (elitism). However, Christ did make amends for the damage done by our rebellion against God's moral government, thus enabling God to show mercy to all who would convert. In rebelling against God, "we . . . practically despised his law and authority." It became "necessary," therefore, "that his authority should be supported, and that it should be made to appear, that sin shall not go without proper tokens of divine displeasure and abhorrence; that God will maintain his law; that his authority and government shall not be allowed to fall into contempt; and that God is a friend to virtue and holiness, and an irreconcilable enemy to transgression, sin, and vice." In short, while not literally saving all humanity by paying the debt for human sin, the atonement has maintained the viability of God's moral government, safeguarding our system of morality and thus clearing the way of salvation for the entire human race.[36]

Most scholars have interpreted the Edwardsian theory of the atonement as an American manifestation of the "Grotian theory," named after the Dutch Arminian legal theorist Hugo Grotius (1583–1645). Though he is perhaps best known for systematizing the modern theory of natural rights, Grotius was also the first major figure to define the atonement in moral government terms. In his landmark *Defensio fidei catholicae de satisfactione Christi adversus F. Socinum* (1614), Grotius attempted to defend the Church's traditional use of satisfactionary language for the atonement against the objections of the liberal Faustus Socinus (1539–1604). Significantly, however, in doing so he avoided the use of the historic "Anselmian" or satisfaction *theory* of the atonement (named after its originator, St. Anselm of Canterbury, d. 1109), which posited that the atonement served primarily to appease or satisfy God's wrath over human sin. Grotius contended that Christ suffered, not for God's sake, but for humanity's. Accordingly, his atonement satisfied, not an offended deity, but divine justice and the moral government it supported. Clearly, the Edwardsian theory of the atonement followed the basic contours set out by Grotius. Its moral government language echoed Grotius's concern to promulgate a general or unlimited theory of the atonement (i.e., one that did not limit its effects to the elect) that yet sustained its objective efficacy (Socinus and other liberals argued that the atonement performed only a subjective function and that Jesus' self-sacrifice served primarily as a moral example or appeal to humanity). Moreover, the Edwardsians did have access to Grotius's work. Jonathan Edwards listed Grotius in his "Catalogue" of readings and Harvard and Yale owned copies of the *Defensio* as early as 1723 and 1733, respectively. But the Edwardsian understanding of the atonement also differed somewhat from that of Arminians such as Grotius, and it is important not to confuse the differences between Arminian and Calvinist uses of the moral government theory. Whereas, for the Arminians, this theory meant that God had chosen to award salvation to anyone upon condition of belief, for the Edwardsians it meant that God had decreed to save the elect by means of moral government. Though Christ did die to atone for the sins of the entire world, his death did not guarantee salvation to anyone. Moral government ensured that all are naturally able to turn to God in faith. But only the elect, a limited number, would ever actually do so. In sharp contrast to the Arminians, the Edwardsians insisted that faith does not elicit, but rather responds to, supernatural grace. Thus, as Kenneth Rowe has noted, the Edwardsian theory did not rely entirely on the Arminian Grotius, but enjoyed a relatively "independent origin in America." One might add that it represented, not a precipitous decline, but a defense of New England Calvinism.[37]

In the tradition of his New Divinity predecessors, Taylor carried forward the Edwardsian theory of the atonement and defended it firmly against what had grown by his day into an organized Universalist movement. He defined the atonement throughout his life as an act that "was necessary to magnify the law, and to vindicate and unfold the justice of God in the pardon of sin." It had not abrogated God's rule of law; God continues to hold sinners responsible for their crimes against our moral government. But it had enabled God to provide a more merciful rule of judgment for this wayward, sinful world. Against Universalists and other "infidels," Taylor contended that a God who does not demonstrate an absolute abhorrence of sin is not a God to be worshiped. In a vivid, early sermon entitled "The Terror of the Lord Persuasive," he declared, "Such a God on the throne of the universe, and every angel would drop his harp—every devil shout in ecstacy. The bands of God's moral dominion would be broken, the pillars of eternal justice would fall, and heaven fall with them; the fires of hell burst forth unchecked, and rebellion stand triumphant on the ruins. Such is the Universalist's God. Let him trust him, if he dare! Thus, while Universalists denied the eternality of Hell on the basis of divine benevolence, Taylor believed the benevolence of God necessitated everlasting punishment. The liberal God "is not benevolent," he argued, "for he is not just." Justice requires that evil be punished and righteousness finally vindicated. When the Universalists entered his parish, then, to attempt the establishment of a church, Taylor pulled out all the stops at his disposal to ensure that they would fail. As George P. Fisher related shortly after his death, the Universalists held two separate meetings there "with a view to a permanent organization." Both times Taylor sneaked in "uninvited" and publicly criticized the preacher's sermon. While the first time the congregation got "so angry, that they extinguished the lights before he had finished his remarks," he finally offered "such a refutation" of their preacher "that they were discouraged from their purpose."[38]

Taylor also supported the moral government theory against the teachings of many high Calvinists who found little to appreciate in the Edwardsians' daring new defense of soteriological orthodoxy. Not everyone had followed the New Divinity away from earlier forensic or transactional conceptions of the atonement. In fact, a considerable number of Calvinists continued to cling to the language of imputation as the best method for expressing the salvific import of Christ's suffering. A limited understanding of the atonement, in which the righteousness of Christ and his passion is said to be imputed directly to the accounts of the elect (and the elect alone), comprised one of the three deterministic angles of the ever-present "triangle" decried by Samuel Whelpley. Further-more, hyper-Calvinist followers of the British theologian William Giles had begun ar-guing that Christ never even intended to die for any but the elect. Traditionally, high Calvinists had argued that, while the work of Christ actually proved *efficient* in atoning only for the sins of the elect, it was *sufficient* in magnitude to cover the sins of the entire world. But proponents of what came to be called the "Gethsemane doctrine" argued that the atonement was not even sufficient for the sins of the non-elect. In a book en-titled *Gethsemane* and reprinted in Philadelphia (1817)—where the ex-Edwardsian Ezra Stiles Ely had moved and begun advocating Gethsemane doctrine—Giles suggested that "the sufferings of Christ were in exact proportion to the guilt of the . . . sinners he had undertaken to redeem." God had simply not intended Christ's passion to atone for the guilt of the rest. Taylor opposed the high Calvinist's limited and forensic understanding of the atonement in whatever form it came. He felt that their satisfaction theory had "re-sulted solely from a false philosophy respecting the principles of law and moral govern-ment, which has not the least plausibility or support from the Scriptures." Advanced al-ways without adequate appreciation for God's moral means of government, it depicted God's "acts of pardon and justification" as "acts of mere arbitrary prerogative." They "are without pretense," he contended, "wholly arbitrary, without a reason or shadow of a rea-son." They "contravene the essential nature and principles of a perfect moral government, imply the right . . . of a lawgiver to annihilate his law by an act of absolute sovereignty, and to rule for the weal or woe of his kingdom, according to his own caprice."[39]

Princeton's B. B. Warfield once criticized the moral government theory of the atone-ment as a "half-way house" on a steep and slippery slope descending from the orthodox or "objective" understanding of Christ's meritorious work to embarrassed modern or "subjective" theories that marginalize the atonement as an act providing little more than an inspiring moral example. "I do not myself think," he argued, "that, at bottom, there is in principle much to choose between the Grotian and the so-called 'subjective' theo-ries. It seems to me only an illusion to suppose that [the Grotian theory] preserves an 'objective' atonement at all." Despite their repudiation of the Princetonians' forensic language of imputation, however, the Taylorites proved staunch defenders of the atonement's objective soteriological efficacy. Their departure from the doctrine of limited atonement did not mean that they had given up on the centrality of Christ's passion in the obtainment of eternal life. It simply meant that the atonement procured salvation in a different way than for high Calvinists. Instead of achieving saving merits that God imputes to the accounts of the elect, it achieved the stability of our moral government and provided a just basis for God's merciful rule of judgment. As Goodrich made clear in a public credo during the fall of 1839, the atonement remained for him "vicarious in its nature, in as much as [Christ's] sufferings are substituted for the penalty of the law, in respect to those who trust in his blood." He insisted only that this substitution occurs within a system of *moral* government. Like nearly all atonement theories, then, the Taylorites' moral government theory employed a variety of themes and images to account for the significance of Christ's suffering. Unlike many of their liberal opponents, for example, they proved unwilling to ignore the unpleasant biblical imagery of propitiation and blood sacrifice. They did give pride of place to the moral government motif. But they also allowed considerable room for satisfactionary and substitutionary elements. For the Taylorites, the substitutionary death of the Savior constituted the most important component of God's plan of salvation.[40]

Moral Science and "The Authority of Truth"

Buttressing all Taylor's theorizing on the dynamics of moral government was his undying dedication to the scientific credibility of Christianity and its moral theology. Trusting in the age-old maxim that all truth is God's truth, Taylor held cogent reasoning in highest esteem and became embarrassed and even angry over the anti-intellectual escapism of weak-minded, fideistic, or authoritarian piety. His students tended to depict him as one logical to a fault. As Theodore Munger once remarked, "he had a supreme regard for theology as a science, and he worshiped at the shrine of his queen with chivalric devotion." B. N. Martin recalled that "at any violation of intellectual integrity or of logical consistency he felt that he did well to be angry; and any professed sacredness of aim did but aggravate the offense." Unwilling to allow the theologians of New England's future to hide behind the veil of piety, Taylor "pursued" the occasional "delinquent into the sanctuary where he sought a refuge, and smote him even at the horns of the altar." As noted earlier, he challenged his charges to "follow the truth if it carries you over Niagra [*sic*]." Fond of an old proverb said to have come from Joseph Bellamy, he recommended it frequently to the boys under his care: "Do not be afraid of investigation and argument—there is no poker in the truth."[41]

Aside from Edwards, Taylor's favorite Christian philosopher was the Anglican bishop Joseph Butler (1692–1752), author of the acclaimed *Analogy of Religion* (1736). He admired Butler's bold rejoinder to the rise of enlightened infidelity and shared fully his confidence in the analogous credibility of sacred and secular science. Just as Butler employed the method of analogy to defend the validity of the Christian religion, moreover, the Taylorites employed this method to defend the evangelical doctrines of grace. In an extended "Review of Butler's Analogy of Natural and Revealed Religion" (1830–31), they contended that, while Butler himself failed to assent to the truths of evangelical Calvinism, his method could be used to legitimate its central soteriological affirmations. Much like secular scientists inducing theories from the facts of nature, evangelicals had induced their own peculiar doctrines from the "facts" of revelation. Indeed, despite (or perhaps because of) their utter confidence in divine revelation, the Taylorites took great interest with Butler in the relationship between natural and revealed theology. Not content to defend their religious views with appeals to biblical authority alone, they frequently sought to ground such appeals by analogy to mundane knowledge. Unbelievers needed to know that Christian claims about moral government held up with or without revelation. Thus, against fellow evangelical moral theorists who declared the Bible the only true guide for living, the Taylorites argued that moral science can and "must be prosecuted on independent grounds." In their view, natural theology was "not to be considered merely as the handmaid of revealed religion." Rather, "like the law, it is as 'a schoolmaster to bring us to Christ.'"[42]

In keeping with their modern interest in the inductive evidence for Christian faith, the New Haven theologians proved ardent critics of the deductive logic of much Protestant scholasticism. Like Bishop Butler, they modeled their own theological methodology after the empiricism of the "new science," castigating the rigid, syllogistic confessionalism of their more Aristotelian Protestant predecessors. In a telling publication on "The Progess of Theological Science Since the Reformation" (1838), the Taylorites chided scholastic Protestants scarcely less than the Catholics they opposed, scoffing:

> As if that dead, eyeless, soulless, senseless, unmoving skeleton, of pagan Aristotle, could help along the ark of the living God, in its return [i.e., from Catholicism] to his holy temple! As if that philosophy which had, beyond all manner of question, wrought out and brought in Popery, and made her empress of nations' consciences, would, after its proper and natural death, assist mightily the sacramental host of God's elect in their conflict, and work out and bring in for them, in like manner, complete success against that mother of abominations.

The Taylorites esteemed Francis Bacon, not Aristotle, as the philosopher for modern Protestantism. They felt he had earned the "chief praise . . . of having taught men better than they knew before, how to discover truth." Aristotelian philosophy had, since the Reformation, produced little more than arcane theological speculation and religious warfare. Baconian inductivism, however, had facilitated the happy "triumph of theological truth." Taylor knew that theology cannot proceed without "a sound, deep philosophy." Yet he argued that such philosophy must be inductive and scientific. "It must," in his words, "be common-sense-philosophy, such as all the world can understand if we would defend orthodox theology."[43]

Taylor's cocksure commitment to common-sense induction attests again to his attachment to Scottish Common Sense Realism. Without a doubt, he considered the Scottish Philosophy the most effective means available for promoting his system of moral government without constant recourse to the authority of divine revelation. With Thomas Reid and Dugald Stewart, he deemed common sense an "infallible umpire . . . in all cases, where it is competent to sit in judgment." Adam's Fall *has* weighed us down with both sin and ignorance, he admitted. But it has not eradicated our basic power to see and to do the good. Surely "a God of infinite benevolence . . . would not so constitute our minds, that any other cause than wilful [*sic*] obliquity . . . could lead its judgment astray, on points of the highest moment to our welfare." In fact, in Taylor's view, even the Bible presented God's system of moral government in a manner intended for and accessible to all. Though frequently perceived incorrectly as the special preserve of the learned or of the saints, "the language of the Scriptures" actually equaled "the language of common use." The Bible laid bare God's system of morals to the man and woman on the street. It constituted a public document, a document to be interpreted simply and literally (whenever possible), and one that never contradicted humanity's common moral sense. Taylor told his students, "Coleridge thinks that common men have not the power to philosophize—that they [stay] in the valley while transcendental Philosophers live in the upper regions." But this was wrong, he argued firmly—at least when it came to essential moral and religious truths.[44]

Again, however, despite the claims of several first-rate historians, Taylor's use of Common Sense philosophy neither set him apart from Edwardsian peers nor placed him in league with Old Calvinism. By the time of the Taylorite controversy, nearly all American moral theorists had adopted the Scottish Philosophy—from the most liberal Unitarians to the most conservative Tylerites and Princetonians. Not even Edwards's most slavish followers had held on to his hybrid of post-Cartesian metaphysics. Having gone the way of most of their counterparts and appropriated the philosophy of Reid and Stewart, it is true that antebellum Edwardsians found themselves in something of an awkward (some would say dissonant) cognitive position. The Scottish realists, though great admirers of Edwards, had defended a libertarian understanding of human free will and proved staunch critics of what they called Edwards's "scheme of Necessity." But Taylor, for one, did not share the Scots' criticism of Edwards on human freedom. As we have seen, his conception of human moral power derived, not from the anthropology of enlightened liberals, but from Edwards himself on natural ability. Indeed, the Taylorites proved outspoken opponents of modern liberalism and the "infidelity" they thought it inspired. They adopted the Scottish Philosophy not in support of its libertarianism, but because, like inductivism and empiricism generally, it could grant an aura of scientific legitimacy to their attempts to delineate God's moral government. As pointed out helpfully by Stanley French, Jr., Common Sense Realism played primarily a formal or methodological role in America and rarely functioned for theologians as a substantive determinant of doctrine. Its use "did not determine theological differences between sects, but sectarian differences determined the manner in which mental philosophy was used."[45]

Neither did Common Sense Realism lead Taylor to anthropocentric rationalism. On a spectrum spanning from fideism at one end to rationalism at the other, Taylor did stand somewhat closer to the latter end than the sage of Northampton himself. In his struggle to disabuse his students, for example, of their assumption that God is arbitrary, Taylor told them that right moral action "is not right because [God] wills it, but he wills it because it is right." Moreover, as evidenced in the *Quarterly Christian Spectator* for June of 1835, the Taylorites could go even so far as to suggest that "there is such a thing as truth, or moral rectitude, independent both of man or God. There are certain unchanging principles, of right and wrong, which have their foundation," not in God, but "in the nature of things." However, lest we conclude too hastily that Taylor abandoned his theocentric inheritance, it is important to bear in mind that Edwards himself often defended the natural "fitness" of God's moral government, and both Edwards and his followers rather quickly became rational apologists for their newfound consistent Calvinism. Furthermore, Taylor testified frankly to the limits of "perverted" human reason and the Taylorites proved consistent defenders of the necessity of divine revelation for complete knowledge of God's moral government. The authority of revelation "is supreme," they wrote, "over all the other sources of knowledge." Unlike "the schemes of religion . . . devised by the pride of human reason . . . , the Gospel comes to every mind, with the authority of truth." Thus, for the Taylorites, while reason, natural theology, and moral science paved the way for revelation, they were "never . . . to be raised above revelation, to become a substitute for it, or deemed sufficient without it."[46]

Rather, in the manner of the great medieval theologian Thomas Aquinas (c. 1225–74), Taylor maintained that revelation builds on, elevates, and perfects human reason. It "recognizes and re-proclaims all that [we] before knew to be true." But it also "lengthens out and supplies" our natural knowledge with new insights, enabling us to apprehend things more fully and clearly. As elucidated in the Taylorites' review of Bishop Butler, "[T]he bible is in religion, what the telescope is in astronomy. It does not contradict any thing before known; it does not annihilate any thing before seen; it carries the eye forward into new worlds, opens it upon more splendid fields of vision, and displays grander systems." Like Aquinas, Taylor also believed in a realm of divine mystery entirely unfathomable by finite minds, denying only (as did Aquinas) that, in the end, its mysteries stood "opposed to reason." As became clear in his commentary on the doctrine of the Trinity, for example, he knew that much of God's internal life remains hidden from our view. The very notion of divine revelation implied that God's ways are beyond our ken. But despite our undeniable epistemic limitations, Taylor maintained that "so far as revelation goes, so far there is light; so far, and no farther, truth, be it little or much, is revealed, and therefore may be understood and believed." Worried that orthodox colleagues had fueled the Unitarians' fire with unnecessarily vague appeals to the mystery of God's triunity, he upheld the reasonableness and consistency of what he thought *had* been revealed. "A doctrine announced in words," he explained, "which cannot be interpreted or understood, is not a *revealed* doctrine. To say *that God is one being in three persons*, is to express some meaning, or it is not. If it expresses no meaning, why say it, or why pretend to believe it?" While Taylor himself did not pretend that trinitarian dogma comprehended God's essence, he did believe that, like all other revealed doctrine, it expressed truths about God that are reasonable, reliable, and consistent.[47]

At the end of the day, Taylor trusted completely in the harmony of reason and revelation. He employed natural theology and moral science, not to shore up the crumbling walls of revealed truth, but to persuade unbelievers that "Christianity, as a system of morals, whether it be of God or not, is true." Desiring desperately to draw an increasingly secular people into the workings of God's moral government, he sought to present his case in terms to which anyone could relate. "The great question," he believed, "is not between Christianity and Infidelity, but between Christianity and nothing. . . . Reject the morals of Christianity as false, and all here is midnight. We can know nothing to be true." Confident, however, that we can indeed know a great deal about our good, the Taylorites held out great hope for the future of moral government. With Bishop Butler, they looked forward to the day when "the order of events, and the deductions of reason, and the decisions of the gospel, will yet be found completely to tally," never doubting that, "though the affairs of the church and the world may yet flow on in somewhat distinct channels, yet they will finally sink into complete and perfect harmony; like two streams rising in distant hills, and rendering fertile different vales, yet at last flowing into the bosom of the same placid and beautiful ocean."[48]

6

"To Make Himself a Holy Heart"

Taylor and the Work of Regeneration

The passion of his life was so to preach—and to instruct and train his pupils so to preach—that conversions should follow, not at some future day, but immediately.

Leonard Bacon

If the doctrine of original sin placed Taylor on America's theological map and the theme of moral government shaped his view of the surrounding terrain, his passion for conversions fired his engine and kept him going down the rough and frequently hazardous road of religious controversy.[1] The doctrine of the new birth, or regeneration, which gave theological expression to this evangelistic fervor, comprised the single most important element in Taylor's corpus. It represented the culmination of his concern both to combat physical conceptions of depravity and to promote a truly moral understanding of divine providence or government. It directed his driving ambition to preach for immediate compliance with God's equitable terms of salvation. As the topic that got Taylor the most excited and enthused, it also yielded the least consistent and most controversial of his theological opinions. Scholars typically identify the New Haven Theology with antebellum debates over original sin and the justice of God. But Taylor actually expended more energy and spilled more polemical ink on the doctrine of regeneration. Arguably the most formative nineteenth-century influence on the more recent and highly publicized evangelical notions of the born-again experience, this investment has enjoyed a remarkable return, making a powerful and enduring impression on the subsequent history of American spirituality.[2]

Immediate Repentance and Sinful Excuses

Faithful to their calling as Edwardsian revivalists, Taylorite preachers inundated New England audiences with constant pleas for immediate repentance. Exasperated by excuses for what they deemed the "criminal" habit of conversional procrastination, they excoriated the still-popular preparationist mentality perpetuated by Old Calvinist rivals. As George P. Fisher once noted of Taylor's preaching style, he aimed "to go before his impenitent hearers, conscious of his ability to beat down every refuge which gave them shelter from the arrows of conscience." The old morphology of conversion, he felt, had become little more than a counterproductive crutch for complacent sinners. Though in the past it may have provided a useful spiritual gauge for active but anxious churchgoers, it now provided pious excuses for the willfully unrepentant. Old Calvinists continued to decry "Hopkinsian" denigrations of historic, means-oriented piety. But, undaunted, Taylor stood fast in proclaiming that "now is the day of salvation." Thrilled by the thousands of conversions achieved during the golden years of New England's Second Great Awakening, he worried for those who remained behind in the wake of the mighty revivals. Conversion is for those who seek it, he preached; one does not simply inherit it after setting up house. In fact, contrary to the glib assumptions of generations of Old Calvinists, resisters who reach adulthood without it "are almost sure never to embrace it."[3]

As a good Edwardsian should, Taylor repudiated the tendency of many New Englanders to rely casually for salvation on the conventional "means of grace." He contended that, in the vast majority of cases, such reliance proved utterly sinful, postponing rather than inaugurating one's new life in Christ. While seekers may "imagine that reading the Scriptures, hearing the gospel preached, and seeking (praying they are wont to call it) for renewing grace, with the heart as actively devoted to the world as ever, is doing what renders their regeneration highly probable," they needed to understand that such acts "are not *using*" but rather "*abusing* the means of regeneration." For Taylor, "the only *use* which a man is authorized to make" of these means "is *instantly to obey*. A moment's delay . . . is not a using of [them] for the purpose of obedience, but of prolonged rebellion." Indeed, "while the selfish principle remains active" in the heart of an anxious sinner, nothing he or she can do will constitute a legitimate "using" of means. Because one's *predominant* volition determines the quality of all one's moral acts, only those performed with a true heart prove acceptable in the sight of God.[4]

The Solicitation of Self-Love

Unlike the Hopkinsians, however, Taylor refused to point the way to Heaven from the foot of a rungless ladder. While he felt that most of the time the "means of grace" turned out to be means of sin, he acknowledged that there are steps one can take that lead to eternal life. He thought the issue of the means had been misconstrued and had led to unnecessary confusion. Wary of the dangers of "unregenerate doings," seekers had too often resolved either to sit idly by in the uncertain hope of divine grace or, worse yet, "to commit sin" boldly "as the necessary means of regeneration." In order "to expose and correct these errors," Taylor believed it "of vital importance to show, that there are acts which are not sinful—and yet which may be done, and which must be done, by the man, or he will never be regenerated." Convinced that this work of God would not take place without the free exercise of human will, Taylor tried diligently to remove the passivity ingrained by Hopkinsian and high Calvinist views of providence.[5]

Like his teaching on native depravity, Taylor's doctrine of regeneration crystallized in response to a treatise by New York's Gardiner Spring. An expatriated New Englander with strong Hopkinsian leanings, Spring in his *Dissertation on the Means of Regeneration* (1827) took a standard Hopkinsian line. Heralding the need for immediate conversion and portraying the use of the means as sinful, it seemed yet again to present the anxious sinner with a goal impossible to attain. Taylor's review of Spring's treatise took up no fewer than 112 pages (more than twice as many as Spring's *Dissertation*) in the newly constituted *Quarterly Christian Spectator* (1829). As the initial essay in New Haven's new series, it set the polemical tone of the Taylorites' official publication. It also provided a comprehensive—if not always fully comprehensible—elaboration of Taylor's doctrine of regeneration. Upset by Spring's smug reversion to the logic of "damned if you do and damned if you don't," Taylor objected to the implication that sinners must "'[do] evil that good may come.'" He commended Spring's insistence on immediate repentance and affirmed his condemnation of the sinful use of means, but he chastised Spring for leaving the penitent bereft of *any* legitimate spiritual recourse. Taylor countered by appealing to a crucial pre-Hopkinsian distinction between selfish and self-interested doings. While selfishness stemmed from a sullied heart and yielded only sin, self-interest stemmed from a perfectly natural desire for happiness—from a morally neutral principle of self-love—and could yield both vice and virtue. "This self-love or desire of happiness," he wrote, "is the primary cause or reason of all acts of preference or choice." When functioning apart from one's selfish principle (or predominant volition), it can lead to acts of genuine benevolence. Especially in the sinner's conversion away from selfishness to benevolence, Taylor contended that the love of self plays a very powerful role. Like Edwards, he described conversion or regeneration (he used these terms synonymously) as an aesthetic, affectional event. If one is to choose God, he explained, over all other possible goods, God—like any other "object of . . . preference"—must be seen and desired as one's own "greatest good." Moreover, inasmuch as many had been drawn to God by appeals to their own best interests, and since the recognition of God and God's will as one's highest good required a suspension of one's disordered, selfish desires, Taylor concluded that one's selfish principle or predominant volition must indeed be suspended during the act of regeneration, and prior to the commencement of one's new life in Christ. In a move that proved as controversial as any he ever made, Taylor suggested that those who prove truly penitent are the ones who convert in a quest for happiness that has been freed from selfish vice. With the Hopkinsians, he agreed that *before* the time when seekers convert, the "means" lead them only to sin. But he claimed that *during* the act of conversion itself, they can (and do) escape from bondage to the selfish principle and pursue salvation from a morally neutral regard to their own self-interest.[6]

As usual, Taylor called down a deluge of criticism with this revision of Hopkinsian dogma. Tylerites reacted with horror, alleging Pelagianism in Taylor's argument. Bennet Tyler himself spearheaded the denunciation with *Strictures* (1829) on Taylor's review, claiming that Taylor had subverted Calvinist orthodoxy across a broad range of soteriological issues. Rehashing the standard rationale for the Hopkinsian view of the means, he maintained:

> If sinners use the means they must use them with a holy heart, or an unholy heart, or no heart at all; that is, with right motives, or wrong motives, or no motive at all. If with right motives, the change is already effected, and the end [i.e., regeneration] precedes the means—If with wrong motives, their actions are sinful, and sin is the means of holiness—If with no motive at all, they act without any design, and cannot be using means for the accomplishment of an end.

Tyler questioned how Taylor could claim that the suspension of the selfish principle took place *prior to* one's union with Christ "without first denying the entire depravity of the unrenewed heart, and thus striking at the foundation of the doctrines of grace." The notion that humans contributed to their own salvation—indeed sinlessly—not only undermined the Edwardsians' disjunctive spirituality, belittling both the primacy of grace in salvation and the Holy Spirit's regenerative role, but also relied on a very non-Edwardsian, "progressive" understanding of conversion. It takes time to use the means, argued Tyler, whether or not such use proves sinful. How did Taylor presume to uphold both the means and immediate repentance?[7]

Taylor replied quickly in defense of his Edwardsian orthodoxy, contesting Tyler's notion "that every motive must be either selfish or holy—either right or wrong." Building on an admission by Tyler that conversion does require motivation and cognition, he questioned what his antagonist really meant by this after all. Was such activity sinful? Was sin, then, a necessary means of regeneration? In Taylor's view, Tyler seemed to be implying that it was. In short, Taylor claimed that Tyler held a "physical" view of both depravity and regeneration that undermined his alleged allegiance to human natural ability:

> If Dr. Tyler will tell us *how* the sinner is able to do his duty, when as he maintains, he cannot do it from right motives, or wrong motives, or no motive at all, he will see the fallacy of his own reasoning. He will see that after all his admissions of the doctrine of the *natural ability* of sinners, his own reasoning proceeds on the assumption of a natural inability; and that what he calls a *moral* inability, is nothing diverse from a natural inability. For what is a natural inability, if that is not, which involves three actually existing physical impossibilities?

As in his doctrine of original sin and his understanding of divine providence, Taylor fought valiantly against the presumption that God operates by force. As even Princeton had contended in the most recent *Biblical Repertory*, regenerative grace works morally, not physically, on our souls.[8]

Taylor's decision to preach a conversion of persuasion rather than compulsion found support in the tradition of eudaemonistic ethics. Founded in the philosophy of Aristotle, Christianized at the hands of the Greek Fathers, and bequeathed to the West in the work of St. Augustine, eudaemonism (from the Greek word *eudaemonia*, meaning "well being" or "happiness") placed a premium on motivation and desire. Defining virtue, like Aristotle, as the ability to pursue one's highest good (*summum bonum*), Christian proponents of this teleologically framed theory sought to synthesize the seemingly antithetical ends of self-love and the love of God. They claimed that humanity's true end, highest good, and greatest happiness lay in union with (or vision of) God. Thus the self—when its affections were rightly ordered—found the satiation of its desires in things divine (*fruitio Dei*). In the tradition of Christian eudaemonism, then, God's call to conversion was also a call to personal fulfillment. As St. Augustine expressed it in the prayerful words at the beginning of his *Confessions* (397–400), "you arouse [us] to take joy in praising you, for you have made us for yourself, and our heart is restless until it rests in you." Though St. Thomas ensured its posterity within his Aristotelian theological synthesis, however, this baptism of human self-interest did not proceed through the Middle Ages uncontested. Beginning in the early twelfth century with the theology of Peter Abelard (1079–1142), and continuing in Duns Scotus (c. 1265–1308), the radical Franciscans, and many late medieval mystics, an alternative tradition emerged much less sanguine about self-love. Claiming ancient Christian roots and seeing little practical difference between self-love and abject selfishness, the Abelardians or ethical rigorists prized abnegation above all. Heralding a willingness to be damned (*resignatio ad infernum*) as the surest sign of regenerate piety, they advocated a disinterested or "pure love" (*castus amor* or, in the French, *pur amour*) that disregarded personal happiness. Achieving their greatest fame (and infamy) in the mystical rigorism of Madame Guyon (1648–1717), by the late seventeenth century they moved to the center stage of international controversy. British moralists, French Jansenists, and colonial Puritans alike, all seemed to be talking about self-love. The world-renowned debate between Guyon's defender, the Abbe Fenelon (1651–1715), and the ecclesiastical statesman, Bishop Bossuet (1625–1704), represented only the most visible instance of this historic and now-momentous conversation.[9]

Like Martin Luther, John Calvin, and most other early Protestants, the Hopkinsians sided generally with the rigorists. While their willingness to be damned is often deemed strange and extreme, it actually enjoyed a long and hallowed history. It did not enjoy the full support of Jonathan Edwards, however, whose own position proved much like St. Augustine's. Edwards did list Fenelon in his "Catalogue" of readings. He also spent a significant portion of his later career opposing modern liberalism's veneration of "enlightened self-interest"—a move that, as Norman Fiering has noted, moved him closer to moral rigorism. But while Edwards worried frequently throughout his career (like most other Christian eudaemonists) about the dangers of *unregulated* self-love, he distinguished these concerns carefully from his confidence in self-love per se. As he explained in his seventh charity sermon, "Charity Contrary to a Selfish Spirit," the "self-love which is the selfishness to which a Christian spirit is contrary is only an *inordinate* self-love":

> A Christian spirit is not contrary to *all* self-love. It is not a thing contrary to Christianity that a man should love himself; or what is the same thing, that he should love his own happiness. Christianity does not tend to destroy a man's love to his own happiness; it would therein tend to destroy the humanity. . . . That a man should love his own happiness is necessary to his nature, as a faculty of will is; and it is impossible that it should be destroyed in any other way than by destroying his being. The saints love their own happiness. . . . Otherwise their happiness, which God has given them, would be no happiness to them; for that which anyone does not love he can enjoy no happiness in.

For Edwards, then, regeneration did not represent an eradication of self-love; rather, it set self-love on the path to its ultimate fulfillment. God's grace redirects our desire and grants it a new telos or final end. It infuses our souls with the very "superior principles" (*donum superadditum*) lost to us in Adam's Fall, reordering our natural appetites and reenabling us to love God truly: "The alteration which is made in a man when he is converted and sanctified is not by diminishing his love to happiness, but only by regulating it with respect to its exercises and influence, and the object to which it leads." Indeed,

> a man may love his own happiness as much as anybody, . . . and yet he may place that happiness so that he may in the same act be in an high exercise of love to God. As for instance, when the happiness for which he longs is to enjoy God, and to behold the glory of God, or to enjoy communion with God. Or a man may place his happiness in glorifying God; it may seem the greatest happiness to him that he can conceive of to give God glory as he ought to do, and he may long for this happiness. Now in longing for this

happiness he loves that which he looks on as his happiness. If he did not love what he esteemed his happiness he would not long for it. And to love his happiness is to love himself. But yet in the same act he loves God, because he places his happiness in God. What can more properly be called love to any being, or any thing, than to place one's happiness in that thing?[10]

Of course, by Taylor's day one need not have appealed to the ancient tradition of eudaemonism to defend the pursuit of personal happiness or the legitimacy of self-love. The fiery dragon of rampant egoism, so fiercely combated in the era of Calvin and Hobbes, no longer frightened the self-confident knights of the age of Enlightenment. But while Bishop Butler's defense of self-love surely inspired Taylor's own, and while Taylor did appeal strategically to Dugald Stewart on the topic, he appropriated such largely conservative spokesmen of the British Enlightenment primarily to buttress an essentially Edwardsian understanding of salvation. Far and away the most frequent appeals in defense of his doctrine of regeneration were made to Jonathan Edwards himself. When not appealing directly to Edwards, moreover, the Taylorites usually appealed to New Divinity men. Joseph Bellamy, Timothy Dwight, and Nathan Strong, for example, were each claimed as precursors of New Haven's view. Even Samuel Hopkins himself, the champion of "unconditional submission," was said to be less rigoristic than was usually assumed.[11]

Indeed, the Taylorites' emphasis on the role of self-love in regeneration stood in marked continuity with Edwards's eudaemonism. Only the twice-born life of true virtue, they claimed, could begin to quench one's thirst for happiness. "Look through the universe," Taylor once preached in utterly Augustinian fashion, "and there is nothing on which the soul of man can fix as an object of contemplation or love which can satisfy it but God." While many Hopkinsians called for conversion by encouraging an abandonment of one's own loves and desires, Taylor pointed out that Edwards himself called for, "not indeed an uninterested, but a *disinterested* affection." He felt that Hopkinsians too often conflated self-love with the sin of downright selfishness, failing to see that "selfishness . . . differs from self-love, not in degree merely, but in kind." Self-love, he explained, "[is] an original impulse of our nature, which fixes on no definite external object." Selfishness, however, "[is] an act of the *will*—a selection and preference of some object, to the exclusion of all that can stand in competition with it." While selfishness, then, is the pursuit of self-interest in *opposition* to God and neighbor, self-love can produce the kind of acts that *accord* with more general benevolence. "Destroy self-love, as some would do," one anonymous Taylorite warned, "and all the motives to holiness which the universe presents, would fall on the sinner's heart powerless as water on the rock. . . . Annihilate self-love . . . and all voluntary action must instantly cease: with no desires to gratify, there would be no motive for action." In Taylor's view, as free citizens of God's moral government we are actually "*capacitated* to love God supremely, from a regard to *happiness*, as distinct from any selfish feeling." He admitted that the one "who seeks his own happiness, in any other way than that of pleasing God, and making others happy, is selfish and sinful. But who is the good man," he wondered aloud, "if he is not, who proposes and finds his highest happiness in pleasing God, and in promoting the greatest sum of happiness?"[12]

This Edwardsian defense of self-love and the pursuit of happiness has seemed to some scholars a manifestation of utilitarianism. It is true that Taylor did study the proto-

utilitarian ethics of William Paley under Timothy Dwight at Yale College. He also upheld Dwight's conviction that "virtue is founded in utility," or in one's apprehension of
the tendency of a moral act to produce goodness and promote happiness. But to posit
with Dwight and Taylor that we pursue virtue for its beneficial consequences is not to
posit a full-blown utilitarianism. These Edwardsians' theological ethics were not intended
to provide criteria for maximizing the subjectively determined happiness of the greatest
possible number. For Taylor, as for Dwight and for Edwards before him, genuine happiness lay not merely in the mind of the beholder, but lay *for all* in reunion with God.
One found the key to the moral life, not in promoting earthly pleasures, but in striving
with all one's strength to inaugurate the reign of Heaven. "The glory of God," Taylor
declared, "is the greatest possible good." All earthly goods paled by comparison. "If all
[the] good that men or angels can conceive might exist it would be but a drop, compared with [the] mighty ocean of good wh[ich] G[od] will communicate [and] uphold."[13]

Thus, while Taylor did employ a form of consequentialist ethical reasoning, he did
so, like Edwards, in a very theocentric way. He taught that God has designed the world,
at least in part, to make us happy. But he believed that, ultimately, human happiness
cannot be had apart from God. This world exhibits an "obvious unsuitableness . . . to
the perfection of the nature of man," he thought. Our souls come equipped with incli-
nations and capacities that we cannot fully actualize here and now. "Who," then, "can
reflect on the nature of [man]" and come away disbelieving "that he is made to be one
with the God who created him—a partaker of his blessedness, a companion of his eternity?" When Taylor mounted New England's pulpits to preach for immediate repentance, then, he promised restless listeners what this world alone cannot provide. He
spoke of eternity with God as the true object of their affections, soliciting conversions
with descriptions of things above. "We must tear away [the] evils of materialism," he
preached, "which hide or obscure our prospect" of eternal bliss. "We must . . . make
heaven a reality," the alluring goal of our deepest desires, "and fondly and intently dwell
on the contemplation of it as our home." Moreover, for those who needed help appreciating the glories of Heaven, Taylor prescribed a goodly dose of the fires of Hell. He
censured the "infidels" of the world for their disdain of "preaching terror" and maintained the necessity of legal sanctions in any worthy moral government. "You may set
before the sinner all the compassion of God, and the tenderness of redeeming love . . .
but if you do not show him that he is lost, he will never embrace a Saviour." Indeed,
"you may call him to accept of the great salvation, but his exposure to an opening hell
must move him or he will never stir." As Eleazar Fitch confirmed against New Haven's
Universalist opponents, "in giving up the doctrine [of eternal punishment], it is certain
that they destroy that most powerful of all appeals in behalf of immediate and thorough
reformation, which arises from the fear of losing the soul to all eternity."[14]

Of course, the Taylorites recognized that the preaching of sanctions "will never of
itself convert the sinner." Yet their respect for the force of the selfish principle in the
unrenewed heart led them to conclude that "no sinner will ever be converted without
it." It takes a powerful appeal to the stark reality of eternity to crack the rock-hard shell
of human selfishness. In fact, the most effective solicitations to evangelical conversion
come from eternity itself. God calls us from Heaven, appealing "not only to the most
powerful spring of human action, but press[ing] that appeal even to the very last vestige
of human sensibility." Thence "surrounded by the fullness of God," moreover, and

"encircled by the pledges of his favor—thus invited, urged and constrained by the riches of his gifts, with what a mighty energy is man impelled to consecrate himself, soul and body, to the service of his Maker!" In keeping with the ways of moral government, however, such heavenly appeals do not necessitate conversion. Though God persuades by presenting us with powerful truths, "obedience to truth cannot be produced by compulsory power." Divine influence is such that it "draws, not compels; [it] attracts, not forces to duty." As Taylor would insist over and over again, "the Spirit of God renews the heart of man through the truth." God appeals to our reason and, through reason, to self-love, enticing us to delight in eternity. Thus, contrary to the teachings of Hopkinsians and Tylerites, the human mind must play a positive role in regeneration. While it is true that the means of grace are quite often abused, salvation does not come until they are rightly used. Divine appeals to the truth about one's own best interests must be responded to in a reasoned act of faith. "The Holy Spirit will not convert a sinner while remaining thoughtless of his God, of his Saviour, and of his own soul. I care not what else is true of him," pronounced Taylor, "be he who he may, while he sleeps in sin, God will not convert him."[15]

For their part, the Tylerites proved quick to concede the value of a reasoned or rightly ordered self-love, particularly as expressed in the theology of Jonathan Edwards himself. Unwilling to allow New Haven to achieve the better part of devotion, they attested awkwardly to the veracity of their hero's eudaemonistic teaching. In an address republished in the very same year as Taylor's review of Spring, Edward Dorr Griffin led the way in this act of homage. In a passage soon to be exploited in the *Quarterly Christian Spectator*, he affirmed that "unless *something* is loved or regarded as desirable, there can be no motive to action, no excitation of feeling, nothing to inflame the passions." He went on: "[W]hen I speak of self-love as the source of sin, I mean self-love *unsubjected by a higher principle*, or *inordinate* self-love, properly denominated *selfishness*. Mere self-love is only the love of happiness, and aversion to misery, and so far from being sinful, is an essential attribute of a rational and even of a sensitive nature." Even Bennet Tyler himself softened his earlier Hopkinsian rhetoric and retreated somewhat from his predecessors' denigration of self-love. In his *Vindication of the Strictures* (1830) he had written on Taylor's review of Spring and denied ever asserting "that every degree of self-love is selfish and sinful." Instead, he claimed that "it is the duty of every man to desire and seek his own happiness" and, like Griffin, affirmed this truth within an affectionally (if not very aesthetically) based doctrine of regeneration.[16]

But despite such concessions on the nature of regeneration and the legitimacy of rightly ordered self-love, the Tylerites refused to recognize any human role in salvation or that self-love could yield a sinless use of means. If all Taylor intended was to echo Edwards's own assertion that conversion marked a reorientation of one's affections, then Tyler, for one, "[had] no dispute with him." However, Tyler was not alone in suspecting that Taylor actually intended to claim much more for self-love than one could find in Edwards's oeuvre. Neither was he alone in complaining that Taylor had "used language . . . in a manner directly calculated to mislead his readers." In fact, Griffin felt that Taylor had espoused an Arminian view of regeneration but had cloaked it with his pretensions to Calvinist orthodoxy. As he complained in his famous treatise on *The Doctrine of Divine Efficiency* (1833), "Taylor every where denies divine efficiency" in his treatment of regeneration "and limits the agency of the Spirit to the mere presentation of motives." Among the orthodox, the idea of divine efficiency had always meant "the effectual power of God immediately applied to the heart to make it holy," and "no man," New Haven's Dr. Taylor not excepted, "has a right to use it in another sense." In sum, the Tylerites charged that Taylor's unprecedented notion of the suspension of the seeker's selfish principle wound up belittling God's omnipotent saving grace. In his effort to clear a way for sinners to pursue their own salvation, Taylor had abandoned the doctrine of total depravity and the supremacy of divine initiative.[17]

The Moment of Conversion

Clearly, the Taylorites did have some explaining to do regarding the relationship in regeneration between divine grace and human activity. While Chauncey Goodrich tried to assure the public that Tylerite worries were unwarranted and that Taylor stood with Edwards after all, in many quarters New Haven's credibility had worn quite thin and his assurances seemed to fall upon deaf ears. Even the scions of the New Divinity could tolerate only so much innovation. Thus, as Tyler continued to condemn Taylor as "Pelagian" and "Arminian," a growing number of other, more dispassionate observers grew dissatisfied as well with New Haven's Edwardsianism au courant.[18]

In response to these growing concerns, Taylor pointed out first that "we have never called in question the doctrine of an immediate or direct agency of the Spirit, on the soul, in regeneration." In fact, no one, boasted Taylor, "attaches higher importance to this doctrine than I do; preaches it more decisively, or appreciates more highly its practical relations and bearings." Braggadocio aside, Taylor was right to insist that he had consistently taught the necessity of this supernatural agency. To teach otherwise, he believed, or to suggest, as Griffin and others had claimed he had done, that the Spirit converts the sinner by "moral suasion" alone, was to employ "Pelagian phraseology" and to commit "Pelagian error." Regeneration "is never produced . . . by moral suasion" alone, or "by the mere influence of truth and motives, as the Pelagians affirm, but is produced by the influence of the Holy Spirit." Now this influence of the Spirit is not coercive, he added. It does not "[violate] the laws of moral action." Yet no one, in the end, receives salvation without it and it is not something earned or guaranteed.[19]

Taylor's doctrine of election supported these claims to have safeguarded this central role of the Holy Spirit. According to Taylor, "a plainer proposition in theology is scarcely conceivable" than that "God has eternally purposed to . . . save a part only of mankind." He distinguished his doctrine of election, moreover, quite clearly from that of the Arminians. While Arminians maintained that election occurred on condition of foreseen faith, Taylor asserted that election took place "according to the good pleasure of [God's] will." As his theodicy and doctrine of the atonement made clear, God does wish that all could be saved; God knows, however, that this simply cannot happen in a system of moral government. The laws of moral government require that its citizens remain free to dissent. Thus, while "God does all that he can wisely do to bring every sinner to repentance," there are some things that even God cannot do in a system such as ours. There are clearly some things that "would result in more evil than good" by impinging on our freedom or affecting others adversely. If the father of a prodigal son, for example, did everything possible to secure his return, he "might occasion the disobedience and ruin of all his other children, or occasion some other evil that would be worse than to leave the prodigal to his own perverseness." Taylor concluded, therefore, that God must "have good reasons for bringing to repentance the very individuals whom he has selected," speculating that the elect might prove "more useful than others in promoting his designs." As George Park Fisher summarized his father-in-law's views on election and moral government, "the system of influence is adapted to sweep into the kingdom of heaven a certain number, and those alone; not from any partiality to them, not because they deserve more than others, but because the system that secures their salvation is the wisest and most beneficent."[20]

The trumped-up charges of many Tylerites to the contrary, Taylor also retained a commitment to human depravity. As he taught with many hundreds of other orthodox Edwardsians, unless God elected one from eternity for true holiness, and unless God's Spirit broke one's bonds to selfish vice, then all one did would result in heinous sin. Because we cannot act rightly from a morally wrong heart, true virtue requires a renovation of our predominant disposition. If benevolence is to flow from the souls of unregenerate sinners, God must "[secure] by his immediate intervention . . . an entire and permanent change in the *choice* which we make between Himself and the world, as objects of supreme affection." Taylor stressed that this change "is not a physical change; not a change in any of the properties or powers of the soul." But while reemphasizing the moral nature of both sin and regeneration, he described this change as the sine qua non of true virtue.[21]

The point at which Taylor did move beyond the views of his Edwardsian predecessors lay in his notion of the suspension of the selfish principle. If there truly were means of regeneration, he thought, then by definition they "must have either some *tendency* to produce regeneration; or some necessary or real *connexion* with it; or must at least be such as will not infallibly *prevent* it." Thus, led by his dissatisfaction with the Hopkinsian notion that the means lead universally to sin, Taylor wondered whether the selfish principle "may be so imperfect in *degree*" at times as to "be subject to occasional intermissions or suspensions, in its active control or influence on the mind." Oftentimes, even in unregenerative moments, our selfishness seems to wane. During revivals, for example, even the vilest of sinners seem affected by gospel preaching. No doubt all could remember times in their lives when their predominant volitions seemed less dominant than usual. For Taylor, these times proved analogous to the moment of regeneration. The difference between such times and the moment of regeneration itself lay in the degree to which the means of grace had weakened the selfish principle. Often the means seem to work for a while but then fail ultimately to transform us. Our selfish principle is blunted, but not entirely disabled. In regeneration, however, the means of grace yield a complete suspension of this predominant volition. While the selfish principle is still losing its hold, our use of the means proves sinful. But at the moment in which that principle is suspended, we employ the means without sin.[22]

For Taylor, however, even those sinless acts that occur in the moment of regeneration depend for their very existence on the power of divine grace. Taylor described regeneration as a "complex act" comprised of a minute series of more simple, separate acts. When viewed in its entirety, or "in the widest and most comprehensive sense of the term," he thought it fair to say that regeneration "is *all* dependent on divine inter-position." The difficulty, according to Taylor, came in deciding *how* God's grace related to each of those simple acts within the series of regeneration. Among many theologians, and as defined in its most technical, "*restricted* sense," regeneration frequently referred more narrowly to that specific "act of the will" that took place at the end of Taylor's series "in which God is preferred to every other object." Taylorites and Tylerites alike agreed that this act required divine interposition. But the Taylorites argued that this act represented only the culmination of one's conversion. "*Some part* of the process," wrote Taylor, "is preliminary to such interposition, and preliminary also to that which, in the limited use of the word, may be called regeneration." The sinless use of means, for instance, took place prior to such interposition and thus prior to regeneration in its most technical and restricted sense. This did not mean, for Taylor, that we use the means without any divine grace at all; only that we use the means without the same kind of grace granted at the culmination of conversion. In a point that is often missed by those who view Taylor through Tylerite lenses, and though Taylor only clarified this point as Tyler pressed him on its details, in the end he distinguished "the strivings of the Spirit" that permit a sinless use of means from "the renewing act of the Spirit" that completes one's second birth. In language that has caused no little confusion among those who prefer to keep theology simple, Taylor explained that he "did not say, as Dr. Tyler makes us, that '[the means] precede the act of divine interposition.'" He "only said that they were preliminary to *that* 'act of divine interposition' which secures regeneration in the *restricted* sense of the term."[23]

Despite this complicated discussion of the complex process of regeneration, moreover, the Taylorites did maintain firmly the instantaneous nature of the experience. Incredulous Tylerites questioned how they presumed to uphold immediate regeneration while portraying the event as a *series* of acts requiring a sinless use of means. Taylor replied, however, by claiming that his position "amounts substantially to nothing more" than what Edwards had said in *Freedom of the Will*. Indeed, much like New Haven's Taylorites, though in less extensive fashion, Edwards himself had also "analyze[d] instantaneous acts, into extended processes of thought and feeling." His well-known maxim that "the will is as the greatest apparent good" implied quite clearly that regeneration must involve acts of reflection and volition. Further, New Haven had never suggested that these acts required a protracted length of time. In fact, the Taylorites had described them as "*contemporaneous*" and as having "*no measurable duration*" whatsoever. That we must discuss them as if they did take place in chronological succession, wrote Taylor, reveals only "the imperfection" of our "language." Indeed, for the Taylorites, to speak of "the priority" of the means in the complex series of regeneration is to "refer rather to the order of nature than of time." As a frustrated Taylor explained to Tylerites who refused to accede this subtle distinction, "the progress of thought and feeling is often as rapid as that of light, and we no more intend to affirm any *measurable* duration between the first and last act in the series, than when we say the sun must exist before it can shine."[24]

Taylor did have to perform some strenuous feats of intellectual gymnastics in order to convince his hearers of their (genuine) ability to convert from the perspective of Edwardsian Calvinism. In the process, he also risked obfuscating the popular perception of his views. But he took these risks for the same reason Edwardsians had always pressed the logic of regeneration—he did so to promote conversions and spread revival. As he stated in his initial critique of Spring's *Dissertation*, he intended to "[overthrow] the standing objection of many unrenewed men, *that they have nothing to do because all they shall do will be either vain or sinful.*" Given the prevalence in New England of the notion of the sinner's utter dependence, he felt that his own views represented "the only way, in which the immediate performance of duty can be regarded as practicable." He felt that seekers must exert themselves or they could never hope to be saved and he liked to quote Edwards on the relationship between such exertion and divine grace: "God produces all," he quoted, but "we act all. For that is what he produces, viz. our own acts." For Taylor, this meant nothing less than that action was required in conversion. God never saves those who remain passive with regard to regeneration. As the Taylorites made very clear in an essay on the doctrine of human dependence,

> [W]e should be careful to distinguish, clearly, between a true and false reliance on God. . . . A true reliance, while it makes God all in all, as the efficient agent in our progress heavenward, includes, also and at every step in our advance in holiness, our own personal activity. God does not make us holy, and fit us for heaven, as mere passive recipients of divine influence; but he does it by leading us, in the exercise of our active powers, to do his will; by exciting us to use in a right manner, the capacities which he has given us; by inclining us to act, as he would have us act, with the powers which we already possess.[25]

Taylor sought to move beyond what William Clebsch has aptly called the New Divinity's "theology of unself-conscious conversion." Convinced as they were that "true revival . . . must come unpredictably and unpredicted," Hopkins and Bellamy "became like the nervous host who vows he will act naturally when his august guest arrives." But Taylor, while still opposed to a lengthy period of preparation, stressed that one must at least open the door to one's heart before God could enter in. In a system of moral government, God does not break into souls by force. Though no one enjoys God's company who has not been elected to this privilege, and though no one invites God in who has not been enabled by divine grace, still God will not come to stay with those who have offered no invitation and who do not go out to greet their Guest with willing hearts and open arms. For Taylor, regeneration came only as a result of self-conscious and earnest effort. While certainly unpredictable and dependent on God's decrees, it did not come unanticipated in the hearts of its recipients. Further, conversion was something that all human beings had a natural capacity to perform. Thus "the sinner should act" in pursuing this goal as if it really were attainable, or "in precisely the same manner as he would were he not dependent on God." In a statement that proved axiomatic throughout all the New Haven Theology, Taylor taught that "the sinner does that through grace which he is competent to do and ought to do without grace." He did not believe with the Arminians "that the Holy Spirit is always ready to convert." But he did believe "that we are authorised to assure any sinner, that it may be true, that the Holy Spirit is now ready to convert." The doctrine of divine dependence, then, should not be employed to discourage anxious sinners, but should rather be used to "prevent utter despair, and consequent inaction." Though preachers could not guarantee conversion to any within their churches, they could assure the inquiring sinner "that he ought to submit to God without grace" and that "he *may*" do so "through grace."[26]

"The Modern Question" and the Duty of Faith

Though Taylor never presented it as such, his doctrine of regeneration actually made a considerable contribution to a century-old, Anglo-American conversation concerning what several English clergymen had termed "the modern question." Popularized by Andrew Fuller (1754–1815), a Baptist minister in Kettering, Northamptonshire, but dating back to several tracts on the topic from the era of the Great Awakening, the modern question concerned whether or not all sinners have an obligation to believe the gospel. Evangelical Calvinists in Great Britain who responded in the affirmative to this question met great resistance from high Calvinists who held that God called only the elect to such belief. Significantly, however, these same evangelical Calvinists found much support for their position in the New Divinity. Edwards's *Freedom of the Will* and Smalley's sermons on natural ability proved especially important to their thinking. In fact, Andrew Fuller, whose *The Gospel Worthy of All Acceptation* (1785) first drew (English) national attention to the modern question, had been influenced by Edwardsian theology to a remarkable extent. Having read *Freedom of the Will* as early as 1777 (at the behest of Edwards's Scottish friend, John Erskine), he was corresponding with Samuel Hopkins by century's end. Though his letters made it clear that he was no radical Hopkinsian, he was definitely devoted to the mainstream Edwardsian tradition. His opponents decided to dub him the "American doctor" and his talk of "duty faith" soon caught on in the newly formed United States.[27]

While both Taylorites and Tylerites proved enthusiastic about Fuller, it was Taylor who did the most with the modern question. Based on his strenuous commitment to human natural ability, he affirmed "the duty of *all* men . . . to confess Christ." The clergy, he declared, "are under solemn responsibility, *so* to preach the Gospel, that men shall feel their obligation to obey it." He knew that "many there are who tell us . . . that a new heart, repentance, &c., are [God's] gift, that they cannot repent themselves, but must wait God's time." To Taylor, however, such talk was but a "casting [of] the blame of their continued impenitence upon God." Fully equipped with gospel truth and with natural ability, sinners had "ample warrant for the conclusion that compliance with the terms of salvation, is an event which may take place the next moment." In fact, nothing held them back from full compliance with God's plan but their own very sinful lack of will. Thus, in Taylor's view, the answer to his British colleagues' modern question could be summed up in a few simple words: God calls every sinner "to make himself a holy heart" and expects, not pious excuses, but faithful action.[28]

Like his associates across the sea, though, Taylor sought to shape a theology that proved both modern and well grounded in evangelical Calvinist orthodoxy. Thus, while he worked with all his might to promote our duty to have faith, he found this effort perfectly consistent "with the doctrine of dependence." For Taylor, as for all other Edwardsians in old and New England alike, all sinners have the power to convert. While there is no way to be certain "that the renewing grace, or the grace which secures the performance of duty, *will attend* any call to duty," this need not leave anxious sinners without hope. God has never promised to save everyone who hears the gospel call. But God has promised to save those who exert a genuine faith. Undeniably, New Haven's rather ambivalent logic of salvation struck many outsiders as woefully idiosyncratic and enigmatic. But Taylor's answer to the modern question seemed, to insiders at least, to represent the most contemporary solution to the problem of perpetuating Edwardsian Calvinism. Edwardsians had always preached, Janus-like, for the sinner's immediate repentance while insisting on the absolute providence of God. So Taylor, who went so far as to state that sinners *could* and *should* convert without any help from God, admitted that sinners never *would* unless elected and enabled for the task. Precisely "here . . . lies the practical power of the doctrine of dependence," he proposed: "in the fearful uncertainty, which it imparts to the great question of the sinner's regeneration." He went on: "[I]t is only when the event of compliance with the terms of life, is seen to depend on the unpromised and uncertain grace of an offended God, that the doctrine of dependence carries its agitating power into the guilty bosom" of the active seeker. Taylor knew quite well that this proverbial "guilty bosom" had provided the tinder for sparking tens of thousands of evangelical conversions. In the train of many other tremendously successful Edwardsian revivalists, then, he exploited this "agitating power" in the saving of souls throughout the North. In the end, his doctrine of regeneration may not have proved as obeisant to Edwards's own phraseology as, in the Tylerites' estimation, it should have. But it did contribute faithfully, indeed more faithfully than the Tylerites often hackneyed clichés, to the great, anxious spirit of Edwardsian revivalism.[29]

III

IMPLICATIONS

7

The Decline and Fall of the Edwardsian Culture

Taylorites, Tylerites, and the Disintegration of New England Calvinism

> It is impossible to write a story about New England life and manners for a
> thoughtless, shallow-minded person. If we represent things as they are, their
> intensity, their depth, their unworldly gravity and earnestness, must inevita-
> bly repel lighter spirits, as the reverse pole of the magnet drives off sticks
> and straws.
>
> Harriet Beecher Stowe, *The Minister's Wooing*

As we have begun to see by now, Taylor's recontextualization of the Edwardsians' "agitating power," while tremendously fecund, also bore devastating consequences for the
Edwardsian theological culture. Taylor perpetuated this culture to great effect at Yale
and beyond, and in part 2 I interpreted this extension of Edwardsian culture in Taylor's
own terms. Accounting for his self-identification as an Edwardsian theologian, I described
what it meant to be an Edwardsian in the 1820s and 1830s, and how it was that Taylor
laid claim to continuity with Edwards's thought.

Now it is time to account for the broader implications of Taylor's views. In a word,
and ironically, Taylor stretched the Edwardsain culture so far that he eventually tore it
apart. His controversial modifications of the main components of the New England
Theology, though carried out on explicitly Edwardsian terms, led to the ultimate dissolution of the very tradition he cherished so dearly. In part 3, then, I shift gears and
narrate this history of dissolution. Along the way, I reinterpret what Haroutunian and
many others have called "the passing of the New England Theology," setting the record
straight with regard to both its nature and its timing. And I conclude with an estimation of Taylor's legacy to America.

The Institutionalization of the Taylorite-Tylerite Schism

Tellingly, while the New Haven Theology had been developing publicly throughout the
1820s, it was not until the end of that fateful decade that Taylorite views received much
criticism. Indeed, before the publication in 1828 of Taylor's *Concio ad Clerum*, New
England's Congregationalists stood largely united on rather conservative Edwardsian
principles. As noted in Beecher's *Autobiography*, "Time was when Taylor, and Stuart,
and Beecher, and Nettleton, and Tyler, and Porter, and Hewitt [sic], and Harvey were
all together, not only in local proximity, but in the warmest unity of belief and feeling."[1]

This claim was not unfounded. In the middle years of the 1820s, these future rivals banded together to battle both Unitarianism back east and Finneyite methods in the west. We have already witnessed the Taylorites' leadership of the Edwardsian defense of New England Calvinism in response to the Unitarian critiques of the 1810s and 1820s. Suffice it to add in this context that the Tylerites supported their labors heartily. In only the best known case of such support, when the Unitarian *Christian Examiner* attempted to divide New England's trinitarians by separating Beecher and New Haven from the region's historic Calvinism, none other than Asahel Nettleton, the fiery conservative soon to serve as the Tylerite party's leading activist, supported Beecher and affirmed the unity of the Edwardsian ranks within Connecticut. "I believe it to be a matter of fact," he claimed, "that you and I are really a different kind of Calvinists from what Unitarians have imagined or been accustomed to manage. Probably [your Unitarian critic] thinks that you are in sentiment at war with the orthodox at the present day, but he is grandly mistaken so far as Connecticut is concerned. . . . We feel no concern for old Calvinism. Let them dispute it as much as they please; we feel bound to make no defense."[2]

When Finneyite progressives in upstate New York threatened to encroach upon their region, moreover, these men joined hands again to keep the "new measures"[3] out of New England. In an early piece of correspondence that Nettleton used widely in New York, Beecher excoriated Finney's revivalism, its reckless methods and rampant emotionalism, declaring that it "brings in its train certainly universal and permanent evil." Soon thereafter, Beecher and Nettleton led the charge in New Lebanon, New York, when a group from New England met Finney's party there in July of 1827 to discuss their very different approaches to revival and gospel ministry. Though nothing much came of their meetings (which lasted for over a week), Beecher is said to have thrown down the gauntlet, challenging Finney with words that Nettleton would not have stated any more strongly. "Finney I know your plan," he exclaimed, "& you know I do; you mean to come to Connecticut & carry a streak of fire to Boston. But if you attempt it, as the Lord liveth I'll meet you at the state line & call out all the artillerymen & fight every inch of the way to Boston & then I'll fight you there." Shortly after these meetings, Beecher and Nettleton went to the press against the "new measures." At the end of 1827, Beecher wrote a letter to the *Christian Spectator* charging the Finneyites with, among other things, "the most marvellous duplicity and double-dealing and lying." He published it separately in pamphlet form, *To the Congregational Ministers and Churches of Connecticut* (1827), and followed it up with a volume of his and Nettleton's *Letters . . . on the "New Measures"* (1828).[4]

Before long, however, things changed along New England's united front and it was only a matter of time before the Edwardsian culture would begin to disintegrate. Nettleton ultimately proved more extreme in his opposition to the Finneyites, and grew terribly disappointed with the inconstancy of Beecher and Taylor. Charles Hambrick-Stowe has quipped that "Nettleton aimed to kill, while Beecher fired warning shots over Finney's head."[5] Having failed to scare Finney off, moreover, Beecher soon decided to help him. As he wrote to Chauncey Goodrich in the spring of 1828,

[T]here is such an amount of truth in the preaching of Finney, [and] so much good hopefully done that if he can be so far restrained as that he shall do more good than evil, then it should be dangerous to oppose him, lest at length we might be found to fight against God; for though some revivals may be so badly managed as to be worse than none; there may to a certain extent be great imperfections in them [and] yet, they be on the whole, blessings to the church.

Three years later, and only four years after Beecher's threatening speech at New Lebanon, Finney was actually preaching revival in the city of Boston with Beecher's support. Beecher confessed that he had erred in his estimation of Finney's ministry. Indeed, he even went so far as to write the following in a letter to Finney: "[W]ith very little difference, & that more on points of discretion unessential, you and I are, as much, perhaps even more, one than almost any two men whom God has been pleased to render conspicuous in his church."[6]

This softening on Finney's ministry, combined with the notoriety of Taylor's *Concio*, set a chain of events in motion that would eventually lead to a full-blown schism. With support from southern Presbyterian friends, a Tylerite network soon emerged to combat what confessional Calvinists throughout America now deemed dangerous tendencies in New Haven.[7]

Nettleton's doctors had urged him to move south soon after the end of the New Lebanon conference. His health had never been good and Finney had worked him into a frenzy. Nettleton obliged them the following winter, staying with Presbyterian colleagues in Virginia and remaining in the south until the spring of 1829. While there, one of his friends, the Presbyterian minister John Holt Rice, received copies of Taylor's *Concio*, as well as the first installment of his "Review of Spring on the Means of Regeneration." These items were covered in the mail by a letter from Chauncey Goodrich attributing Nettleton's own success as a gospel preacher to Taylorite views. To Nettleton's utter embarrassment, Rice and company found Taylor heretical, denouncing the New Haven Theology as "Pelagian." Furious now with Taylor and fearing guilt by association, Nettleton labored strenuously to distance himself from Yale.[8]

Upon his return to New England, he tried to quiet the Taylorites down, hoping to avert any future embarrassments with Presbyterian friends to the south. Failing this, he took up his pen and launched a letter-writing campaign, casting aspersions about Taylor's theology throughout the region. Taylor's "speculations are working mischief wherever his pupils go," he claimed. "His sermon [the *Concio*] shows more metaphysical darkness & weakness than I could imagine would ever come from his pen." Taylor had fallen into heresy, Nettleton argued, especially on sin. He was sliding down the slippery slope to Arminianism and beyond, and attempting along the way "to demolish orthodoxy."[9]

This tactic proved somewhat persuasive among the leaders of Andover Seminary, whose president Ebenezer Porter and senior theologian Leonard Woods soon joined the ranks of those who opposed the New Haven Theology. Soon after Nettleton's return to New England, Porter decided to enter the fray himself, complaining to Beecher that "in all the annals of theological discussion, I have seen no match for Dr. Taylor's obscurity."[10] Determined to meet this matter head on, Porter then called a meeting in his study at home on the day after Andover's anniversary celebration in September of 1829. All the region's luminaries attended—Taylor, Beecher, Goodrich, Nettleton, Woods, Stuart, and several others. But while managing to air their differences charitably, they left the meeting unreconciled. And after what proved to be their last concerted effort to keep the peace, relations turned quite sour in the Edwardsian camp. Woods, who had been holding back in the hope of reclaiming his friends in New Haven, now published his captious series of *Letters to Rev. Nathaniel W. Taylor*—and a battle for control of the Edwardsian culture had been joined.[11]

Before this tragic meeting, Beecher had promised to remain a theological peacemaker, telling Porter, "[W]ith me it is a fundamental maxim not to expend my strength in contending with the friends of Christ, when so much effort is needed to turn back his enemies." But after the meeting, he spun around nearly 180 degrees, encouraging Taylor to respond to Woods with decisive force. "Attack," he wrote to his friend, so that Woods will "never . . . peep again or mutter. . . . I would have him exposed and pushed with great directness and power, and unsparingly, leaving of his temple not one stone upon another." Always more aggressive than the academicians in New Haven, Beecher now was playing the part of New Haven's battlefield commander. "We are not to be browbeaten," he exclaimed, "and driven off the ground of New England divinity—Bible divinity—by a feeble and ignorant philosophy."[12]

Making matters worse, by this time Beecher had already ruined his friendship with Nettleton, having tried to intimidate him during a conversation held, quite literally, in Beecher's woodshed. Though, as might have been expected, these men interpreted the encounter differently, both allowed that it took place in October of 1829 after a meeting of Boston-area clergy held in Beecher's own home at which Nettleton publicized his opposition to Taylor's theology.[13] After the meeting, Beecher and Nettleton spent time alone in Beecher's woodshed, Beecher chopping wood while the younger Nettleton looked on. At a memorable point in their conversation, Beecher shook his axe at Nettleton and said, "Taylor and I have made you what you are, and if you do not behave yourself we will hew you down." Beecher always remembered this as "a mere playful act of humor," claiming that Nettleton had understood it as such himself. But when word of it spread southward down the seaboard Nettleton fumed in humiliation and the story of their encounter generated discomfort wherever it went.[14]

Meanwhile, Taylor's views were stirring up strife in the religious periodicals and theological quarterlies, in which he was gaining a notoriety that would soon catch up with him back home. Much of this strife is discussed earlier. Taylor attracted the most popular attention, however, not for his scholarly publications, but for a highly publicized exchange on his creedal commitments with Joel Hawes, a friend and colleague who served as pastor of Hartford's First Church. Published originally in the *Connecticut Observer* in February of 1832, this exchange was reprinted numerous times in other places. Hawes intended it as an opportunity for Taylor to clarify his orthodoxy in response to the many criticisms he had received in the wake of the *Concio*. But it wound up provoking further dissension—not over the 11 articles Taylor laid out in a basic statement of his beliefs (which he had phrased in fairly traditional Edwardsian terms), but over his annotations to the articles (stamped much more clearly with Taylorite symbols), which struck many as suspiciously elaborate and ambiguous. While charging Taylor repeatedly now with both Arminian and Pelagian heresy, Joseph Harvey asked why, "if the eleven articles of this creed . . . really expresses [sic] the sentiments of Dr. Taylor," it "was . . . necessary to add so many and elaborate marks by way of explanation?" He went on to contend on behalf of the Tylerites that "it is unusual, in creeds or confessions of faith, to adopt terms so ambiguous, as to require an explanation longer than the confession itself." And he suggested that Hawes's widely rumored (though never specified) editorial emendations to the published version of this exchange rendered him suspect along with Taylor and the journals that published it.[15]

Beecher took steps immediately to reclaim New Haven's reputation, engaging Woods in the *Spirit of the Pilgrims* in a friendly exchange of correspondence. Comprising six different installments, and covering 65 pages in all, their letters focused on the fundamental principles of the New England Theology, principles that Beecher argued all of New England's Calvinists still affirmed. Their dialogue culminated in another, much more simple theological creed that Beecher offered to Woods in the hope of rallying New England's Calvinists around the basics of Edwardsian doctrine. Woods responded to Beecher's creed in words that appeared to promise rapprochement. "I cordially agree with you," Woods assured him. "The cordial belief of these doctrines is, I think, a solid basis of ministerial fellowship and cooperation, though there may be a variety of opinions on other subjects, and on some subjects which are by no means unimportant." Though this statement was qualified, Beecher was thrilled and looked for better days to come. But as it turned out, this gesture of fellowship was both too little and too late. It paled in the light of the fires already blazing throughout New England, and went largely unheeded by the rest of New Haven's opponents.[16]

In fact, by August of 1834 Taylor faced heresy charges at home, as the controversy he had ignited began to burn in his own back yard. The previous April, the Yale Corporation had assigned two of its members, the Revs. Abel McEwen and Daniel Dow, to attend and report on the examinations of Yale's graduate students in theology. According to McEwen, all went well. But Dow, a 10-year veteran of the corporation who was growing suspicious of Taylor's orthodoxy, took the occasion to object to Taylor's teaching, as well as complain of his refusal to adhere literally to Connecticut's historic (and Calvinistic) Saybrook Platform (1708).[17]

An investigation was held and Taylor was called to defend his views. In a formal "Statement" and "Explanation" of his theology to the trustees, he made clear that he still adhered to the Saybrook Platform. But as he argued in his defense:

> According to the established usage of this College, at the time when I gave my assent to the Saybrook Platform [1822], such assent was required only to "the substance of doctrine therein contained." It was therefore in this sense only, that the founders of the Dwight Professorship can be understood, on the established principles of legal construction, to have required this assent. From the system of theology long taught in the Institution, from the well known views of the Corporation at that time, and those of the founders as fully and repeatedly expressed, there was every reason to believe that if I had maintained the doctrines of that Confession with all their minutia . . . , it would have been considered a decisive disqualification for the office in question. It is well known that some parts of that Platform, have been universally rejected by the congregational clergy of New England, and it is believed, by every member of this Board.[18]

After some checking, the corporation concluded that Taylor was correct, that throughout the college's history, "excepting the period from 1753 to 1778, it has been an established principle, that the assent to the Confession of faith in question, is to be understood, as only an assent to 'the substance of doctrine therein contained.'" Consequently, Dow was required either to substantiate or to withdraw his charges of heresy against Taylor. Reluctantly, and while protesting that mere assent to "substance of doctrine" was so elusive and indefinite as to be no assent at all, Dow withdrew his heresy charges and Taylor received a full acquittal. Realizing now that their only recourse was to try Taylor in the media, the Tylerites quickly exposed this episode to the religious press. Dow departed Yale determined to thwart its innovations. And New Haven acquired a reputation for theological legerdemain.[19]

The Taylorites disowned this reputation whenever they had the chance, contesting the Tylerites' frequent claim to be New England's true Edwardsians. They contended that the spirit of the New England Theology had always been one of investigation, of creative advancement of the gospel, not a spirit of fearful clinging to the past. Though the Tylerites seemed to think "that the Congregational ministers of New England should never dream of making a single advance upon the views of Bellamy and Edwards,—that nothing shall be deemed not heretical, except the exact phraseology adopted by these divines," this "was not the spirit of Edwards," they insisted—"Not at all."[20]

The Taylorites also felt that they had been largely misunderstood, and that New England's theologians held more in common than they knew. They pleaded for unity both in print and in their private correspondence "between those who agree in the cardinal points of Calvinism,—decrees, election, total depravity by nature, regeneration by the special and direct influence of the spirit, and final perseverance of saints."[21] They viewed the Tylerites as their friends, as Taylor made unmistakably clear early in 1843 when he visited Nettleton on what everyone thought would be his deathbed. As remembered by Leonard Bacon, "there were no dry eyes in that chamber of suffering when Taylor fell weeping on the neck of Nettleton and kissed him."[22] And Taylor repeated on many occasions what all of his friends knew to be true, that "nothing could have been farther from my wishes than to be drawn into a theological controversy with the Rev. Dr. Tyler of Portland; a man for whom an intimate friendship, in early life, has made it impossible for me to entertain any sentiments but those of respect and affection."[23]

But the Tylerites refused to accept the olive branch their friends extended. Taylor had simply gone too far in his dilution of Edwardsian Calvinism and the future of New England's churches was at stake. The Taylorites remained the most popular religious party in the region. And Yale's Theological Department burgeoned throughout this period of theological tumult. As George Park Fisher would note, "[T]he more that young men in other colleges and schools of theology were warned against Dr. Taylor, the more they flocked to his lecture-room."[24] Further, Taylor remained a popular churchman even while inundated with criticism, serving in 1830 as both moderator and preacher at the meeting of the Connecticut General Association (in Wethersfield), and as moderator of the meetings of 1838 (in Norwalk) and 1841 (in New Haven).[25] But despite Taylor's success, he never managed to find a way to stem the rising tide of criticism. And Beecher's removal to Cincinnati in the crucial year of 1832 (when he assumed the presidency of Lane Seminary) severely weakened his party's ability to maintain unity by strategic diplomacy.[26]

Indeed, by the time of Beecher's removal, the Tylerites had already begun to plan for an ecclesiastical separation. They disagreed among themselves over the extent to which they should separate. But they all believed that they should "separate as soon as possible." As one anonymous Tylerite wrote, "[I]t is mere affectation to say or pretend that we are not a divided denomination [already]. And the division has occurred on grounds, and in respect to subjects, which will satisfy any reflecting mind that it is deep and will be permanent. . . . By continued contact," the writer warned, "the evil [of Taylorism] will secretly spread, until the whole mass be corrupt. . . . Until we have a separate organization, and are united in our exertions to exclude false teachers from our churches, there will be no effectual barrier to their influx."[27]

After a secret meeting in Norwich on October 12, 1831, at which they formed their own Doctrinal Tract Society, planned their own *Evangelical Magazine*,[28] and developed a constitution that would govern the proceedings of their group, the Tylerites met again in Hartford on January 9, 1833, to work on a list of doctrinal Articles of Agreement.[29] This process culminated in a larger meeting on September 10-11, 1833, held quite symbolically in East Windsor, Jonathan Edwards's hometown. It was there that the Tylerites launched their separate Pastoral Union formally, electing the Rev. George Calhoun as their founding president. About 40 clergymen attended from all across the state of Connecticut, adopting the Tylerite constitution and Articles of Agreement developed earlier, and stipulating that future members of their union would have to be nominated from within and then approved by a two-thirds vote at the annual meeting.[30]

Most importantly, the new Tylerite union planned the establishment of a seminary, a manual labor school that they hoped would provide an alternative to Yale both theologically and economically.[31] Worrying not only the Taylorites with their plans but also some faculty members at Andover, all of whom questioned whether New England could support three evangelical seminaries,[32] the Pastoral Union agreed to break ground only after raising $20,000 in pledges. According to Tylerite lore, they "opened a subscription on the spot" (i.e., at their September meeting). And in the only slightly exaggerated words of Bennet Tyler, the school's first president, "the twenty thousand dollars were subscribed in the course of a few weeks."[33]

Naming their school the Theological Institute of Connecticut (TIC), the Pastoral Union appointed trustees who determined to locate in East Windsor, literally right down the street from Edwards's birthplace. On May 14 of the following year (1834), they took the Edwards family doorstep and laid it symbolically and ceremoniously as the cornerstone of their new building. Every speaker at the service stressed the significance of this gesture, noting that the TIC did not represent a new departure in New England theology, but an effort to preserve the Edwardsian culture from the acids of Taylorism. Referring to President Tyler's desire to "find the hallowed spot, where he may cast down the mantle of the Bellamys, of the Dwights, of the Smalleys, of the Backuses, and the Strongs," one local minister spoke in words that reverberated all day long:

> Venerated and happy man! You are permitted, this day, in your own person, and by your own solemn acts, to unite the events of two great Eras in our Israel! You are permitted the satisfaction to take from the dilapidated ruins of the Mansion, in which Edwards, the great Champion of New England Calvinism, was born and nurtured, a stone, which you have laid here as a repairer of the breach,—a renewal of the ancient foundation on which he built.

These sentiments culminated in Tyler's inaugural address, a speech in which he confirmed his desire to build an Edwardsian bulwark in East Windsor. "The doctrines which we maintain," he declared in no uncertain terms, "are the doctrines which have been maintained by the orthodox of New England from generation to generation. They are the doctrines which were taught by Edwards, by Bellamy, by Dwight, by Strong, by Smalley, and by a host of divines who have been the glory of New England."[34]

By October of 1834, the TIC was open for business and training pastors to preach its own interpretation of Edwardsian themes. President Tyler served as the school's first regular professor of theology. And the Rev. William Thompson (of North Bridgewater, Massachusetts) served as the founding professor of biblical literature.[35]

"The Little End of Time's Telescope"

For all intents and purposes, the Taylorites and the Tylerites now moved in different clerical networks—the most acrimonious days of their dispute lay in the past. Leonard Bacon and George Calhoun would wage a paper war at decade's end.[36] By midcentury, moreover, the Tylerites would begin to squabble among themselves.[37] But in the near term, the Tylerite leaders of the Connecticut's renegade Pastoral Union began to associate more closely with the emergent Old School Presbyterians than with their neighbors and former colleagues in New England.

In fact, the Tylerites had been in touch with Presbyterians in and around Princeton since the beginning of their dispute with the Yale theologians. As shown by Sherry Pierpont May, they sought an alliance with the moderates in what would become the Old School party that would not only fortify their efforts among New England's Congregationalists but might also help to avert a schism in the Presbyterian church. The best evidence of this alliance is in the fraternal correspondence between Tylerites such as Woods and Nettleton, and Princetonians such as Ashbel Green, Charles Hodge, and Samuel Miller. In one such piece of correspondence, Miller wrote Nettleton the following words, speaking for himself and Princeton's patriarch, Professor Archibald Alexander:

> Our views [and] feelings with respect to the 'Pastoral Union of Con.,' are not only amicable, but cordial [and] fraternal. We view it as a most desirable [and] important association, embarked in a great [and] good cause, [and] likely to accomplish a very important object. True, indeed, in looking over their published Confession of Faith, we do not find every word exactly as we could have wished; but we find quite enough in it that we approve, to be a basis of affectionate confidence, [and] unfeigned good will.[38]

This alliance made for trouble within Connecticut's General Association after the Presbyterian schism of 1837–38. For at its annual meeting in June of 1839, Dr. Samuel H. Cox of New York's Laight-Street Presbyterian Church presented a formal commission to serve as a delegate from the New School General Assembly, thereby requesting the perpetuation of normal relations with his constituency (i.e., with the churches represented by what was now the New School). A major debate ensued, the Tylerite minority resisting the overture and opposing anything that would seem to favor the largely Taylorite New School.[39] After numerous attempts at spin control by both the Taylorites and the Tylerites, the Congregationalists remained deadlocked and Cox withdrew his request for fellowship. In the end, the Connecticut clergy decided to send delegates of their own to both the Old School and the New School Presbyterian General Assemblies, refusing to do anything that would make them a party to the Presbyterian contest.[40]

Despite their informal alliance with moderate Old School Presbyterians, however, the Tylerites would never muster sufficient material support to succeed in building a viable anti-Taylorite counterculture. To be sure, both the Pastoral Union and the TIC attracted a great deal of attention in the 1830s. But even during the most bitter years of the Taylorite-Tylerite struggle, Yale's Theological Department outpaced the growth of the TIC by a wide margin. As late as 1859, the year after Tyler's death and a quarter century after opening its doors, the TIC had graduated only 148 students. Taylor, by comparison, who died in the very same year as Tyler, taught a total of 815 students during his 35 years at Yale. In its best year alone (1837–38), 82 seminarians enrolled at Yale. And by 1840, only 18 years after Taylor launched its divinity program, Yale had the fifth largest seminary in the country. As Beecher bragged to Taylor in March of 1846, "You and I are the same as when we projected the Christian Spectator, and battled about the means of grace and episcopacy, and Hartford College [i.e., the TIC], and Nettleton, and Tyler, and Woods, and Harvey, if you remember such a one. But now, like Bonaparte's battles and marshals, have all these gone through the little end of Time's telescope into the dim but not uninteresting distance."[41]

Indeed, the most significant long-term consequence of Tylerite antagonism was not the defeat of Taylor, who remained the most popular clergyman in New England, but the fragmentation and dissolution of the Edwardsian theological culture. On an individual basis, many Edwardsian ministers would continue to thrive. And here and there, Edwardsian revivals continued to grace the New England scene.[42] But in the wake of the Taylorite controversy, the social and institutional network that had so long supported the Edwardsian movement began to break apart, foreshadowing the decline of the movement itself.

Taylor's reputation notwithstanding, Yale's own Theological Department began to decline in the mid-1840s, reaching a point of near "total collapse" by the time of his death. As I will explain more fully below, this had little to do with Tyler and a lot to do with mismanagement and broader social and cultural trends. But things eventually got so bad that by March of 1858 (when Taylor died) Yale had only 22 divinity students enrolled. In addition to its low enrollments, the school was running out of money. As George P. Fisher remembered, "[W]hen Dr. Taylor died the Seminary was possessed of an endowment amounting only to about fifty thousand dollars, together with a building for the accommodation of students, which contained no lecture-rooms, and was erected under a stipulation that it might be taken at its appraised value by the Academical Department whenever that Department should need it." Further, "no pains had been taken for many years to increase the revenues of the institution." As a result, "it was impossible to appoint a successor to Dr. Taylor, because the income of the chair was so small." (Not until 1866 was Taylor's Dwight chair filled when Samuel Harris began to serve as Yale's Professor of Didactic Theology.)[43]

In fact, by 1855 resources at both Yale and the TIC had dwindled to the point that these erstwhile rivals considered a merger. According to a plan proposed by the Tylerites in December of that year, the TIC would move to New Haven and share the resources of Yale College, its Pastoral Union would have the power to nominate new professors in theology, and the Yale Corporation would retain the right to make all appointments.[44] Yale ultimately refused this proposal, fearing that it would give the Pastoral Union too great a foothold in New Haven. Taylor himself, moreover, was said to have damned the proposal with faint praise. As reported in *The Independent*:

Rev. Dr. Taylor said that he had nothing to say in objection to such a "plan of union" as that which had been suggested. Let East Windsor come there in welcome; and Princeton too, for that matter. The more, the better! There is no harm in any such juxtaposition as that. But as for *cooperation and consolidation*, the less said of that the better. Which institution would give up to the other the exclusive control of any department—for instance that of Didactic Theology? I do not, said he, speak for myself. I am an old man, and compared with what I once was, I am feeble. I am ready to step aside any day, or any moment, when it may be thought best. But I say that the harmony of these two bodies thus contiguous would depend on their entire distinctness. I would welcome the East Windsor students to our rooms, and our library; yes, and to our lectures, and I should not fear for the interests of Truth in such a juxtaposition. I will endeavor to keep the peace as far as I am concerned; but I do not believe it can be secured, short of perfect independence.[45]

But despite this mild resistance, it was now clear to most in New England that the Edwardsian clergy were reeling from a ruinous civil war, and that there was now a need for healing and religious reconciliation. For all intents and purposes, Taylor and Tyler had finished fighting. The smoke was clearing and, as it did, the soldiers on both sides began to see that the religious landscape was changing rapidly and that their differences were no longer as important to the life of the churches as they had been. Two subsequent merger proposals failed.[46] And the TIC moved down to Hartford in 1865, changing its name along the way to Hartford Theological Seminary. But it now modified its tone with regard to Taylorism as well, virtually desisting from its polemics altogether. For his part, Taylor had refrained from publishing a single word against the Tylerites since the height of their dispute in the mid-1830s. What is more, since the mid-1840s he had been plagued with other problems.

Foremost among them was an ugly affair exposed by Beecher's daughter Catharine involving Leonard Bacon's sister and one of Taylor's favorite students. Both Delia Bacon (1811–59) and Alexander MacWhorter (1822–80) were big supporters of Taylor and Yale. Best known outside of New Haven for her theory that Francis Bacon and some of his followers were the real authors of Shakespeare's plays, Delia Bacon was known in New Haven mainly as the sister of Leonard Bacon and the daughter of David and Alice (Parks) Bacon, pioneering home missionaries inspired by Edwards's *Life of Brainerd*. Born in the town of Tallmadge, Ohio, where her family had helped to settle the Western Reserve, Delia returned to New England when her father died in 1817. She studied in Catharine and Mary Beecher's school in Hartford (the Hartford Female Seminary) in the 1820s. And she professed conversion at the age of 15 under the ministry of Joel Hawes, Taylor's friend who served as pastor of Hartford's First Church.[47]

Alexander MacWhorter, whose friends called him "Mac," was a wealthy young man from Newark, New Jersey, who had recently graduated from Yale's Theological Department. After receiving his license to preach, he remained in town to do further linguistic research with Professor Josiah Gibbs. He lived in the Taylor family home while pursuing his postgraduate studies. And he later published a widely read essay based in part on this work with Gibbs, *Yahveh Christ, or, The Memorial Name* (1856), introduced with a brief but laudative note by Taylor.[48]

The Bacon-MacWhorter affair began in 1845 when Mac and Delia fell in love while Mac was living with the Taylors. Eleven years younger than Delia (who was now working as a local teacher), Mac appears to have behaved as a spoiled and equivocating son of privilege. He courted Delia like a puppy, speaking to her of marriage before he had any intention of settling down. Delia's friends expressed concern that Mac was leading her on indecently. And when Delia failed to protect her own interests, Catharine Beecher forced the issue by spreading the word that Mac had proposed. Mac got nervous and defensive, dispelling the rumor that he had proposed and portraying Delia to his friends as an aggressive, designing woman. Delia feared for her reputation as a lady and a scholar; her brother Leonard, who had never liked Mac, became incensed.[49]

In the hope of redeeming his sister's reputation, Leonard Bacon charged Mac with "slander, falsehood, and conduct dishonorable to the Christian ministry" before the New Haven West Association in 1847. A trial was held, pitting the plaintiff—to the shame of all—against his friend Taylor, who proved to be Mac's most ardent supporter throughout the affair. Stubbornly committed to the defense of Yale and Connecticut's Congregational clergy, Taylor had tried to silence Delia in the hope that the crisis would disappear. When she refused to go away or sweep her grievance under a rug, Taylor treated her as a threat to the gospel ministry in Connecticut and did his best to ensure that Mac would survive the scandal unscathed. To no one's surprise, then, Mac emerged with little more than a slap on the wrist. But Catharine Beecher went on to publish a blistering account of the whole affair, entitled *Truth Stranger Than Fiction: A Narrative of Recent Transactions, Involving Inquiries in Regard to the Principles of Honor, Truth, and Justice, Which Obtain in a Distinguished American University* (1850). While not naming any names, she referred to the principals by their initials, depicting Taylor and his Yale colleagues (who had rallied to protect their threatened alumnus) as a bunch of scheming, insensitive hypocrites. Ironically, Mac endured the barrage of negative publicity as well as any, marrying another woman, Henrietta Blake, just five years after his clerical trial. But tragically, Delia, on whose behalf Beecher had written her exposé (but who protested its publication), never managed to recover fully from the ordeal. Having suffered intensely from emotional trauma throughout her troubled life, she died in 1859 in an asylum for the mentally ill.[50]

Humiliated by the scandal, Taylor scrambled to salvage his honor, as well as to restore his treasured friendships with the Bacons and the Beechers. The details of his restitution with Leonard Bacon no longer remain, though we know that by 1851 "a reconciliation [had] been effected through the kind offices of Miss Delia,"[51] and that Taylor lived out his final years as Bacon's friend and partner in ministry. The details of Taylor's future with the Beechers are better known. To his chagrin, however, they constituted a thicket of personal problems.

Catharine Beecher (1800–1878) had been a friend of the Taylor family for many years, and was no stranger to the Edwardsian culture or to the world of religious controversy. A minister's daughter by birth, an intellectual by temperament, and an educator by training, Catherine was led by the accidental death of her fiancé in 1822 and the tragic suicide of her clergyman brother in 1843 (among other, less important events) into the realm theological speculation. Living in Franklin, Massachusetts, and attending Nathanael Emmons's church while grieving the loss of her young lover, Alexander Metcalf Fisher, Beecher complained in a note to her father that Emmons's preaching "contributed . . . to bewilder and irritate my wounded heart," repining that Edwardsian clergy "teach" their peculiarities "more than they feel" them (a sentiment echoed later in some of her sister Harriet's novels). Soon thereafter she launched a career in education and domestic reform, contending for the importance of feminine nurture and the Christian home to American society—and moving away subtly from the disjunctive piety of her childhood. By the time of her brother George's death over two decades later, Catharine had become a mature and widely respected social and cultural critic. And she was ready now to publicize her uneasiness with the Edwardsians.[52]

Beecher had already published—in addition to several domestic and pedagogical works—a rather innocuous collection of *Letters on the Difficulties of Religion* (1836), which had received a brief but positive notice in Yale's *Quarterly Christian Spectator*. But after her brother's death, she released his *Biographical Remains* (1844), wherein she indicted New England Calvinism for the damage it did to the human psyche. She began to suggest publicly that traditional views of divine sovereignty, original sin, and human depravity undercut common sense, religious nurture, and mental health. This suggestion was soon confirmed for her in the Bacon-MacWhorter affair, a scandal that seemed to demonstrate the Edwardsians' insensitivity to the concerns of women, and their neglect of the needs of any but those promoting or pursuing conversion.[53]

By October of 1850, when she alleged in the *New York Tribune* that the men of her famous family had supported the release of *Truth Stranger Than Fiction*, Beecher had clearly become a public relations problem for Taylor and Yale. Taylor wrote to Lyman Beecher, begging for something that he could use to assure the public that Catharine's family did not condone her exposé. But even though the Beecher men had tried to stop its publication, and remained upset about the ways in which Catharine had smeared the Taylor family, they refused to oppose her publicly and Taylor received no ammunition.[54]

By the end of Taylor's life things had only gotten worse, for Catharine Beecher began to affirm the Pelagian heresy on Taylorite grounds, adding to Taylor's reputation as a dangerous influence on the laity. Beecher had always maintained a commitment, both confusing and confused, to her father's Taylorite views—even while detesting Taylor personally or denouncing the principles of Edwardsian Calvinism. As explained by Kathryn Kish Sklar, "Taylor represented the religious and cultural heritage that she had alternately denounced and supported but had never transcended. For a quarter of a century she had tried to find her place within and define her relationship to this heritage. Her ambivalent attitude toward it was closely bound up with her ambivalent attitude toward her father." Whatever its source, Beecher's ambivalence came to a head with the publication of *Common Sense Applied to Religion* (1857), released just months before Taylor's death.[55]

Though ill conceived and inconsistent in its theological argumentation, in *Common Sense* Beecher embraced the arch-heresy of western Christendom, attacking Calvinism with what she thought to be the support of the Yale school. Shocking all her father's friends, she stated that "Pelagius promulgated the common-sense views on the nature of mind . . . set forth in this volume," adding that the Taylorites taught "the doctrine of Pelagius in opposition to that of Augustine." To be sure, she admitted, the New Haven men did refer to themselves as Calvinists. And they exhibited ambivalence and confusion on the issue of human ability. But in the main they opposed the Calvinists in their reliance on common sense, and in their emphasis on human freedom as the basis of moral reform. Beecher wondered, in fact, "how it is possible that men so intelligent and so honest should maintain that on this subject they had not departed from the system of New England divinity as exhibited by Edwards." Clearly "the ancient follow-ers of Pelagius, the modern Unitarians, and the leaders of the New Haven school of divines, all hold exactly the position set forth in this work." At this point, moreover, Beecher was proud to be a Taylorite. And Taylor himself, now in his seventies, nearing death and very weak, could not explain that Beecher's pride had been misplaced.[56]

Taylor would never receive the sort of public support from Lyman Beecher needed to distance himself from the criticisms and the heterodoxy of Catharine. But the two remained close even while Beecher protected his daughter, maintaining a devotion to one another that endured these final stresses and strains. Beecher's private support of Taylor is found throughout his correspondence, but expressed most poignantly in a letter written in December of 1850:

> And as to you, my brother, with whom for forty years I have been associated in affection, and confidence, and counsels, and prayers, and revivals, and missions, and reformations, and joys, and sorrows, till the shades of evening begin to fall upon us, and the light of other suns through faith begin to brighten upon our upward vision, what shall I say? Had others seen and known what I have seen and known of the integrity of your heart and the grief of your soul from the commencement of these trials, you would need no other exposition or advocate; and all that now I have to say or need to say is, very pre-cious hast thou been unto me, my brother, and precious art thou still, and precious for-ever wilt thou be, I doubt not, in the presence and glory of our common Lord.

Though the two men lived at a distance for almost all of Taylor's life, they went to their graves in the Grove Street Cemetery with a bond of friendship never broken.[57]

The Death of Taylor and Dissolution of the New England Theology

Little else is known about the end of Taylor's life, though several sources provide ac-counts of Taylor's death. In an obituary notice published the day on which he died, Chauncey Goodrich said of his friend that he "died of no specific disease. He was sim-ply worn out by hard study." Indeed, true to form, Taylor worked until the end, caring for students until his body would no longer let him. Though he resigned his Dwight chair in the summer of 1857, he continued to teach through most of the fall. By year's end, reports suggest, he was meeting his classes at home in his parlor, one of the stu-dents reading his lectures while Taylor expounded on them himself. Moreover, as Samuel Dutton recalled, he was giving the students fresh material. He drafted his last lecture ever "not more than two months before his death." And even then he longed to preach on his lecture topic from the pulpit. When his wife, Rebecca, implored, "'How I wish that could be put into the form of a sermon, and that you could preach it!'" Taylor is said to have responded exuberantly, "'O, that I could be permitted to preach again, and to preach to ministers!'"[58]

By February, however, Taylor could no longer work at all. Too weak to do much but rest, he had plenty of time to prepare for death. He began to tell his friends that he wanted to die like the martyr Stephen. "I wish to go," he said, praying "Lord Jesus, receive my spirit" [Acts 7:59]. Confined to his bed by the end of the month, Taylor knew that his time had come. He asked his wife to let him go and began to drift in and out of consciousness. Dreaming frequently of heaven, he repeated the words of a favorite hymn as if enthralled in a state of delirium:

> See Salem's golden spire
> In beauteous prospect rise!
> And brighter crowns than angels wear,
> Which sparkle through the skies!

He died in the early hours of March 10, though it was said that "he passed . . . so quietly" no one knew the time of his death. Not long after midnight, one of the loved ones keeping vigil at his bedside had noticed that Taylor "was sleeping more quietly than usual." Sometime later, having noticed that Taylor had also "slept longer than usual," this anonymous friend finally "went to him, and found that he was dead."[59]

Taylor's funeral filled the Center Church with people pressing to pay their respects, many from as far away as New York City. The church was draped in black, as Leonard Bacon, Yale's President Woolsey and Chauncey Goodrich conducted the service. Bacon lamented in his eulogy that "a great light has been extinguished: no, not extinguished, but removed to shine on us, henceforth, only from the historic past; removed to shine in that high and blessed sphere where 'they that are wise shall shine as the brightness of the firmament, and they that turn many to righteousness, as the stars forever and ever'" [Dan. 12:3]. Whatever one's view of the afterlife, Bacon's metaphor was apt. For Taylor's light had been growing dimmer in New England for 20 years. And like those of the other Edwardsian luminaries who once lit up the region's churches, Taylor's star now only gleamed on them from afar.[60]

Thus, in the wake of Taylorite controversy, the Edwardsian tradition did decline. Taylor remained an esteemed patriarch of the Congregationalists throughout his life. By the time of his death, however, the New England Theology was clearly dying too. An era had ended. Everyone knew it, though some would protest for years to come. New England's churches faced new challenges. And the Edwardsian movement had run out of steam.

Again, however, this is not to echo the traditional jeremiad regarding the passing of the New England Theology. Rather, to sum up the argument offered here, the Edwardsians did not languish, but actually flourished during the first four decades of the nineteenth century, forming America's first indigenous theological movement— perhaps the most popular movement of indigenous theology in American evangelical history. Their great success proved a two-edged sword, however, as they eventually grew so large and diverse that they tore themselves apart, leaving their culture too weak to sustain a vital tradition of religious reflection.

Indeed, as urbanization and industrialization altered the region's religious landscape, and German idealism, biblical criticism, and Darwinian science revolutionized theology, the Edwardsian culture proved as weak as it had been since the eighteenth century, and its leaders, now tired and aging, lacked the resources with which to respond. The coming generation of churchmen began to look elsewhere for intellectual guidance, seeking new and creative solutions to problems the Edwardsians had not addressed. And by the eve of the Civil War, even their teachers began to respond by paying homage to Edwardsian ancestors while offering a much more expansive theological curriculum.

At Andover, Edwards A. Park would try to drag the movement forward, writing histories of the New England Theology that papered over its cracks and fissures. But "progressive orthodoxy" would soon win the hearts and minds of most at Park's own seminary, and its proponents viewed Park and his passions as curious remnants from the past.[61] At Yale, men such as Bacon, Porter, Fisher, and Samuel Harris continued to appropriate Edwardsian themes as well. But they did so more forthrightly in selective acts of historical retrieval. In their increasingly secular, cosmopolitan world, none tried to revive the tradition whole, ill-adapted as it always remained to the problems of modern, urban America.[62] Perhaps Porter put it best. When asked about his father-in-law's death in March of 1858, he replied, "It was not too soon." Taylor "belonged to another world than that now coming on, and he would not have been happy in it."[63]

To be sure, external forces also contributed to their demise, forces recognized by the successors of Taylor, Beecher, Tyler, and Nettleton. But these forces neither co-opted nor overwhelmed New England's Edwardsians. Rather, the problem was that these ministers—these ardent proponents of "spiritual politics"—failed to engage them much at all. Indeed, one looks in vain to the New England Theology for any serious, sustained analysis of the challenges that proved most pressing to Christian ministers in the mid-nineteenth century. The Edwardsians largely neglected the new opportunities for urban ministry. They proved more lethargic than Baptists and Methodists in planting churches on the frontier. They disrespected German idealism, even as many of their students devoured Coleridge. And by 1859, when Darwin published *The Origin of Species* and higher criticism began to make inroads into American theological studies, both Taylor and Tyler were dead, their movement was disintegrating, and their followers were struggling simply to hold on to what was left.

In his important recent work on the long history of the New England Theology, American historian Bruce Kuklick attributes the Edwardsians' eventual extinction to the intellectual commitments of their leaders. One of the few major interpreters to take the later Edwardsians seriously, Kuklick argues that they declined in the face of indomitable critical challenges. In short, according to Kuklick, Charles Darwin undermined the Edwardsians' traditional dependence on British empiricism, and especially on the psychology and epistemology of Common Sense Realism. Or in Kuklick's own words, evolutionary theory "made untenable commitments to a Christian philosophy based on Scottish thought," and thus "[destroyed] . . . the philosophical basis of all American religious orthodoxy."[64] While this is not the place for a full-fledged response to Kuklick's argument, perhaps it is the place to point out that many religious philosophers today espouse a version of Scottish Realism,[65] and religious orthodoxies of many kinds continue to thrive. The Edwardsians never expressed much fear or confusion regarding Darwin. In fact, they largely ignored the new science, underestimating its eventual influence.[66]

No, the Edwardsians were not the losers of the mid-nineteenth-century culture wars. The fact of the matter is that they hardly entered them at all. The New England Theology did not wilt in the face of insurmountable obstacles. Rather, it declined primarily because its leaders had long ago become self-absorbed, expending most of their energy on internal struggles for control of their movement's vast resources. As a result, they failed to respond effectively to the changing needs of the world around them. And, after a while, that changing world just passed them by.

8

Taylor's Edwardsian Legacy

New Haven and the Religious Culture of Evangelical America

You cannot deny that [New England] has a very peculiar character & has made that character felt over great interests of man. Now a Philosopher's ambition is to *make* that character, to let his own thought & will live in whole nations of men, to let his own system of belief . . . pervade society & to let it mould & alter whole masses of the people. . . . Jonathan Edwards has done this very thing. Dwight & Emmons & Hopkins & Edwards & Bellamy have *begotten* New England & these all are the one mans [sic] pupils & actual disciples. And tho' the faults of New England spring from the same philosophy yet there is something glorious in having named in the quiet of a study by one individual intelligence the thoughts & the character of whole generations of the people. . . . The ambition of a Philosopher is to be what Edwards now is[,] a man absolutely growing brighter & better known as the times advance. . . . I want to revolutionize philosophy. I want to be an Augustine or an Edwards.

John Miller to Sally McDowell

My father was a man of intense convictions and of intense purposes, and the power of propagating them. These qualities, combined with a nature both sympathetic and courageous, enabled him to exert a wide influence in the theological world and in the community where he lived for nearly fifty years. Professor Silliman said to me after his death that no death had occurred since that of Dr. Dwight which had been so deeply felt in all New England.

Rebecca Taylor Hatch, *Personal Reminiscences and Memorials*

We may believe . . . that the New England theology will have this reproduction of its essential ideas, at least, in the new evangelical creed of the future. . . . It may prove to be the case that the traditional theology has, in a general way, set a type from which the Christian mind as a whole will never depart.

George A. Gordon, "The Collapse of the New England Theology"

As we have seen throughout this analysis of Taylor's share in Edwards's legacy, Taylor's claims to Edwardsian paternity were well-founded.[1] In ways personal, professional, institutional, and theological, his life took most of its shape from a uniquely Edwardsian theological culture. His perpetuation of that culture did entail an expansion of its boundaries, a greater expansion than it had ever experienced before. Indeed, his insistence that natural ability obviated the seeker's need for grace (though only in theory) proved more far-reaching than even the Taylorites would have wished. It inadvertently took an unstable set of Edwardsian cultural boundaries and helped to tax them beyond the point of no return. Thus, by the end of Taylor's life, despite the efforts of Edwards Park (and other, less adamant New England patriots) to shore up the walls of a religious culture that was now crumbling all around, the Edwardsian tradition was on the wane—henceforth, it would live on mainly in the "mystic cords" of historical memory.[2] Edward Shils is surely right that "traditions, to survive, must be fitting to the circumstances in which they operate."[3] But as Edwardsian history shows, adaptation has its limits. Though remarkably resilient, the Edwardsian culture was not as elastic as Taylor and company had dared to hope. Or put in yet another way, it would not prove possible for Taylor's disciples to take up his challenge and "go over Niagara" without either crashing on the rocks below or learning to swim in other waters.

But though the Tylerites, Princetonians, and recent historians of American religion have seized on Taylor as a scapegoat for the dissolution of Edwards's legacy, the Edwardsian movement grew exponentially during the early nineteenth century and thus its precarious cultural expansion was inevitable. As thousands upon thousands joined the rolls of New England's "pure" churches, diversification and disagreements were to be expected. Taylor was certainly not the first Edwardsian—nor would he be the last—to retool the doctrines of his teachers for a new generation of American sinners. In fact, if anything was unique about New Haven's theological agenda, it was the extent to which it succeeded in pervading America's evangelical churches. Contrary to one recent interpreter, "Taylor's influence" did not "[prove] ephemeral." Nor did New Haven's most famous thinker become "only a footnote in American theology."[4] Rather, by scattering Edwardsian seed broadly over the fertile soil of the new nation, Taylor enabled it to take root and bear fruit in a bewildering variety of ways.

In conclusion, then, I move beyond the usual story of Edwardsian declension to a summary of Taylor's own substantial legacy to post-Edwardsian America. After surveying his oft-attested influence among Congregationalists (both in New England and to the west) and Presbyterians (especially those of the New School), I address his broader contributions to American religious and cultural history.

"The New England Conscience"

At Yale, Taylor lived on in the preaching and teaching of his successors. He had tried hard *not* to make disciples, encouraging his students to think for themselves and promoting a recontextualization of Edwards more than his own peculiar opinions. After his death, moreover, Yale underwent a period of marked secularization during which theological study was eclipsed by the rise of modern science. Taylor's name and views were hallowed there for the rest of the nineteenth century, however, and his example lived on in the scholarship of even those who surpassed his thought.[5]

In May of 1872, at the Divinity School's semicentennial celebration, George Park Fisher delivered an address that confirmed the strength of Taylor's reputation as well as its identification with Edwards and the opening up of the Edwardsian culture. Charting the history of Yale Divinity School and Taylor's predominant place within it, he took pains to characterize New Haven Theology as a subspecies of Edwardsian thought, describing Taylor as the most important late promoter of the New England Theology. I have quoted this speech in chapter 00 to show that Taylor's colleagues deemed him an Edwardsian. I mention it here to add a word about his legacy. It is worthy of note that after all that had taken place in the contested history of Edwardsian thought, in 1872 Yale continued to consider itself a faithful steward of Edwards's legacy—and viewed Taylor's own significance largely in broader Edwardsian terms. Indeed, at one of the high points of his speech, Fisher claimed Edwards as Yale's own in words that were sure to offend his colleagues down in Princeton. Alluding vividly to the (biblical) patriarch Joseph's desire to be buried in the land of promise—not in Egypt, his home in exile and eventually a land of bondage for the people of God—Fisher declared that although Edwards was now buried in Princeton's cemetery, "had he lived in these days of easy and swift conveyance, he would have given a commandment respecting his bones like that which Joseph gave to his brethren," that is, "ye shall carry up my bones from hence" and bury them in Canaan (Gen. 50: 24–25).[6]

Those whose lives Taylor touched most deeply exhibited a similar approach to his legacy, putting their Taylorite inheritance to use in the extension of broader New England perspectives. Moving past the debates of the 1830s over the details of Taylor's doctrine, most of them championed New Haven Theology for its crucial place in Edwardsian history. Noah Porter, Taylor's son-in-law and a leader at Yale for 40 years (serving as president of the college from 1871 to 1886), remained a Taylorite all his life—even after imbibing Coleridge, studying in Germany and expanding his purview. Leonard Bacon, who succeeded Taylor both at the Center Church and at Yale (where he taught theology for 15 years), likewise remained "an ardent, though not undiscriminating, adherent of the New Haven theology." And a host of others at Yale as well, from Fisher himself to Samuel Harris, while not embracing all of Taylor's pronouncements, nevertheless promoted his legacy as their century's greatest Edwardsian.[7]

Outside New Haven, Taylor's views contributed powerfully to American culture, primarily by infusing the moral ethos of the Edwardsian theological culture into the recesses of what Perry Miller once described as "the New England conscience"—a conscience "created in New England by the geographical isolation of the region and solidified under the pressure of the climate," but a conscience, according to Miller, that "proved to be an exportable commodity."[8]

In New England itself, as we have seen, Taylor's influence was widely felt. Not only did his theology manage to divide Connecticut's General Association but his opening up of the Edwardsian culture changed the face of New England Theology. Even at Andover, where President Porter had been so suspicious of Taylor's views and where the faculty proved quite reluctant to speak directly about New Haven, leading thinkers like Stuart and Park proved sympathetic to Taylor's thought.

Moses Stuart had been claimed in the 1830s by both the Taylorites and the Tylerites and, as a cautious biblical scholar, usually avoided intramural disputes. But as a student of Timothy Dwight, former pastor of New Haven's Center Church and a contributor to the *Christian Spectator*, he had a soft place in his heart for New Haven Theology. Consequently, he came up for criticism (along with Taylor) in Spring's *Dissertation on Native Depravity*. And as John H. Giltner has shown in his recent treatment of Stuart's biblical scholarship, Stuart's work on original sin, "though unoriginal, . . . was important because of its exegetical thoroughness. His contribution was to provide the New Haven 'liberals,' Taylor chief among them, a solid exegetical ground for their speculative conclusions."[9]

Edwards Park was too young to be claimed by either party in the 1830s. And as he matured, he devoted his energies primarily to unifying the Edwardsians. But by the time that he assumed the Abbot Chair at Andover in 1847, it is fair to say that he, too, had been won over to New Haven Theology.[10] Though he had done his training in divinity under Leonard Woods at Andover Seminary, he became disappointed (like Taylor himself) with Woods's engagement of Unitarianism and dissatisfied as well with Woods's critique of Taylor's *Concio*. Thus after a two-year stint in ministry to the people of Braintree, Massachusetts, where Park earned a reputation as a winsome revival preacher, he ventured forth to Yale to study Taylorism at its source. He spent much of the winter of 1834–35 sitting in on Taylor's lectures before embarking on his own theological career. When he emerged a decade later as Woods's heir apparent to the Abbot Chair, his divergence from Woods and Andover's old guard caused no minor in-house quarrel. On almost everything that mattered—from natural ability to original sin and from theodicy to regeneration—Park had adopted essentially Taylorite views. He did not label himself a Taylorite. Nor did he simply parrot Taylor's teachings. But the similarities were unmistakable for all who had eyes to see.[11]

It is not surprising, then, that Park's vision of the tradition of the New England Theology proved much more expansive than the vision of the Tylerites. As one who relished the cultural ascendancy of Jonathan Edwards's New Divinity throughout the Calvinistic churches of New England, Park was loath to allow the recondite rivalry of a few academics to divide the swelling ranks of Edwardsian orthodoxy. He had inherited the Taylorite penchant for evangelical ecumenism, viewing rifts among the orthodox as private family affairs. Since the Unitarians had begun sharing the trinitarian Congregationalists' backyard, moreover, he tried to keep from hanging dirty laundry on the line. He often covered up the discord within New England's Edwardsian tradition by applying a liberal measure of what he called "the theology of the feelings." Where differences seemed irreconcilable between the Tasters and the Exercisers or between Taylor and his more high Calvinistic foes, Park's approach to Edwardsian history was to focus on the forest and ignore the tangled underbrush below (tangled by what he termed the more polemical and precisionistic "theology of the intellect"). While, in doing so, he did provide a map of the New England Theology that proved more useful in the air than on the ground, he did not fabricate or invent the continuity of his cherished tradition by simply projecting a deep-felt wish to get along.[12]

To the west, Taylor's dilation of New England's traditional regional orthodoxies paved the way for the spread of its churches and their theology on the frontier. This proved especially attractive to denominational officials involved in church planting and home missions, and working to establish truly national denominational structures. Among Congregationalists, Taylor's distension of the Edwardsian culture aided the efforts of church leaders to resolve the tensions that had been mounting between theologians back east and church planters out west over evangelistic methods and the utility of Calvinist dogma. In so doing, it eased the development of a national Congregationalist identity that was no longer tethered quite so tightly to New England's historic Calvinism, or divided quite so clearly in its ministries by the Appalachians. This development culminated in the first national meeting of the denomination, held in Albany, New York, in October of 1852, where resolutions were passed repairing now-damaged relations between east and west, condemning careless accusations of western heresy made by the Tylerites (who had grown rather nervous about doctrinal laxity on the frontier),[13] and encouraging a spirit of cooperation among denominational leaders across the country in building a uniquely Congregational ministry outside New England.[14]

As a result of Taylor's role in building bridges to the west, Taylorite clergy made major inroads into the land beyond the mountains. Just as turnpikes, canals, steamboats, railroads, and rapid outmigration began to connect provincial New England to the world beyond its borders, New England's support for the work of home missions connected the Edwardsian culture personally to the millions of Americans who now inhabited that world. New Haven's churches and Yale College supported numerous missions to the west, some as far away as California and the Sandwich Islands. And of the hundreds of Taylor students who left New Haven to serve the churches, we know that one out of every four settled west of Pennsylvania.[15]

Inasmuch as Taylor's interest in the religious culture of the west was eventually compounded exponentially by his students and their colleagues, a brief survey of the highlights of his influence must suffice. A number of Taylorites served as pioneering Edwardsian missionaries to the Sandwich Islands, leaving New Haven to plant new churches there beginning in 1822. In fact, as one nineteenth-century historian boasted:

> The missionary movement to those islands originated in New Haven and was for many years largely supported by the churches on the Green. To these churches therefore it is principally due that that young republic to-day is controlled by American institutions and American influence, instead of being an appendage of Great Britain or France. In recognition of this fact, when the interior of the Center Church was renovated in 1843, its pulpit was sent to the Sandwich Islands at the request of the people there and set up in the First Church of Honolulu as a memorial of New Haven, upon whose Green not only that church but the Hawaiian nation itself may be fairly said to have been founded.[16]

As the Hawaiian mission was developing (and as discussed in chapter 3), Julian Sturtevant and the "Illinois Band" left Yale in 1829 to settle the Mississippi Valley for the Edwardsians. Sturtevant himself was such a Taylorite that in 1833 he and his colleague Edward Beecher (Lyman's son) were tried for heresy before their colleagues within the newly founded and hotly contested Illinois Presbytery. Eventually exonerated of heresy, these Taylorites continued to establish churches, colleges (such as Illinois, Beloit, and Grinnell), and benevolent societies that clearly reflected the Edwardsian values of their homeland.[17] Meanwhile, Jeremiah Root Barnes left Yale for frontier Indiana, where he preached and helped plant churches beginning in 1836. He went on to become a financial agent of Marietta College (in Ohio), to found the Young Ladies Seminary near Cincinnati in 1850, and eventually to help establish Carleton College in Minnesota.[18] Joseph Benton, a Yale alumnus and yet another ardent Taylorite, headed to California during the gold rush of 1849. He served as chaplain of the Boston and California Joint Stock Mining and Trading Company, becoming just one of several Taylor students to cultivate California's religious culture. Founding the First Church of Christ in Sacramento, Benton went on to serve as founding coeditor of *The Pacific* (the first major religious periodical in California). He served as a founding member of the board of trustees of the College of California (later the University of California), as the first moderator of the General Association of California's Congregational clergy, and as the founding professor of theological studies in Pacific Theological Seminary (later the Pacific School of Religion).[19]

In almost every case, Taylorite efforts to export Edwardsian culture were met with resistance and creative engagement by other settlers in the west. Consequently, Edwardsian culture looked somewhat different on the frontiers, having adapted by necessity to local cultures and practical exigencies. As the best of the western historians remind us, wherever New England's ambassadors traveled to "redeem" the peoples of the west, they wound up negotiating cultural settlements for the sake of expediency and effectiveness. But one might argue that their very flexibility with regard to cultural adaptation had been facilitated by Taylor's expansion of Edwardsian culture back in New England. Indeed, Edwardsians in the west succeeded in spreading New England values at least in part *because* they compromised and cooperated for the sake of the gospel. This often upset more confessional Protestants. But it also enabled Edwardsian ministers to exert great influence, Edwardsian influence, wherever they went.[20]

"The New Divinity Tried"

Many of Taylor's best students, at least 172, served either as Presbyterian or "Presbygational" clergy.[21] And as alluded to above, Taylor's appeal among both groups proved a major source of friction in the Presbyterian Church. The Presbygationalists owed their origins to a long-standing Plan of Union (1801), devised by Connecticut Congregationalists and Presbyterians in the North who sought to facilitate frontier evangelism by joining missionary forces. By the 1830s, their union churches, which became Presbyterian more often than not, aroused suspicion among denominational purists. Attracted from the beginning to the evangelical earnestness of the New Divinity, by the 1830s most Presbygationalists exhibited pronounced New Haven tendencies. Thus, when their "New School" party arose to a position of dominance in the North, "Old School" opponents reacted harshly, fearing infection from New England. They annulled the Plan of Union and severed four synods that it had produced after mustering a majority at the General Assembly of 1837. When the New School decided, in turn, to form their own denomination, Old Schoolers had every reason to place the bulk of the blame on Taylor. As even Zebulon Crocker, a Connecticut Congregationalist and a defender of Taylor, admitted of the notorious Presbyterian schism of 1837, "there can be no doubt" that it owed its "origin and result to the controversies in Connecticut, more than to any other single cause."[22]

Historians have long debated how best to interpret this story of schism, whose several subplots included the heresy trials of high-profile New School clergymen—most notably Lyman Beecher (1835) and Albert Barnes (1830–31, 1835)—and even the founding in New York City of the largely New School Union Seminary (1836).[23] Some have argued for close connections between the schism and the issue of slavery. But most have agreed that Taylor and/or the expansion of New England Theology that Taylor had encouraged played the most significant role in the Presbyterian disruption.[24] This is certainly not the place for a major discussion of Presbyterian history. But it should be noted that the vast majority of Taylor's contemporaries also attributed these developments to the role he played in infusing a liberal dose of Edwardsian culture into north-eastern evangelicalism.[25]

It should also be noted that Taylor himself supported the Presbyterian schism. He wrote to Lyman Beecher in March of 1837:

> [W]hat I long to see in the Presbyterian Church is a thorough separation of Old School and New School, brought about in the right way. I am fully convinced that the errors of Old School are calamitous, and too much so to seem to be countenanced by New School in that manner and degree in which they have been by union. The Old School men will never rest; and the question is, How much time and strength shall be expended in conflict? God means to effect a division ultimately—on the ground of essentials I do not say, but on the ground of expediency; and if I were king, I should say to the next General Assembly, Divide—not on the ground of heresy, and with mutual hate and denunciation, but divide for peace's sake, with mutual toleration, as sects differing so much, and with such conscience of the speculative importance of the differences that the cause of God will be better promoted. To the New School I should say, show your magnanimity by giving up Princeton Seminary and all Old School funds to the Old School party, and begin anew for yourselves. In five years and less you will have more funds, more seminaries, more power for God and his cause than the whole Presbyterian Church now possesses, and have it unclogged and unencumbered by that incubus which has so long made her strength weakness.[26]

As one with a long-standing interest in the Presbyterian Church, Taylor was sent to the General Assembly of 1838 as a delegate of Connecticut's General Association. And after arriving in Philadelphia to find two separate Assemblies meeting, he presented himself forthwith to the New School Assembly in Washington Square, which was meeting, somewhat ironically, in Albert Barnes's First Presbyterian Church—a congregation that Taylor had once been asked to serve.[27] He quickly became the main attraction, declaring confidently to the New School that "as a delegate from the General Association of Connecticut at this crisis, I have no hesitation in assuring this body of the cordial sympathy of the great majority of our ministers and churches"—a declaration soon denounced by both the Old School and the Tyerlites.[28]

Certainly, other factors were at work in the Presbyterian disruption—regional tensions, moral differences, divergent views of the church and its ministries. But none of these received as much attention during the schism as New Haven. Perhaps Pope has put it best: "Taylorism in itself did not precipitate the final disruption of the Presbyterian Church, but Taylorism and the misunderstandings which arose over it, coalescing with the deep unresolved tensions which had developed over New England Calvinism, conspired with ecclesiastical and social factors to bring about a major crisis, thus making the division of the Church appear not only necessary but also highly desirable to many of its leaders."[29]

Though not a student of Taylor himself, and though he had left the denomination well before 1837, Charles G. Finney was the most prominent early New School Presbyterian. Not coincidentally, Finney also did more than anyone else to popularize—some would say bastardize—Taylorite views. Scholars have often found it difficult to categorize Finney's thought, not least because he was a maverick who seldom acknowledged intellectual debts. Taking their cues from his opponents, many historians have portrayed Finney as the archetypal Jacksonian Arminian, a democratic critic of the leading traditions of American Calvinism.[30] Others have exaggerated Finney's ties to New Haven's strain of New England Calvinism, calling him Taylor's "true successor" and "chief disciple."[31] Most careful observers, however, have come down somewhere between these still-popular views, depicting Finney for what he was—a rather unusual and inconsistent New Haven–style Edwardsian preacher.[32]

His relationship with Taylor was never very warm. And Finney never enjoyed much respect from any of his more sophisticated seaboard colleagues. Moreover, during the height of the Taylorite controversy, Taylor worked hard to distance himself from Finney's agenda, going so far as to ask Finney himself to make their differences clear to the public.[33] But New Haven also defended its Finneyite colleagues from caustic Old School and Tylerite pundits attempting to whitewash their "New Divinity" in broad and careless Taylorite strokes. Most notoriously, when Asa Rand, who edited the sharply Tylerite *Volunteer*, tried to blame Taylor and Beecher for the worst of new measures revivalism, the response was sure and swift against what Beecher called Rand's "gall and bile," the Taylorites mounting a firm critique of his bully tactics.[34]

James H. Fairchild, Finney's student, colleague, editor, and successor to the presidency of Oberlin College, offered what is arguably the most accurate description of Finney's views: "His system of doctrine, when he came to Oberlin, was the New School Calvinism, in its essential features the theology of such men as Lyman Beecher and N. W. Taylor— what has come to be recognized as the advanced New England Theology. . . . This Theology he inculcated in his classes, and with a few modifications, or improvements, as Mr. Finney regarded them, it became the Oberlin Theology as it has sometimes been called."

Indeed, the best interpreters of Finney's thought have recognized the veracity of Fairchild's assessment, as well as the power of Finney's ministry in amplifying (if also distorting) Taylor's legacy. In sum, though Finney was not a disciple of Taylor, his revivalistic emphases on natural ability and immediate repentance served to ingrain the potent dye of Taylor's theology indelibly into the fiber of the evangelical mind.[35]

"The Main Bridge"

As Finney's connection to Taylor makes clear, despite the efforts made by the Taylorites to keep tight reigns on their theology, many contemporaries exploited it for ends that Taylor himself did not uphold. Through the work of Finney alone, Taylorite doctrine was used to support evangelical feminism, abolitionism, even Liberty Party politics.[36] More troublesome to Taylor than Finney was William Lloyd Garrison, who attended Lyman Beecher's Hanover Street Church upon his move to Boston in 1826 and found support for his doctrine of immediate abolition in the Edwardsian doctrine of immediate repentance.[37] Even John Humphrey Noyes, the Oneida Community founder who studied theology with Taylor at Yale until expelled for perfectionism in 1834, exploited his teacher's understanding of human natural ability in support his own, much more radical anthropology.[38]

Indeed, Taylor's thought informed not only those whose religious commitments resembled his own but also many who left the evangelical movement entirely. The New Theology of later liberals, the tradition of American Pragmatism, even the politics of the progressives, have all been said to have grown from the forbidding soil of Edwardsian New England—but only after its aeration at the hands of Taylor and his associates.[39] To be sure, Taylor's promotion of critical thinking and evangelical ecumenicity attracted even students of his at Yale like Horace Bushnell and Theodore Munger. And while such men moved on eventually to repudiate their teacher's Edwardsian views, constituting the leadership of postbellum America's liberal Protestant religious establishment, they did so on methodological grounds first shown to them by Taylor. As Munger remembered of Bushnell, "Dr. Bushnell, late in life, said, 'Taylor taught me one thing— that it doesn't hurt a man to think for himself.'"[40] Anson Stokes would put it well: "Taylor was the last, as Edwards was the first, of the great minds who built up the New England Theology. His thought formed the main bridge from the inherited orthodoxy of the eighteenth century to the liberal tendencies of later Congregationalism. In doctrinal belief he was nearer the first group; in the spirit of free inquiry, and of earnest and fearless search after truth, he was nearer the last."[41]

For Taylor, as for millions of his American successors, the proof of one's theology lay in the preaching and virtuous living.[42] And though the success of this pragmatic criterion has often tended to undermine respect for religious tradition (even Taylor's own), this is certainly not what Taylor himself intended. His own perpetuation of the Edwardsian theological tradition did favor the preachers and churches of the present over the guardians of the past. But it also contributed to the diffusion and accessibility of Edwards's influence throughout America in a manner unprecedented among New England's more cautious custodians. As recent scholarship has revealed, Edwards's legacy has been appropriated in countless arenas of American culture (not to mention around the world) at a rate of speed that has only accelerated since the decline of New England Calvinism.[43] Harriet Beecher Stowe said well just prior to Taylor's death, the Edwardsians have "made the theological deep of New England to boil like a pot." Indeed, "the agitation of [their] course remains to this day."[44]

But if Taylor extended Edwardsian influence among those outside of evangelicalism— fueling the engines of groups that supplanted the evangelicals and their cultural leadership—he certainly also exerted an influence on later evangelicals as well, those left behind and disinherited during what George Marsden has aptly described as the long transition in American culture "from Protestant establishment to established non-belief."[45] As Marsden himself has argued, Taylor played a significant role in the rise of fundamentalism.[46] And while it would take another book to map out the ways in which this is true, clearly his emphasis on revival and conversion, his intense concern for individual souls, not to mention his sunny view of disestablishment and "spiritual politics," all contributed not only to the "great reversal" discussed earlier, but also to the sustenance of evangelicals who would live on the margins of American culture.

As Taylor lay dying, yet another major revival was underway, one that adumbrated the future of evangelical cultural engagement while recapitulating the course of Taylor's ministry. Known as the "businessmen's revival" of 1857–58, its lay leaders proclaimed the power of prayer—and of their numerous prayer meetings—in the transformation of American hearts, as well as the need for a new awakening of American culture from below.[47] Taylor had called for such a revival in August of 1856 at a meeting of the alumni of Yale Divinity School. Referring to the decline of Congregationalism since the days of disestablishment,[48] he pointed to grassroots Methodist activism as the spiritual wave of the future. "The pastoral relation has done much for the churches," he said, "but it will not do all. We must have a laborious church. Look at the Methodists, if you want to see what this will do! Here in New-Haven, I can remember when there were only two of them, and one used to preach to the other. Every man of them has been at work including some that might better have left it alone." Taylor went on to herald lay ministry as a crucial means to spiritual revival in a day and age when New England's established spiritual leadership was growing lethargic. In so doing, he symbolized personally the transition of Edwardsian evangelicals from magisterial cultural authorities to increasingly marginal cultural prophets.[49]

In February of 1858 this new revival hit Yale College. As reported enthusiastically by H. B. Wright:

> The Yale revival started on the day of prayer for colleges and . . . was characterized by multiplied and crowded prayer-meetings, which sometimes embraced every member of a given college class. There were no special preachers. The members of the faculty most prominent in the meetings were President Woolsey, Dr. Fisher, Professors Goodrich and Thacher, and Tutor Hutchison. No special church services were held. There were early morning entry prayer groups, and large numbers of the students took part in the morning meetings held in Centre Church by the townspeople. On Sundays many students went by twos to surrounding towns and held evangelistic services, one livery stable-keeper, Philemon Hoadley, who never let horses on Sunday, giving free use of his teams for this purpose during the revival. The college church was greatly augmented by the conversions at this time.[50]

Apparently, so were other local churches. For at the state convention of Sunday School teachers held in New Haven later that year, it was estimated that 8,000 of Connecticut's children had converted in the revival.[51]

A fitting ending to Taylor's life. And if he had any inkling on his deathbed of the scope of this revival, he must have departed his friends and family a happy man. For though he had fractured the Edwardsian culture, dividing the ranks of Edwards's heirs, in the process he had also set loose the forces of Edwardsian spirituality to empower the religious life of American culture at large. He went out in glory, to be sure—though, as he surely would have insisted, it was a glory not his own.

Notes

Introduction

1. Taylor's vast influence is detailed in chapter 8.

2. I have made this argument in abbreviated form in "Nathaniel William Taylor and the Edwardsian Tradition: A Reassessment," in *Jonathan Edwards's Writings: Text, Context, Interpretation*, ed. Stephen J. Stein (Bloomington: Indiana University Press, 1996), pp. 139-58.

3. As I will discuss later, I am building here on historian Thomas Bender's conceptualization of what he calls "the cultures of intellectual life." See "The Cultures of Intellectual Life: The City and the Professions," reprinted in his *Intellect and Public Life: Essays on the Social History of Academic Intellectuals in the United States* (Baltimore, Md.: Johns Hopkins University Press, 1993), pp. 3-15; and Thomas Bender, *New York Intellect: A History of Intellectual Life in New York City, from 1750 to the Beginnings of Our Own Time* (New York: Alfred A. Knopf, 1987).

4. Technically speaking, "the New England Theology" was the tradition of Protestant thought that stemmed from the work of Edwards and flourished, I will argue, until the middle of the nineteenth century. As distinguished from the rest of New England theology, "the New England Theology" was uniquely Edwardsian. A tradition of variations on certain key Edwardsian themes, it represented the first indigenous theological movement in America.

5. Nathaniel W. Taylor, *Concio ad Clerum: A Sermon Delivered in the Chapel of Yale College, September 10, 1828* (New Haven, Conn.: H. Howe, 1828).

6. On this quest and its historiographical significance, see my recent article entitled "Edwards and His Mantle: The Historiography of the New England Theology," *New England Quarterly* 71 (March 1998): 97-119.

7. As will be discussed in chapter 2, New England's "Old Calvinists" emerged in the years following the Great Awakening to oppose the Edwardsian "New Divinity" and advocate a moderate, means-oriented approach to Christian conversion.

8. Sidney Mead, *Nathaniel William Taylor, 1786-1858: A Connecticut Liberal* (Chicago: University of Chicago Press, 1942), pp. 12-23, 95-127 (quotations taken from pp. 124, ix); and Sidney E. Mead, *The Old Religion in the Brave New World: Reflections on the Relation Between Christendom and the Republic* (Berkeley: University of California Press, 1977), pp. 51-54, 105-32. On Mead's view of Taylor, see also Sidney E. Mead, *The Lively Experiment: The Shaping of Christianity in America* (New York: Harper and Row, 1963), pp. 123-24, 185. For background to Mead's interpretation of Taylor and of American religious history generally, see the Festschrift for Mead edited by Jerald C. Brauer, *The Lively Experiment Continued* (Macon, Ga.: Mercer University Press, 1987), esp. pp. 3-67.

9. Zebulon Crocker, whose *The Catastrophe of the Presbyterian Church, in 1837, Including a Full View of the Recent Theological Controversies in New England* (New Haven, Conn.: B. and W. Noyes, 1838) Mead had read, associated Taylor with the Old Calvinists (p. 295); and George Leon Walker, *Some Aspects of the Religious Life of New England with Special Reference to the Congregationalists* (New York: Silver, Burdett, and Company, 1897), p. 151, wrote that Taylor's understanding of the role of self-love in regeneration "did little more . . . than revert to the Old-Calvinist position."

10. George Nye Boardman, *A History of New England Theology* (New York: A.D.F. Randolph Company, 1899), and Frank Hugh Foster, *A Genetic History of the New England Theology* (Chicago: University of Chicago Press, 1907).

11. Mark A. Noll, "Moses Mather (Old Calvinist) and the Evolution of Edwardseanism," *Church History* 49 (September 1980): 273–85; Allen C. Guelzo, *Edwards on the Will: A Century of American Theological Debate* (Middletown, Conn.: Wesleyan University Press, 1989), pp. 218–71; David W. Kling, *A Field of Divine Wonders: The New Divinity and Village Revivals in North-western Connecticut, 1792–1822* (University Park: Pennsylvania State University Press, 1993), pp. 91–93, 232–43; and William R. Sutton, "Benevolent Calvinism and the Moral Government of God: The Influence of Nathaniel W. Taylor on Revivalism in the Second Great Awakening," *Religion and American Culture* 2 (Winter 1992): 28–29, 40.

12. William G. McLoughlin, "Introduction: The American Evangelicals: 1800–1900," in *The American Evangelicals, 1800–1900: An Anthology,* ed. William G. McLoughlin (New York: Harper and Row, 1968), pp. 4–5; and William G. McLoughlin, *Revivals, Awakenings, and Reform: An Essay on Religion and Social Change in America, 1607–1977,* Chicago History of American Religion (Chicago: University of Chicago Press, 1978), p. 113.

There are both implicit and explicit portrayals of Taylor as an Arminianizer. Of course, Joseph Haroutunian, *Piety Versus Moralism: The Passing of the New England Theology* (New York: Henry Holt, 1932), pp. 266–80, represents the most significant of the implicit portrayals. For a sampling of other implicit portrayals, see Henry B. Smith, "The Theological System of Emmons," in *Faith and Philosophy: Discourses and Essays,* ed. George L. Prentiss (New York: Scribner, Armstrong, and Co., 1877), pp. 215–63; Alexander V. G. Allen, "The Transition in New England Theology," *Atlantic Monthly* 68 (December 1891): 774, 775; Timothy L. Smith, *Revivalism and Social Reform in Mid-Nineteenth-Century America* (New York: Abingdon Press, 1957), for whom Taylor plays a significant role in "revivalism's triumph over Calvinism" (pp. 28, 88–89, 92); Kenneth E. Rowe, "Nestor of Orthodoxy New England Style: A Study in the Theology of Edwards Amasa Park, 1808–1900" (Ph.D. diss., Drew University, 1969), p. 240; George M. Marsden, *The Evangelical Mind and the New School Presbyterian Experience: A Case Study of Thought and Theology in Nineteenth-Century America* (New Haven, Conn.: Yale University Press, 1970) p. 58; and Iain H. Murray, *Revival and Revivalism: The Making and Marring of American Evangelicalism, 1750–1858* (Carlisle, Penn.: Banner of Truth Trust, 1994), pp. 259–63.

For a sampling of explicit portrayals, see Benjamin Breckenridge Warfield, "Edwards and the New England Theology," in *Encyclopedia of Religion and Ethics,* vol. 5, ed. James Hastings (New York: Charles Scribner's Sons, 1912), p. 226; Whitney R. Cross, *The Burned-Over District: The Social and Intellectual History of Enthusiastic Religion in Western New York, 1800–1850* (Ithaca, N.Y.: Cornell University Press, 1950), p. 27; Otto W. Heick, *A History of Christian Thought* (Philadelphia: Fortress Press, 1966), 2: 424; John F. Thornbury, *God Sent Revival: The Story of Asahel Nettleton and the Second Great Awakening* (Grand Rapids, Mich.: Evangelical Press, 1977), pp. 189–94; Joseph W. Phillips, *Jedidiah Morse and New England Congregationalism* (New Brunswick, N.J.: Rutgers University Press, 1983), pp. 7–8; Keith J. Hardman, *The Spiritual Awakeners: American Revivalists from Solomon Stoddard to D. L. Moody* (Chicago: Moody Press, 1983), p. 127; Walter H. Conser, Jr., *Church and Confession: Conservative Theologians in Ger-*

many, England, and America 1815-1866 (Macon, Ga.: Mercer University Press, 1984), p. 236; Paul Goodman, *Towards a Christian Republic: Antimasonry and the Great Transition in New England, 1826-1836* (New York: Oxford University Press, 1988), p. 62; Leonard I. Sweet, "Nineteenth-Century Evangelicalism," in Charles H. Lippy and Peter H. Williams, eds., *Encyclopedia of the American Religious Experience: Studies of Traditions and Movements* (New York: Charles Scribner's Sons, 1988), 2: 876; Charles Sellers, *The Market Revolution: Jacksonian America, 1815-1846* (New York: Oxford University Press, 1991), p. 210; John H. Gerstner, *The Rational Biblical Theology of Jonathan Edwards*, 3 vols. (Powhatan, Va.: Berea Publications, 1991-), 1: 552-63; Julius H. Rubin, *Religious Melancholy and Protestant Experience in America*, Religion in America Series (New York: Oxford University Press, 1994), pp. 131-32, and 125-55 passim; and Paul K. Conkin, *The Uneasy Center: Reformed Christianity in Antebellum America* (Chapel Hill: University of North Carolina Press, 1995), pp. 220, 264.

13. Noteworthy exceptions to this rule include H. Shelton Smith, *Changing Conceptions of Original Sin: A Study in American Theology since 1750* (New York: Charles Scribner's Sons, 1955), p. 112, who characterized the Taylorites as "liberal Edwardeans" and who characterized Taylor's opponents as "conservative Edwardeans"; Earl Pope, *New England Calvinism and the Disruption of the Presbyterian Church* (New York: Garland, 1987; 1962), pp. 67-68, who thought that "the liberal strands in both Edwardeanism and Old Calvinism converged in Taylor" and argued that, while "Mead was correct in pointing out affinities of Taylor's idea to Old Calvinism," he "failed to recognize . . . that despite his innovations Taylor was still an Edwardean at heart"; Bruce Kuklick, *Churchmen and Philosophers: From Jonathan Edwards to John Dewey* (New Haven, Conn.: Yale University Press, 1985), pp. 94-111, who portrays Taylor ambivalently as both an Edwardsian and one whose "significance for later American theological and philosophical debate was his role in the rise of anti-Calvinist tendencies" (though Kuklick realizes that this role "is more diffuse and complex than commentators have realized" [pp. 108-9]); Robert C. Whittemore, *The Transformation of the New England Theology* (New York: Peter Lang, 1987), pp. 240-88; and Leo P. Hirrel, *Children of Wrath: New School Calvinism and Antebellum Reform* (Lexington: University Press of Kentucky, 1998), who recognizes that "Taylor borrowed liberally from many traditions" (p. 27), but tends to portray him primarily as a rationalistic accommodator to the enlightened spirit of his times (pp. 1-2, 25-28).

14. Again, a fuller analysis of these historiographical developments can be found in "Edwards and His Mantle."

15. Joseph Conforti has made this case well in "Edwards A. Park and the Creation of the New England Theology, 1840-1870," in Stein, ed., *Jonathan Edwards's Writings*. The seamlessness of Park's creation is most readily apparent in his essay "New England Theology; With Comments on a Third Article in the Biblical Repertory and Princeton Review, Relating to a Convention Sermon," BS 9 (January 1852): 170-220.

16. For the very nontheological focus of the new religious history, see Philip R. VanderMeer and Robert P. Swierenga, "Introduction: Progress and Prospects in the New Religious History," in *Belief and Behavior: Essays in the New Religious History*, ed. Philip R. VanderMeer and Robert P. Swierenga (New Brunswick, N.J.: Rutgers University Press, 1991), pp. 1-14; and Jay Dolan, "The New Religious History," *Reviews in American History* 15 (September 1987): 449-54. Among the many recent collections of essays in the new religious history, see esp. Harry S. Stout and D. G. Hart, eds., *New Directions in American Religoius History* (New York: Oxford University Press, 1997); David D. Hall, ed., *Lived Religion in America: Toward a History of Practice* (Princeton, N.J.: Princeton University Press, 1997); Thomas A. Tweed, ed., *Retelling U. S. Religious History* (Berkeley: University of California Press, 1997); and Jon Butler and Harry S. Stout, eds., *Religion in American History: A Reader* (New York: Oxford University Press, 1998).

17. Charles L. Cohen, "The Post-Puritan Paradigm of Early American Religious History," *William and Mary Quarterly* 54 (October 1997): 700.

18. Rodney Stark, *The Rise of Christianity: A Sociologist Reconsiders History* (Princeton, N.J.: Princeton University Press, 1996), p. 209; and David S. Shields, "Joy and Dread among the Early Americanists," *William and Mary Quarterly* 57 (July 2000): 639.

19. Edward Shils, *Tradition* (Chicago: University of Chicago Press, 1981), p. 44.

20. Shils, *Tradition*, p. 258. Shils's work is quite useful for anyone seeking to understand the development and significance of intellectual traditions. For understanding the innovations of the later Edwardsians, the following theme from Shils's chapter "Why Traditions Change: Endogenous Factors" is also helpful: "There is something in tradition which calls forth a desire to change it by making improvements in it. There is an unceasing striving in the strongest human minds for 'better' truth, for greater clarity and coherence, and for adequacy of expression" (p. 214).

21. See esp. Joseph Conforti, *Samuel Hopkins and the New Divinity Movement: Calvinism, the Congregational Ministry, and Reform in New England Between the Great Awakenings* (Grand Rapids, Mich.: Christian University Press, 1981); Joseph Conforti, *Jonathan Edwards, Religious Tradition, and American Culture* (Chapel Hill: University of North Carolina Press, 1995); Kling, *Field of Divine Wonders*; and Mark Valeri, *Law and Providence in Joseph Bellamy's New England: The Origins of the New Divinity in Revolutionary America*, Religion in America Series (New York: Oxford University Press, 1994).

Chapter 1

1. Samuel Orcutt, *History of the Towns of New Milford and Bridgewater, Connecticut, 1703–1882* (Hartford: Case, Lockwood, and Brainard Company, 1882), pp. 201–2, the most comprehensive source on New Milford's early history.

2. What little we do know of this patriarch of the Taylor clan in Connecticut comes primarily from Samuel Orcutt, *History of the Towns of New Milford and Bridgewater*, p. 773. But see also Mead, *Nathaniel William Taylor*, p. 3, who offers a fine account of Taylor's family heritage; the Taylor family genealogical file at the New Milford Historical Society; and John Taylor's will, composed on November 24, 1645, on file in the Probate Office of Hartford, Connecticut. On early Windsor, Connecticut, see Henry R. Stiles, *History of Ancient Windsor* (n.p., 1859).

3. Cotton Mather, *Magnalia Christi Americana; or, The Ecclesiastical History of New-England; From Its First Planting, in the Year 1620, unto the Year of Our Lord 1698. In Seven Books* (Hartford, Conn.: Silas Andrus and Son, 1853; 1702), 1, 6. 6.

4. Henry Wadsworth Longfellow, "Phantom Ship," in *The Complete Poetical Works of Longfellow*, The Cambridge Poets (Boston: Houghton Mifflin Company, [1893]), p. 188.

5. As made evident in John Taylor's will, Rhoda had now been widowed twice, for she had been a widowed mother of an unspecified number of daughters when Taylor married her. Taylor provided for Rhoda as well as her daughters in his will.

6. Orcutt, *History of the Towns of New Milford and Bridgewater*, pp. 773–74; the Taylor family genealogical file at the New Milford Historical Society; and Mead, *Nathaniel William Taylor*, pp. 3–4. The first name of Nathaniel William Taylor's grandfather has been rendered both "Nathanael" and "Nathaniel." For the sake of clarity and consistency, I have adopted the former spelling.

7. Orcutt, *History of the Towns of New Milford and Bridgewater*, pp. 623–25; the Taylor family genealogical file at the New Milford Historical Society; AAP, 1: 467–69; and Mead, *Nathaniel William Taylor*, p. 4. The unanimity of Taylor's call was made possible by the recent departure from the First Church of a minority group of radical New Lights who had been contending for control of the congregation. These New Lights were not allowed to build their own meetinghouse until 1753. Technically speaking, then, while largely absent from most congregational activities, they remained Taylor's parishioners and stirred up a great deal of religious strife during the early years of Taylor's ministry.

Tamar Boardman Taylor (1723–95) died on June 27, 1795, and Taylor was remarried in March of 1797 to Mrs. Zipporah Bennett (née Strong) of Huntington, New York.

8. The Rev. Thomas Robbins to Samuel Orcutt, September 9, 1851, printed in Orcutt's *History of the Towns of New Milford and Bridgewater*, pp. 624–25; and Stanley Griswold, *The Good Man's Prospects in the Hour of Death;–and His Voice from the World Beyond. Two Discourses, Delivered at New-Milford, Dec. 14th, 1800. Being the Sabbath Next After the Decease of The Rev. Nathanael Taylor, Late Pastor of the First Church of Christ in Said New-Milford* (New Milford, Conn.: n.p., 1800), p. 24.

9. The Taylor children were Urania (b. 1751), Nathaniel (b. 1753), Augustine (b. 1755), Tamar (b. 1759), and William (b. 1764).

10. In addition to the sources cited earlier, on the history of New Milford's First Church see also the booklet written by local historian Ross Detwiler, *History of The First Congregational Church, New Milford, Connecticut* (New Milford, Conn.: privately published, 1983).

11. Mead, *Nathaniel William Taylor*, pp. 12–23.

12. Robins to Orcutt, September 9, 1851, in Orcutt's *History of the Towns of New Milford and Bridgewater*, p. 625. While in theory Taylor adhered to the Half-Way Covenant (and was bound by the terms of his contract to uphold the Saybrook Platform), after midcentury the number of people joining New Milford's First Church as half-way members proved so much greater than the number joining in full communion that the church leadership became worried. Many parishioners began absenting themselves from worship (either from religious laxity or overscrupulosity regarding the terms of full communion) and proved difficult to reclaim. To make matters worse, the Episcopal church in town accepted members to full communion without a conversion relation, and New Milford's Separate Church began to attract a growing number of evangelical conversionists. In an attempt to counteract this problem and shore up its membership, the First Church voted in 1769 "that there is no half-way covenant" and began admitting half-way members to communion. Further, in 1772 it was voted that "all who are in covenant have a right to vote in the church meetings," whether or not they had related a conversion experience. In effect, then, Taylor and his congregation wound up adopting Stoddardean measures. See Orcutt, *History of the Towns of New Milford and Bridgewater*, pp. 145–49, 176–90 (quotations from p. 185). For evidence of the friendship of Taylor and Stiles, see esp. Franklin B. Dexter, ed., *The Literary Diary of Ezra Stiles*, 3 vols. (New York: Charles Scribner's Sons, 1901), 2: 208, 498–99; 3: 4, 368, 413, 436, 445–46, 490, 548.

13. Taylor's sermon to Connecticut's soldiers was entitled *Praise Due to God for All the Dispensations of His Wise and Holy Providence: A Sermon Preached at Crown-Point, at the Close of the Campaign, 1762* (New Haven, Conn.: J. Parker and Company, 1762). On Taylor's Revolutionary-era patriotism, see *AAP*, 1:468; Rebecca Taylor Hatch, *Personal Reminiscences and Memorials* (New York: Gillis Press, 1905), p. 1; and *Two Centuries of New Milford, Connecticut: An Account of the Bi-Centennial Celebration of the Founding of the Town Held June 15, 16, 17 and 18, 1907, with a Number of Historical Articles and Reminiscences* (New York: Grafton Press, 1907), p. 15. Roger Sherman served as a deacon in Taylor's church beginning in 1757, functioning as treasurer of the First Church Society as well.

14. For his part, Stanley Griswold served in New Milford only until 1802, when he left to pursue a career in journalism, politics, and public service on behalf of the Jeffersonian Democrats. Though highly esteemed in New Milford, his political allegiances got him in trouble with other clergymen in the region, the vast majority of whom remained ardent Federalists. See Orcutt, *History of the Towns of New Milford and Bridgewater*, pp. 268–70; Payne Kenyon Kilbourne, *A Biographical History of the County of Litchfield, Connecticut* (New York: Clark, Austin, and Co., 1851), pp. 84–88; *AAP*, 1: 468; and Franklin Bowditch Dexter, *Biographical Sketches of the Graduates of Yale College*, 6 vols. (New Haven, Conn.: Yale University Press, 1885–1912), 4: 476–81.

15. See Samuel Orcutt, *History of the Towns of New Milford and Bridgewater*, pp. 190, 265, 469–71; and Rachel D. Carley, ed., *Voices from the Past: A History as Told by the New Milford Historical Society's Portraits and Paintings* (West Kennebunk, Maine: Phoenix, 2000), p. 11. On the increasingly Edwardsian flavor of religious life in Litchfield County during this period, see especially Arthur Goodenough, *The Clergy of Litchfield County* (n.p.: Litchfield County University Club, 1909), pp. 10–17, 29–38, 40–42; and Kling, *A Field of Divine Wonders*, pp. 14–15, 145–47, 183–85, 244–50. On the religious culture of the Housatonic River valley more generally, see esp. Chard Powers Smith, *The Housatonic: Puritan River*, The Rivers of America (New York: Rinehart, 1946). Interestingly, Nathaniel William Taylor's son-in-law, Noah Porter, a Taylorite-Edwardsian at the time, served as pastor of the New Milford Church from 1836 to 1843.

16. According to Charles Beach Barlow, the current owner of the Taylor house and an amateur historian of New Milford, the Rev. Nathanael Taylor deeded the house and its lot to his son Nathaniel on May 4, 1778. It currently sits at 34 Main Street, New Milford. See also Carley, ed., *Voices from the Past*, p. 62. Ann Northrop Taylor died on April 10, 1810. Two years later Nathaniel Taylor married Susanna Noble Gunn, widow of Captain Abner Gunn, Jr.

17. Nathaniel Taylor, father of Nathaniel William Taylor, appears to have had quite an extensive range of financial interests and an equally extensive amount of capital. He owned a gristmill, he sat in the first rank (of six) in New Milford's meetinghouse and paid a tax of $1,468 for his pew, he had a financial interest in the marble quarries of Marbledale, Connecticut, and he was one of the original subscribers to the Union Library of New Milford, founded in 1796. See Orcutt's *History of the Towns of New Milford and Bridgewater*, pp. 202, 261, and 342.

Among the sources available on the early life of Nathaniel William Taylor, see esp. Leonard Bacon, Samuel W. S. Dutton, and George P. Fisher, *Memorial of Nathaniel W. Taylor, D.D., Three Sermons* (New Haven, Conn.: Thomas H. Pease, 1858); and Hatch, *Personal Reminiscences and Memorials*. Dutton's "A Sketch of the Life and Character of Rev. Nathaniel W. Taylor, D.D.," *The Congregational Quarterly* 2 (July 1860): 245–66, is a slightly later, more comprehensive version of the eulogy included in the *Memorial*.

18. Orcutt, *History of the Towns of New Milford and Bridgewater*, pp. 625–26; Hatch, *Personal Reminiscences and Memorials*, p. 3; and George P. Fisher, "A Sermon Preached in the Chapel of Yale College, March 14, 1858, the First Sunday after the Death of Rev. Nathaniel W. Taylor, D.D., Dwight Professor of Didactic Theology," in *Memorial of Nathaniel W. Taylor, D.D.*, p. 26.

19. Orcutt, *History of the Towns of New Milford and Bridgewater*, pp. 625–28; Hatch, *Personal Reminiscences and Memorials*, p. 3; and George P. Fisher, "A Sermon Preached in the Chapel of Yale College, March 14, 1858," p. 26.

20. For more on Azel Backus and his relationship to Taylor, see "Sketch of the Life of Rev. Azel Backus, S.T.D., First President of Hamilton College," in *Sermons on Important Subjects, by the Late Rev. Azel Backus, S.T.D., First President of Hamilton College* (Utica, N.Y.: William Williams, 1824), pp. v–xxxvii; "Azel Backus, D.D.," in *AAP*, 2: 281–87; Fisher, "A Sermon Preached in the Chapel of Yale College, March 14, 1858," p. 26; Dutton, "A Sketch of the Life and Character of Rev. Nathaniel W. Taylor, D.D.," p. 246; and Goodenough, *The Clergy of Litchfield County*, pp. 42–43. While Mead noted the relationship between Taylor and Backus, he did not acknowledge Backus's New Divinity commitments and he underestimated the role of Litchfield County generally in shaping Taylor's early predilections.

21. Bennet Tyler to William B. Sprague, January 14, 1848, in *AAP*, 2: 285. On Backus's winsome preaching, see also Luther F. Dimmick's letter to Sprague in *AAP*, 2: 287.

22. *An Address of the General Association of Connecticut, to the Congregational Ministers and Churches of the State, on the Importance of United Endeavours to Revive Gospel Discipline* (Litchfield, Conn.: Hosmer and Goodwin, 1808), pp. 3–4, 10, 15.

23. "Sketch of the Life of Rev. Azel Backus," pp. xxix, xxxvi.

24. Dutton, "A Sketch of the Life and Character of Rev. Nathaniel W. Taylor," p. 246.

Chapter 2

1. "Dr. Taylor's Lectures on the Moral Government of God," *BR* 31 (July 1859): 490–91, 494.

2. At this point, my work differs significantly from the recent materialist intellectual history of scholars such as Darren Marcus Staloff and Peter S. Field. Based as their work is on what Field calls a "cultural materialist ontology," this new materialist history continues to reduce the study of intellectual life to a (now post-Marxian) form of class analysis. Such analysis can prove quite illuminative. But its usefulness in the context of early American history is somewhat limited (and anachronistic). And its cynical hermeneutics of suspicion fails to account fully for the genuinely religious commitments, beliefs, and perceptions of subjects such as the Edwardsians, whose intellectual traditions were rooted in a variety of social and economic backgrounds, and whose leadership (as will be argued below) rarely wielded a great deal of economic or political power. See Staloff's programmatic essay, "Intellectual History Naturalized: Materialism and the 'Thinking Class,'" *William and Mary Quarterly*, 3d ser., 50 (April 1993): 406–17. And for the application of this method in the context of early American religious history, see Darren Staloff, *The Making of an American Thinking Class: Intellectuals and Intelligentsia in Puritan Massachusetts* (New York: Oxford University Press, 1998); and Peter S. Field, *The Crisis of the Standing Order: Clerical Intellectuals and Cultural Authority in Massachusetts, 1780–1833* (Amherst: University of Massachusetts Press, 1998).

3. The best single volume on Timothy Dwight and his theology is the recent book by John R. Fitzmier, *New England's Moral Legislator: Timothy Dwight, 1752–1817*, Religion in North America (Bloomington: Indiana University Press, 1998). But see also the works listed in the notes that follow.

4. Orcutt, *History of the Towns of New Milford and Bridgewater*, p. 626. Tellingly, Taylor's grandfather died on December 9, 1800, just a couple of months after Taylor enrolled at Yale.

5. This in a period of extensive urbanization throughout America. Between 1830 and 1860, America's urban population grew by over 700 percent, from 500,000 to 3.8 million residents. Even more impressively, between 1800 and 1890 America's urban population increased 87-fold, while the general population grew by a factor of 12. See Robert A. Orsi, ed., *Gods of the City: Religion and the American Urban Landscape*, Religion in North America (Bloomington: Indiana University Press, 1999), pp. 13–14.

6. Rollin G. Osterweis, *Three Centuries of New Haven, 1638–1938* (New Haven, Conn.: Yale University Press, 1953), pp. 191–92, 200–204, 317–18; and Oscar Edward Maurer, *A Puritan Church and Its Relation to Community, State, and Nation: Addresses Delivered in Preparation for the Three Hundredth Anniversary of the Settlement of New Haven* (New Haven, Conn.: Yale University Press, 1938), pp. 103–6. Cf. Edward E. Atwater, ed., *History of the City of New Haven to the Present Time* (New York: W. W. Munsell, 1887); Henry T. Blake, *Chronicles of New Haven Green from 1632 to 1862: A Series of Papers Read Before the New Haven Colony Historical Society* (New Haven, Conn.: Tuttle, Morehouse, and Taylor, 1898); and William L. Philie, *Change and Tradition: New Haven, Connecticut, 1780–1830*, Garland Studies in Entrepreneurship (New York: Garland, 1989).

7. Nathaniel W. Taylor to William B. Sprague, February 20, 1844, in *AAP*, 2: 162. Taylor's eye trouble was actually quite common among hardworking students before the rise of opthalmology. For recent physiological and psychological analyses, see Fitzmier, *New England's Moral Legislator*, pp. 8–12, who suggests that Timothy Dwight's similar (but much more serious) visual impairment may have resulted from a severe form of myopia that produced ocular migraine headaches;

and Robert D. Richardson, *Emerson: The Mind on Fire* (Berkeley: University of California Press, 1995), p. 63, who surmises that Ralph Waldo Emerson may have suffered from uveitis, a rheumatic inflammation of the eye that also produces headaches.

8. Hatch, *Personal Reminiscences and Memorials*, p. 4 (the story of Dwight's prayer and "bruised reed" allusion is also recounted in Fisher, "A Sermon Preached in the Chapel of Yale College, March 14, 1858," p. 27); Dutton, "A Sketch of the Life and Character of Rev. Nathaniel W. Taylor, D.D.," p. 247; and Taylor to Sprague, February 20, 1844, in *AAP*, 2: 163–64 .

9. Hatch, *Personal Reminiscences and Memorials*, p. 26; Fisher, "A Sermon Preached in the Chapel of Yale College, March 14, 1858," p. 28; and Orcutt, *History of the Towns of New Milford and Bridgewater*, p. 626.

10. Leonard Bacon, "A Sermon at the Funeral of Nathaniel W. Taylor, D.D.," p. 6; and Taylor to Sprague, February 20, 1844, in *AAP*, 2: 161–64. Fitzmier's discussion of Dwight's blindness is found in *New England's Moral Legislator*, pp. 8–12.

11. Timothy Dwight, *Remarks on the Review of Inchiquin's Letters* (New York: Garrett Press, 1970; 1815), p. 107; Dwight, *Travels in New England and New York*, 4: 227–31; and Dwight to John Ryland, March 16, 1805, Folder 3, Box 1, Series I, Dwight Family Papers, Sterling Memorial Library, Yale University. For Dwight's early infatuation with his Edwardsian heritage, see the heroic and mythic (though anonymous) significance of Edwards in Dwight's epic poem *The Triumph of Infidelity: A Poem* (Printed in the World, 1788), pp. 22ff. For his eradication of the Half-Way Covenant at Greenfield, see Charles E. Cuningham, *Timothy Dwight, 1752–1817: A Biography* (New York: Macmillan, 1942), pp. 106–9. For Dwight's theological opposition to the Half-Way Covenant, see sermon 159, "The Extraordinary Means of Grace.—No Infants, but the Children of Believers, Proper Subjects of Baptism.—Mode of Administration," in Dwight's *Theology Explained and Defended in a Series of Sermons*, 12th ed. (New York: Harper and Brothers, 1858), 4: 338–54. For his Edwardsian curriculum at Yale, see Lyman Beecher, *The Autobiography of Lyman Beecher*, 2 vols., ed. Barbara M. Cross (Cambridge, Mass.: Belknap Press of Harvard University Press, 1961; 1864), 1: 44–45; and Cuningham, *Timothy Dwight*, p. 228. For an example of Taylor's reverence for and fidelity to Dwight's theology, see the preface to Nathaniel W. Taylor, *Concio ad Clerum: A Sermon Delivered in the Chapel of Yale College, September 10, 1828* (New Haven, Conn.: A. H. Maltby and Homan Hallock, 1842; 1828). As George Park Fisher would note, Taylor "loved and honored" Dwight more than "any other mortal." George P. Fisher, "Historical Address," in *The Semi-Centennial Anniversary of the Divinity School of Yale College, May 15th and 16th, 1872* (New Haven, Conn.: Tuttle, Morehouse, and Taylor, 1872), p. 11.

12. Perry Miller, "Jonathan Edwards' Sociology of the Great Awakening," *New England Quarterly* 21 (March 1948): 51, 53. Cf. Gerald R. McDermott, *One Holy and Happy Society: The Public Theology of Jonathan Edwards* (University Park: Pennsylvania State University Press, 1991). Regarding Edwards's lack of political savvy, his uncle, Ephraim Williams, Jr., once said, "I am sorry that a head so full of divinity should be so empty of politics." Quoted in Wyllis E. Wright, ed., *Colonel Ephraim Williams: A Documentary Life* (Pittsfield, Mass.: Berkshire County Historical Society, 1970), p. 61.

13. On Edwards's notebooks and their significance for understanding the development of his thought, see esp. Wilson H. Kimnach, "General Introduction to the Sermons: Jonathan Edwards' Art of Prophesying," in Jonathan Edwards, *Sermons and Discourses, 1720–1723*, WJE, vol. 10 (Yale, 1992), pp. 42–74; and Thomas Schafer's "Editor's Introduction" to Edwards's *Miscellanies*, WJE, vol. 13 (Yale, 1994), pp. 1–109.

14. See esp. Jon Butler, "Enthusiasm Described and Decried: The Great Awakening as Interpretive Fiction," *Journal of American History* 69 (September 1982): 305–25; and Joseph Conforti, "The Invention of the Great Awakening, 1795–1842," *Early American Literature* 26 (1991):99–118. But contrast these essays with the recent work of Timothy D. Hall, *Contested Boundaries: Itinerancy and the Reshaping of the Colonial American Religious World* (Durham, N.C.:

Duke University Press, 1994), esp. pp. 2–3, 7–12, who offers a useful analysis of the historiography of the Great Awakening and demonstrates that this concept was not an invention of the nineteenth century. Rather, many colonists themselves described the revivals as an immense, pan-colonial phenomenon. According to Hall, the vast scope of the revivals and the itinerancy that often tied them together signaled the decline of localism in the colonies and the consequent "struggle over meanings, over order, over alternative ways of living" in the colonists' "rapidly expanding social world" (p. 12). See also the somewhat more conservative recent spin on Butler's and Conforti's interpretations in Frank Lambert, *Inventing the "Great Awakening"* (Princeton, N.J.: Princeton University Press, 1999), a book that provides the most up-to-date summary available of the history of these revivals. On the historiography of the Great Awakening, see also the excellent recent essays by Allen C. Guelzo, "God's Designs: The Literature of the Colonial Revivals of Religion, 1735–1760," in Harry S. Stout and D. G. Hart, eds., *New Directions in American Religious History* (New York: Oxford University Press, 1997), pp. 141–72; and Christopher Grasso, "Appendix 3: A Note on the Historiography of the Great Awakening," in his *A Speaking Aristocracy: Transforming Public Discourse in Eighteenth-Century Connecticut* (Chapel Hill: University of North Carolina Press, 1999), pp. 495–98.

15. Edwin S. Gaustad, "The Theological Effects of the Great Awakening in New England," *Mississippi Valley Historical Review* 40 (March 1954): 683. See also Edwin S. Gaustad, "Society and the Great Awakening in New England," *William and Mary Quarterly*, 3d ser., 11 (October 1954): 566–77; and Edwin Scott Gaustad, *The Great Awakening in New England* (Chicago: Quadrangle Books, 1968; 1957). The most prominent recent proponent of the notion of a great and unified eighteenth-century revival, not only throughout America but in Great Britain and on the Continent as well, is W. R. Ward, *The Protestant Evangelical Awakening* (Cambridge: Cambridge University Press, 1992), who argues, p. 355, "however ruthlessly cut down to size, the Great Awakening is not to be dismissed by critics as 'invention' or 'interpretative fiction.'"

16. Jonathan Edwards, *A Faithful Narrative*, in *The Great Awakening*, WJE, vol. 4 (Yale, 1972), p. 146. Perry Miller, *The New England Mind: From Colony to Province* (Cambridge, Mass.: Harvard University Press, 1953), pp. 19–146, remains the standard argument for religious declension in the period preceding the Great Awakening. For criticism of the declension thesis, see esp. Robert G. Pope, "New England Versus the New England Mind: The Myth of Declension," *Journal of Social History* 3 (1969–70), 95–108; Patricia U. Bonomi and Peter R. Eisenstadt, "Church Adherence in the Eighteenth-Century British American Colonies," *William and Mary Quarterly*, 3d ser., 39 (April 1982): 245–86; Charles E. Hambrick-Stowe, *The Practice of Piety: Puritan Devotional Disciplines in Seventeenth-Century New England* (Chapel Hill,: University of North Carolina Press, 1982); Patricia U. Bonomi, *Under the Cope of Heaven: Religion, Society, and Politics in Colonial America* (New York: Oxford University Press, 1986); and Harry S. Stout, *The New England Soul: Preaching and Religious Culture in Colonial New England* (New York: Oxford University Press, 1986). For a brief presentation of the debate over the cyclical interpretation of America's religious awakenings, see the "Symposium on Religious Awakenings," *Sociological Analysis* 44 (Summer 1983): 81–122. See also Kathryn Long, "The Power of Interpretation: The Revival of 1857–58 and the Historiography of Revivalism in America," *Religion and American Culture* 4 (Winter 1994): 77–105, and Kathryn Teresa Long, *The Revival of 1857–58: Interpreting an American Religious Awakening*, Religion in America Series (New York: Oxford University Press, 1998), for an insightful analysis of this interpretation.

17. For critical analysis of the somewhat indiscriminate use of the "myth of Arminianism" by Calvinists in this period, see esp. Francis A. Christie, "The Beginnings of Arminianism in New England," *Papers of the American Society of Church History*, 2d ser., 3 (1912): 152–72; Edmund Morgan, *The Gentle Puritan: A Life of Ezra Stiles* (New Haven, Conn.: Yale University Press, 1962), pp. 15–19; and Gerald J. Goodwin, "The Myth of 'Arminian-Calvinism' in Eighteenth-Century New England," *New England Quarterly* 41 (June 1968); 213–37. For confirmation that

Arminianism, loosely defined, did constitute a real threat to Calvinist New England in this period, see Conrad Wright, *The Beginnings of Unitarianism in America* (Boston: Starr King Press, 1955), pp. 9–27; C. C. Goen, "Editor's Introduction," in Jonathan Edwards, *The Great Awakening,* WJE, vol. 4 (Yale, 1972), pp. 4–18; and Robert J. Wilson III, *The Benevolent Deity: Ebenezer Gay and the Rise of Rational Religion in New England, 1696–1787* (Philadelphia: University of Pennsylvania Press, 1984), pp. 61–79. For a fine summary analysis of the meaning of the term Arminianism in colonial New England, see Clyde A. Holbrook, "Editor's Introduction," in Jonathan Edwards, *Original Sin,* WJE, vol. 3 (Yale, 1970), pp. 4–5, n. 9. A brief but useful survey of "The Influence of Arminius on American Theology" may be found in Gerald O. McCulloh's essay by that title in Gerald O. McCulloh, ed., *Man's Faith and Freedom: The Theological Influence of Jacobus Arminius* (New York: Abingdon Press, 1962), pp. 64–87.

18. Edwards, *A Faithful Narrative,* p. 148. For Edwards's sermon series on justification, see *Five Discourses on Important Subjects, Nearly Concerning the Great Affair of the Soul's Eternal Salvation,* in *WJE* (BTT), 1: 620–89. Note, however, that the fifth of these sermons, "The Excellency of Jesus Christ," was not part of the original series but was added for publication in 1738.

19. See Breitenbach's "New Divinity Theology and the Ideal of Moral Accountability," pp. 102–11, "The Consistent Calvinism of the New Divinity Movement," pp. 263–64, "Piety and Moralism," and "Religious Affections and Religious Affectations: Antinomianism and Hypocrisy in the Writings of Edwards and Franklin," in Barbara B. Oberg and Harry S. Stout, eds., *Benjamin Franklin, Jonathan Edwards, and the Representation of American Culture* (New York: Oxford University Press, 1993) pp. 13–26.

20. Jonathan Edwards to John Erskine, July 5, 1750, in Sereno E. Dwight, *Memoirs of Jonathan Edwards, A.M.,* in *WJE* (BTT), 1: cxviii, and Joseph Bellamy, *True Religion Delineated* (Boston: S. Kneeland, 1750), pp. ii–iii. Edwards's own works on this topic in the period of the Great Awakening included *The Distinguishing Marks of a Work of the Spirit of God* (Boston: S. Kneeland and T. Green, 1741), *Some Thoughts Concerning the Present Revival of Religion in New-England* (Boston: S. Kneeland and T. Green, 1742), and *A Treatise Concerning Religious Affections* (Boston: S. Kneeland and T. Green, 1746). Samuel Hopkins (among others) would pursue this topic later in a major treatise entitled *An Inquiry into the Nature of True Holiness* (Newport, Conn.: Solomon Southwick, 1773).

21. Gaustad, "The Theological Effects of the Great Awakening in New England," p. 697; Gaustad, *The Great Awakening in New England,* p. 136; and Harriet Beecher Stowe, *Oldtown Folks,* in Kathryn Kish Sklar, ed., *Harriet Beecher Stowe: Three Novels,* Library of America (New York: Literary Classics of the United States, 1982), p. 1243.

22. James Patrick Walsh, "The Pure Church in Eighteenth-Century Connecticut" (Ph.D. diss., Columbia University, 1967), p. 127; Elizabeth Currier Nordbeck, "The New England Diaspora: A Study of the Religious Culture of Maine and New Hampshire, 1613–1763" (Ph.D. diss., Harvard University, 1978), p. 352 and passim; Stephen A. Marini, *Radical Sects of Revolutionary New England* (Cambridge, Mass.: Harvard University Press, 1982), p. 38 and passim. For more on the rise of Separatism and sectarianism in the wake of New England's Great Awakening, see C. C. Goen, *Revivalism and Separatism in New England, 1740–1800: Strict Congregationalists and Separate Baptists in the Great Awakening* (Middletown, Conn.: Wesleyan University Press, 1987; 1962); Howard Frederic Vos, "The Great Awakening in Connecticut" (Ph.D. diss., Northwestern University, 1967), pp. 187–242; Mary Catherine Foster, "Hampshire County, Massachusetts, 1729–1754: A Covenant Society in Transition" (Ph.D. diss., University of Michigan, 1967); David S. Lovejoy, *Religious Enthusiasm in the New World: Heresy to Revolution* (Cambridge, Mass.: Harvard University Press, 1985); Elizabeth C. Nordbeck, "Almost Awakened: The Great Revival in New Hampshire and Maine, 1727–1748," *Historical New Hampshire* 35 (Spring 1980): 23–58; Douglas Hardy Sweet, "Church and Community: Town Life and Ministerial Ideals in Revolutionary New Hampshire" (Ph.D. diss., Columbia Univer-

sity, 1978); and the handy recent summary of these developments provided in Louis Billington, "'The Perfect Law of Liberty': Radical Religion and the Democratization of New England, 1780–1840," in David K. Adams and Cornelius A. van Minnen, eds., *Religious and Secular Reform in America* (New York: New York University Press, 1999), pp. 29–49. On the New Light revival in Canada, see also Maurice W. Armstrong, *The Great Awakening in Nova Scotia, 1776–1809*, vol. 7 of *Studies in Church History* (Hartford, Conn.: American Society of Church History, 1948); J. M. Bumsted, *Henry Alline, 1748–1784* (Toronto: University of Toronto Press, 1971); Gordon T. Stewart, ed., *Documents Relating to the Great Awakening in Nova Scotia* (Toronto: Champlain Society, 1982); G. A. Rawlyk, *Ravished by the Spirit: Religious Revivals, Baptists, and Henry Alline* (Kingston, Ont.: McGill-Queen's University Press, 1984), pp. 32–54; and G. A. Rawlyk, *The Canada Fire: Radical Evangelicalism in British North America, 1775–1812* (Kingston, Ont.: McGill-Queen's University Press, 1994).

23. On the Old Lights, see Conrad Wright, *The Beginnings of Unitarianism in America* (Boston: Starr King, 1955) pp. 28–58; Gaustad, *The Great Awakening in New England*, pp. 61–79; Charles W. Akers, *Called Unto Liberty: A Life of Jonathan Mayhew, 1720–1766* (Cambridge, Mass.: Harvard University Press, 1964); Edward Griffen, *Old Brick of Boston: Charles Chauncy* (Minneapolis: University of Minnesota Press, 1980); Charles H. Lippy, *Seasonable Revolutionary: The Mind of Charles Chauncy* (Chicago: Nelson-Hall, 1981); Wilson, *The Benevolent Deity*; John Corrigan, *The Hidden Balance: Religion and the Social Theories of Charles Chauncy and Jonathan Mayhew* (New York: Cambridge University Press, 1987); and *The Prism of Piety: Catholick Congregational Clergy at the Beginning of the Enlightenment*, Religion in America Series (New York: Oxford University Press, 1991), some of whose moderates leaned toward the New Light rather than the Old Light camp; and Amy Schrager Lang, "'A Flood of Errors': Chauncy and Edwards in the Great Awakening," in Nathan O. Hatch and Harry S. Stout, eds., *Jonathan Edwards and the American Experience* (New York: Oxford University Press, 1988), pp. 160–73; On the activities of New Light radicals such as Davenport and Croswell, see esp. Harry S. Stout and Peter S. Onuf, "James Davenport and the Great Awakening in New London," *Journal of American History* 71 (December 1983): 556–78; and Leigh Eric Schmidt, "'A Second and Glorious Reformation,': The New Light Extremism of Andrew Croswell," *William and Mary Quarterly*, 3d ser., 43 (April 1986): 214–44.

24. Charles E. Hambrick-Stowe, "The Spirit of the Old Writers: Print Media, the Great Awakening, and Continuity in New England," in *Communication and Change in American Religious History*, ed. Leonard I. Sweet (Grand Rapids: Eerdmans, 1993), pp. 126–40; Hambrick-Stowe, "The Spirit of the Old Writers: The Great Awakening and the Persistence of Puritan Piety," in Francis J. Bremer, ed., *Puritanism: Transatlantic Perspectives on a Seventeenth-Century Anglo-American Faith* (Boston: Massachusetts Historical Society, 1993), pp. 277–91; and Gerald Francis Moran, "The Puritan Saint: Religious Experience, Church Membership, and Piety in Connecticut, 1636–1776" (Ph.D. diss., Rutgers University, 1974), p. 230.

25. Though a large number of historians have discussed the Old Calvinists, very few have attempted to define Old Calvinism. For the basic outlines, consult Sydney E. Ahlstrom, *A Religious History of the American People*, 2 vols. (Garden City, N.Y.: Image Books, 1975; 1972), 1: 489–90; Morgan, *The Gentle Puritan*: pp. 172–76; Breitenbach, "The Consistent Calvinism of the New Divinity Movement," pp. 241–42; David Harlan, *The Clergy and the Great Awakening in New England*, Studies in American History and Culture, No. 15 (Ann Arbor, Mich.: UMI Research Press, 1980), esp. pp. 58–96; and Guelzo, *Edwards on the Will*, pp. 140–75. For an example of the derisive Old Calvinist use of the "New Divinity" label, see Jedidiah Mills, *An Inquiry Concerning the State of the Unregenerate under the Gospel* (New Haven, Conn.: B. Mecom, 1767). Old Calvinist William Hart coined the term "Hopkintonian" in 1769. See his *Brief Remarks on a Number of False Propositions, and Dangerous Errors, Which Are Spreading in the Country* (New London, Conn.: Timothy Green, 1769), and his satirical *Sermon of a New Kind . . . Containing*

a Collection of Doctrines, Belonging to the Hopkintonian Scheme of Orthodoxy; Or the Marrow of the Most Modern Divinity (New Haven, Conn.: T. and S. Green, [1769]), which was disseminated as part of an Old Calvinist effort to block Hopkins's installation at the First Congregational Church in Newport, Rhode Island.

26. While one might divide New England's religious adherents into many more than four identifiable subgroups (Anglicans, Quakers, and Jews comprised other noteworthy religious communities), the four constituencies presented here did represent the leading forces in the region's religious life in this period. Miller, "Jonathan Edwards' Sociology of the Great Awakening," p. 50, discussed only "two wings" following the revivals, one headed by Edwards and the other by Chauncy. Gaustad, *The Great Awakening in New England,* p. 134, and Goen, *Revivalism and Separatism in New England,* p. 34, each identified only three major factions, Gaustad neglecting to include the Separates/sectarians and Goen neglecting the Old Calvinists. But as historical work has progressed on eighteenth-century New England, our picture of the region's religious landscape has become more complex. Richard L. Bushman's *From Puritan to Yankee: Character and the Social Order in Connecticut, 1690–1765* (Cambridge, Mass.: Harvard University Press, 1967) has led the way in this regard. More recently, Marini, *Radical Sects of Revolutionary New England,* and Lovejoy, *Religious Enthusiasm in the New World,* have contributed to a more nuanced understanding of New England's sectarians, while John Corrigan's *The Hidden Balance* and *The Prism of Piety* have added new hues and shades to our picture of the Boston area's more "catholick" Congregationalists. Christopher Grasso offers a useful critique of what he terms the older, "bipolar" or "two-party model" of post-Awakening ecclesiastical history in *A Speaking Aristocracy,* pp. 103–8.

27. The extent to which the Great Awakening was responsible for the rise of sectarianism and religious pluralism in New England depends in large measure on the degree of religious hegemony in pre-Awakening New England. Over the past generation, a growing number of historians have detailed the ways in which various nonconformists resisted the forces of mainstream Puritan culture in the seventeenth century. See, for example, Darrett Rutman, *American Puritanism: Faith and Practice* (Philadelphia: Lippincott, 1970); Philip Gura, *A Glimpse of Sion's Glory: Puritan Radicalism in New England, 1620–1660* (Middletown, Conn: Wesleyan University Press, 1984); and Stephen Foster, *The Long Argument: English Puritanism and the Shaping of New England Culture, 1570–1700* (Chapel Hill: University of North Carolina Press, 1991). More recently, Janice Knight, *Orthodoxies in Massachusetts: Rereading American Puritanism* (Cambridge, Mass.: Harvard University Press, 1994), has built on more pluralistic readings of the Puritan mainstream itself such as Andrew Delbanco's *The Puritan Ordeal* (Cambridge, Mass.: Harvard University Press, 1989), to argue that the Puritans' allegedly hegemonic orthodoxy was contested even from within the establishment. Knight sees "the production of a single [New England] 'orthodoxy' as a volatile process that has only come to seem inevitable in subsequent narrative accounts" (p. 11). My argument for the proliferation of sectarianism after the Great Awakening does not mean that earlier Puritan culture was monolithic, only that its diversity was more successfully suppressed by mainstream Puritans and, therefore, that it was significantly less pluralistic.

28. Park, "New England Theology," p. 214.

29. Gaustad, "The Theological Effects of the Great Awakening in New England," p. 695; and Gaustad, *The Great Awakening in New England,* p. 134.

30. Donald H. Meyer, *The Democratic Enlightenment* (New York: Capricorn Books, 1976), p. 7.

31. For debate over the extent to which the innovations of the New England Theology derived from Edwards's own thought, consult my "Edwards and His Mantle." The literature debating Edwards's alleged modernity is voluminous. However, there are a few recent works on the broader relationship between the revivals and the Enlightenment worth singling out. Henry D. Rack, *Reasonable Enthusiast: John Wesley and the Rise of Methodism* (Philadelphia: Trinity Press International, 1989), for example, argues that "the relationship between 'Enlightenment'

and 'Revival' in this period is more complex than is allowed for by simple notions of the latter being a 'reaction' against the former." The evangelicals "did not escape the accents of their time" (pp. 32–33). And for helpful, recent reassessments of the Edwardsian engagement with Enlightenment themes, see especially D. W. Bebbington, "Evangelical Christianity and the Enlightenment," *Crux* 25 (December 1989): 29–36, who overstates his nonetheless insightful argument that "to posit a sharp contrast between Evangelicalism on the one hand and the Enlightenment on the other is entirely mistaken. It can be shown that, on the contrary, Evangelicalism was actually started by the Enlightenment" (p. 32), and who contends that "Edwards must not be seen as a traditional Calvinist resisting the Enlightenment. . . . Rather, he was an Enlightenment thinker adapting the received body of Protestant thought to the new modes of thinking of his day" (p. 33); D. W. Bebbington, *Evangelicalism in Modern Britain: A History from the 1730s to the 1980s* (London: Unwin Hyman, 1989), pp. 34–74; and A. Owen Aldridge, "Enlightenment and Awakening in Edwards and Franklin," in Oberg and Stout, eds., *Benjamin Franklin, Jonathan Edwards, and the Representation of American Culture*, pp. 27–41. The best survey of American theological history in the century or so after Edwards is found in Mark A. Noll, *America's God, from Jonathan Edwards to Abraham Lincoln* (New York: Oxford University Press, 2002).

32. On this theme, see Conforti, *Samuel Hopkins and the New Divinity Movement*, pp. 159–74.

33. Samuel Hopkins to Samuel Miller, January 23, 1801, Folder 79, Box 7, Samuel Miller Papers, PUL.

34. Jonathan Edwards, Jr. to Samuel Hopkins, October 29, 1793, printed in Park, *Memoir*, 1: 204–7; and Joseph H. Jones, ed., *The Life of Ashbel Green, V.D.M., Begun to Be Written by Himself in His Eighty-Second Year and Continued to His Eighty-Fourth* (New York: Robert Carter and Brothers, 1849), pp. 239–40. For further discussion of intramural Edwardsian disagreement, see Samuel Hopkins to Stephen West, January 12, 1770, Samuel Hopkins Papers, Trask, where Hopkins worried quite early on in the history of the New Divinity movement that "the *few* Edwardeans" were getting "into divisions among themselves"; and *The Literary Diary of Ezra Stiles*, 1: 261 and 3: 273–75. For the consistent historiographical tendency to note at least two different Edwardsian subtraditions, see Leonard Woods, *History of the Andover Theological Seminary* (Boston: James R. Osgood, 1885), pp. 29–32; Williston Walker, *A History of the Congregational Churches in the United States*, The American Church History Series, vol.3 (New York: Christian Literature, 1894), p. 299; Foster, *A Genetic History of the New England Theology*, p. 189; Stephen E. Berk, *Calvinism Versus Democracy: Timothy Dwight and the Origins of American Evangelical Orthodoxy* (Hamden, Conn.: Archon Books, 1974) pp. 49–73; and Conforti, *Samuel Hopkins and the New Divinity Movement*, p. 3.

35. Breitenbach, "The Consistent Calvinism of the New Divinity Movement," p. 257; Breitenbach, "Unregenerate Doings," p. 484; and Mead, *Nathaniel William Taylor*, p. 105. Theodore Davenport Bacon, *Leonard Bacon: A Statesman in the Church*, ed. Benjamin W. Bacon (New Haven, Conn.: Yale University Press, 1931), p. 110, calls the natural/moral ability distinction "the peculiarity of the New England Theology." Allen Guelzo as well, in *Edwards on the Will*, reveals how powerful the distinction proved to be in the unfolding of New Divinity doctrine. For testimony from the Edwardsians about the importance of this distinction, see esp. Jonathan Edwards, Jr., "Remarks on the Improvements Made in Theology by His Father, President Edwards," in *The Works of Jonathan Edwards, D.D., Late President of Union College*, 2 vols. (Andover, Mass.: Allen, Morrill, and Wardwell, 1842), 1: 481–84.

36. Jonathan Edwards, *True Grace Distinguished from the Experience of Devils*, BTT, 2:42. As Edwards had preached to his Northampton congregation years before the publication of his treatise on the *Freedom of the Will*, "men are under no such inability to any moral good Required of him [*sic*] as is owing to any defect in the Capacity of his nature." "[I]f it were so," he argued, they would be like "a stone or tree, a Brute Crea[ture]." Further, humans are "naturally

capable of Knowing G[od], Loving him. . . . [I]f his [man's] Heart were but Right his Capacity is as much fitted for such things as [for] any acts that he Performs." See Edwards's sermon on Deut. 29:4 (September 1745), Edwards Papers, Beinecke, L. 11r-L. 11v.

37. Jonathan Edwards, *Freedom of the Will*, ed. Paul Ramsey, WJE, vol. 1 (Yale, 1957), pp. 362–63. The phrase "he can if he will" may be found in one form or another throughout this work. A good example of the many Edwardsian appropriations of this crucial Edwardsian distinction may be found in John Smalley, *The Consistency of the Sinner's Ability to Comply with the Gospel; with His Inexcusable Guilt in Not Complying with It, Illustrated and Confirmed* (Hartford, Conn.: Green and Watson, 1769).

38. It should be pointed out here that the Edwardsians held to what Norman Fiering calls an "Augustinian" rather than a "scholastic" voluntarism. While I think that Fiering, "Will and Intellect in the New England Mind," *William and Mary Quarterly*, 3d ser., 29 (October 1972): 515–58, draws too sharp a distinction between what he terms intellectualism, Augustinian voluntarism, and scholastic voluntarism in this essay, it is nonetheless important to note that Edwardsian voluntarism differed from that which one finds among many late medieval scholastics or among the Arminians, for example, both of which groups posited the will's power to act arbitrarily or indifferently. While the Edwardsian doctrines of the atonement, disinterested benevolence, and unconditional submission may be found in a great number of primary sources, the best places to start are Edwards A. Park, ed., *The Atonement. Discourses and Treatises by Edwards, Smalley, Maxcy, Emmons, Griffin, Burge, and Weeks* (Boston: Congregational Board of Publication, 1859), on the atonement; Hopkins, *An Inquiry into the Nature of True Holiness*, on disinterested benevolence (though Hopkins's articulation of this doctrine proved more ultra than some of his Edwardsian colleagues would have liked); and on unconditional submission, Samuel Hopkins, *A Dialogue between a Calvinist and a Semi-Calvinist*, in Stephen West, ed., *Sketches of the Life of the Late Rev. Samuel Hopkins, D.D.* (Hartford, Conn.: Hudson and Goodwin, 1805), pp. 141–67, and Nathanael Emmons to Sarah Ann Hopkins (his niece), May 8, 1820, Small Collection, Rare Book Room, CL, a wonderful 18-page manuscript source wherein Emmons defended his doctrine of resignation against his niece's doubts (printed in slightly revised form in Jacob Ide, ed., *The Works of Nathanael Emmons, D.D.* [Boston: Crocker and Brewster, 1842], 1: lxxxiii–lxxxviii). For an anlysis of Charles G. Finney's "Oberlin perfectionism" as a product of the Edwadsian doctrine of natural ability, see Allen C. Guelzo, "Oberlin Perfectionism and Its Edwardsean Origins, 1835–1870," in Stein, ed., *Jonathan Edwards's Writings*, pp. 159–74. For Luther on the egocentric or concupiscent self, see especially his commentary on Galatians 5:16, *Lectures on Galatians* (1535), in *Luther's Works*, vol. 27, ed. Jaroslav Pelikan (Saint Louis: Concordia, 1964), pp. 63–70.

39. The best place to begin for an understanding of the New Divinity critique of unregenerate doings is Samuel Hopkins's *Enquiry Concerning the Promises of the Gospel; Whether Any of Them Are Made to the Exercises and Doings of Persons in an Unregenerate State* (Boston: W. M'Alpine and J. Fleeming, 1765). On preparation for salvation, the use of means, and the morphology of conversion in the Puritan tradition, see especially Edmund S. Morgan, *Visible Saints: The History of a Puritan Idea* (Ithaca, N.Y.: Cornell University Press, 1965; 1963), who coined the phrase "morphology of conversion" (p. 66) in his discussion of the Puritan concern to identify predictable stages of the typically unpredictable conversion experience; Norman Pettit, *The Heart Prepared: Grace and Conversion in Puritan Spiritual Life* (New Haven, Conn.: Yale University Press, 1966); and Charles Lloyd Cohen, *God's Caress: The Psychology of Puritan Religious Experience* (New York: Oxford University Press, 1986). On the Edwardsian abbreviation of the traditional morphology of conversion, see Edwards's *Faithful Narrative*, pp. 160–76; and Goen, *Revivalism and Separatism in New England*, pp. 13–15, and "Editor's Introduction," pp. 26–29. Kenneth P. Minkema, in "The East Windsor Conversion Relations, 1700–1725," *Connecticut Historical Society Bulletin*" 51 (1986): 9–63, and "A Great Awakening Conversion: The Relation

of Samuel Belcher," *William and Mary Quarterly*, 3d ser., 44 (January 1987): 121–26, demonstrates that Edwards's father, the Rev. Timothy Edwards of East Windsor, Connecticut, though a committed preparationist, also abbreviated the traditional morphology in a way that anticipated the innovations of his son.

40. George Bancroft, "Jonathan Edwards," in George Ripley and Charles A. Dana, eds., *The New American Cyclopaedia: A Popular Dictionary of General Knowledge* (New York: D. Appleton and Company, 1860–63), 7: 15; and Guelzo, *Edwards on the Will*, p. 124. For Edwards's reversal of Stoddard's sacramental polity, see Edwards's *Ecclesiastical Writings*, ed. David D. Hall, WJE, vol. 12, in which he also opposed the Half-Way Covenant (pp. 314–19). This latter point was demonstrated first by George L. Walker, "Jonathan Edwards and the Half-Way Covenant," *NE* 43 (September 1884): 601–14. Opposition to the Half-Way Covenant would become a hallmark of the New Divinity. Joseph Bellamy would lead the way in virtually eradicating its use by century's end. See esp. his *The Half-Way-Covenant. A Dialogue* (New Haven: Thomas and Samuel Green, 1769), the first of four such dialogues around which a paper war raged over halfway measures with various Old Calvinists; and Valeri, *Law and Providence in Joseph Bellamy's New England*, pp. 145–50. On sacramental theology generally in eighteenth-century New England, see Michael Ryan McCoy, "In Defense of the Covenant: The Sacramental Debates of Eighteenth-Century New England (Puritanism)" (Ph.D. diss., Emory University, 1986). E. Brooks Holifield, *The Covenant Sealed: The Development of Puritan Sacramental Theology in Old and New England, 1570–1720* (New Haven, Conn.: Yale University Press, 1974), pp. 228–29, has argued that the Edwardsian abrogation of Stoddardean and half-way measures undermined what Holifield views as a "sacramental renaissance" (or resurgence of means-oriented spirituality) in pre-Awakening New England. His point is well taken. But it is also important to note the intensity of Edwards's sacramental vision of reality. On this theme, see esp. Edwards's manuscript notebook "Images of Divine Things," ed. Wallace E. Anderson, in Edwards's *Typological Writings*, WJE, vol. 11 (Yale, 1993), pp. 50–142; and see Christa Marie Thompson, O.S.F., "Apocalyptic Piety: The Franciscan Spirit and Tradition in Jonathan Edwards' Works" (Ph.D. diss., University of Notre Dame, 1982), pp. 148–49 and passim, and Lisa Mary McCartney, R.S.M., "Form and Voice in Selected American Puritan Spiritual Autobiographies" (Ph.D. diss., University of Notre Dame, 1982), pp. 21–22, 68–102. For the image of the rungless ladder, see Harriet Beecher Stowe, *The Minister's Wooing*, in Sklar, ed., *Harriet Beecher Stowe*, pp. 579–80. See also Charles H. Foster, *The Rungless Ladder: Harriet Beecher Stowe and New England Puritanism* (Durham, N.C.: Duke University Press, 1954), and Marie Caskey, *Chariot of Fire: Religion and the Beecher Family*, Yale Historical Publications, Miscellany 117 (New Haven, Conn.: Yale University Press, 1978), pp. 184–87. Interestingly, and in the tradition of Sacvan Bercovitch, Werner Sollors, *Beyond Ethnicity: Consent and Descent in American Culture* (New York: Oxford University Press, 1986), pp. 81–86, connects the Edwardsian abrogation of the Half-Way Covenant with his own consensual (rather than hereditary) model for American culture and nationality.

41. On the importance of such forms of social organization in maintaining and promoting a revivalistic ethos, see J. Stephen Kroll-Smith, "Transmitting a Revival Culture: The Organizational Dynamic of the Baptist Movement in Colonial Virginia, 1760–1777," *Journal of Southern History* 50 (November 1984): 551–68. On the essential role of boundary definition in the construction and maintenance of cultures, see Mary Douglas's *Purity and Danger: An Analysis of the Concepts of Pollution and Taboo* (London: Ark Paperbacks, 1984; 1966), and *Natural Symbols: Explorations in Cosmology* (New York: Pantheon Books, 1982; 1970), which build on Emile Durkheim's analyses of social deviance and collective consciousness. For useful applications of this theme to American religious history, see Kai T. Erikson, *Wayward Puritans: A Study in the Sociology of Deviance* (New York: John Wiley and Sons, 1966), and Robert Wuthnow, *The Restructuring of American Religion: Society and Faith Since World War II* (Princeton, N.J.: Princeton University Press, 1988).

42. In "The Cultures of Intellectual Life," Bender unpacks his understanding of intellectual cultures and their significance: "Men and women of ideas work within a social matrix that constitutes an audience or public for them. Within this context they seek legitimacy and are supplied with the collective concepts, the vocabulary of motives, and the key questions that give shape to their work. These communities of discourse, which I am here calling *cultures of intellectual life*, are historically constructed and are held together by mutual attachment to a cluster of shared meanings and intellectual purposes. They socialize the life of the mind and give institutional force to the paradigms that guide the creative intellect. . . . A consideration of the historical development of these cultures of intellectual life brings us to an insufficiently studied but vital point where intellectual history and social history touch. To discern the character of these networks of intellectual discourse, to assess their relative significance over time, and to discover their pattern of interaction promise to illuminate the social foundations of intellectual life in America" (pp. 3–4).

43. Valeri, *Law and Providence in Joseph Bellamy's New England*, p. 4. On New Divinity schools of the prophets, see David W. Kling, "The New Divinity and Schools of the Prophets, 1750–1825," in R. Albert Mohler and D. G. Hart, eds., *Theological Education in the Evangelical Tradition* (Grand Rapids, Mich.: Baker Books, 1996), pp. 129–47; David W. Kling, "New Divinity Schools of the Prophets, 1750–1825: A Case Study in Ministerial Education," *History of Education Quarterly* 37 (Summer 1997): 185–206; Mary Latimer Gambrell, *Ministerial Training in Eighteenth-Century New England* (New York: Columbia University Press, 1937), pp. 101–41; Roland H. Bainton, *Yale and the Ministry: A History of Education for the Christian Ministry at Yale from the Founding in 1701* (New York: Harper and Row, 1957), pp. 49–61; and Conforti, *Samuel Hopkins and the New Divinity Movement*, pp. 23–40 (quote from p. 39). For a close-up look at the schools of Bellamy and Emmons, see Glenn Paul Anderson, "Joseph Bellamy (1719–1790): the Man and His Work" (Ph.D. diss., Boston University, 1971), pp. 370–452; John T. Dahlquist, "Nathanael Emmons: His Life and Work" (Ph.D. diss., Boston University, 1963), pp. 201–4; and Park, *Memoir of Nathanael Emmons*, pp. 215–65. On the tremendous significance of these schools in shaping the theology of New England, see *Contributions to the Ecclesiastical History of Connecticut; Prepared Under the Direction of the General Association, to Commemorate the Completion of One Hundred and Fifty Years Since Its First Annual Assembly* (New Haven, Conn.: William L. Kingsley, 1861), pp. 296–97. A helpful, rudimentary tree charting the lines of intellectual descent that flowed through these schools may be found in Kling, *A Field of Divine Wonders*, p. 31.

44. Park, *Memoir of Nathanael Emmons*, p. 121. For the common background and close ties of the New Divinity clergymen, see especially Conforti, *Samuel Hopkins and the New Divinity Movement*, pp. 9–22, 41–58; and Kling, *A Field of Divine Wonders*, pp. 16–42, 62–74. On Edwards Jr.'s work on his father's works, see Kenneth Pieter Minkema, "The Edwardses: A Ministerial Family in Eighteenth-Century New England" (Ph.D. diss., University of Connecticut, 1988), pp. 430–36, 561–62. The largest collections of New Divinity correspondence are held by the Case Memorial Library at Hartford Seminary, the Sterling Memorial Library at Yale University, the Franklin Trask Library at Andover-Newton Theological Seminary, the Historical Society of Pennsylvania in Philadelphia, and the Connecticut Historical Society in Hartford.

45. Kling, *A Field of Divine Wonders*; Michael P. Anderson, "The Pope of Litchfield County: An Intellectual Biography of Joseph Bellamy, 1719–1790" (Ph.D. diss., Claremont Graduate School, 1980), pp. 289–90; Conforti, *Samuel Hopkins and the New Divinity Movement*, p. 58; Albert Hopkins, "Historical Discourse," in *Proceedings at the Centennial Commemoration of the Organization of the Berkshire Association of Congregational Ministers, Held at Stockbridge, Mass., October 28, 1863* (Boston: J. E. Farwell, 1864), pp. 5–6; Richard D. Birdsall, *Berkshire County: A Cultural History* (New Haven, Conn.: Yale University Press, 1959), pp. 53–54; Samuel M. Worcester, *The Life and Labors of Rev. Samuel Worcester, D.D.*, 2 vols. (Boston: Crocker and

Brewster, 1852), 2: 24–25; *The Diary of William Bentley, D.D., Pastor of the East Church, Salem, Massachusetts*, 4 vols. (Gloucester, Mass.: Peter Smith, 1962; 1905), 3: 113; Mortimer Blake, *A Centurial History of the Mendon Association of Congregational Ministers, with the Centennial Address, Delivered at Franklin, Mass., Nov. 19, 1851, and Biographical Sketches of the Members and Licentiates* (Boston: Sewall Harding, 1853), pp. 29–34, 62–72 (quotation from p. 30), who attributed the tremendous growth of the Mendon Association to its Edwardsian theology; and Dahlquist, "Nathanael Emmons," pp. 174–75. On the general history of the association movement, consult Alonzo H. Quint, "The Origin of Ministerial Associations in New England," *Congregational Quarterly* 2 (April 1860): 203–12; Alonzo H. Quint, "Some Account of Ministerial Associations," *Congregational Quarterly* 5 (October 1863): 293–304; J. William T. Youngs, Jr., *God's Messengers: Religious Leadership in Colonial New England, 1700–1750* (Baltimore, Md.: Johns Hopkins University Press, 1976), pp. 67–78; and Harlan, *The Clergy and the Great Awakening in New England*, pp. 99–113.

46. Walsh, "The Pure Church in Eighteenth-Century Connecticut," pp. 228, 218, 89; Goen, *Revivalism and Separatism in New England*, p. 203; Joseph Tracy, *The Great Awakening: A History of the Revival of Religion in the Time of Edwards and Whitefield* (Carlisle, Penn.: Banner of Truth Trust, 1976; 1842), pp. ix–xiii, 406–13; and Samuel W. S. Dutton, *The History of the North Church in New Haven, from Its Formation in May, 1742, During the Great Awakening, to the Completion of the Century in May, 1842. In Three Sermons* (New Haven, Conn.: A. H. Maltby, 1842), p. 97. For a vivid account of one local, New Divinity-inspired dispute over the Half-Way Covenant, see Mark L. Sargent, "The New Divinity in the Old Colony: Chandler Robbins and the Legend of the Pilgrims," in *Puritanism in America: The Seventeenth Through the Nineteenth Centuries*, Studies in Puritan American Spirituality, vol. 4 (Lewiston, N.Y.: Edwin Mellen Press, 1994), pp. 155–84.

47. This is a major theme of Miller's *Jonathan Edwards* as well.

48. The most useful formal analysis of countercultures is J. Milton Yinger, *Countercultures: The Promise and the Peril of a World Turned Upside Down* (New York: Free Press, 1982). On the difficulty in attaining conceptual definition of the term *counterculture*, see also Harry H. Bash, "Counterculture: Some Problems in the Quest for Sociological Theory," in Seymour Leventman, ed., *Counterculture and Social Transformation: Essays on Negativistic Themes in Sociological Theory* (Springfield, Ill.: Charles C. Thomas, 1982), pp. 19–47. For applications of this concept to religious history, see the entire issue of *Church History* 40 (March 1971). For more on New Divinity counterculturalism, see James R. Rohrer, *Keepers of the Covenant: Frontier Missions and the Decline of Congregationalism, 1774–1818*, Religion in America Series (New York: Oxford University Press, 1995), pp. 148–52.

49. Edwards, "Images of Divine Things," p. 127.

50. See esp. Patricia J. Tracy, *Jonathan Edwards, Pastor: Religion and Society in Eighteenth-Century Northampton*, American Century Series (New York: Hill and Wang, 1979); Jon Pahl, "Jonathan Edwards and the Aristocracy of Grace," *Fides et Historia* 25 (Winter/Spring 1993): 62–72, and *Paradox Lost: Free Will and Political Liberty in American Culture, 1630–1760*, New Studies in American Intellectual and Cultural History (Baltimore, Md.: Johns Hopkins University Press, 1992), pp. 147–61; and even Perry Miller himself in "Jonathan Edwards and the Great Awakening," in *Errand into the Wilderness* (Cambridge, Mass.: The Belknap Press of Harvard University Press, 1956), p. 162.

51. For the text of the covenant, see Edwards's writings on *The Great Awakening*, ed. C. C. Goen, pp. 550–54 (quotation from p. 551).

52. Jonathan Edwards, "Charity Contrary to a Selfish Spirit," in Edwards's *Ethical Writings*, ed. Paul Ramsey, WJE, vol. 8 (Yale, 1989), p. 271. On Edwards's concern for justice and social welfare, see esp. McDermott, *One Holy and Happy Society*; but also Clyde A. Holbrook, *The Ethics of Jonathan Edwards: Morality and Aesthetics* (Ann Arbor: University of Michigan Press,

1973), pp. 78–96; Roland A. Delattre, "Beauty and Politics: A Problematic Legacy of Jonathan Edwards," in *American Philosophy from Edwards to Quine*, ed. Robert W. Shahan and Kenneth R. Merrill (Norman: University of Oklahoma Press, 1977), pp. 20–48; Mark Valeri, "The Economic Thought of Jonathan Edwards," *Church History* 60 (March 1991): 37–54; Mark Valeri, "Editor's Introduction," in Jonathan Edwards, *Sermons and Discourses, 1730–1733*, WJE, vol. 17 (Yale, 1999), pp. 17–44; and Richard A. S. Hall, *The Neglected Northampton Texts of Jonathan Edwards: Edwards on Society and Politics*, Studies in American Religion, vol. 52 (Lewiston, N.Y.: Edwin Mellen Press, 1990).

53. Though scholars disagree over the pace of these social changes and the extent to which they undermined a previously unified Puritan culture, all agree on their importance for New England's transition from a Puritan to a Yankee society. See esp. Gaspare John Saladino, "The Economic Revolution in Late Eighteenth-Century Connecticut" (Ph.D. diss., University of Wisconsin, 1964); Bushman, *From Puritan to Yankee*; William Floyd Willingham, "Windham, Connecticut: Profile of a Revolutionary Community, 1755–1818" (Ph.D. diss., Northwestern University, 1972); J. E. Crowley, *This Sheba, Self: The Conceptualization of Economic Life in Eighteenth-Century America* (Baltimore, Md.: Johns Hopkins University Press, 1974); Daniel Scott Smith, "Parental Power and Marriage Patterns: An Analysis of Historical Trends in Hingham, Massachusetts," in Michael Gordon, ed., *The American Family in Social Historical Perspective*, 2d ed. (New York: St. Martin's, 1978), pp. 87–100; Bruce C. Daniels, *The Connecticut Town: Growth and Development, 1635–1790* (Middletown, Conn.: Wesleyan University Press, 1979); Douglas Lamar Jones, *Village and Seaport: Migration and Society in Eighteenth-Century Massachusetts* (Hanover, N.H.: University Press of New England, 1981); William E. Nelson, *Dispute and Conflict Resolution in Plymouth County, Massachusetts, 1725–1825*, Studies in Legal History (Chapel Hill: University of North Carolina Press, 1981); Jay Fliegelman, *Prodigals and Pilgrims: The American Revolution Against Patriarchal Authority, 1750–1800* (Cambridge: Cambridge University Press, 1982); George Selement, *Keepers of the Vineyard: The Puritan Ministry and Collective Culture in Colonial New England* (Lanham, Md.: University Press of America, 1984); Bruce H. Mann, *Neighbors and Strangers: Law and Community in Early Connecticut* (Chapel Hill: University of North Carolina Press, 1987); Gloria L. Main and Jackson T. Main, "Economic Growth and the Standard of Living in Southern New England, 1640–1774," *The Journal of Economic History* 48 (March 1988): 27–46; Richard D. Brown, *Knowledge Is Power: The Diffusion of Information in Early America, 1700–1865* (New York: Oxford University Press, 1989); William J. Gilmore, *Reading Becomes a Necessity of Life: Material and Cultural Life in Rural New England, 1780–1835* (Knoxville: University of Tennessee Press, 1989); John J. McCusker and Russell R. Menard, *The Economy of British America, 1607–1789* (Chapel Hill: University of North Carolina Press, 1991); Winifred Barr Rothenberg, *From Market-Places to a Market Economy: The Transformation of Rural Massachusetts, 1750–1850* (Chicago: University of Chicago Press, 1992); Gerald F. Moran and Maris A. Vinovskis, "Troubled Youth: Children at Risk in Early Modern England, Colonial America, and Nineteenth-Century America," in *Religion, Family, and the Life Course: Explorations in the Social History of Early America*, ed. Gerald F. Moran and Maris A. Vinovskis (Ann Arbor: University of Michigan Press, 1992), pp. 141–80; Margaret Ellen Newell, *From Dependency to Independence: Economic Revolution in Colonial New England* (Ithaca, N.Y.: Cornell University Press, 1998); and the special January 1999 issue of the *William and Mary Quarterly* (vol. 56), devoted to "The Economy of British North America." Jon Butler's *Becoming America: The Revolution Before 1776* (Cambridge, Mass.: Harvard University Press, 2000), is an outstanding synthesis of the recent literature on this transformation throughout the American colonies. Joyce Appleby's *Inheriting the Revolution: The First Generation of Americans* (Cambridge, Mass.: Belknap Press of Harvard University Press, 2000), extends this synthesis into the post-Revolutionary period.

54. Nathan O. Hatch, *The Democratization of American Christianity* (New Haven, Conn.: Yale University Press, 1989), p. 125. On the rise of the language of republicanism and civic

humanism in New England and America, see esp. Bernard Bailyn, *The Ideological Origins of the American Revolution* (Cambridge, Mass.: Belknap Press of Harvard University Press, 1967), and Gordon S. Wood, *The Creation of the American Republic, 1776–1787* (Chapel Hill: University of North Carolina Press, 1969). Nathan Hatch, *The Sacred Cause of Liberty: Republican Thought and the Millennium in Revolutionary New England* (New Haven, Conn.: Yale University Press, 1977), several works by Mark A. Noll, most notably "The American Revolution and Protestant Evangelicalism," *Journal of Interdisciplinary History* 23 (Winter 1993): 615–38, and Gerald Robert McDermott, "Civil Religion in the American Revolutionary Period: An Historiographic Analysis," *Christian Scholar's Review* 18 (June 1989): 346–62, discuss this rise and its role in the gradual marginalization of theological discourse in America's public sphere. Their work is contextualized well by Grasso, *A Speaking Aristocracy*, which offers a comprehensive look at the transformation of public discourse generally in eighteenth-century New England, and Michael Warner, *The Letters of the Republic: Publication and the Public Sphere in Eighteenth-Century America* (Cambridge, Mass.: Harvard University Press, 1990), which offers an insightful analysis of the transformations in public printing and the press. On the permanent decline in the biblical naming of children beginning in this period, see David W. Dumas, "The Naming of Children in New England, 1780–1850," *The New England Historical and Genealogical Register* 132 (July 1978): 196–210; Daniel Scott Smith, "Child-Naming Practices, Kinship Ties, and Change in Family Attitudes in Hingham, Massachusetts, 1641 to 1880," *Journal of Social History* 18 (Summer 1985): 541–66; David Hackett Fischer, "Forenames and the Family in New England: An Exercise in Historical Onomastics," in Robert M. Taylor, Jr., and Ralph J. Crandall, eds., *Generations and Change: Genealogical Perspectives in Social History* (Macon, Ga.: Mercer University Press, 1986), pp. 215–41; Harry S. Stout and Catherine Brekus, "A New England Congregation: Center Church, New Haven, 1638–1989," in James P. Wind and James W. Lewis, eds., *American Congregations: Portraits of Twelve Religious Communities*, Congregational History Project (Chicago: University of Chicago Press, 1994), p. 38; and Gloria L. Main, "Naming Children in Early New England," *Journal of Interdisciplinary History* 27 (Summer 1996): 1–27. On the importance of biblical naming in the Calvinist tradition, see also W. G. Naphy, "Baptisms, Church Riots, and Social Unrest in Calvin's Geneva," *Sixteenth Century Journal* 26 (Spring 1995): 87–97. On the decline in prestige and cultural authority on the part of the New England clergy, see Daniel H. Calhoun, *Professional Lives in America: Structure and Aspiration, 1750–1850* (Cambridge, Mass.: Harvard University Press, 1965); Mary Catherine Foster, "Hampshire County, Massachusetts, 1729–1754: A Covenant Society in Transition" (Ph.D. diss., University of Michigan, 1967), pp. 290–311; Youngs, *God's Messengers*, pp. 92–108, 120–41; Donald M. Scott, *From Office to Profession: The New England Ministry, 1750–1850* (Philadelphia: University of Pennsylvania Press, 1978); Patricia A. Watson, *The Angelical Conjunction: The Preacher-Physicians of Colonial New England* (Knoxville: University of Tennessee Press, 1991); Maris A. Vinovskis, "'Aged Servants of the Lord': Changes in the Status and Treatment of Elderly Ministers in Colonial America," in *Religion, Family, and the Life Course*, ed. Moran and Vinovskis, pp. 181–208; and Robert A. Ferguson, *The American Enlightenment, 1750–1820* (Cambridge, Mass.: Harvard University Press, 1997), pp. 44–79 (esp. pp. 73–74). Several of these developments and their significance are conceptualized well in the recent article by T. H. Breen and Timothy Hall, "Structuring Provincial Imagination: The Rhetoric and Experience of Social Change in Eighteenth-Century New England," *American Historical Review* 103 (December 1998): 1411–39.

55. Harry S. Stout, *The New England Soul: Preaching and Religious Culture in Colonial New England* (New York: Oxford University Press, 1986), pp. 185–211 (quotation from p. 208). Cf. Gregory H. Nobles, *Divisions Throughout the Whole: Politics and Society in Hampshire County, Massachusetts, 1740–1775* (New York: Cambridge University Press, 1983), pp. 36–58.

56. Berk, *Calvinism Versus Democracy*, pp. 13–16 and passim, argues hyperbolically for a strong and enduring politicization of Edwardsianism that led to grasping attempts at revivalistic

social control. However, as Ruth H. Bloch, "Religion and Ideological Change in the American Revolution," in *Religion and American Politics*, ed. Noll, pp. 44–61, has shown, the clerical fusion of religion and politics was actually rather short-lived. On the fundamentally gospel-oriented nature of the Edwardsian ministry that resisted co-optation by more secular, political concerns, see Stout, *The New England Soul*, pp. 268–71, and passim; Harry S. Stout, "Rhetoric and Reality in the Early Republic", in *Religion and American Politics*, ed. Mark A. Noll (New York: Oxford University Press, 1989); and Kling, *A Field of Divine Wonders*, pp. 54–57. And on the powerful effect of Edwardsian *theology* in resisting the trend toward secularization in New England's and America's public life, see also William Casto, "Oliver Ellsworth's Calvinism: A Biographical Essay on Religion and Political Psychology in the Early Republic," *Journal of Church and State* 36 (Summer 1994): 507–26, which reveals that, in the life of the third chief justice of the United States, republican political ideology was subsumed and interpreted within a heavily Edwardsian theological world view (i.e., rather than vice-versa). Reliable analyses of Edwardsian political preaching during the Revolutionary era may be found in Weber, *Rhetoric and History in Revolutionary New England*; Valeri, *Law and Providence in Joseph Bellamy's New England*, pp. 140–72; and Valeri, "The New Divinity and the American Revolution." On the political thought of the New England clergy generally during this period, see Dale S. Kuehne, *Massachusetts Congregationalist Political Thought, 1760–1790: The Design of Heaven* (Columbia: University of Missouri Press, 1996), who confirms, p. 144, that "the ministers were Christians first; their political thought can only be understood if their religion is held to be primary." And for important new insight regarding the frequent Francophobia of New England Protestants, see Charles P. Hanson, *Necessary Virtue: The Pragmatic Origins of Religious Liberty in New England* (Charlottesville: University Press of Virginia, 1998), who discusses the significance of French Catholic military assistance during the American Revolution for the eventual disestablishment of the Standing Order and secularization of American politics.

57. Ward, *The Protestant Evangelical Awakening*, p. 353.

58. On the dissatisfaction of Bellamy, Hopkins, and Emmons with enlightened self-interest, see especially Valeri, *Law and Providence in Joseph Bellamy's New England*, pp. 77–101; Conforti, *Samuel Hopkins and the New Divinity Movement*, pp. 5–6, 109–24, and Sellers, *The Market Revolution: Jacksonian America, 1815–1846*, pp. 206–8, 214. William Warren Sweet, *The Story of Religion in America*, 2d rev. ed. (New York: Harper and Brothers, 1950), p. 171, refers to Hopkins (exaggeratedly) as "the father of the antislavery movement in America." On Edwardsian antislavery reform, see also Conforti, *Samuel Hopkins and the New Divinity Movement*, pp. 125–58; David S. Lovejoy, "Samuel Hopkins: Religion, Slavery, and the Revolution," *New England Quarterly* 40 (June 1967): 227–43; John Saillant, "Slavery and Divine Providence in New England Congregationalism: The New Divinity and a Black Protest, 1775–1805," *New England Quarterly* 68 (December 1995): 584–608; Minkema, "The Edwardses," pp. 503–12; David E. Swift, "Samuel Hopkins: Calvinist Social Concern in Eighteenth-Century New England," *Journal of Presbyterian History* 47 (March 1969): 31–54; Edwards A. Park, *Memoir*, in *The Works of Samuel Hopkins, D.D.*, 3 vols. (Boston: Doctrinal Tract Society, 1852), 1: 114–66; and Lorenzo Johnston Greene, *The Negro in Colonial New England, 1620–1776*, Studies in History, Economics, and Public Law, No. 494 (New York: Columbia University Press, 1942), pp. 277–79. On the evangelistic aspects of the colonization movement, Sylvia M. Jacobs, "Black Americans and the Missionary Movement in Africa: A Bibliography," in Sylvia M. Jacobs, ed., *Black Americans and the Missionary Movement in Africa*, Contributions in Afro-American and African Studies, No. 66 (Westpost, Conn.: Greenwood Press, 1982), pp. 229–37, is somewhat dated but still quite useful. Far and away the best source on black evangelism in West Africa and its role in shaping West African social and political history is Lamin Sanneh, *Abolitionists Abroad: American Blacks and the Making of Modern West Africa* (Cambridge, Mass.: Harvard University Press, 1999). But see also the recent discussion of black leadership of the Liberian mission in Janet Duitsman Cornelius, *Slave*

Missions and the Black Church in the Antebellum South (Columbia: University of South Carolina Press, 1999), pp. 159–74. For a concise, reliable history of black attitudes toward colonization, see Wilson Jeremiah Moses's more recent introduction to *Liberian Dreams: Back-to-Africa Narratives from the 1850s,* ed. Wilson Jeremiah Moses (University Park: Pennsylvania State University Press, 1998), pp. xiii–xxxiv. On Lemuel Haynes, see Timothy M. Cooley, *Sketches of the Life and Character of the Rev. Lemuel Haynes* (New York: Harper and Brothers, 1837); Helen MacLam, "Black Puritan on the Northern Frontier: The Vermont Ministry of Lemuel Haynes," in Richard Newman, ed., *Black Preacher to White America: The Collected Writings of Lemuel Haynes, 1774–1833* (Brooklyn, N.Y.: Carlson, 1990), pp. xix–xxxviii; and John Saillant, "Lemuel Haynes and the Revolutionary Origins of Black Theology, 1776–1801," *Religion and American Culture* 2 (Winter 1992): 79–102. On Emmons's opposition to slavery and Freemasonry, see Park, *Memoir of Nathanael Emmons,* pp. 444–46. For the ongoing opposition of Emmons and other Hopkinsians (especially the ex-mason Rev. Moses Thacher of Wrentham, Mass.) to Freemasonry, see Paul Goodman, *Towards a Christian Republic: Antimasonry and the Great Transition in New England, 1826–1836* (New York: Oxford University Press, 1988), pp. 54–79, 163–76; Park, *Memoir,* 1: 113; Dahlquist, "Nathanael Emmons," pp. 182–84; and John L. Brooke, *The Heart of the Commonwealth: Society and Political Culture in Worcester County, Massachusetts, 1713–1861* (New York: Cambridge University Press, 1989), pp. 344–46. On Dwight and the Illuminati, see Timothy Dwight, *The Duty of Americans at the Present Crisis, Illustrated in a Discourse, Preached on the Fourth of July, 1798, at the Request of the Citizens of New-Haven* (New Haven: Thomas and Samuel Green, 1798), and Vernon W. Stauffer, *New England and the Bavarian Illuminati* (New York: Russell and Russell, 1967). On the capacity of Edwardsian millennial speculation to generate radical cultural criticism, see M. Darrol Bryant, "From Edwards to Hopkins: A Millennialist Critique of Political Culture," in M. Darrol Bryant and Donald W. Dayton, eds., *The Coming Kingdom: Essays in American Millennialism and Eschatology* (Barrytown, N.Y.: New Era Books, 1983), pp. 45–70. On the depoliticization of Edwardsian religion after the Revolution, and on Edwardsian efforts to effect change by converting individuals rather than Christianizing the social order, consult Richard D. Birdsall, "The Second Great Awakening and the New England Social Order," *Church History* 39 (September 1970): 345–64; and Rohrer, *Keepers of the Covenant,* pp. 62–69. The Edwardsians have often been described as dyed-in-the-wool Federalists, but this argument is misleading. Even among the most politically oriented Edwardsian clergy, not all were Federalist sympathizers. See Richard D. Birdsall, "The Reverend Thomas Allen: Jeffersonian Calvinist," *NEQ* 30 (June 1957): 147–65. For a forceful (yet overdrawn) argument that New Divinity theology proved much more conducive to liberal individualism and market capitalism than historians have typically assumed, see James D. German, "The Preacher and the New Light Revolution in Connecticut: The Pulpit Theology of Benjamin Trumbull, 1760–1800" (Ph.D. diss., University of California, Riverside, 1989); and James German, "The Social Utility of Wicked Self-Love: Calvinism, Capitalism, and Public Policy in Revolutionary New England," *Journal of American History* 82 (December 1995): 965–98. More helpful is Breitenbach, "Unregenerate Doings," pp. 500–502, who argues, not that New Divinity thought proved conducive to these trends, but that it gave New Englanders a way to be Calvinistic capitalists. Because it taught that "saints would respect limits," New Englanders could "venture into market relations with something approaching confidence." See also Grasso, *A Speaking Aristocracy,* p. 368, who concludes wisely that "no single Edwardsean social and political theory guided the thought and practice of New Divinity men in the later eighteenth century"; and Paul Gilje, ed., "Special Issue on Capitalism in the Early Republic," *Journal of the Early Republic* 16 (Summer 1996): 159–308, for a reliable sampling of the historiography on the rise of capitalism in the early republic.

59. Jonathan Edwards, Jr., to [John Erskine], February 8, 1787, Jonathan Edwards, Jr., Papers, Trask; Park, *Memoir,* 1: 238. On late eighteenth-century Edwardsian strength, see also "Essays

upon Hopkinsianism," *HM* 1 (February 1824): 42–43; and note the early presence of the Edwardsians or "Hopkinsians" as a school to be reckoned with in Hannah Adams's historical encyclopedia of religious groups: Hannah Adams, *An Alphabetical Compendium of the Various Sects Which Have Appeared in the World from the Beginning of the Christian Era to the Present Day* (Boston: B. Edes and Sons, 1784), pp. 79–86; and Hannah Adams, *A View of Religions* (Boston: John West Folsom, 1791), pp. 96–104.

60. In recent years, the concept of America's "Second Great Awakening" has suffered a fate similar to that of the first "Great Awakening." For historical analysis of the problems involved in employing this concept, see John R. Fitzmier, *New England's Moral Legislator: Timothy Dwight, 1752–1817,* Religion in North America (Bloomington: Indiana University Press, 1998), esp. pp. 228–33; Conkin, *The Uneasy Center,* pp. 128–30; and Hatch, *The Democratization of American Christianity,* pp. 220–26. The best general treatment of New Divinity preaching is Kling, *A Field of Divine Wonders,* pp. 110–43. But see also Conforti, *Samuel Hopkins and the New Divinity Movement,* pp. 175–90, on Hopkins; Valeri, *Law and Providence in Joseph Bellamy's New England,* on Bellamy; and Donald Weber, *Rhetoric and History in Revolutionary New England* (New York: Oxford University Press, 1988). In his famous "Letters on Revivals of Religion" (1832), the Edwardsian Ebenezer Porter characterized the New Divinity preaching of New England's Second Great Awakening, not as dry and esoteric, but as "doctrino-practical." It steered a middle course, he argued, "between the precincts of a sterile, heartless morality on the one hand, and of a useless speculation on the other." Ebenezer Porter, "Dr. Porter's Letters on Revivals of Religion," *SP* 5 (June 1832): 320.

Joseph Conforti especially, but also Bruce Kuklick, have argued, in Conforti's words, that Edwards's broad-based popularity and cultural influence "was far more a creation of the nineteenth century than a lineal, continuous evolution from the eighteenth." While this is true to a certain extent, it is important not to neglect the gradual growth of the Edwardsian theological culture throughout the latter part of the eighteenth century. The early New Divinity social and intellectual network sank the roots that made the growth of nineteenth-century Edwardsianism possible. Conforti, "Mary Lyon," (quotation from p. 84); Conforti, "Antebellum Evangelicals"; Conforti, "The Invention of the Great Awakening,"; and Bruce Kuklick, "The Two Cultures in Eighteenth-Century America," in Oberg and Stout, eds., *Benjamin Franklin, Jonathan Edwards, and the Representation of American Culture,* pp. 101–13. The persuasive power of the argument for a cultural revival of Edwardsianism after a period of relative Edwardsian obscurity in the eighteenth century derives in part from the once-popular but now-tenuous notion that religious vitality in America reached its low ebb after the Revolution. While it is true that New England Congregationalism as a whole suffered substantial institutional losses during the Revolution, and though the Edwardsians themselves employed the myth of declension in an effort to promote the successes of the Second Great Awakening, the low-ebb thesis has been roundly criticized in recent years. See Douglas H. Sweet, "Church Vitality and the American Revolution: Historiographical Consensus and Thoughts Toward a New Perspective," *Church History* 45 (September 1976): 341–57; Shiels, "The Second Great Awakening in Connecticut"; Richard W. Pointer, *Protestant Pluralism and the New York Experience: A Study of Eighteenth-Century Religious Diversity,* Religion in North America (Bloomington: Indiana University Press, 1988), pp. 107ff.; Harry S. Stout and Catherine A. Brekus, "Declension, Gender, and the 'New Religious History,'" in Vandermeer and Swierenga, eds., *Belief and Behavior,* pp. 15–37; Roger Finke and Rodney Stark, *The Churching of America, 1776–1990: Winners and Losers in Our Religious Economy* (New Brunswick, N.J.: Rutgers University Press, 1992), pp. 3–4, 56–59; and Stephen A. Marini, "Religion, Politics, and Ratification," in Ronald Hoffman and Peter J. Albert, eds., *Religion in a Revolutionary Age* (Charlottesville: University Press of Virginia, 1994), pp. 184–217.

61. On New Divinity concerts of prayer, circular fasts, conference meetings, and cooperative revivalism generally, see Richard Douglas Shiels, "The Connecticut Clergy in the Second Great

Awakening" (Ph.D. diss., Boston University, 1976), pp. 40–86; and Kling, *A Field of Divine Wonders*, pp. 67–73.

62. Kling, *A Field of Divine Wonders*, p. 19. See also Conforti, *Samuel Hopkins and the New Divinity Movement*, pp. 175–90. On the New England revivals generally, Mary Hewitt Mitchell, *The Great Awakening and Other Revivals in the Religious Life of Connecticut* (New Haven, Conn.: Yale University Press, 1934), pp. 23–51, remains a rich resource.

63. *The Diary of William Bentley, D.D., Pastor of the East Church, Salem, Massachusetts*, 4 vols. (Gloucester, Mass.: Peter Smith, 1962; 1905), 4: 302 (for further supercilious testimony from Bentley concerning the prevalence of Edwardsianism, see 1: 160, 196–97, and 3: 113, 364–65, 412); David D. Field, ed., *A History of the County of Berkshire, Massachusetts; In Two Parts. The First Being a General View of the County; The Second, an Account of the Several Towns* (Pittsfield, Mass.: Samuel W. Bush, 1829), p. 229; [Archibald Alexander], "An Inquiry into That Inability under Which the Sinner Labours, and Whether It Furnishes Any Excuse for His Neglect of Duty," *BR*, n.s., 3 (July 1831): 362; Samuel Miller, *Life of Jonathan Edwards*, The Library of American Biography (Boston: Hilliard, Gray, and Co., 1837), p. 215; Bennet Tyler, *Memoir of the Life and Character of Rev. Asahel Nettleton, D.D.*, 2d ed. (Hartford, Conn.: Robins and Smith, 1845; 1844), p. 274; Worcester, *The Life and Labors of Rev. Samuel Worcester*, 1: 211; and Blake, *A Centurial History of the Mendon Association*, p. 31. For other testimonials to the powerful influence of the Edwardsian theological culture during the first two-thirds of the nineteenth century, see the anonymous author of the *Essays on Hopkinsianism* [Boston?: n.p., c. 1820], p. 42, who contended that "many of the students of the theological seminary, at Auburn, . . . one half of the students of the theological seminary at Princeton, . . . [and a] large proportion, some think almost half of the Presbyterian ministers in the United States, adopt the leading sentiments of the Hopkinsian system"; Porter, "Dr. Porter's Letters on Revivals of Religion," p. 318; [Joseph Harvey], *Letters on the Present State and Probable Results of Theological Speculations in Connecticut* (n.p., 1832), pp. 41–42; Lyman Beecher, "Letter from Dr. Beecher to Dr. Woods," *SP* 5 (July 1832): 394; Eliza Buckminster Lee, *Memoirs of Rev. Joseph Buckminster, D.D., and of His Son, Rev. Joseph Stevens Buckminster* (Boston: Wm. Crosby and H. P. Nichols, 1849), p. 330; [Harriet Beecher Stowe], "New England Ministers," *Atlantic Monthly* 1 (February 1858): 487; Leonard Bacon, "Historical Discourse," in *Contributions to the Ecclesiastical History of Connecticut; Prepared Under the Direction of the General Association, to Commemorate the Completion of One Hundred and Fifty Years Since Its First Annual Assembly* (New Haven, Conn: William L. Kingsley, 1861), p. 61; Frederick Denison Maurice, *Modern Philosophy; Or, A Treatise of Moral and Metaphysical Philosophy from the Fourteenth Century to the French Revolution, with a Glimpse into the Nineteenth Century* (London: Griffin, Bohn, and Company, 1862), p. 469; Leonard Woods, *History of the Andover Theological Seminary* (Boston: James R. Osgood and Company, 1885), pp. 28–41; and Theodore S. Woolsey, "Theodore Dwight Woolsey—A Biographical Sketch," *Yale Review*, n.s., 1 (January 1912): 246.

64. Thomas H. Johnson, *The Printed Writings of Jonathan Edwards, 1703–1758: A Bibliography* (Princeton, N.J.: Princeton University Press, 1940), p. xi; and "Review of the Works of President Edwards," *CS* 3 (June 1821): 298–99. For publication statistics, see also Conforti, "Antebellum Evangelicals." On the tremendous popular appeal of Edwards's writings among both clergy and laity, see Norman Pettit, "Editor's Introduction," in Jonathan Edwards, *The Life of David Brainerd*, ed. Norman Pettit, WJE, vol. 7 (Yale, 1985), pp. 1–4; Conforti, "Jonathan Edwards's Most Popular Work"; Conforti, "David Brainerd"; Ola Elizabeth Winslow, *Jonathan Edwards 1703–1758: A Biography* (New York: Macmillan, 1940), quotation from p. 240; John F. Wilson, "Editor's Introduction," in Jonathan Edwards, *A History of the Work of Redemption*, ed. John F. Wilson, WJE, vol. 9 (Yale, 1989), p. 82; and Guelzo, *Edwards on the Will*. For Brainerd's vast influence on evangelical spirituality and mental health, see also David L. Weddle, "The Melancholy Saint: Jonathan Edwards's Interpretation of David Brainerd as a Model of

Evangelical Spirituality," *Harvard Theological Review* 81 (July 1988): 297–318; and Rubin, *Religious Melancholy and Protestant Experience in America*, pp. 94–103.

65. H. P. Beach, "Yale's Contribution to Foreign Missions," in James B. Reynolds, Samuel H. Fisher, and Henry B. Wright, eds., *Two Centuries of Christian Activity at Yale* (New York: G. P. Putnam's Sons, 1901), p. 289, and N. L. L. Beman to Edwards Amasa Park, October 31, 1860, BPL. On the significance of Brainerd's grave, see *AAP*, 3: 116. For his influence in the rise of American missions, see Oliver Wendell Elsbree, *The Rise of the Missionary Spirit in America, 1790–1815* (Philadelphia: Porcupine Press, 1980; 1928), pp. 17–20, 57. Hopkinsians dominated the Massachusetts Missionary Society from its beginning in 1799. Nathanael Emmons became the society's founding president and also served for a time as editor of its publication, the *Massachusetts Missionary Magazine*. While the General Association of Connecticut controlled the Connecticut Missionary Society, it too was dominated by Edwardsians. The Connecticut society originated in 1797–98 out of the concerns of the Edwardsian Hartfield North Association and Edwardsians such as Nathan Strong, John Smalley, Jeremiah Day, and Levi Hart played leading roles in the founding and maintenance of its publication, the *Connecticut Evangelical Magazine*. For a small sampling of the large body of literature on the influence of Edwardsianism in the rise of Protestant world missions, see esp. Samuel Hopkins to Andrew Fuller, October 15, 1799, in Park, *Memoir*, 1: 236; Park, *Memoir of Nathanael Emmons*, pp. 176–200; Elsbree, *The Rise of the Missionary Spirit in America*, pp. 138–42, 146–52; James A. De Jong, *As the Waters Cover the Sea: Millennial Expectations in the Rise of Anglo-American Missions, 1640–1810* (Kampen, Netherlands: J. H. Kok, 1970), pp. 199–227; William R. Hutchison, *Errand to the World: American Protestant Thought and Foreign Missions* (Chicago: University of Chicago Press, 1987), pp. 49–51; Ronald Edwin Davies, "Prepare Ye the Way of the Lord: The Missiological Thought and Practice of Jonathan Edwards (1703–1758)" (Ph.D. diss., Fuller Theological Seminary, 1989); and David W. Kling, "The New Divinity and the Origins of the American Board of Commissioners for Foreign Missions," in Wilbert R. Shenk, ed., *North American Foreign Missions, 1810–1914: Theology, Theory, and Policy* (Grand Rapids, Mich.: Eerdmans, in press). For the roles of Edwardsians at Williams College and Andover Seminary in the missions movement, see also *Memoirs of American Missionaries, Formerly Connected with the Society of Inquiry Respecting Missions, in the Andover Theological Seminary* (Boston: Peirce and Parker, 1833); David W. Kling, "The New Divinity and Williams College, 1793–1836," *Religion and American Culture* 6 (Summer 1996): 195–223; and Glenn T. Miller, *Piety and Intellect: The Aims and Purposes of Ante-Bellum Theological Education* (Atlanta, Ga.: Scholars Press, 1990), whose analysis of Andover as "the missionary seminary" may be found on pp. 77–79. On New England Congregationalist missions generally during this period, see also John A. Andrew III, *Rebuilding the Christian Commonwealth: New England Congregationalists and Foreign Missions, 1800–1830* (Lexington: University Press of Kentucky, 1976).

66. Social control analyses of New England's revivalistic benevolent reform include Mead, *Nathaniel William Taylor*, pp. 47–49; Clifford S. Griffin, *Their Brothers' Keepers: Moral Stewardship in the United States, 1800–1865* (New Brunswick, N.J.: Rutgers University Press, 1960); W. David Lewis, "The Reformer as Conservative: Protestant Counter-Subversion in the Early Republic," in *The Development of an American Culture*, ed. Stanley Coben and Lorman Ratner (Englewood Cliffs, N.J.: Prentice-Hall, 1970), pp. 64–91; McLoughlin, *New England Dissent*, 2: 918; and Berk, *Calvinism Versus Democracy*, pp. 161–93. In recent years, several scholars have moved beyond this condescending analytical framework and offered more useful interpretations of evangelical benevolence. See, for example, Donald G. Mathews, "The Second Great Awakening as an Organizing Process, 1780–1830: An Hypothesis," *American Quarterly* 21 (Spring 1969): 23–43; Birdsall, "The Second Great Awakening and the New England Social Order"; Daniel Walker Howe, *The Political Culture of the American Whigs* (Chicago: The University of Chicago Press, 1979), pp. 150–80; and George M. Thomas, *Revivalism and Cultural Change: Christian-*

ity, Nation Building, and the Market in the Nineteenth-Century United States (Chicago: University of Chicago Press, 1989). The best general treatment of religion and reform in this period is Robert H. Abzug, *Cosmos Crumbling: American Reform and the Religious Imagination* (New York: Oxford University Press, 1994). Two recent works that point, significantly, to ongoing evangelical dissent from the status quo in this period of evangelical dominance are Mark Y. Hanley, *Beyond a Christian Commonwealth: The Protestant Quarrel with the American Republic, 1830–1860* (Chapel Hill: University of North Carolina Press, 1994); and William R. Sutton, *Journeymen for Jesus: Evangelical Artisans Confront Capitalism in Jacksonian Baltimore* (University Park: Pennsylvania State University Press, 1998). And as Mark S. Schantz argues helpfully in *Piety in Providence: Class Dimensions of Religious Experience in Antebellum Rhode Island* (Ithaca, N.Y.: Cornell University Press, 2000), "Evangelical Christianity was not the possession of a single social class or constituency in the industrializing Northeast. It served simultaneously to bolster the rising power of the American bourgeoisie and to create an alternative religious culture that fueled opposition to that power" (p. 2).

67. Taylorite/Edwardsian benevolent reform will be discussed later. For examples of latter-day Hopkinsian opposition to slavery, see "American Colonization Society," *HM* 1 (May 1825): 430–31; "On Slave Labor," *HM* 4 (December 1831): 281–82; and "The Slave Question," *HM* 4 (June 1832): 411–12. On the antislavery reform of New England's evangelical Calvinists generally in this period, see Victor B. Howard, *Conscience and Slavery: The Evangelistic Calvinist Domestic Missions, 1837–1861* (Kent, Oh.: Kent State University Press, 1990). The leaders of the Edwardsian opposition to Indian removal were Jeremiah Evarts (a member of New Haven's Center Church) and his pupil, the Cherokee missionary Samuel A. Worcester (nephew of the Edwardsian Dr. Samuel Worcester of Salem, Massachusetts). See John A. Andrew III, *From Revivals to Removal: Jeremiah Evarts, the Cherokee Nation, and the Search for the Soul of America* (Athens: University of Georgia Press, 1991); Althea Bass, *Cherokee Messenger* (Norman: University of Oklahoma Press, 1936); William G. McLoughlin, *Cherokees and Missionaries, 1789–1839* (New Haven: Yale University Press, 1984), pp. 239–65; and William G. McLoughlin, "Two Bostonian Missions to the Frontier Indians, 1810–1860," in Conrad Edick Wright, ed., *Massachusetts and the New Nation*, Studies in American History and Culture, No. 2 (Boston: Massachusetts Historical Society, 1992), pp. 175–80. See also the several articles against U.S. treatment of the Indians in the heavily Edwardsian periodical *The Spirit of the Pilgrims* (discussed later), which both Evarts and Worcester helped to establish: "Review of an Article in the North American Review," *SP* 3 (March 1830): 141–61; "Speeches on the Indian Bill," *SP* 3 (September 1830): 492–500, and (October 1830): 517–32; "Review of the Case of the Cherokees against Georgia," *SP* 4 (September 1831): 492–513; "Review of Pamphlets on the Death of Jeremiah Evarts, Esq.," *SP* 4 (November 1831): 599–613; and "Review of Thatcher's Lives of the Indians," *SP* 6 (January 1833): 41–47. An excellent recent discussion of the historical significance of Edwardsian and other forms of resistance to Indian removal may be found in Mary Hershberger, "Mobilizing Women, Anticipating Abolition: The Struggle Against Indian Removal in the 1830s," *Journal of American History* 86 (June 1999): 15–40. For an example of latter-day Hopkinsian opposition to intemperance, see "Intemperance," *HM* 3 (November 1828): 248–53, and (February 1829): 316–21.

68. Not all Edwardsians would remain content within the limits of the colonizationist agenda, but the position of the Andover Seminary faculty proved fairly representative. In 1835, after nearly one-fourth of its students had joined the immediatist cause, Andover's faculty won them back for colonizationism by arguing that radical abolitionism was unscriptural, divisive, and would distract them unnecessarily from their ministerial preparation. See J. Earl Thompson, Jr., "Abolitionism and Theological Education at Andover," *New England Quarterly* 47 (June 1974): 238–61. That same year, John Greenleaf Whittier would quip, "anti-slavery is going on well in spite of mobs, Andover Seminary, and rum." John Greenleaf Whittier to Abijah Wyman Thayer,

November 29, 1835, in John B. Pickard, ed., *The Letters of John Greenleaf Whittier, vol. 1, 1828–1845* (Cambridge, Mass.: Belknap Press of Harvard University Press, 1975), p. 177. Lewis Perry, *Childhood, Marriage, and Reform: Henry Clarke Wright, 1797–1870* (Chicago: University of Chicago Press, 1980), pp. 15–16, 144–45, offers another useful perspective on the weakly defined opposition to slavery at Andover. On antislavery reform generally among evangelicals in this period, see Bertram Wyatt-Brown, *Lewis Tappan and the Evangelical War Against Slavery* (Cleveland, Ohio: The Press of Case Western Reserve University, 1969). On the failure of the colonizationists' mission in Liberia, see Sanneh, *Abolitionists Abroad*, pp. 182–237. On the moral and spiritual pilgrimage of one important, erstwhile Edwardsian who became disappointed with both evangelical reform and the piety from which it sprang, see Robert H. Abzug, *Passionate Liberator: Theodore Dwight Weld and the Dilemma of Reform* (New York: Oxford University Press, 1980).

69. By contrast, the Brahmins of Boston responded to these cultural and political changes with a series of rearguard tactics intended to shore up and even extend their cultural authority. "Regarding culture in general as an extension of politics," they "launched a broad and many-faceted cultural crusade designed to impose their values on the nation, and thereby to ensure the salvation of the republic." See the helpful recent book by Harlow W. Sheidley, *Sectional Nationalism: Massachusetts Conservative Leaders and the Transformation of America, 1815–1836* (Boston: Northeastern University Press, 1998), p. xi and passim.

70. James H. Moorhead, "Social Reform and the Divided Conscience of Antebellum Protestantism," *Church History* 48 (December 1979): 416–30, has made a similar argument concerning American evangelicalism as a whole in this era. Though he emphasizes the evangelical neglect of social reform more than I, his point is well taken: "Creating a vast reservoir of moral anxiety and a boundless commitment to do good, evangelicalism inspired its adherents to strain every nerve in pursuit of new channels for benevolence. . . . But by resting hopes for improvement upon the willingness of individuals to act benevolently, Protestantism also came close, on occasion, to making good intentions a substitute for reform" (p. 429).

71. See Claude M. Fuess, *Amherst: The Story of a New England College* (Boston: Little, Brown, 1935), p. 30; Leon Burr Richardson, *History of Dartmouth College* (Hanover, N.H.: Dartmouth College Publications, 1932), 1: 239–40; Conforti, "Mary Lyon"; Kling, "The New Divinity and Williams College"; Frederick Rudolph, *Mark Hopkins and the Log: Williams College, 1836–1872*, Yale Historical Publications (New Haven, Conn.: Yale University Press, 1956), pp. 89–132; and Amanda Porterfield, *Mary Lyon and the Mount Holyoke Missionaries* (New York: Oxford University Press, 1997). Significantly, before Griffin assumed the Williams presidency, Taylor's colleague Chauncey Goodrich was asked to serve (at the tender age of 31), but declined due to ill health and the need to care for his aging father. See Goodrich's two letters, to Alvan Hyde and to Timothy M. Cooley, August 24, 1821, Ferdinand J. Dreer Autograph Collection, Historical Society of Pennsylvania.

The Edwardsian enculturation process extended outside of New England as well during this period, most notably to New York and East Tennessee. On developments in New York, especially at Union College (whose second, third, and fourth presidents were the Edwardsians Jonathan Edwards, Jr., Jonathan Maxcy [the former president of Rhode Island College], and Eliphalet Nott, respectively), Hamilton College, and Auburn Seminary (which was dominated by the Edwardsian theologians James Richards and Matthew La Rue Perrine beginning in the early 1820s), see esp. Codman Hislop, *Eliphalet Nott* (Middletown, Conn.: Wesleyan University Press, 1971); Samuel H. Gridley's "Biographical Sketch" of Richards in Gridley, ed., *Lectures on Mental Philosophy and Theology. By James Richards, D.D.* (New York: M. W. Dodd, 1846), pp. 9–96; *AAP*, 4: 99–112, 237–41; and John Quincy Adams, *A History of Auburn Theological Seminary, 1818–1918* (Auburn, N.Y.: Auburn Seminary Press, 1918), pp. 72–80. On developments in East Tennessee, where Edwardsians Hezekiah Balch and Charles Coffin (to a lesser extent) led in the founding and early development of Greeneville College (later Tusculum College) beginning in 1794, Edwardsian Isaac Anderson (student of the Hopkinsian missionary Gideon Blackburn) led in the founding of Southern and Western Theological Seminary in 1819 (later Maryville College), and other Edwardsians founded a Brainerd Mission to the Cherokees in Chattanooga, see esp. Joseph T. Fuhrmann, *The Life and Times of Tusculum College* (Greeneville, Tenn.: Tusculum College, 1986); Allen E. Ragan, *A History of Tusculum College, 1794–1944* (Bristol, Tenn.: Tusculum Sesquicentennial Committee, 1945); John Joseph Robinson, *Memoir of Rev. Isaac Anderson, D.D.* (Knoxville, Tenn.: J. A. Rayl, 1860); Samuel Tyndale Wilson, *A Century of Maryville College, 1819–1919: A Story of Altruism* (Maryville, Tenn.: Directors of Maryville College, 1919); Samuel Tyndale Wilson, *Isaac Anderson: Founder and First President of Maryville College; A Memorial Sketch* (Maryville, Tenn.: Kindred of Dr. Anderson, 1932); Ralph Waldo Lloyd, *Maryville College: A History of 150 Years, 1819–1969* (Maryville, Tenn.: Maryville College Press, 1969), pp. 74–81; Robert Sparks Walker, *Torchlights to the Cherokees: The Brainerd Mission* (New York: Macmillan, 1931); and Altha Leah Bierbower Bass, *The Cherokee Messenger* (Norman: University of Oklahoma Press, 1936). Cf. *AAP*, 3: 308–19, and 4: 43–58, 246–56; Ernest Trice Thompson, *Presbyterians in the South, Volume 1: 1607–1861* (Richmond, Va.: John Knox Press, 1963), pp. 269–72, 353–55, 409–11; and Elwyn A. Smith, "The Doctrine of Imputation and the Presbyterian Schism of 1837–1838," *Journal of the Presbyterian Historical Society* 38 (September 1960): 129–51 (these Edwardsian developments prepared the way for the dominance of New School Presbyterianism in Tennessee beginning in 1837). Significantly, in 1827 Coffin resigned the presidency of Greeneville College to become president of East Tennessee College, which was later renamed the University of Tennessee. Thanks go to Richard C. Goode of Nashville's Lipscomb University for information on the Brainerd Mission.

72. For the differences between the Tasters and the Exercisers, see Breitenbach, "New Divinity Theology and the Ideal of Moral Accountability,"pp. 215–35; Kuklick, *Churchmen and Philosophers*, pp. 55–59; Guelzo, *Edwards on the Will*, pp. 108–11; and James Hoopes, *Consciousness in New England: From Puritanism and Ideas to Psychoanalysis and Semiotic*, New Studies in American Intellectual and Cultural History (Baltimore, Md.: Johns Hopkins University Press, 1989), pp. 95–124.

73. James King Morse, *Jedidiah Morse: A Champion of New England Orthodoxy* (New York: Columbia University Press, 1939), pp. 40–41, 121–49, 148, 160; Enoch Pond, *Sketches of the Theological History of New England* (Boston: Congregational Publishing Society, 1880), pp. 55–59, 74–75; and Fisher, *A Discourse, Commemorative of the History of the Church of Christ in Yale College*, pp. 80–82. See also Harlan, *The Clergy and the Great Awakening in New England*, p. 5 and passim; William Breitenbach, "The Consistent Calvinism of the New Divinity Movement," *William and Mary Quarterly*, 3d ser., 41 (April 1984): 242; Hirrel, *Children of Wrath*, p. 69, who notes that Morse's sons Sidney, Richard, and Samuel became supporters of New Haven Edwardsianism; and Elsbree, *The Rise of the Missionary Spirit in America*, pp. 91–93, who writes: "So influential did the aggressive Edwardean revivalists become that there was soon no middle ground possible between the liberalism of the Boston Unitarians and the dogmatism of the New Calvinists. Forced to make a choice, the Old Calvinists, for the most part, cast in their lot with the revivalists."

74. *Diary of William Bentley*, 3: 403. For further liberal criticism of Hopkinsian strength at Andover, see "Theological Seminary," *The Monthly Anthology* 5 (November 1808): 602–14; and see the liberal belletrist Charles Prentiss's (1774–1820) anti-Hopkinsian essay *The Trial: Calvin and Hopkins Versus the Bible and Common Sense. To Which Are Added Some Remarks on the Andover Constitution*, 2d ed. (Boston: n.p., 1819), esp. pp. 28ff.

75. Henry K. Rowe, *History of Andover Theological Seminary* (Newton, Mass.: Thomas Todd Company, 1933), pp. 16, 20, 48–58; and Leonard Bacon, *A Commemorative Discourse, on the Completion of Fifty Years from the Founding of the Theological Seminary at Andover* (Andover: Mass.: W. F. Draper, 1858), p. 39. On Andover's early years, see also William B. Sprague, *The Life of*

Jedidiah Morse (New York: Anson D. F. Randolph and Company, 1874), p.110; Woods, *History of the Andover Theological Seminary*, pp. 93-131, 257-60, 333-52; Ephraim Abbot to Edwards A. Park, December 23, 1859, Folder 4, Box 2, Ephraim Abbot Papers, AAS; Edwards A. Park, *Memoir of Nathanael Emmons; with Sketches of His Friends and Pupils* (Boston: Congregational Board of Publication, 1861), pp. 209-10; Morse, *Jedidiah Morse*, who notes that "in conference after conference and in the dealings between the two groups seeking to unite, . . . the moderate Calvinists yielded before the definite and insistent demands of the Hopkinsians" (p. 114); Harold Young Vanderpool, "The Andover Conservatives: Apologetics, Biblical Criticism, and Theological Change at the Andover Theological Seminary, 1808-1880" (Ph.D. diss., Harvard University, 1971), esp. p. 348; and Richard J. Moss, *The Life of Jedidiah Morse: A Station of Peculiar Exposure* (Knoxville: University of Tennessee Press, 1995), pp. 90-92.

76. Oliver Wendell Holmes, "The Deacon's Masterpiece: or The Wonderful 'One-Hoss-Shay,'" *Atlantic Monthly* 2 (September 1858): 496-97. Elsewhere, Holmes wrote that "Edwards's whole system had too much of the character of the savage people by whom the wilderness had so recently been tenanted," and "Edwards's system seems, in the light of to-day, to the last degree barbaric, mechanical, materialistic, pessimistic." Oliver Wendell Holmes, "Jonathan Edwards," in *Pages from an Old Volume of Life: A Collection of Essays, 1857-1881* (Boston: Houghton Mifflin, 1892), pp. 392, 395.

77. Stowe, *The Minister's Wooing*, p. 728. Stowe portrays the ways in which ordinary laypeople appropriated the New England Theology in *Oldtown Folks* (1869) and *Poganuc People* (1878). As Henry Ward Beecher's Dr. Wentworth comments in *Norwood: Or, Village Life in New England* (New York: Fords, Howard, and Hulbert, 1887; 1867), pp. 133-34, "It may be that at any given time, a high doctrinal sermon is not so edifying as a simple practical one would be. But a community brought up, through a hundred years, to task their thought upon themes remote, difficult, and infinite, will be far nobler than if they had been fed upon easy thought. . . . Look at the history of New England mind in a large way. I think we owe every thing to her theologians, and most to the most doctrinal. . . . Such men as Edwards, Hopkins, Smalley, West, Bellamy, Backus, Burton, Emmons, lifted up the New England mind into a range of speculation and conviction that ennobled and strengthened it as art never could have done."

78. Howe, *The Political Culture of the American Whigs*, pp. 6-7; Daniel Walker Howe, *Making the American Self: Jonathan Edwards to Abraham Lincoln* (Cambridge, Mass.: Harvard University Press, 1997), p. 2; Smith, "The Theological System of Emmons," p. 253; and [Stowe], "New England Ministers," pp. 486-87. On the widespread accessibility and lay appropriation of earlier New England theology, see also David D. Hall, "Toward a History of Popular Religion in Early New England," *William and Mary Quarterly*, 3d ser., 41 (January 1984): 49-55; Selement, *Keepers of the Vineyard*, pp. 43-56; Michael McGiffert, "The People Speak: Confessions of Lay Men and Women," in Michael McGiffert, ed., *God's Plot: Puritan Spirituality in Thomas Shepard's Cambridge*, rev. ed. (Amherst: University of Massachusetts Press, 1994), pp. 135-48; David D. Hall, "Narrating Puritanism," in Harry S. Stout and D. G. Hart, eds., *New Directions in American Religious History* (New York: Oxford University Press, 1997), pp. 64, 71; and James F. Cooper, Jr., *Tenacious of Their Liberties: The Congregationalists in Colonial Massachusetts*, Religion in America Series (New York: Oxford University Press, 1999). On literacy rates, see esp. David D. Hall, "Readers and Writers in Early New England," in *A History of the Book in America*, vol. 1, *The Colonial Book in the Atlantic World*, ed. Hugh Amory and David D. Hall (Cambridge: Cambridge University Press, 2000), pp. 117-51; David D. Hall, "Readers and Reading in America: Historical and Critical Perspectives," *Proceedings of the American Antiquarian Society* 103 (October 1993): 337-57; David D. Hall, *Worlds of Wonder, Days of Judgment: Popular Religious Belief in Early New England* (New York: Alfred A. Knopf, 1989), pp. 21-70; Kenneth Lockridge, *Literacy in Colonial New England* (New York: Norton, 1974); Cathy N. Davidson, *Revolution and the Word: The Rise of the Novel in America* (New York: Oxford University Press, 1986), pp. 55-

79; Gilmore, *Reading Becomes a Necessity of Life*; and Timothy Dwight, *Travels in New England and New York*, ed. Barbara Miller Solomon, with the assistance of Patricia M. King (Cambridge, Mass.: Belknap Press of Harvard University Press, 1969), 1: 336–38. Yale's Eleazar T. Fitch, *National Prosperity Perpetuated: A Discourse: Delivered in the Chapel of Yale College; on the Day of the Annual Thanksgiving: November 29, 1827* (New Haven, Conn.: Treadway and Adams, 1828), p. 9, once declared with joy: "How rare is that phenomenon at least in New-England, that is so common in other nations;—an adult who cannot read!" For more on the close relationship between pulpit and pew in the Edwardsian tradition, see Park, *Memoir of Nathanael Emmons*, 344–54, and Kling, *A Field of Divine Wonders*, pp. 169–228.

79. See Edwards's *Faithful Narrative*, pp. 191–205, and *Some Thoughts*, pp. 331–41. For more on Sarah Edwards's piety, see Elisabeth D. Dodds, *Marriage to a Difficult Man: The "Uncommon Union" of Jonathan and Sarah Edwards* (Philadelphia: Westminster Press, 1971), and Amanda Porterfield, *Feminine Spirituality in America: From Sarah Edwards to Martha Graham* (Philadelphia: Temple University Press, 1980), pp. 19–50. For further examples of Edwardsian female piety, see the Diary of Mary Cleaveland, Cleaveland Family Papers, EI; Carol F. Karlsen and Laurie Crumpacker, eds., *The Journal of Esther Edwards Burr, 1754–1757* (New Haven, Conn.: Yale University Press, 1984); Ann Taves, ed., *Religion and Domestic Violence in Early New England: The Memoirs of Abigail Abbot Bailey*, Religion in North America (Bloomington: Indiana University Press, 1989); Samuel Hopkins, *The Life and Character of Miss Susanna Anthony* (Worcester, Mass.: Leonard Worcester, 1796); Samuel Hopkins, *Memoirs of the Life of Mrs. Sarah Osborn* (Worcester, Mass.: Leonard Worcester, 1799); Sarah Osborn and Susanna Anthony, *Familiar Letters, Written by Mrs. Sarah Osborn, and Miss Susanna Anthony, Late of Newport, Rhode Island* (Newport, R.I.: Newport Mercury, 1807); *The Life and Writings of Mrs. Harriet Newell*, rev. ed. (Philadelphia: American Sunday School Union, 1832); Genevieve McCoy, "The Women of the ABCFM Oregon Mission and the Conflicted Language of Calvinism," *Church History* 64 (March 1995): 62–82; and the accounts of female conversion in the *Connecticut Evangelical Magazine* during the Second Great Awakening. See also Virginia Lieson Brereton, *From Sin to Salvation: Stories of Women's Conversions, 1800 to the Present* (Bloomington: Indiana University Press, 1991), who notes, pp. 10–12, that Edwards's *Personal Narrative* comprised the most significant American model for early nineteenth-century women's conversion narratives.

80. Edwards argued in his sermon on "The Importance and Advantage of a Thorough Knowledge of Divine Truth," in *The Sermons of Jonathan Edwards: A Reader*, ed. Wilson H. Kimnach, Kenneth P. Minkema, and Douglas A. Sweeney (New Haven, Conn.: Yale University Press, 1999), p. 35, that divine things are "proper to be studied, not only by men of learning, but by persons of every character, learned and unlearned, young and old, men and women." Park, *Memoir*, 1: 22, emphasizes the powerful influence that Sarah Edwards's own willingness to be damned for the glory of God had on Hopkins's commitment to the doctrine of resignation. Cuningham, *Timothy Dwight*, pp. 10–18, discusses the major role played by Mary Edwards Dwight, Timothy Dwight's mother, in readying her son for college and in instilling him with Edwardsian theology. B. B. Edwards, *Memoir of the Rev. Elias Cornelius* (Boston: Perkins and Marvin, 1833), p. 22, notes that Cornelius used Hopkins's *Life and Character of Miss Susanna Anthony* (1796) to guide himself through the straights of conversion while a college student at Yale in 1813. William A. Hallock, *"Light and Love." A Sketch of the Life and Labors of the Rev. Justin Edwards, D.D.* (New York: American Tract Society, 1855), pp. 11–12, reports that Justin Edwards, the famous social reformer and president of Andover Seminary from 1836 to 1842, was converted under the influence of the elderly Phebe Bartlet. On the rise of women's influence as nurturers of piety or moral mothers in this period, see Ruth H. Bloch, "American Feminine Ideals in Transition: The Rise of the Moral Mother, 1785–1815," *Feminist Studies* 4 (June 1978): 101–26.

81. On the role of women in Edwardsian revivalism, see esp. Kling, *A Field of Divine Wonders*, pp. 215–27. On Edwardsian women in missions, see McCoy, "The Women of the ABCFM Oregon Mission and the Conflicted Language of Calvinism," and Dana L. Robert, *American Women in Mission: A Social History of Their Thought and Practice*, The Modern Mission Era, 1792–1992, An Appraisal (Macon, Ga.: Mercer University Press, 1996), pp. 1–124 passim. On women in the rise of the Sunday School movement, see Anne M. Boylan, *Sunday School: The Formation of an American Institution 1790–1880* (New Haven, Conn.: Yale University Press, 1988), pp. 114–26.

82. See especially the deeply personal correspondence between Hopkins, Osborn, and Anthony held in the Samuel Hopkins Papers at the Trask Library, the Simon Gratz and American Colonial Clergy Collections of the HSP, and the BPL; and see also the correspondece held in the Sarah Osborn collection of the AAS and the Osborn diaries held at the Newport Historical Society, the Beinecke, and the CHS. The most comprehensive treatment of Osborn is Sheryl Anne Kujawa, "'A Precious Season at the Throne of Grace': Sarah Haggar Wheaten Osborn, 1714–1796" (Ph.D. diss., Boston College, 1993). But see also Mary Beth Norton, ed., "'My Resting Reaping Times': Sarah Osborn's Defense of Her 'Unfeminine' Activities, 1767," *Signs: Journal of Women in Culture and Society* 2 (Winter 1976): 515–29; Conforti, *Samuel Hopkins and the New Divinity Movement*, pp. 102–8; and Charles E. Hambrick-Stowe, "The Spiritual Pilgrimage of Sarah Osborn (1714–1796)," *Church History* 61 (December 1992): 408–21.

83. Park, *Memoir of Nathanael Emmons*, pp. 96–97.

84. See Conforti, "Mary Lyon"; and Porterfield, *Mary Lyon and the Mount Holyoke Missionaries*.

85. On the feminization of New England Congregationalism during the Revolutionary and early national periods, see Richard D. Shiels, "The Feminization of American Congregationalism, 1730–1835," *American Quarterly* 33 (Spring 1981): 46–62; Stephen R. Grossbart, "Seeking the Divine Favor: Conversion and Church Admission in Eastern Connecticut, 1711–1832," *William and Mary Quarterly*, 3d ser., 46 (October 1989): 732–35; Stout and Brekus, "Declension, Gender, and the 'New Religious History,'" p. 28; and Kling, *A Field of Divine Wonders*, pp. 10, 179, 206, 230–31. For Douglas's view of feminization, see Ann Douglas, *The Feminization of American Culture* (New York: Alfred A. Knopf, 1977). On the subject of religion, two of the best critiques of Douglas are David S. Reynolds, "The Feminization Controversy: Sexual Stereotypes and the Paradoxes of Piety in Nineteenth-Century America," *New England Quarterly* 53 (March 1980): 96–106, who argues that, in its opposition to the defeatism and passivity of Calvinist determinism, the rise of liberal theology manifested very "masculine" as well as "feminine" qualities; and Terry D. Bilhartz, "Sex and the Second Great Awakening: The Feminization of American Religion Reconsidered," in Vandermeer and Swierenga, eds., *Belief and Behavior*, pp. 117–35, who admits that American religion underwent feminization in this period, but argues that this occurred only in spite of the efforts of new measures revivalists to draw men into the churches. See also the trailblazing recent book by Catherine A. Brekus, *Strangers and Pilgrims: Female Preaching in America, 1740–1845*, Gender and American Culture (Chapel Hill: University of North Carolina Press, 1998), pp. 207–16, whose female preachers "clearly did not embrace a 'feminized' or sentimental faith" (p. 213). Indeed, "despite their rejection of Calvinism," many of these women "clung to an older, traditional faith in an angry God who would wreak vengeance on those who persecuted the poor and the weak" (p. 214).

Chapter 3

1. Epigraph taken from Theodore T. Munger to Elisha Mulford, 1856, as quoted in Anson Phelps Stokes, *Memorials of Eminent Yale Men: A Biographical Study of Student Life and University Influences During the Eighteenth and Nineteenth Centuries* (New Haven, Conn.: Yale University Press, 1914), 1:66–67.

2. Hatch, *Personal Reminiscences and Memorials*, pp. 27–28.

3. Theodore T. Munger, "Dr. Nathaniel W. Taylor—Master Theologian," *Yale Divinity Quarterly* 5 (February 1909): 238; Rev. Thomas Davies to Rev. Charles Beecher, n.d., in Beecher's *Autobiography*, 1: 282–83; Constance Mayfield Rourke, *Trumpets of Jubilee: Henry Ward Beecher, Harriet Beecher Stowe, Lyman Beecher, Horace Greeley, P. T. Barnum* (New York: Harcourt, Brace and Company, 1927), pp. 3–86; Hatch, *Personal Reminiscences and Memorials*, pp. 28–29 and passim;

4. Hatch, *Personal Reminiscences and Memorials*, pp. 31–33.

5. Hatch, *Personal Reminiscences and Memorials*, p. 33. This is corroborated in Dutton, "A Sketch of the Life and Character of Rev. Nathaniel W. Taylor, D.D.," p. 265. "Now that Dr. Taylor is gone," wrote Dutton, "Dr. Beecher, in the infirmities of his extreme age, goes to the house of Dr. Taylor's son-in-law, in Brooklyn; and there he stands before an excellent portrait of his friend, and weeps, and, as he expresses it, 'talks to Taylor.'"

6. As explained by Dutton, "A Sketch of the Life and Character of Rev. Nathaniel W. Taylor, D.D.," p. 265, Rebecca "was of his kindred, and the daughter of his cousin. Her maternal grandfather and his mother were brother and sister, of the name of Northrop."

7. Hatch, *Personal Reminiscences and Memorials*, pp. 5–6. On Noah Webster and his family, see esp. the recent work by Harlow Giles Unger, *Noah Webster: The Life and Times of an American Patriot* (New York: John Wiley, 1998). Fowler's reminiscences of Taylor are found in William Chauncey Fowler, *Essays: Historical, Literary, Educational* (Hartford, Conn.: Case, Lockwood, and Brainard Co., 1876), pp. 1–71.

8. Hatch, *Personal Reminiscences and Memorials*, pp. 6–8; Fowler, *Essays*, pp. 17–18, 58; Dutton, "A Sketch of the Life and Character of Rev. Nathaniel W. Taylor, D.D.," pp. 246, 250; and Munger, "Dr. Nathaniel W. Taylor—Master Theologian," pp. 233–34.

9. Hatch, *Personal Reminiscences and Memorials*, pp. 7–8.

10. Dutton, "A Sketch of the Life and Character of Rev. Nathaniel W. Taylor, D.D.," p. 265; and Hatch, *Personal Reminiscences and Memorials*, p. 9.

11. Hatch, *Personal Reminiscences and Memorials*, p. 36; and Dutton, "A Sketch of the Life and Character of Rev. Nathaniel W. Taylor, D.D.," pp. 245–46. The Taylors' house was built in 1806 for John H. Lynde (Yale class of 1796), but was bought by New Haven's First Church and deeded to the Taylors in 1812 (soon after Taylor settled as the church's pastor—more on this later). Its original address was 48 Temple St., later changed to 326 Temple St. (though the house remained in the same place). In 1868, soon after Rebecca Taylor died, it was sold back to the First Church for use as a parsonage. In 1919 it was acquired by Yale University, and is now used as the University chaplain's residence. In 1922 Yale built a new entrance onto the house, facing Wall St., and the address was changed yet again to 66 Wall St. On the house and its history, see "Buildings and Grounds of Yale University, September 1979," "Yale University Planner's Office: Buildings Survey," and Yale Treasurer's Records, Thomas W. Farnam's Building Files, YRG 5-B, Ser. 6, Box 512, all in the archives of SML.

12. Stories survive of his experiments with Morse code and early telegraphy out back in the family stables.

13. Dutton, "A Sketch of the Life and Character of Rev. Nathaniel W. Taylor, D.D.," p. 265; and George S. Merriam, ed., *Noah Porter: A Memorial by Friends* (New York: Charles Scribner's Sons, 1893), pp. 34–35.

14. Another child, Emily Webster, died at the age of 18 months. Merriam, ed., *Noah Porter*, p. 35; and Hatch, *Personal Reminiscences and Memorials*, p. 62. For more on the Taylors' children, see Mead, *Nathaniel William Taylor*, pp. 164–68.

15. Dutton, "A Sketch of the Life and Character of Rev. Nathaniel W. Taylor, D.D.," p. 265; and Merriam, ed., *Noah Porter*, pp. 35–36.

16. See Fowler, "The Appointment of Nathaniel William Taylor to the Chair of the Dwight Professorship of Didactic Theology in Yale College," in Fowler's *Essays*, p. 50.

17. Orcutt, *History of the Towns of New Milford and Bridgewater*, p. 627; and Mead, *Nathaniel William Taylor*, pp. 34–35.

18. See the New Haven, Connecticut, First Ecclesiastical Society Records, CSL, pp. 91–96, which reveal that Taylor's apprehension may also have had something to do with the overcrowding of the church's meetinghouse on Sunday mornings, and thus the congregation's need to finance and build a new facility; *AAP*, 2:163; and Lyman Matthews, *Memoir of the Life and Character of Ebenezer Porter, D.D.* (Boston: Perkins and Marvin, 1837), pp. 50–52, which reveals that Taylor was called only after the Center Church had failed to secure the services of the Rev. Ebenezer Porter (later president of Andover Seminary), and so may have felt like a second choice.

19. The ordination sermon was later printed in Dwight's *Sermons*, 2 vols. (New Haven, Conn.: Hezekiah Howe, and Durrie and Peck, 1828),: 2: 453–78. On Taylor's opposition to the Universalists' effort to establish a congregation in New Haven, see Fisher, "A Sermon Preached in the Chapel of Yale College, March 14, 1858," pp. 34–35. On Taylor as an ecclesiastical disciplinarian, see Mead, *Nathaniel William Taylor*, pp. 70–75. And note that William L. Philie, *Change and Tradition: New Haven, Connecticut, 1780–1830*, Garland Studies in Entrepreneurship (New York: Garland Publishing, Inc., 1989), pp. 93–95, exaggerates the controversy this discipline provoked as well as the level of Taylor's opposition to Episcopal Rector Harry Croswell (Philie does this both by misconstruing Mead's coverage of the topic and by mistaking Congregational clergyman Bennet Tyler as a "pseudonym for Taylor"). On Taylor's short-lived desire to enroll at Andover "for the purpose of supplying what he deemed to be deficiencies in his culture," see Fisher, "A Sermon Preached in the Chapel of Yale College, March 14, 1858," p. 32 (though we do not know which deficiencies he had in mind, we do know that Taylor never learned Hebrew or German). On Taylor's $500 bonus, see Oscar Edward Maurer, *A Puritan Church and Its Relation to Community, State, and Nation: Addresses Delivered in Preparation for the Three Hundredth Anniversary of the Settlement of New Haven* (New Haven, Conn.: Yale University Press, 1938), p. 93, who notes that the church did this in part to help the Taylors cover their costs during the period of rapid inflation that followed the War of 1812. On the high-profile membership of the Center Church (which, at one time or another during Taylor's ministry there, included Senator Hillhouse, Jedidiah and Samuel F. B. Morse, Noah Webster, and Eli Whitney, among other dignitaries), consult Franklin Bowditch Dexter, *Historical Catalogue of the Members of the First Church of Christ in New Haven, Connecticut (Center Church), A.D. 1639–1914* (New Haven, Conn.: n.p., 1914).

20. Bacon, "A Sermon at the Funeral of Nathaniel W. Taylor, D.D.," pp. 5–6; Edwards A. Park, *A Discourse Delivered at the Funeral of Professor Moses Stuart* (Boston: Tappan and Whittemore, 1852), pp. 21–24; Dutton, "A Sketch of the Life and Character of Rev. Nathaniel W. Taylor," pp. 248–49; Fowler, "The Appointment," p. 47; John H. Giltner, *Moses Stuart: The Father of Biblical Science in America* (Atlanta, Ga.: Scholars Press, 1988), pp. 2–3; Newman Smyth, *The Historical Discourse Delivered at the Two Hundred and Fiftieth Anniversary of The First Church in New Haven, April 22d, 1888* (New Haven, Conn.: privately published, 1888), p. 11; Blake, *Chronicles of New Haven Green*, p. 99; and Stout and Brekus, "A New England Congregation," pp. 52–54. See also Maurer, *A Puritan Church*, p. 98, who must have read Smyth before he repeated that "Dr. Taylor's ministry brought to flood tide the gracious movement which had begun under Moses Stuart"; and Leonard Bacon, *Thirteen Historical Discourses, on the Completion of Two Hundred Years, from the Beginning of the First Church in New Haven, with an Appendix* (New Haven, Conn.: Durrie and Peck, 1839), pp. 276–77. For the Center Church's 1809 "Confession, Covenant, and Articles of Practice," consult the Records of the First Church of Christ and Ecclesiastical Society, New Haven, Connecticut, vol. 4, 1773–1840, CSL, pp. 26–30 (many thanks to Jim Walsh for tracking down the Center Church's adoption of pure church polity). And for the record of the church's nine-month struggle to settle Stuart as

pastor, first as Dana's "Colleague Pastor," but later (after Dana objected, Stuart withdrew, and Dana was fired for his recalcitrance) as senior pastor, see New Haven, Connecticut, First Ecclesiastical Society Records, 1715–1892, vol. 2, CSL, pp. 32–58.

While Taylor did not publish on the issue of church membership (by his day the Edwardsian pure church model had already triumphed), he did maintain an Edwardsian commitment to a membership of regenerate or "real" Christians only. See, for example, William H. Goodrich (Chauncey's son), "Notes of Lectures Delivered by Nathaniel W. Taylor, D.D. on Mental Philosophy, Moral Philosophy, Moral Government, Natural Theology, Evidences of Christianity, Revealed Theology, 1845–6," owned by John R. Fitzmier, Claremont, California, pp. 204–5. For published adherence to the Edwardsian pure church model in the Taylorites' *QCS*, see [Luther Hart], "Review on the Early History of the Congregational Churches of New-England," *QCS* 2 (June 1830): 328–30; "Review of the Works of President Edwards," *QCS* 3 (September 1831): 349–50; "Review of Harvey's Inquiry," *QCS* 3 (December 1831): 552–56; and [Luther Hart], "A View of the Religious Declension in New England, and of Its Causes, During the Latter Half of the Eighteenth Century," *QCS* 5 (June 1833): 228–29. For Beecher's opposition to the Half-Way Covenant, see also his sermon delivered in 1814 at the installation of the Rev. John Keyes in the Congregational Church of Wolcott, Connecticut, "The Building of Waste Places," in Lyman Beecher, *Sermons, Delivered on Various Occasions* (Boston: John P. Jewett and Company, 1852), pp. 117–21.

21. Maurer, *A Puritan Church*, p. 83; and New Haven, Connecticut, First Ecclesiastical Society Records, 1715–1892, vol. 2, CSL, p. 99. On the history of antagonism between Dana and the Edwardsians, see esp. Anderson, "Joseph Bellamy," pp. 529–49.

22. The syndicate that built the new building was comprised of William Leffingwell, Henry Daggett, Jr., William W. Woolsey, Isaac Mills, James Goodrich, Gad Peck, and Abraham Bradley III. See Maurer, *A Puritan Church*, pp. 93–95; Blake, *Chronicles of New Haven Green*, pp. 27–28, 253; and Charles W. Whittlesey, *The Fourth Meeting House: A Description and Account of the Fourth Meeting House of the First Church of Christ in New Haven, Conn., and of the First Ecclesiastical Society* (n.p., 1938–a photostatic copy of this publication is available at the CSL), pp. 5–7, who discusses briefly the building of the third meetinghouse as well, explaining that the Center Church eventually regretted the deal it had struck with the local syndicate: "The society must have been carried away by the apparent simplicity of the plan of raising money to build, and leaving it to the contractors to get their own pay as it were. . . . As it worked out the simplicity of the plan resulted in most intricate complications in later years, and the dissatisfaction with it must have become apparent soon after its accomplishment, for we find in 1831 . . . an effort to have the Society obtain title to its pews so that it could have control of its property without the encumbrance of titles to portions of the property within the walls of its own building. The Society had to raise the money eventually to pay for the pews, so in the end it did really pay for the Meeting House, but as a matter of fact the Meeting House was not really paid for until the last pew was bought by the Society and the last stock certificate redeemed. And this did not happen until that memorable Sunday early in 1888 when, among other debts, that which was incurred for clearing up the ownership of the pews, was cleared." Coincidentally, the church's neighbors to the north and south also began to construct new buildings at this time, each of them gaining permits at the same town meeting in 1812. The Center Church building was completed first, but by decade's end New Haven's green looked completely different than it had when Taylor began his ministry there. For a brief summary of the practice of selling and renting pews among British and American Reformed churches, see Charles D. Cashdollar, *A Spiritual Home: Life in British and American Reformed Congregations, 1830–1915* (University Park: Pennsylvania State University Press, 2000), pp. 166–74 (though Cashdollar pays insufficient attention to the moral critics of such funding systems).

23. Blake, *Chronicles of New Haven Green*, pp. 27–28, 251–54; and Maurer, *A Puritan Church*, p. 97.

24. Fowler, *Essays*, p. 58.

25. Fisher, "A Sermon Preached in the Chapel of Yale College, March 14, 1858," p. 30; and Munger, "Dr. Nathaniel W. Taylor–Master Theologian," p. 237.

26. The Hodge quotation is taken from a letter he wrote to Leonard Bacon quoted in *The Semi-Centennial Anniversary of the Divinity School of Yale College*, p. 103, where Hodge continues: "His [Taylor's] name is never mentioned without awakening in me a glow of grateful and affectionate remembrance." See also Lyman H. Atwater, "Address of Rev. Dr. Atwater," in *The Semi-Centennial Anniversary of the Divinity School of Yale College*, p. 100; Bacon, "A Sermon at the Funeral of Nathaniel W. Taylor, D.D.," p. 9; Fowler, *Essays*, pp. 57, 60; and Fisher, "A Sermon Preached in the Chapel of Yale College, March 14, 1858," p. 30. Tellingly, Taylor's successor at the Center Church, Leonard Bacon, always found it difficult living up to the homiletical standards Taylor had set. See Davis, *Leonard Bacon*, pp. 47–50.

27. Fisher, "A Sermon Preached in the Chapel of Yale College, March 14, 1858," p. 31; Dutton, "A Sketch of the Life and Character of Rev. Nathaniel W. Taylor," p. 250; and Orcutt, *History of the Towns of New Milford and Bridgewater*, p. 627.

28. See esp. the memoir of Dwight written by his brother, the Rev. William T. Dwight of Portland's Third Congregational Church, in William T. Dwight, ed., *Selected Discourses of Sereno Edwards Dwight, D.D., Pastor of Park Street Church, Boston, and President of Hamilton College, in New York. With a Memoir of His Life* (Boston: Crocker and Brewster, 1851), pp. vii–lxviii. Dwight's biography of Edwards was published in his edition of Edwards's works, *The Works of President Edwards . . . in Ten Volumes* (New York: S. Converse, 1829–1830).

29. Fisher, "A Sermon Preached in the Chapel of Yale College, March 14, 1858," p. 34; and Bacon, "A Sermon at the Funeral of Nathaniel W. Taylor, D.D.," p. 7. On the visit of President James Monroe to the Center Church in June of 1817, see the New Haven *Register* (June 21 and 28, 1817); and Rollin G. Osterweis, *Three Centuries of New Haven, 1638–1938* (New Haven, Conn.: Yale University Press, 1953), p. 307.

30. Fisher, "Historical Address," p. 12; and Taylor to Sprague, February 20, 1844, in *AAP*, 2: 161–62.

31. Fowler, *Essays*, pp. 1–2. Significantly, the two young men who first approached Fitch were Fowler himself and the friend who talked Fowler into this, Samuel B. Ingersoll. On the founding of Yale Divinity School, see esp. Fisher, "Historical Address," pp. 13–14; Fisher, *A Discourse, Commemorative of the History of the Church of Christ in Yale College*, pp. 92–93; and Wayland, *The Theological Department in Yale College*.

32. *Contributions to the Ecclesiastical History of Connecticut*, p. 182; Fowler, *Essays*, pp. 17–26, who reprints the letter from Fitch to the Prudential Committee of Yale College, April 23, 1822, recommending the foundation of a Theological Department and the appointment of a new professor to lead it; and Wayland, *The Theological Department in Yale College*, pp. 54, 120–24.

33. Fowler, *Essays*, pp. 5–6, 52–53; and Bacon, "A Sermon at the Funeral of Nathaniel W. Taylor, D.D.," p. 7. The Union College Trustees' Minutes of July 23, 1823, include a resolution granting Taylor the Doctor of Divinity degree, but the Union College archives contain no other information about the occasion of this award. Thanks go to Dorothy Barnes, Assistant Librarian, Schaffer Library, Union College, for this information.

34. Interestingly, Chauncey Goodrich would serve as chief editor of Webster's dictionary from the time of Webster's death in 1843 until his own death in 1847. Noah Porter then took over for Goodrich, serving as chief editor of the dictionary until his death in 1892.

35. Fisher, "Historical Address," pp. 17–18; Munger, "Dr. Nathaniel W. Taylor–Master Theologian," pp. 234–36; Bacon, "A Sermon at the Funeral of Nathaniel W. Taylor, D.D.," p. 7; Julian M. Sturtevant, *An Autobiography*, ed. J. M. Sturtevant, Jr. (New York: Fleming H. Revell Company, 1896), p. 121; Timothy Dwight, *Memories of Yale Life and Men, 1845–1899* (New York: Dodd, Mead, and Company, 1903), p. 173; Fisher, "A Sermon Preached in the

Chapel of Yale College, March 14, 1858," p. 35; and Stokes, *Memorials of Eminent Yale Men*, 2:368. Cf. Merriam, ed., *Noah Porter*, p. 31; and Benjamin Wisner Bacon, *Theodore Thornton Munger: New England Minister* (New Haven, Conn.: Yale University Press, 1913), pp. 37, 56, 68, 72–74.

36. Merriam, ed., *Noah Porter*, p. 31; and Munger, "Dr. Nathaniel W. Taylor—Master Theologian," p. 235. Cf. Dwight, *Memories of Yale Life and Men*, p. 257; and Munger, idem., p. 234, who adds that "Professor Silliman [Yale's geologist] used to labor with Dr. Taylor for using tobacco—the only professor in the college who was addicted to its use; and Dr. Taylor labored with him for contradicting the Bible as to creation. Professor Silliman, upon whom the first rays of modern exegesis had begun to fall, pointed to the fossils in the cemetery wall, and assigned a date of some millions, to which Dr. Taylor replied, 'God can create fossils in stone, and you can't prove that he didn't.' Of course, Professor Silliman could not, and the victory rested with theology." Taylor would return to the issue of creation near the very end of his life. As noted by Fisher, "A Sermon Preached in the Chapel of Yale College, March 14, 1858," p. 36, about a year before his death "he occupied himself with the composition of an ingenious essay on the cosmogony of Genesis, as compared with the teachings of Geology." Unfortunately, this essay no longer survives.

37. Dutton, "A Sketch of the Life and Character of Rev. Nathaniel W. Taylor, D.D.," pp. 253–54, 236; Nathaniel W. Taylor, "Mental Philosophy," Folder 1, Box I, Ms 93234, CHS, unpaginated; and Fisher, "A Sermon Preached in the Chapel of Yale College, March 14, 1858," pp. 28–29. Cf. B. N. Martin, "Dr. Taylor on Moral Government," *NE* 17 (November 1859): 904.

38. Bacon, "A Sermon at the Funeral of Nathaniel W. Taylor," pp. 7–8. On Taylor's on-going work as an evangelist and revivalist in and around New Haven, see also *RI* 15 (26 March 1831): 680–81, (23 April 1831): 751; vol. 16 (28 January 1832): 558, (21 April 1832): 744, 751; *Contributions to the Ecclesiastical History of Connecticut*, pp. 439–40; Chauncey A. Goodrich, "Obituary Notice," in *Memorial of Nathaniel W. Taylor*, pp. 41–43; Dutton, "A Sketch of the Life and Character of the Rev. Nathaniel W. Taylor," pp. 250–52; and Ralph Henry Gabriel, *Religion and Learning at Yale: The Church of Christ in the College and University, 1757–1957* (New Haven, Conn.: Yale University Press, 1958), pp. 132–33. And on Taylor's work in build-ing up New Haven's network of Congregational churches, see esp. the following congregational histories: Theodore T. Munger, *Historical Discourse Preached on the One Hundred and Fiftieth Anniversary of the Organization of the United Church, May 8th, 1892* (New Haven, Conn.: United Church, 1892), pp. 5, 36–37; Mary Hewitt Mitchell, *History of The United Church of New Haven* (New Haven, Conn.: United Church, 1942), pp. 34–46; *A History of Plymouth Congregational Church in New Haven, Connecticut, 1831–1942* (New Haven, Conn.: Published for the Church by the Committee on History, 1942), pp. 3–4; Gerard Hallock, *History of the South Congrega-tional Church, New Haven, from Its Origin in 1852 till January 1, 1865* (New Haven, Conn.: Tuttle, Morehouse, and Taylor, 1865), p. 43; and Samuel W. S. Dutton (a Taylor student), *History of the North Church in New Haven. From Its Formation, During the Great Awakening, to the Completion of the Century in May, 1842. In Three Sermons* (New Haven, Conn.: A. H. Maltby, 1842). For an example of the effectiveness of Taylor's ongoing revivalistic preaching, see "Dr. Taylor's Preaching," *RI* 18 (15 March 1834): 662.

39. Hatch, *Personal Reminiscences and Memorials*, pp. 14–15; Fisher, "A Sermon Preached in the Chapel of Yale College, March 14, 1858," p. 31; and Munger, "Dr. Nathaniel W. Tay-lor—Master Theologian," p. 236.

40. On the unity and cooperation of the New Haven theologians, see Dwight, *Memories of Yale Life and Men*, pp. 254, 197; and the more immediate and personal testimony of an anony-mous Yale student in his 35-page "Journal, Commenced March 6th, 1831, Yale College," owned by Kenneth P. Minkema, Hamden, Connecticut. On the intimate, often beautiful, friendship between Taylor and Beecher, see esp. Hatch, *Personal Reminiscences*, pp. 27–35. For biographi-

cal information on Goodrich and Fitch and eyewitness accounts of their revivalistic preaching, see J. M. Hoppin, "Professor Fitch as a Preacher," *NE* 30 (April 1871): 215–30; "Dr. Fitch's Sermons," *NE* 30 (October 1871): 739–44; O. E. Daggett, "Reminiscences of Professor Fitch," in *The Semi-Centennial Anniversary*, pp. 73–79; I. N. Tarbox, "Life and Services of Professor Goodrich," in *The Semi-Centennial Anniversary*, pp. 87–91; William Chauncey Fowler, "Origin of the Theological School of Yale College," in Fowler, *Essays*, p. 4; W. W. Andrews, "Student at Yale," in Merriam, ed., *Noah Porter*, p. 14; H. B. Wright, "Professor Goodrich and the Growth and Outcome of the Revival Movement," and Timothy Dwight, "The College Pastorate," both in Reynolds, Fisher, and Wright, eds., *Two Centuries of Christian Activity at Yale*, pp. 73–95, 146–50; Dwight, *Memories of Yale Life and Men*, pp. 76–89; Harris Elwood Starr, "Goodrich, Chauncey Allen," in *Dictionary of American Biography*, vol. 7, ed. Allen Johnson and Dumas Malone (New York: Charles Scribner's Sons, 1931), pp. 399–400; John T. Wayland, *The Theological Department in Yale College, 1822–1858*, American Religious Thought of the eighteenth and nineteenth Centuries (New York: Garland, 1987; 1933), 78–118; Sidney Mead, "Fitch, Eleazar Thompson" and "Goodrich, Chauncey Allen," in Vergilius Ferm, ed., *An Encyclopedia of Religion* (New York: Philosophical Library, 1945), pp. 281, 307. On Goodrich's offer of the Williams presidency and course on revivals at Yale, see Chauncey A. Goodrich to Alvan Hyde and Timothy M. Cooley, August 24, 1821, Ferdinand J. Dreer Autograph Collection, HSP, and Chauncey A. Goodrich, notes to lectures on "Revivals of Religion," Ms. Vault File, Beinecke. On the history of revivals at Yale, see Chauncey A. Goodrich, "Narrative of Revivals of Religion in Yale College, from Its Commencement to the Present Time," *American Quarterly Register* 10 (February 1838): 289–310; and Wright, "Professor Goodrich and the Growth and Outcome of the Revival Movement," who notes (p. 77) that "the years 1820, 1821, 1822, 1823, and 1824 [alone] were each marked by a revival of religion. The total number of converts in these five awakenings must have been considerably over one hundred and fifty." For the New Haven school's promotion and theoretical defense of revivalism, see "Review of Letters on Revivals of Religion," *QCS* 2 (June 1830): 234–46; "Farr on Revivals," *QCS* 4 (March 1832): 25–33; "On the Obstacles to Revivals of Religion," *QCS* 4 (June 1832): 277–90; "Sprague on Revivals of Religion," *QCS* 5 (March 1833): 20–45; "Memoirs of the Rev. George Whitefield," *QCS* 6 (March 1834): 88–118; and "Practical View of Revivals of Religion," *QCS* 10 (August 1838): 387–408.

    41. Wayland, *The Theological Department in Yale College*, p. 238.

    42. For a summary of Beecher's role in the publication of these periodicals, see James W. Fraser, *Pedagogue for God's Kingdom: Lyman Beecher and the Second Great Awakening* (Lanham, Md.: University Press of America, 1985), pp. 75–92.

    43. On the Doctrinal Tract Society and the rise of the *Christian Spectator*, see [Joseph Harvey], *Letters, on the Present State and Probable Results of Theological Speculations in Connecticut* (n.p., 1832), p. 15; "Sketch of the Life and Character of the Rev. Luther Hart," *QCS* 6 (September 1834): 486; Lyman Beecher to Nathaniel W. Taylor, September 30, 1816, Folder 65, Box 2, Beecher-Scoville Family Papers, SML; and Beecher, *Autobiography*, 1: 218–19, 241, 245–47. For the early *Spectator* quotations praising Edwards and Edwards, Jr., see "Review of the Works of President Edwards," *CS* 3 (June 1821): 300, and "Review of Edwards' Sermon," *CS* 5 (January 1823): 39. For the Taylorites' claims to the Edwardsian legacy in later volumes of the *Quarterly Christian Spectator* (the name given the periodical after Goodrich's purchase), see esp. "Review of True Religion Delineated," *QCS* 2 (September 1830): 397–424; another "Review of the Works of President Edwards," *QCS* 3 (September 1831): 337–57; [Luther Hart], "Character and Writings of Dr. Strong," *QCS* 5 (September 1833): 337–63 ("prince of divines" quote taken from p. 355); and "Sketch of the Life and Character of the Rev. Luther Hart," 490–91, which defends Hart's earlier claims to Strong (and Bellamy) against the objections of the Tylerites.

    44. On the early years of *The Spirit of the Pilgrims*, see Enoch Pond, *The Autobiography of the Rev. Enoch Pond, D.D.*, ed. Edwin Pond Parker (Boston: Congregational Sunday School and

Publishing Society, 1883), pp. 54–61, and Frank Luther Mott, *A History of American Magazines, 1741–1850*, 3 vols. (New York: D. Appleton and Company, 1930), 1: 569–72. For the reprinting of the Hopkins and Emmons sermons, see *SP* 3 (November 1830): 582–91, and 594–97. On the Edwardsian character of the journal's guiding orthodoxy, see "Introduction," *SP* 4 (January 1831): 5.

45. "Moral Characteristics of the Nineteenth Century," *QCS* 5 (June 1833): 201; and "Review of Hawes' Tribute to the Memory of the Pilgrims," *QCS* 3 (September 1831): 389. See also "Who Are the True Conservatives?" *QCS* 10 (November 1838): 618–19.

46. For Taylorite support of the temperance movement, see Nathaniel W. Taylor, *A Sermon, Addressed to the Legislature of the State of Connecticut, at the Annual Election in Hartford, May 7, 1823* (Hartford, Conn.: Charles Babcock, 1823), pp. 28–30, 36–37, who contended that "the single sin of drunkenness may obtain a prevalence in a community, that will prostrate all moral influence, and paralyze all moral sensibility" (p. 29); "The Use and Abuse of Ardent Spirits," *CS* 8 (June 1826): 300–304; "Discourses on Intemperance," *CS*, n.s., 1 (November 1827): 587–604, and (December 1827): 645–55; "The Philosophy and Influence of Habit, in Its Relation to Intemperance," *QCS* 6 (September 1834): 370–81; and "Seventh Report of the American Temperance Society," *QCS* 6 (December 1834): 596–609. For Taylorite support of the Sunday School movement, see "Review of the Report of the American Sunday School Union," *QCS* 2 (September 1830): 425–34; and "Review of President Wayland's Sermon, in Behalf of the American Sunday School Union," *QCS* 3 (March 1831): 32–56. On the rise of the Sunday School movement in New Haven and at Yale, see Maurer, *A Puritan Church*, p. 91; and Wayland, *The Theological Department in Yale College, 1822–1858*, pp. 361–66. The Taylorites' ardent support of this movement belies Peter Y. De Jong's claim, in *The Covenant Idea in New England Theology, 1620–1847* (Grand Rapids, Mich.: Eerdmans, 1945), pp. 178, 181–82, that latter-day Edwardsians, as individualistic revival preachers moving away from the organic themes of covenantal piety, largely neglected the nurture of children within the churches. For Taylorite roles in the New Haven, Connecticut, and American Bible Societies (Taylor was the founding secretary of the New Haven Bible Society), see New Haven's *RI* 1 (June 1, 1816): 8, (Sept. 28, 1816): 288, (Oct. 12, 1816): 320, and (Oct. 26, 1816): 344–45; Charles Roy Keller, *The Second Great Awakening in Connecticut* (New Haven, Conn.: Yale University Press, 1942), pp. 113–14; and Henry Otis Dwight, *The Centennial History of the American Bible Society* (New York: Macmillan, 1916), p. 22, who notes that Taylor served as a delegate of the Connecticut Bible Society at the first convention of the American Bible Society in 1816, a convention which Beecher served as a secretary and member of the constitution committee (on this latter point, see also Lacy, *The Word Carrying Giant*, pp. 7–8). Taylor also served for a time as secretary of the Charitable Society for the Education of Pious Young Men for the Ministry of the Gospel, whose annual meeting was held in New Haven in 1816 (see the *RI* 1 [Sept. 7, 1816]: 240). On Taylorite anti-masonry, see Goodman, *Towards a Christian Republic*, who notes correctly that Taylor and the *Quarterly Christian Spectator* "kept silent on the question of Masonry" (p. 225), but who shows that Beecher came out publicly (though cautiously) against the Masons beginning in July of 1831 (p. 64). For Taylorite opposition to the theater, see "Theatrical Amusements," *QCS* 10 (November 1838): 557–72. Fraser, *Pedagogue for God's Kingdom*, offers a useful summary and interpretation of Beecher's major role in antebellum benevolent reform. For a well-constructed (though slightly exaggerated) portrayal of the religious agenda that gave Beecher's reform efforts a cosmic significance, see also Abzug, *Cosmos Crumbling*, pp. 30–56.

47. *RI* 1 (June 22, 1816); 63–64; (July 27, 1816): 137, where we learn that Taylor was appointed to a five-man "Committee of Missions" within the Domestic Missionary Society "with power to appoint Missionaries, and designate their fields of labour in the recess of this Board [i.e., the society]"; and (July 27, 1816): 138–42, where we find an "Address" written by Abel Flint (chairman of the society) and Taylor to rouse up support for the society from among

Connecticut's churches; *RI* 1 (Nov. 2, 1816): 360, where we learn that Taylor had recently been elected one of the vice-presidents of the New Haven Foreign Mission Society; Maurer, *A Puritan Church*, pp. 87–88; Charles P. Bush, "Yale Theological Seminary and Foreign Missions," in *The Semi-Centennial Anniversary of the Divinity School of Yale College*, p. 38; S. G. Buckingham, "Remarks by Rev. S. G. Buckingham, D.D.," in ibid., pp. 63–64; J. M. Sturtevant (leader of the Illinois Band and founding president of Illinois College), "Yale Theological Seminary and Home Missions," in ibid., pp. 64–72; Julian M. Sturtevant, *An Autobiography*, ed. J. M. Sturtevant, Jr. (New York: Fleming H. Revell Company, 1896), pp. 135–276; John Randolph Willis, *God's Frontiersmen: The Yale Band in Illinois* (Washington, D.C.: University Press of America, 1979); Beach, "Yale's Contribution to Foreign Missions," pp. 285–307; "Review of the Report of the A. H. M. Society," *QCS* 3 (December 1831): 513; and Bainton, *Yale and the Ministry*, pp. 131– 35. On the role of Yale alumni in the founding of Christian colleges in the Mississippi Valley, see esp. Iver F. Yeager, *Julian M. Sturtevant, 1805–1886: President of Illinois College, Ardent Churchman, Reflective Author* (Jacksonville: Trustees of Illinois College, 1999), the best and most up-to-date treatment of Sturtevant and the founding of Illinois College—esp. chapter 1, "Preparing for Christian Service," in which "Taylor's influence" on Sturtevant is confirmed to have been "greater than that of any other person" (p. 31); C. E. Barton, *The Founders and Founding of Illinois College* (Jacksonville, Ill.: John K. Long, 1902); Travis Keene Hedrick, Jr., "Julian Monson Sturtevant and the Moral Machinery of Society: The New England Struggle against Pluralism in the Old Northwest, 1829–1877" (Ph.D. diss., Brown University, 1974); *Aaron Lucius Chapin, D.D., LL.D.: Memorial Service Held by the Alumni of Beloit College, in the College Chapel, July 20, 1893* (Chicago: P. F. Pettibone and Co., 1893), on the Yale alumnus who became the founding president of Beloit College in 1849; and Joseph Frazier Wall, *Grinnell College in the Nineteenth Century: From Salvation to Service* (Ames: Iowa State University Press, 1997), on the founding of Iowa College (later Grinnell) and the work of President George F. Magoun (an alumnus of Yale Divinity School). For a partial listing of Yale graduates who served on the mission field, see Fisher, *A Discourse, Commemorative of the History of the Church of Christ in Yale College*, pp. 93– 95. For more Taylorite support of home missions, see "Claims of the West," *QCS* 6 (December 1834): 513–24, and "Beecher's Plea for the West," *QCS* 7 (September 1835): 481–503. For Taylorite interest in foreign missions and in missions generally, see "Review on Missions to China," *QCS* 2 (June 1830): 299–321; "Causes Which Have Impeded the Spread of Christianity," *QCS* 4 (September 1832): 401–18; "Difficulties in the Way of Converting the Heathen," *QCS* 10 (February 1838): 1–17; and "New Order of Missionaries," *QCS* 10 (May 1838): 285– 99. For the invocation of the spirit of Brainerd in New Haven, see "Review of Memoirs of Brainerd," *CS* 5 (March 1823): 135–45; "On the Obstacles to Revivals of Religion," *QCS* 4 (June 1832): 284; and Goodrich, "Narrative of Revivals of Religion in Yale College," p. 310. Significantly, Lyman Beecher stands out among Edwardsians for his aversion to Brainerd's diary and piety, which he thought exhibited "a state of permanent hypochondria." Beecher, *Autobiography*, 1: 29–30.

48. On the general trends, see esp. George Rogers Taylor, *The Transportation Revolution, 1815–1860* (White Plains, N.Y.: M. E. Sharpe, 1951), and Sellers, *The Market Revolution*. For a sampling of the recent debates regarding the historical significance of these trends, see Melvin Stokes and Stephen Conway, eds., *The Market Revolution in America: Social, Political, and Religious Expressions* (Charlottesville: University Press of Virginia, 1996). On the relationship between evangelical Protestantism and the market revolution, see the recent essay by Mark S. Schantz, "Religious Tracts, Evangelical Reform, and the Market Revolution in Antebellum America," *Journal of the Early Republic* 17 (Fall 1997), and esp. the works he cites on pp. 426–28, n. 3. Several fine studies trace the local impact of these changes in New England. See Peter J. Coleman, *The Transformation of Rhode Island, 1790–1860* (Westport, Conn.: Greenwood Press, 1985; 1963); Stephen Robert Davis, "From Plowshares to Spindles: Dedham, Massachusetts, 1790–1840"

(Ph.D. diss., University of Wisconsin, 1973); Richard Holmes, *Communities in Transition: Bedford and Lincoln, Massachusetts, 1729–1850*, Studies in American History and Culture (Ann Arbor: UMI Research Press, 1980; 1978); Carl Siracusa, *A Mechanical People: Perceptions of the Industrial Order in Massachusetts, 1815–1880* (Middletown, Conn.: Wesleyan University Press, 1979); Randolph A. Roth, *The Democratic Dilemma: Religion, Reform, and the Social Order in the Connecticut River Valley of Vermont, 1791–1850* (Cambridge: Cambridge University Press, 1987); and, most recently, Catherine E. Kelly, *In the New England Fashion: Reshaping Women's Lives in the Nineteenth Century* (Ithaca, N.Y.: Cornell University Press, 1999). Hal S. Barron, *Those Who Stayed Behind: Rural Society in Nineteenth-Century New England* (Cambridge: Cambridge University Press, 1984), studies those older rural areas that remained largely unaffected by these changes. On the history of these changes in Connecticut, two classic studies remain especially useful as well: Richard J. Purcell, *Connecticut in Transition, 1775–1818*, new ed. (Middletown, Conn.: Wesleyan University Press, 1963; 1918); and Jarvis Means Morse, *A Neglected Period of Connecticut's History, 1818–1850* (New Haven, Conn.: Yale University Press, 1933).

49. On the rise of Democratic-Republicanism in New Haven and the demise of the Federalist Standing Order, see esp. Philie, *Change and Tradition*, pp. 31–55, 81–113.

50. Mary Hewitt Mitchell, *History of the United Church of New Haven*, pp. 240–41. To this extent, the Taylorites adumbrated the "private" Protestantism of the later years of Martin Marty's "righteous empire," as well as the "great reversal" (at century's end) of their role as avant-garde social reformers. But the very "public" significance of their allegedly "private" religious agenda suggests that Marty's "two-party system" motif for the interpretation of modern American Protestantism may need revision. Indeed, as Marty himself has argued in recent years, while conversionistic Protestants lost their most visible roles as shapers of national culture in the late nineteenth century, they have continued to play many other very important public roles, exerting a profound influence on American social life. For the explication of Marty's "two-party system," see Martin E. Marty, *Righteous Empire: The Protestant Experience in America* (New York: Harper Torchbooks, 1977; 1970), pp. 177–187. See also Jean Miller Schmidt, *Souls or the Social Order: The Two-Party System in American Protestantism* (Brooklyn, N.Y.: Carlson, 1991); Sandra Sizer, "Politics and Apolitical Religion: The Great Urban Revivals of the Late Nineteenth Century," *CH* 48 (March 1979): 81–98, who helps to complicate the story of the emergence of the two-party system by reminding us that "the supposed 'otherworldliness' of revivalism was never complete," referring ironically to the tradition of evangelical revivalism as "the apolitical political religion of America" (pp. 90, 98); and Long, *The Revival of 1857–58*, who locates what she calls the "privatization of northern revivalism" in the 1840s and 1850s, when social reform was increasingly politicized and revival was increasingly spiritualized. For recent revision of the concept of a two-part system, see esp. Douglas Jacobsen and William Vance Trollinger, Jr., *Re-Forming the Center: American Protestantism, 1900 to the Present* (Grand Rapids, Mich.: Eerdmans, 1998), which includes important concessions from Marty himself. See also Marty's "Public and Private: Congregation as Meeting Place," in James P. Wind and James W. Lewis, eds., *American Congregations, Volume 2: New Perspectives in the Study of Congregations* (Chicago: University of Chicago Press, 1994), pp. 133–66, as well as the good work of Marty's "Public Religion Project," funded by the Pew Charitable Trusts, esp. Martin E. Marty with Jonathan Moore, *Politics, Religion, and the Common Good* (San Francisco: Jossey-Bass, 2000). The classic source on the "great reversal" is David O. Moberg, *The Great Reversal: Evangelism versus Social Concern*, Evangelical Perspectives (Philadelphia: Lippincott, 1972).

Jonathan Sassi's interpretation of the public Christianity of the post-Revolutionary New England clergy arrived too late to be incorporated sufficiently in this chapter. It deserves notice, however, as an important recent treatment of this topic. For though Sassi exaggerates the extent to which New England's evangelical clergymen functioned as social theorists, his book offers an excellent assessment of the public significance of their ministries. See Jonathan D. Sassi, *A Republic of Righteousness: The Public Christianity of the Post-Revolutionary New England Clergy* (New York: Oxford University Press, 2001), esp. pp. 145–84 (on the period of Taylor's public emergence).

51. Eleazar T. Fitch, *National Prosperity Perpetuated: A Discourse: Delivered in the Chapel of Yale College; on the Day of the Annual Thanksgiving: November 29, 1827* (New Haven, Conn.: Treadway and Adams, 1828), p. 33. In a letter to Edmund Tuttle of Meridan, Connecticut, that implicitly supported Henry Clay's presidential candidacy in 1844, Taylor advocated Christian suffrage even in elections that included no ideal candidates. In response to Tuttle's query whether a Christian, "consistently with the word of God, [could] cast his vote for either a duelist [Clay] or an oppressor of the poor [James K. Polk], for Chief Magistrate of this Nation," Taylor responded in the affirmative: "To put a stronger case," he wrote, "suppose that there is no reasonable doubt, that one of two devils, one of which is less a devil than the other, will be actually elected, let the Christian vote as he may; and that his vote will therefore be utterly lost, if he does not vote for one of them; I think that an enlightened Christian would vote for the least devil of the two." See "Letter from the Rev. Dr. Taylor," *The Christian Freeman* (November 28, 1844). Cf. [Horace Bushnell], "Reply to Dr. Taylor," *The Christian Freeman* (December 12, 1844). For Taylor at his most political and republican, see *A Sermon, Addressed to the Legislature of the State of Connecticut.* Significantly, though he expressed lament in this sermon regarding the popular antipathy toward the institutional church represented by disestablishment, he confessed that "there were dangers and evils without the change . . . greater than exist with it" (p. 25). On the relationship between evangelical Congregationalism and Whig politics, see also Daniel Walker Howe, "Religion and Politics in the Antebellum North," in Noll, ed., *Religion and American Politics*, pp. 121–45; Daniel Walker Howe, "The Evangelical Movement and Political Culture in the North during the Second Party System," *Journal of American History* 77 (March 1991): 1216–39; Curtis D. Johnson, *Redeeming America: Evangelicals and the Road to Civil War*, The American Way Series (Chicago: Ivan R. Dee, 1993), whose heavy dependence on Howe has led to a politicized view of northeastern evangelicals generally (Johnson's "formalists"); Richard Carwardine, "Evangelicals, Whigs, and the Election of William Henry Harrison," *Journal of American Studies* 17 (April 1983): 47–75; Richard J. Carwardine, *Evangelicals and Politics in Antebellum America* (New Haven, Conn.: Yale University Press, 1993), pp. 123–24; John G. West, Jr., *The Politics of Revelation and Reason: Religion and Civic Life in the New Nation*, American Political Thought (Lawrence: University Press of Kansas, 1996), esp. pp. 79–136; and Michael F. Holt, *The Rise and Fall of the American Whig Party: Jacksonian Politics and the Onset of the Civil War* (New York: Oxford University Press, 1999), now the definitive history of the Whig party, and one that also relies quite heavily on Howe for its portrayal of northeastern religion (see esp. pp. 30–32, 117, and 991, n. 36).

52. Howe, *The Political Culture of the American Whigs*, pp. 159–60; and Douglas M. Strong, *Perfectionist Politics: Abolitionism and the Religious Tensions of American Democracy*, Religion and Politics (Syracuse, N.Y.: Syracuse University Press, 1999), pp. 27–29, 50, 71–72. Like Howe, Richard Carwardine has argued that "the great majority of devout evangelicals rallied to the Whigs," but Carwardine offers a qualifier that ought to be taken more seriously: "In very many cases Whiggish ministers, conscious of the partisan divisions within their congregations and fearful of the detrimental effect on religious faith of political excitement, remained publicly discreet in their political posture." See Carwardine, "Evangelicals, Whigs and the Election of William Henry Harrison," p. 70. Recently, Charles E. Hambrick-Stowe has argued that even Charles Finney advocated a largely spiritual approach to American politics, believing that "the ultimate answer to the sins of the United States was moral suasion, not the false god of direct political action. Spiritual revival was what the country required." Charles E. Hambrick-Stowe, *Charles G. Finney and the Spirit of American Evangelicalism*, Library of Religious Biography (Grand Rapids, Mich.: Eerdmans, 1996), pp. 88–93, 203 (quotation from p. 203). James F. Cooper, Jr.'s commentary on "the Great Awakening and the privatization of piety" offers an insightful analysis of the eighteenth-century roots of the Taylorites' increasingly spiritual approach to issues of public

welfare. See Cooper, *Tenacious of Their Liberties*, pp. 197–214. For confirmation of the Taylorites' largely spiritual approach to politics, see Hirrel, *Children of Wrath*, pp. 76–77, 79, 155–69.

53. "Christian Politics," QCS 7 (December 1835): 540, 544.

54. Ibid., p. 543. For more of the Taylorites' spiritualized and gradualist law-and-order approach to social issues, see "Winslow on Social and Civil Duties," QCS 8 (March 1836): 151–60; "The Dangers of Our Country," QCS 8 (December 1836): 505–19, and "Barnes on the Supremacy of the Laws," QCS 10 (August 1838): 490–500.

55. On this theme, see Sellers, *The Market Revolution*, p. 211; Paul E. Johnson, "Democracy, Patriarchy, and American Revivals, 1780–1830," *Journal of Social History* 24 (Summer 1991): 843–50; Paul E. Johnson and Sean Wilentz, *The Kingdom of Matthias* (New York: Oxford University Press, 1994), pp. 6–11; and Teresa Anne Murphy, *Ten Hours' Labor: Religion, Reform, and Gender in Early New England* (Ithaca, N.Y.: Cornell University Press, 1992). See also the recent book by Nobel prize laureate Robert William Fogel, *The Fourth Great Awakening and the Future of Egalitarianism* (Chicago: University of Chicago Press, 2000), on the slowness of the leaders of the Second Great Awakening to recognize that their heavily spiritual approach to social reform "was no longer adequate in a world of confrontations between powerful big businesses and alienated workers" (p. 174). While Taylor expended comparatively little energy on social or economic criticism, he did speak out against Yankee profiteering. See, for example, his sermon on "The Rule and the Test of Morality," in Nathaniel W. Taylor, *Practical Sermons* (New York: Clark, Austin, and Smith, 1858), pp. 137–38. On the general failure of America's most prominent evangelicals to maintain a major critique of American capitalism in this period, see Robert A. Wauzzinski, *Between God and Gold: Protestant Evangelicalism and the Industrial Revolution, 1820–1914* (Rutherford, N.J.: Fairleigh Dickinson University Press, 1993). But see also Sutton, *Journeymen for Jesus*, who has uncovered a strong current of more radical "artisan evangelicalism" in this period that supported a large amount of "anticapitalist militancy." William R. Sutton, "Tied to the Whipping Post: New Labor History and Evangelical Artisans in the Early Republic," *Labor History* 37 (Fall 1995): 251–81, provides a useful analysis of recent treatments of evangelicals among nineteenth-century labor historians.

56. Indeed, Jehudi Ashmun, the first agent of the African Colonization Society in Monrovia, Liberia, was buried in New Haven's Grove Street Cemetery. And as Steven Spielberg's movie production *Amistad* has recently publicized (in a movie that does not do justice to the role of New Haven's Christians in its story), New Haven played a significant role in aiding the Mendi tribesmen arrested for the Amistad rebellion. In fact, it was Yale theologian Josiah Willard Gibbs who succeeded in breaking down the communication barrier between the Mendi and their attorneys (significantly, Gibbs had the help of James Covey, an 18-year-old from Sierra Leone who understood the Mendi dialect). On New Haven's role in this affair, see Osterweis, Three Centuries of New Haven, 1638–1938, pp. 297–302; Mitchell, *History of the United Church of New Haven*, pp. 96–97; and Antony Dugdale, J. J. Fueser, and J. Celso de Castro Alves, *Yale, Slavery and Abolition* (New Haven, Conn.: Amistad Committee, 2001), pp. 22–23.

57. *College for Colored Youth. An Account of the New-Haven City Meeting and Resolutions, with Recommendations of the College, and Strictures upon the Doings of New-Haven* (New York: Published by the Committee, 1831); [Lewis Tappan], *The Life of Arthur Tappan* (New York: Hurd and Houghton, 1870), pp. 146–52; Robert Austin Warner, *New Haven Negroes: A Social History* (New Haven, Conn.: Yale University Press, 1940), pp. 53–60; Osterweis, *Three Centuries of New Haven, 1638–1938*, p. 289; Leon F. Litwack, *North of Slavery: The Negro in the Free States, 1790–1860* (Chicago: University of Chicago Press, 1961), pp. 123–26; Horatio T. Strother, *The Underground Railroad in Connecticut* (Middletown, Conn.: Wesleyan University Press, 1962), pp. 28–30; Wyatt-Brown, *Lewis Tappan*, pp. 87–89; Philie, *Change and Tradition*, pp. 177–92; Davis, *Leonard Bacon*, pp. 75–76; and Dugdale, Fueser, and Alves, *Yale, Slavery and Abolition*, pp. 16–18, 21. As would be expected, the 1830 U.S. census provides a somewhat lower

estimate of New Haven's total black population (567 blacks out of a total population of 10,946) than has been common among local historians.

58. Maurer, *A Puritan Church*, pp. 123–41. On the African Improvement Society and its efforts to ameliorate the living conditions of New Haven's black community, see esp. Davis, *Leonard Bacon*, pp. 57–58. New Haven did have one of the earliest antislavery societies in New England (founded in 1833). But neither it nor its leading clergy—most notably Simeon Jocelyn—were able to put much of a dent in local prejudice. As Osterweis notes, *Three Centuries of New Haven, 1638–1938*, p. 215, New Haven's black community was growing so rapidly in this period that Jocelyn's church could not accommodate the swelling numbers. Five more African churches were formed between 1840 and 1855. On the sour fruit of the moderates' halfhearted colonizing efforts in Liberia, see Sanneh, *Abolitionists Abroad*, pp. 182–237.

59. At a union meeting in New Haven on Oct. 24, 1850, Taylor argued that it was "lawful to deliver up fugitives for the high, the great, the momentous interests of the South." See *The Proceedings of the Union Meeting, Held at Brewster's Hall, October 24, 1850* (New Haven, Conn.: William H. Stanley, 1851), esp. pp. 38–42; quoted in Strother, *The Underground Railroad in Connecticut*, p. 96, who relates that "in the end, the meeting produced a petition stating that 'any alteration of the Compromise Measures adopted at the last Session of Congress is not only inexpedient, but that it is the duty of every good citizen of this Republic to support and vindicate the same.' Not less than 1746 signatures were appended to this document." For confirmation of Taylor's willingness to condone the subjugation of slaves for what he deemed the welfare of the nation at large, see the entry for Thursday, August 1, 1850 in Moseley, ed., *Diary of James Hadley*, p. 82: "Mr. Storrs of Brooklyn (lately here, called on Taylor) loquitur: 'Sell a human being! I would as soon think of selling an angel.' Dr. Taylor: 'I would sell an angel quick, if it was for the greatest good.'" And see the depiction of Taylor as an outright "pro-slavery" advocate in Dugdale, Fueser, and Alves, *Yale, Slavery, and Abolition*, pp. 23–25 (though it should be noted that this depiction is somewhat strained, and that the authors' extrapolations from the minutes of Yale's Rhetorical Society are both excessive and misleading).

60. See *Speeches and Other Proceedings at the Anti-Nebraska Meetings Held in New Haven, Connecticut, March 8th and 10th, 1854* (New Haven, Conn.: John H. Austin, 1854), pp. 10, 13; and Nathaniel W. Taylor et al. to President James Buchanan, [July 1857], James Buchanan Papers, Reel 33, HSP. On the church history of New Haven's Kansas meeting, see Mary Hewitt Mitchell, *History of The United Church of New Haven* (New Haven, Conn.: United Church, 1942), pp. 98–99; Richard H. Clapp, "An Historical Paper," in *Addresses Given at the Meeting in Commemoration of the Two Hundredth Anniversary of the Founding of the United Church of New Haven, Connecticut, Held in the Church Building Thursday Evening, May 7, 1942* (New Haven, Conn.?: n.p., 1942?), n.p.; and Theodore T. Munger, *Historical Discourse Preached on the One Hundred and Fiftieth Anniversary of the Organization of the United Church, May 8th, 1892* (New Haven, Conn.: United Church, 1892), p. 36. On the role of New England's religious leaders in the early fight for Kansas, see also Eli Thayer, *The New England Emigrant Aid Company and Its Influence, through the Kansas Contest, upon National History* (Worcester, Mass.: Franklin P. Rice, 1887). The New Havenites' memorial to Buchanan, Buchanan's response, and a subsequent rejoinder from New Haven were published together as *The New Haven Memorial to the President, Protesting against the Use of the United-States Army to Enforce the Bogus Laws of Kansas; the Answer of President Buchanan; and the Reply of the Memorialists* (Boston: John Wilson and Son, n.d.). In 1856, a group of nearly 100 pioneers (including men, women, and children) from New Haven and the surrounding area emigrated to Kansas to try to ensure that it would become a free state. See Osterweis, Three Centuries of New Haven, 1638–1938, pp. 304–5. For the Taylorites' ongoing commitment to colonizationism, see "Review of Edwards' Sermon," CS 5 (January 1823): 39–48; "Review on African Colonization," QCS 2 (September 1830): 459–82; "Free People of Color," QCS 4 (June 1832): 311–34; [Leonard Bacon], "Slavery and Coloniza-

tion," QCS 5 (March 1833): 145–68; [Leonard Bacon], "Slavery," QCS 5 (December 1833): 631–55; [Leonard Bacon], "The Abolition of Slavery," QCS 6 (June 1834): 332–44; "Mrs. Child's Appeal in Favor of the Africans," QCS 6 (September 1834): 445–56; "Colonization and Anti-Colonization," QCS 7 (September 1835): 503–20, and (December 1835): 521–40; [Leonard Bacon], "Present State of the Slavery Question," QCS 8 (March 1836): 112–27; [Leonard Bacon], "Andrews on Slavery," QCS 8 (March 1836): 160–70; and "Memoir of Lovejoy," QCS 10 (May 1838): 299–318. Even in the years immediately preceding the war, the Taylorites favored restricting northern evangelical commentary on slavery to its personal, moral aspects and avoiding political criticism of southern practices. See Chauncey A. Goodrich, *A Letter to the Secretaries of the American Tract Society, Written in Behalf of the Rev. Jeremiah Day, D.D., LL.D., Eleazar T. Fitch, D.D., and Others* (New Haven, Conn.: Thomas H. Pease, 1858?). For further testimony to the weak-kneed nature of the Taylorites' antislavery stance, see Moseley, ed., *Diary of James Hadley*, pp. 82, 154; Wayland, *The Theological Department in Yale College*, pp. 298–300; and Howard, *Conscience and Slavery*, pp. 13, 26. For more on Leonard Bacon's antislavery activities, see esp. Leonard Bacon, *Slavery Discussed in Occasional Essays, from 1833 to 1846* (New York: Baker and Scribner, 1846); Bacon, *Leonard Bacon*, pp. 179–273, 385–95, and passim; Howard, *Conscience and Slavery*, pp. 11, 17, 97, 132–34; and esp. Davis, *Leonard Bacon*. On the effort to persuade northern Christians to join the immediatist ranks, see John R. McKivigan, *The War against Proslavery Religion: Abolitionism and the Northern Churches, 1830–1865* (Ithaca, N.Y.: Cornell University Press, 1984). And for the most powerful recent testimony to the persistence of racism among all kinds of post-Revolutionary New England gradualists, see Joanne Pope Melish, *Disowning Slavery: Gradual Emancipation and "Race" in New England, 1780–1860* (Ithaca, N.Y.: Cornell University Press, 1998).

61. As Taylor's former student B. N. Martin, "Dr. Taylor on Moral Government," NE 17 (November 1869): 910, once said, "probably no one ever equalled him in the familiarity of his acquaintance with the great works of this eminent divine [Edwards]." See Hatch, *Personal Reminiscences*, pp. 11, 28, 34; Noah Porter, "Introduction," to Taylor's *Lectures on the Moral Government of God*, 2 vols. (New York: Clark, Austin, and Smith, 1859), 1: vi; Noah Porter, "Dr. Taylor and His Theology," in *The Semi-Centennial Anniversary of the Divinity School of Yale College*, pp. 92–97; Noah Porter, "Philosophy in Great Britain and America: A Supplementary Sketch," Appendix 1 in *History of Philosophy from Thales to the Present Time*, vol. 2, *History of Modern Philosophy*, by Friedrich Ueberweg, trans. George S. Morris (New York: Scribner, Armstrong, and Co., 1874), p. 452; Bacon, "A Sermon at the Funeral of Nathaniel W. Taylor," p. 8; Fisher, "A Sermon Preached in the Chapel of Yale College, March 14, 1858," pp. 32, 35; Fisher, "Historical Address," pp. 20, 27–28; George Park Fisher, *History of Christian Doctrine* (Edinburgh: T. and T. Clark, 1949; 1896), pp. 414–17; Beecher, *Autobiography*, 2: 348, 177; and Stuart C. Henry, *Unvanquished Puritan: A Portrait of Lyman Beecher* (Westport, Conn.: Greenwood Press, 1986; 1973), p. 254. For just one of many other occasions when Beecher waved the Edwardsian flag, see his *Autobiography*, 2: 294. For an instance of Beecher's repudiation of Arminianism, see his correspondence with Ebenezer Porter in June of 1829, *Autobiography*, 2: 122–43. Even Beecher's cagey *Views in Theology*, 2d ed. (Cincinnati, Ohio: Truman and Smith, 1836), proved very Edwardsian, as well over half the book was devoted to the Edwardsian distinction between natural and moral ability. For Beecher's opposition to Old Calvinism, see his letter to Bennet Tyler, March 1830, *Autobiography*, 2: 153; and see Beecher to Benjamin Wisner, January 28, 1833, *Autobiography*, 2: 223–25.

62. See, for example, "On Heaven," in *Practical Sermons*, p. 190; Nathaniel W. Taylor, *Man, A Free Agent without the Aid of Divine Grace*, Tracts, Designed to Illustrate and Enforce the Most Important Doctrines of the Gospel, No. 2 (New Haven, Conn.: n.p., 1818); and Nathaniel W. Taylor, "Letter from Rev. Dr. Taylor," SP 5 (March 1832): 175–76. For the work of Taylor's colleagues against Arminianism, see [Ralph? Emerson], "Review of Adam Clarke's Discourses,"

QCS 1 (December 1829): 575-80; [Ebenezer? Porter], "Review of the Doctrine and Discipline of the Methodist Episcopal Church," QCS 2 (September 1830): 483-504; [Chauncey Goodrich], "Review of High Church and Arminian Principles," QCS 2 (December 1830): 730-31; and [Eleazar T. Fitch], "Fisk on Predestination and Election," QCS 3 (December 1831): 597-640. Like other Edwardsians, the Taylorites opposed not only the Arminian soteriology of the Methodists, but their rapid growth through unorthodox and often uncontrolled revivalistic methods as well. See [Emerson], "Review of Adam Clarke's Discourses," pp. 553-55, and [Porter], "Review of the Doctrine and Discipline of the Methodist Episcopal Church," pp. 496-504. Methodist growth in Connecticut in this period was significant but should not be exaggerated. While Francis Asbury visited New Haven as early as 1790 and a Methodist church was planted in town not long thereafter, this church did not have enough support to raise its own building until 1820 (see Osterweis, *Three Centuries of New Haven, 1638-1938*, pp. 214-15). On the rise of Methodism in New England generally, see James Mudge, *History of the New England Conference of the Methodist Episcopal Church* (Boston: The Conference, 1910); George Claude Baker, Jr., *An Introduction to the History of Early New England Methodism, 1789-1839* (Durham, N.C.: Duke University Press, 1941); William Thomas Umbel, "The Making of an American Denomination: Methodism in New England Religious Culture, 1790-1860" (Ph.D. diss., Johns Hopkins University, 1992), who discusses the interaction between New England's Methodists and Edwardsians/Taylorites on pp. 61-115; and Rennetts C. Miller, ed., *Souvenir History of the New England Southern Conference*, 3 vols. (Nantasket, Mass.: Rennetts C. Miller, 1897). See also Stanford E. Demars, "The Camp Meeting Vacation Resort in New England," *Henceforth* 21 (Spring 1994): 8-18, who notes that while Methodists did begin holding camp meetings in New England in the 1830s and 1840s, the camp meeting movement did not flourish in New England until the 1870s, when about one-third of New England's roughly one hundred camp meetings were established. And note the estimate in Finke and Stark, *The Churching of America*, pp. 282-83, that by 1850 devout Methodists still comprised only 6 percent of New England's population (cf. the helpful statistical tables in John H. Wigger, *Taking Heaven by Storm: Methodism and the Popularization of American Christianity*, Religion in America [New York: Oxford University Press, 1998], pp. 197-200). Contrast Richard D. Shiels. "The Methodist Invasion of Congregational New England," in Nathan D. Hatch and John H. Wigger, eds., *Methodism and the Shaping of American Culture* (Nashville: Kingswood Books, 2001), pp. 257-80, an insightful analysis of the rise of Methodism in New England over the course of the nineteenth century but one that exaggerates this rise during the first part of the nineteenth century: "when the Second Great Awakening had passed, Methodist churches were nearly as prominent as Congregational churches in New England" (p. 258). On the relatively conservative nature of Taylorite revivalism, see "Review on the Employment of Evangelists in Our Older Settlements," QCS 1 (September 1829): 425-38. A major Methodist response to Taylorite criticisms may be found in Wilbur Fisk, *Calvinistic Controversy: Embracing a Sermon on Predestination and Election; and Several Numbers on the Same Subject, Originally Published in the Christian Advocate and Journal* (New York: T. Mason and G. Lane, 1837). Taylor's writings bear the ubiquitous presence of Edwards and the Edwardsians. They, rather than the Old Calvinists, were his theological ancestors, those from whose thought his own thinking began and those to whom he referred when in need of an authoritative pronouncement. To cite all the examples of this would require far too much space, but see [Nathaniel W. Taylor], "Review of Spring on the Means of Regeneration," QCS 1 (June 1829): 225, (September 1829): 497-98, 505 (December 1829): 695, 702-3; and [Taylor], "Review of Dr. Tyler's Strictures on the Christian Spectator," pp. 154-58, 162, 169, 184. For the way in which Edwardsian figures and themes pervaded Taylor's lectures at Yale, see the several extant copies of student lecture notes held at Yale's Sterling and Divinity libraries. For example, Alexander MacWhorter, "Notes on a Course of Lectures in Revealed Theology by Nathaniel W. Taylor, D.D.," 1844, Folder 147A, Box 30, Yale Lectures, SML, pp. 147, 151, 152, 403, 404, and passim.

Chapter 4

1. Hatch, *Personal Reminiscences*, p. 15.

2. For an early example of the Unitarians' divide-and-conquer strategy, see "Mutations of Orthodoxy and Heresy," *The Christian Disciple* 2 (June 1814): 166–69, (August 1814): 236–37, (September 1814): 273–75, and (November 1814): 328–30. For Old Calvinists and liberals/ Unitarians alike, the most authoritative expressions of the traditional Calvinist doctrine of sin were found in the *Westminster Confession of Faith* (1647), 6, where humans since the Fall are described as "dead in sin, and wholly defiled in all the faculties and parts of soul and body," and the *Westminster Shorter Catechism*, Q. 18, where original sin is defined as "the corruption of his [one's] whole nature."

3. Henry Ware, *Letters Addressed to Trinitarians and Calvinists, Occasioned by Dr. Woods' Letters to Unitarians* (Cambridge, Mass.: Hilliard and Metcalf, 1820), pp. 106–07. For a general, blow-by-blow account of the Wood and Ware debate and of the subsequent paper wars over original sin with comprehensive bibliographical citations, see Smith, *Changing Conceptions of Original Sin.*

4. Bennet Tyler, *Letters on the Origin and Progress of the New Haven Theology* (New York: Robert Carter and Ezra Collier, 1837), p. 6; and Foster, *A Genetic History of the New England Theology*, p. 369. Relatedly, Beecher grew concerned in 1820 about complaints he had received concerning dull ministers coming out of Andover Seminary. Their preaching was said to lack animation and Beecher feared Andover (and New England) would lose students to Princeton. See Lyman Beecher to Leonard Woods, November 12 1820, in Beecher's *Autobiography*, 1: 324–25. Significantly, the Unitarian Andrews Norton's "Views of Calvinism," *The Christian Disciple*, n.s., 4 (July and August 1822): 244–80, comprised a divide-and-conquer attack on Calvinism that struck the Taylorites even closer to home, for Norton's essay emerged from a squabble with the editors of the *Christian Spectator*. For the emergence of this squabble, see the *Spectator* 4 (May 1822): 249–64; (June 1822): 299–318; and (August 1822): 445–48. For the *Spectator*'s response to Norton, see "Review of Norton's Views of Calvinism," *CS* 5 (April 1823): 196–224. For the full-blown paper war, see "State of the Calvinistic Controversy," *The Christian Disciple*, n.s., 5 (May and June 1823): 212–35; and "Review Reviewed," *CS* 6 (June 1824): 310–21, (July 1824): 360–74. For a sampling of later Taylorite counterattacks against Unitarianism, see Lyman Beecher, "Reply to the Christian Examiner, by the Author of the Sermon Reviewed in the First Number of That Work," *CS* 7 (February 1825): 94–108, (March 1825): 154–61, (April 1825): 210–22, (May 1825): 265–78, and (June 1825): 300–16; "Thoughts on the Unitarian Controversy," *QCS* 5 (March 1833): 64–87; "Norton's Reasons," *QCS* 5 (September 1833): 421–47; and see Taylor's response to Ware's argument "that the total depravity of man by nature is inconsistent with the free moral agency of man" in his *Essays, Lectures, Etc.*, pp. 206–12. For a general account of the battle between Taylor, Beecher, and the Unitarians in the 1820s, see Mead, *Nathaniel William Taylor*, pp. 171–99.

5. On Goodrich's early lectures on sin, see Tyler, *Letters on the Origin and Progress of the New Haven Theology*. For his later, published view of original sin, see [Chauncey Goodrich], "Review of Taylor and Harvey on Human Depravity," *QCS* 1 (June 1829): 343–84. For Fitch's contributions to the New Haven doctrine, see Eleazar T. Fitch, *Two Discourses on the Nature of Sin; Delivered before the Students of Yale College, July 30th, 1826* (New Haven, Conn.: Treadway and Adams, 1826), and Eleazar T. Fitch, *An Inquiry into the Nature of Sin: In Which the Views Advanced in 'Two Discourse on the Nature of Sin,' Are Pursued; and Vindicated from Objections, Stated in the Christian Advocate* (New Haven, Conn.: A. H. Maltby, 1827).

It should be pointed out here that Fitch's definition of sin was more finely nuanced than those of many western, Finneyite evangelicals who popularized the New Haven Theology. Both in the *Two Discourses*, pp. 5-6, and in the *Inquiry*, pp. 14-20, he made clear that his definition of sin was much more comprehensive than many suspected, including so-called sins of ignorance, sins of the heart, and sins of omission: "Sins of ignorance are those acts in which the moral agent transgresses the known obligation to acquaint himself with laws that were applicable, or some known general obligation of morality from which he might have inferred the given law." As to sins of the heart: "[T]he forbidden preference which is involved in coveting and envying, is as strictly an act of selfish preference, as when it is followed with the volition of some external act." Sins of omission, furthermore, stem from an active preference or volition to do something other than one's duty.

6. The Taste and Exercise schemes will be discussed further later. For secondary treatments of their differences, see chapter 2, n. 72.

7. [Ashbel Green], "Fitch's Discourses on the Nature of Sin," *The Christian Advocate* 5 (March 1827): 136, and (April 1827): 164, 166, 167; and Examiner, "Examination of Prof. Fitch's Theory of the Nature of Sin," CS, n.s., 2 (January 1828): 18–19. For the quotation from Nettleton's (unpreserved) letter, see Tyler, *Letters on the Origin and Progress of the New Haven Theology*, pp. 8–9. For a useful account of Nettleton's opposition to the Taylorites, see Sherry Pierpont May, "Asahel Nettleton: Nineteenth-Century American Revivalist" (Ph.D. diss., Drew University, 1969), pp. 276–426.

8. Chauncey Goodrich to Lyman Beecher, January 6, 1822, in Beecher's *Autobiography*, 1: 348; Fitch, *Two Discourses*, p. 38; and Fitch, *An Inquiry into the Nature of Sin*, pp. 54–57 (quotation from p. 57). Further examples of the Taylorite commitment to the Edwardsian natural/moral ability distinction may be found in "The Sermons of Dr. Samuel Clark," CS, n.s., 1 (December 1827): 640–41; Lyman Beecher, *Dependence and Free Agency. A Sermon Delivered in the Chapel of the Theological Seminary, Andover, July 16, 1832* (Boston: Perkins and Marvin, 1832); and "An Inquiry into the True Way of Preaching on Ability," QCS 7 (June 1835): 223–57.

9. Crocker, *The Catastrophe of the Presbyterian Church*, pp. 121–22.

10. Nathaniel W. Taylor, *Concio ad Clerum: A Sermon Delivered in the Chapel of Yale College, September 10, 1828* (New Haven, Conn.: A. H. Maltby and Homan Hallock, 1842; 1828). On the earlier coalescence of the New Haven Theology, see, for example, Lyman Beecher to Asahel Hooker, March 13, 1825, in Beecher's *Autobiography*, 2: 15, where Beecher defends Taylor's orthodoxy and notes that he has known Taylor's view of original sin "perhaps for ten years"; and Mead, *Nathaniel William Taylor*, p. 222.

11. Taylor, *Concio ad Clerum*, pp. 8–11, 13–14.

12. As noted in an entry for September 10, 1828, in Increase N. Tarbox, ed., *Diary of Thomas Robbins, D.D., 1796–1854*, 2 vols. (Boston: Beacon Press, 1887), 2: 107, "there was a rather unpleasant meeting of the clerrgy after the sermon" (i.e., after Taylor preached the *Concio*). The most significant early criticisms of the *Concio* came from the Congregational clergyman Joseph Harvey of Westchester, Connecticut, and Leonard Woods of Andover Seminary. See Harvey's *A Review of a Sermon, Delivered in the Chapel of Yale College, September 10, 1828* (Hartford, Conn.: Goodwin and Co., 1829), and Woods's *Letters to Rev. Nathaniel W. Taylor* (1830), in *The Works of Leonard Woods, D.D.*, vol. 4 (Andover: John D. Flagg, 1850), pp. 343–459. For an interesting and very sarcastic response from the conservative, latter-day Hopkinsians, see Brother Jonathan, "Letter to the Students in the Theological Seminary in New Haven," HM 3 (January 1829): 303–8, and (February 1829): 322–25.

13. Lyman Beecher, *Dependence and Free Agency: A Sermon Delivered in the Chapel of the Theological Seminary* pp. 22–28. On the distinction between compulsion and necessity in Calvin, see his *Institutes of the Christian Religion*, 2. 3. 5; 2. 4. 1; and 2. 1. 9–11 (quotations taken from the Ford Lewis Battles translation, ed. John T. McNeill [Philadelphia: Westminster Press, 1960]). For Calvin's general opposition to the natural ability espoused by Edwards, see ibid., 2. 1. 11–2. 2. 1. But note that, while Calvin clearly did not maintain a doctrine of natural ability himself, the evangelistic purpose of Edwards's doctrine accords with Calvin's suggestion that "when man has been taught that no good thing remains in his power, and that he is hedged about on all sides by most miserable necessity, in spite of this he should nevertheless be instructed to aspire

to a good of which he is empty, to a freedom of which he has been deprived. In fact, he may thus be more sharply aroused from inactivity than if it were supposed that he was endowed with the highest virtues" (ibid., 2. 2. 1). Though Augustine proved more concerned than Calvin to stress that our natural necessity is imposed internally (by improper willing that has acquired the force of habit and thus become "second nature") rather than externally, and while his theology thus served as something of a precursor to the Edwardsian doctrine of free will, similar language can be found in his work. See *On Man's Perfection in Righteousness*, 4. 9, and *On Nature and Grace* , 66., 79. For a passage in Augustine that was quite conducive to the Edwardsians' affectional understanding of necessity and human freedom, see his *Lectures or Tractates on the Gospel According to St. John*, 26. 1–4. Useful summaries of Augustine's doctrine of necessity can be found in Eugene TeSelle's unpublished introduction to Augustine's sermons on Romans 7-9; and John M. Rist, *Augustine: Ancient Thought Baptized* (Cambridge: Cambridge University Press, 1994), pp. 175-77, 265.

14. A well-known anti-Protestant polemicist, Bellarmine was quite familiar to the British and may well have exerted an influence on the Protestant distinction between natural and moral ability. He considered the English Calvinist William Whitaker his greatest opponent and had a portrait of Whitaker in his room. On the theology of Bellarmine, consult Joseph de La Servière, *La théologie de Bellarmin* (Paris: Beauchesne, 1909). For a useful introduction in English to Bellarmine's understanding of original sin and its effects on human ability, and to the dispute between Banez and Molina, see John O. Riedl, "Bellarmine and the Dignity of Man," and Anton C. Pegis, "Molina and Human Liberty," respectively, both in Gerald Smith, ed., *Jesuit Thinkers of the Renaissance* (Milwaukee, Wis.: Marquette University Press, 1939), pp. 193-226, 75-131. On the familiarity of Bellarmine and the British, and for the reference to Whitaker's portrait on Bellarmine's wall, see A. G. Dickens, *The Counter Reformation* (New York: Norton, and 1968), pp. 186-87. Suarez, too, was widely read among all sorts of Protestant theologians. On his influence among Dutch Protestants especially and, through them, on Jonathan Edwards, consult John Platt, *Reformed Thought and Scholasticism: The Argument for the Existence of God in Dutch Theology, 1575–1650*, Studies in the History of Christian Thought (Leiden, Netherlands: E. J. Brill, 1982); and William Sparkes Morris, *The Young Jonathan Edwards: A Reconstruction*, Chicago Studies in the History of American Religion (Brooklyn, N.Y.: Carlson Publishing, 1991).

15. The most thorough treatments in English of Cameron and the Amyraldians are F. P. Van Stam, *The Controversy over the Theology of Saumur, 1635–1650: Disrupting Debates Among the Huguenots in Complicated Circumstances* (Amsterdam: APA–Holland University Press, 1988), and Brian G. Armstrong, *Calvinism and the Amyraut Heresy: Protestant Scholasticism and Humanism in Seventeenth-Century France* (Madison: University of Wisconsin Press, 1969). An important recent discussion of Cameron's role in the history of Scottish theology may be found in Thomas F. Torrance, *Scottish Theology: From John Knox to John McLeod Campbell* (Edinburgh: T and T Clark, 1996), esp. pp. 64-66. For Amyraut's defense of the natural/moral ability distinction, see his *Brief Traitté de la predestination et de ses principales dépendances* (Saumur, France: J. Lesnier, 1634), and *Fidei Mosis Amyraldi, circa errores arminianorum declaratio* (Saumur, France: J. Lesnier, 1646).

16. In a famous letter to his student and friend Joseph Bellamy, Edwards recommended Turretin as an "excellent" theologian, especially "on polemical divinity; on the Five Points, and other controversial points." See Jonathan Edwards to the Rev. Joseph Bellamy, 15 January 1746/ 7, in Jonathan Edwards, *Letters and Personal Writings*, WJE, vol. 16 (Yale, 1998), p. 217. Further evidence of Edwards's high regard for Turrettini may be found in Edwards's treatise on the *Religious Affections*, ed. John E. Smith, WJE, vol. 2 (Yale, 1959), p. 289, n. 4.

17. The natural/moral ability distinction is condemned in Canons 21 and 22 of the *Helvetic Formula Consensus*. I have quoted from the recent English translation by Martin I. Klauber, "The Helvetic Formula Consensus (1675): An Introduction and Translation," *Trinity Journal* 11 (Spring 1990): 103-23. For useful background information on this Swiss confessional document, viewed by many as the acme of high Calvinist scholaticism, see Martin I. Klauber, *Between Reformed Scholasti-*

cism and Pan-Protestantism: Jean-Alphonse Turretin (1671–1737) and Enlightenend Orthodoxy at the Academy of Geneva (Selinsgrove, Penn.: Susquehanna University Press, 1994), pp. 25–35.

18. While the latest and perhaps best-known example of this perpetuation is found in *An End of Doctrinal Controversies, Which Have Lately Troubled the Churches by Reconciling Explication Without Much Disputing* (London: John Salusbury, 1691), Baxter perpetuated the distinction in various places, not always as clearly and consistently as Edwards, but with great force nonetheless. For a useful summary of Baxter's advocacy of natural ability, see George P. Fisher, "The Theology of Richard Baxter," *BS* 9 (January 1852): 150–52. See also anon., "Richard Baxter's 'End of Controversy,'" *BS* 12 (April 1855): 356–62, whose author notes that on the theme of moral agency Baxter "has anticipated . . . many of the distinctions usually ascribed to President Edwards" (p. 356). The best works on Baxter's theology are the classic treatment by James I. Packer, "The Redemption and Restoration of Man in the Thought of Richard Baxter" (D.Phil. diss., University of Oxford, 1954), and the more up-to-date discussion by Hans Boersma, *A Hot Pepper Corn: Richard Baxter's Doctrine of Justification in Its Seventeenth-Century Context of Controversy* (Zoetermeer, Netherlands: Uitgeverij Boekencentrum, 1993). But see also the advocacy of Baxterian theology in Alan C. Clifford, *Atonement and Justification: English Evangelical Theology 1640–1790: An Evaluation* (Oxford, England: Clarendon Press, 1990). As Baxter was one of the best-known clergymen of seventeenth-century England, Edwards was well aware of his theology. There are numerous references to Baxter in Edwards's "Catalogue" of reading. Relatedly, helpful discussions of several other Puritan views regarding the "natural man" and the role of human nature in conversion may be found in William K. B. Stoever, *"A Faire and Easie Way to Heaven": Covenant Theology and Antinomianism in Early Massachusetts* (Middletown, Conn.: Wesleyan University Press, 1978), esp. pp. 3–20; Norman Pettit, *The Heart Prepared: Grace and Conversion in Puritan Spiritual Life*, 2d ed. (Middletown, Conn.: Wesleyan University Press, 1989; 1966); and Charles Lloyd Cohen, *God's Caress: The Psychology of Puritan Religious Experience*, esp. pp. 25–46.

19. The most lively critique of the distinction during Taylor's adult life appeared in Ezra Stiles Ely's *A Contrast Between Calvinism and Hopkinsianism* (New York: S. Whiting and Co., 1811), pp. 53–55. A New England native who had recently repudiated Hopkinsianism, Ely ministered in New York as a stated Presbyterian preacher in the city's hospital and almshouse. With the zeal of a convert, he denounced the distinction as a misleading ruse. "You may thus charm, with the music of words," he wrote, "but will not convince the man of sound mind" (p. 54). The best example of the Princetonian adoption of the distinction may be found in [Alexander], "An Inquiry into That Inability Under Which the Sinner Labours." Very few scholars have noted the prehistory of Edwards's natural/moral ability distinction. Early in this century, Charles A. Briggs, *Theological Symbolics* (New York: Charles Scribner's Sons, 1914), pp. 373–81, and *History of the Study of Theology*, prepared for publication by Emilie Grace Briggs, (New York: Charles Scribner's Sons, 1916), 2: 173, discussed the importance of Amyraldian themes to Edwards and, through the Edwardsians, to "New School" Calvinists generally on this side of the Atlantic. The Dutch theologian Herman Bavinck, *Gereformeerde Dogmatiek*, vol. 3 (Kampen, Netherlands: J. H. Kok, 1918), p. 116, noted this connection briefly as well. More recently, Norman Fiering, *Jonathan Edwards's Moral Thought and Its British Context* (Chapel Hill: University of North Carolina Press, 1981), p. 304, n. 124, has suggested that Edwards picked the distinction up from his "Arminian" opponent Samuel Clarke (1675-1729). As a liberal Anglican, Clarke used the distinction to much different ends than Edwards but Edwards was familiar with his work. However, while Clarke surely represents one source of Edwards's knowledge of the natural/moral ability distinction, he is not the only source. While neither Bellarmine nor the Amyraldians appear on Edwards's manuscript "Catalogue" of works read or to be read, Edwards referred to Amyraldian writings second-hand in "Miscellanies" entries on unrelated topics (see Miscellanies # 956 and #961, in Jonathan Edwards, *"Miscellanies," 833–1152*, ed. Amy Plantinga Pauw, WJE [Yale, forthcoming], where Edwards quotes Theophilus Gale's refer-

ences to the Amyraldians in *Court of the Gentiles* [1669-77; 1682]). Edwards had also read Turrettini's *Institutio Theologiae Elencticae* (Geneva, 1679-85), which engages the teachings of the Saumur Academy throughout. And he might have encountered the Amyraldians through Friderico Adolpho Lampe, *Synopsis Historiae Sacrae et Ecclesiasticae* (Trajecti ad Rhenum: Gysbertum Paddenburg, 1726), 2. 13. 3, 22, and 2. 4. 7, 23, or J. Basnage, *Histoire de la Religion des Eglises Reformeés* (Rotterdam: Abraham Acher, 1690), 2. 3. 3, as well, two other works on Edwards's "Catalogue" that, while not discussing the natural/moral ability distinction, did discuss Amyraldianism. Edwards would have been at least indirectly familiar with the philosophy of Suarez through the writings of Franciscus Burgersdicius and Adrian Heereboord, the Dutch Suaresian Calvinist scholastics whose philosophical works were used to teach logic at Harvard and Yale before the introduction of Locke. On Edwards's familiarity with Burgersdicius and Heereboord, see Morris, *The Young Jonathan Edwards*.

20. Taylor, *Essays, Lectures, Etc.*, p. 210; and [Nathaniel W. Taylor], "Review of Dr. Tyler's Strictures on the Christian Spectator," *QCS* 2 (March 1830): 195. See also Taylor, *Man, A Free Agent Without the Aid of Divine Grace*, pp. 10-11; and Nathaniel W. Taylor, "Dr. Taylor's Reply to Dr. Tyler's Examination," *SP* 5 (August 1832): 428-29.

21. This issue will be discussed further below. For a survey of Taylor's critique of the language of physical depravity—which all Edwardsians repudiated whether or not any of them inadvertently lapsed into it—see especially his *Concio ad Clerum*, 5-6, 8, 14-15, 27; [Nathaniel W. Taylor], "Application of the Principles of Common Sense to Certain Disputed Doctrines," *QCS* 3 (September 1831): 462-67; Nathaniel W. Taylor, "Dr. Taylor's Reply to Dr. Tyler," *SP* 6 (January 1833): 5-12, 16-18; Taylor, *Essays, Lectures, Etc.*, pp. 135-36, 167-68, 183-94, 213-33; and Nathaniel W. Taylor, "The Peculiar Power of the Gospel on the Human Mind, as Determining the Mode of Preaching It," ms. sermon preached at the installation of Noah Porter, January 12, 1843 in Springfield, Massachusetts. Folder 737, Box 19, Yale Miscellaneous Mss., SML, p. 27.

22. Quotation from *Essays, Lectures, Etc.*, p. 213.

23. Nathaniel W. Taylor to Lyman Beecher, January 14, 1819, in Beecher's *Autobiography*, 1: 284-87. For Taylor's response to the catchphrase "he can if he will," see J. A. Saxton, "Notes of Dr. Taylor's Lectures: Taken, in Part at the Lectures, and Compiled, in Part from the Notes of Dutton, Kitchel, and Whittlesey" (1838), 2: 338, Folder 155, Box 32, Yale Lectures, SML; Taylor, "The Peculiar Power of the Gospel," p. 26; and Taylor to Edward Dorr Griffin, March 20, 1832, in William B. Sprague, *Memoir of Rev. Dr. Griffin*, in Sprague, ed., *Sermons by the Late Rev. Edward D. Griffin, D.D.* (New York: John S. Taylor, 1839), 1: 178.

24. As Taylor knew well, Edwards himself had admitted in *Freedom of the Will* (see esp. pp. 159-62) that, technically speaking, the words "necessity" and "inability" do not apply in the moral realm. By definition, "necessity" and "inability" imply the existence of a contrary will/inclination. And since, in Edwards's view, such a contrary will exists only in cases of *natural* necessity, these terms were to be used with great caution in the field of ethics. Consequently, whereas Edwards described "necessity" *in terms of* "certainty," Taylor *distinguished* between "certainty" and "necessity" so as to maintain Edwards's doctrine that "the will always is as the greatest apparent good is" (the central doctrine in Edwards's own understanding of human volition—see *Freedom of the Will*, pp. 141-55), while avoiding the oxymoronic character that Edwards himself attributed to the notion of "moral necessity." Clearly, Edwards himself did not go as far as Taylor in claiming that moral agents possess a genuine "power to the contrary." But Taylor was within his rights in claiming that, in order to avoid depicting the "full and fixed connection" between the unconverted and their sin in terms of "natural necessity," Edwardsians had to say something of the kind. For a fuller analysis of this theme in Taylor than I am able to provide here, see Jason A. Nicholls, "'Certainty' with 'Power to the Contrary': Nathaniel William Taylor (1786-1858) on the Will" (Ph.D. diss., Marquette University, forthcoming).

25. Taylor, *Lectures on the Moral Government of God*, 2: 134; Sprague, *Memoir*, 1: 180; and Goodrich, "Notes," p. 152. For further examples of the Taylorites' synonymous use of the moral/ natural inability and certainty/necessity distinctions, see Saxton, "Notes," 2: 340; "Review of the Works of President Edwards," *QCS* 3 (September 1831): 337–57; and Fitch, *Two Discourses on the Nature of Sin*, p. 38.

26. For Harvey's critique, see Joseph Harvey, *An Examination of the Pelagian and Arminian Theory of Moral Agency as Recently Advocated by Dr. Beecher in His 'Views in Theology'* (New York: Ezra Collier, 1837). Hodge criticized the Taylorite doctrine nearly every year in his lectures on didactic theology. For examples, see Henry V. Rankin, "Notes from Lectures on Didactic Theology by Charles Hodge, 1845–46," 2: 318, Folder 2, Box 35, The Charles Hodge Ms. Collection, PSA; Thomas R. Markham, "Notes from Lectures on Didactic Theology by Charles Hodge, 1850–51," 2: 232, Folder 1, Box 39, The Charles Hodge Ms. Collection, PSA; and Caspar W. Hodge, Sr., "Notes from Lectures on Didactic Theology by Charles Hodge, 1852–53," 1: 288–89, Folder 1, Box 40, The Charles Hodge Ms. Collection, PSA (quotation from the Rankin notebook). Princeton's Archibald Alexander, though more accepting of the natural/moral ability distinction than Hodge, also worried at times that it could function as a misleading legerdemain when put forward by those who do not take human inability seriously enough. Alexander grew especially worried about those he called the "new preachers," presumably in New York and out west who, "in their addresses to the impenitent sinner, say nothing about natural and moral inability. They preach, that man is in possession of every ability which is requisite for the discharge of his duty." See John Lloyd, "Lecture Notes on Archibald Alexander's Didactic Theology, 1842–43," unpaginated, Folder 2, Box 5, Alexander Papers, PSA; and [Alexander], "An Inquiry into That Inability under Which the Sinner Labours," pp. 370–71. For Atwater's comments, see Lyman A. Atwater to [Charles Hodge], July 25, 1853, Folder 32, Box 13, Ser. 14, Charles Hodge Papers, PUL. Cf. [Lyman Atwater], "The Power of the Contrary Choice," *BR* 12 (October 1840): 532–49, which claimed erroneously that the notion of a power to the contrary "really amounts" to the Arminian "liberty of indifference" (p. 538); and [Lyman Atwater], "Modern Explanations of the Doctrine of Inability," *BR* 26 (April 1854): 217–46.

27. See, for example, Edwards's *Freedom of the Will*, pp. 149–55.

28. Jonathan Edwards, "Remarks on the *Essays on the Principles of Morality and Natural Religion*, in a Letter to a Minister of the Church of Scotland: By the Rev. Mr. Jonathan Edwards, President of the College of New Jersey, and Author of the Late *Inquiry into the Modern Notions of the Freedom of the Will*," in Ramsey, ed., *Freedom of the Will*, p. 456 (emphasis mine). The American editors of Edwards's works published this letter along with *Freedom of the Will* beginning with the third edition of the latter work (1768). For the Taylorite quotations, see "An Inquiry into the True Way of Preaching on Ability," *QCS* 7 (June 1835): 233; and "Day on the Will," *QCS* 10 (February 1838): 181. Significantly, "Day on the Will" was a review of *An Inquiry Respecting the Self-Determining Power of the Will; Or Contingent Volition* (New Haven, Conn.: Herrick and Noyes, 1838), written by Yale's conservative and highly respected Calvinist president, Jeremiah Day. The Taylorites heaped their highest praise on this anti-Arminian volume, claiming that Day had articulated that which they had been saying all along. In a tellingly acrimonious response, however, Bennet Tyler claimed Day for the Tylerites and objected to his abduction by Yale's theologians. See Tyler, *A Review of President Day's Treatise on the Will* (Hartford, Conn.: Elihu Geer, 1838). On the continuity of Taylor's doctrine of "certainty without necessity" with the earlier Edwardsian understanding of natural ability, cf. Pope, *New England Calvinism and the Disruption of the Presbyterian Church*, p. 105, and Earl A. Pope, "The Rise of the New Haven Theology," *Journal of Presbyterian History* 44 (June 1966): 115.

29. Banez and his followers are the best known advocates of describing sin and grace in physical terms. They argued that efficacious grace operated as a "physical premotion" (*praemotio physica*) on the will and thereby determined its free acts. Significantly, however, neither the

Banezians nor any other proponents of this or similar language (including the sixteenth-century Lutheran Matthias Flacius, who taught that original sin comprised the substance or essence of human nature and that conversion thus marked a transformation of human nature itself) have viewed sin and grace as corporeal entities. By depicting God's power as a physical cause, Banez meant only to portray it as exerting an intrinsic effect on the faculty of the will that was conceptually prior to and thus caused or actualized the will's own causal powers. On the doctrine of physical premotion, see R. Garrigou-Lagrange, *"Premotion Physique," Dictionnaire de Théologie Catholique* (Paris: Librarie Letouzey et Ané, 1936), 13: 31–77; T. C. O'Brien, "Premotion, Physical," *New Catholic Encyclopedia* (New York: McGraw-Hill, 1967), 11: 741–43; and Reginald Garrigou-Lagrange, *Grace: Commentary on the Summa theologica of St. Thomas, Ia Iae, q. 109–14* (St. Louis, Mo.: B. Herder, 1952). For Flacius's doctrine of original sin, see his *De peccati originalis aut veteris Adami appellationibus et essentia,* appended to his *Clavis Scripturae Sacrae* (Basileae: Ioannem Oporinum and Eusebium Episcopium, 1567).

30. Quotations from Leonard Woods, *An Essay on Native Depravity* (Boston: William Peirce, 1835), pp. 197, 207, and Bennet Tyler, *Lectures on Theology* (Boston: J. E. Tilton and Company, 1859), p. 189. For the most significant early reactions of Harvey and Tyler to Taylor's doctrine of original sin, see Joseph Harvey, *A Review of a Sermon, Delivered in the Chapel of Yale College, September 10, 1828* (Hartford, Conn.: Goodwin and Co., 1829); [Joseph Harvey], *Examination of a Review of Dr. Taylor's Sermon on Human Depravity and Mr. Harvey's Strictures on that Sermon* (Hartford, Conn.: Goodwin and Co., 1829); and Bennet Tyler's contributions to the *Spirit of the Pilgrims,* "Dr. Tyler's Examination of Dr. Taylor's Theological Views," "Dr. Tyler's Reply to Dr. Taylor," and "Dr. Tyler's Letter to the Editor of the Spirit of the Pilgrims," in vol. 5 (June 1832): 325–36, (September 1832): 508–23, (October 1832): 545–63, and vol. 6 (May 1833): 284–306.

31. [Nathaniel W. Taylor et al.], "Wardlaw's Christian Ethics," QCS 7 (September 1835): 415; and Taylor, *Essays, Lectures, Etc.,* pp. 167–68. On the fallacy and heterodoxy of physical depravity, see also Taylor, *Concio ad Clerum,* pp. 5–6, 14–15, 27. Significantly, the Taylorites opposed the notion of hereditary, physical depravity on consistently (and explicitly) Edwardsian grounds. Against Unitarians who argued that Edwards himself taught physical depravity and Tylerites who seemed unwittingly to confirm their argument, the Taylorites perceived themselves as defending authentic Edwardsianism by repudiating physical depravity and natural inability together. See, for example, T.R., "Edwards's View of Original Sin," CS 6 (November 1824): 567–75; Taylor, "Dr. Taylor's Reply to Dr. Tyler's Examination," pp. 428–29; [Chauncey Goodrich], "Dr. Tyler's Remarks and Dr. Taylor's Reply," QCS 4 (September 1832): 458–64; and Taylor, "Dr. Taylor's Reply to Dr. Tyler," pp. 16–18. An interesting recent example of a pro-Edwardsian Calvinist arguing (well, though inaccurately) that Edwards taught physical depravity may be found in C. Samuel Storms, *Tragedy in Eden: Original Sin in the Theology of Jonathan Edwards* (Lanham, Md.: University Press of America, 1985), pp. 136–37, n. 64.

32. For Taylor's critique of physical depravity, see his works cited in n. 21. Quotations taken from his *Essays, Lectures, Etc.,* p. 186, and Taylor, "The Peculiar Power of the Gospel on the Human Mind," p. 27. For Goodrich's use of Edwards, see [Goodrich], "Review of Taylor and Harvey on Human Depravity," p. 367. The source of this quotation may be found in Edwards' *Original Sin,* p. 380. For the premium Taylorite revivalists placed on sustaining their listeners' sense of guilt and responsibility for sin, see also [Albert Barnes], "How Can the Sinner Be Made to Feel His Guilt?" QCS 5 (June 1833): 169–92. On the rise of forensic psychology and the legal doctrine of *mens rea,* see Janet Ann Tighe, "A Question of Responsibility: The Development of American Forensic Psychiatry, 1838–1930" (Ph.D. diss., University of Pennsylvania, 1983), pp. 1–76; James C. Mohr, *Doctors and the Law: Medical Jurisprudence in Nineteenth-Century America* (New York: Oxford University Press, 1993), pp. 140–53; Daniel N. Robinson, *Wild Beasts and Idle Humours: The Insanity Defense from Antiquity to the Present* (Cambridge,

Mass.: Harvard University Press, 1996); and Hoopes, *Consciousness in New England*, pp. 97-98. The greatest symbol of this rise in the second quarter of the nineteenth century was the publication of the physician Isaac Ray's *Treatise on the Medical Jurisprudence of Insanity* (Boston: C. Little and J. Brown, 1838). For a general history of the Supreme Court in this foundational period, see G. Edward White, *The Marshall Court and Cultural Change, 1815-35*, History of the Supreme Court of the United States, vols. 3-4 (New York: Macmillan, 1988).

33. On Augustine's struggle to come to terms with the question of the origin of souls, consult the works of Robert J. O'Connell, especially his *The Origin of the Soul in St. Augustine's Later Works* (New York: Fordham University Press, 1987). Calvin's opposition to traducianism and mild commitment to creationism may be found in his *Institutes*, 1. 15. 5, and 2. 2. 7. For a useful summary of the subsequent Calvinist commitment to creationism, consult Heinrich Heppe, *Reformed Dogmatics: Set Out and Illustrated from the Sources*, ed. Ernst Bizer (Grand Rapids, Mich.: Baker Book House, 1978; 1950), pp. 227-31.

34. See esp. Edwards's *Original Sin*, pp. 397-409. Cf. his "Miscellanies" #1358, Edwards Papers, Beinecke. For Edwards's creationism, see also "Miscellanies" #541, #1174 (at objection #7) and #1263 (toward the end), and see his manuscript sermon on Romans 7: 14 (written early in 1730), Edwards Papers, Beinecke. While Ava Chamberlain's recent article "The Immaculate Ovum: Jonathan Edwards and the Construction of the Female Body," *WMQ* 57 (April 2000): 289-322, offers an insightful interpretation of Edwards's doctrine of original sin within the context of early modern biological science, Chamberlain is in error when she suggests that Edwards was a traducianist (p. 311). For more on Edwards's occasionalist understanding of continuous creation, see Douglas J. Elwood, *The Philosophical Theology of Jonathan Edwards* (New York: Columbia University Press, 1960), pp. 33-64; Sang Hyun Lee, *The Philosophical Theology of Jonathan Edwards* (Princeton, N.J.: Princeton University Press, 1988), pp. 47-75, and Norman Fiering, "The Rationalist Foundations of Jonathan Edwards's Metaphysics," in Hatch and Stout, eds., *Jonathan Edwards and the American Experience*, esp. pp. 79-81. On the philosophical background to Edwards's occasionalism, see esp. Charles J. McCracken, *Malebranche and British Philosophy* (Oxford, England: Clarendon Press, 1983). For more on the creationist view of the soul implied by this doctrine, see George P. Fisher, "The Philosophy of Jonathan Edwards," in *Discussions in History and Theology* (New York: Charles Scribner's Sons, 1880), pp. 240-41, and George Park Fisher, *History of Christian Doctrine* (Edinburgh: T. and T. Clark, 1949; 1896), p. 403. For a classic but somewhat strained theological interpretation of Edwards as a traducianist, see William G. T. Shedd, *A History of Christian Doctrine*, 9th ed. (New York: Charles Scribner's Sons, 1887; 1863), 2: 25.

35. See Bellamy, *True Religion Delineated*, pp. 153-54, 171; Nathanael Emmons, "Man's Activity and Dependence Illustrated and Reconciled," in *The Works of Nathanael Emmons*, 4: 356-57; and Dwight, *Theology Explained and Defended*, 1: 477-88 (quotation from p. 480). Though most Edwardsians who discussed the soul and its origin were creationists, Samuel Hopkins, *Works*, 1: 289, showed that Edwardsian metaphysics might also allow for traducianism: "It is a mistake which some have made who have supposed that the parents of a child are the parents or authors of the body, and are instruments of producing that only, and not the soul of the child. They are the cause of one as much as the other, and no more. They are not the efficient cause of either. . . . The mother, therefore, according to a law of nature, conceives both the soul and body of her son; she does as much towards the one as towards the other, and is equally the instrumental cause of both; and God is as much the efficient and immediate cause of the existence of the one as of the other." The degree to which an Edwardsian affirmed creationism often depended on the balance struck between divine efficiency and secondary causes.

36. For the Taylorites' defense of creationism, see esp. "An Inquiry Concerning the Soul," *QCS* 8 (June 1836): 285-86, 289-90 (quotation from p. 290). For an example of the Tylerites' repudiation of physical depravity, see "Review of Spring on Native Depravity," *EM* 1 (June 1833):

446. For the controversy over physical depravity, see esp. the debate between Taylor and Harvey in Harvey, *A Review of a Sermon*, Taylor, *An Inquiry into the Nature of Sin*, and [Harvey], *Examination of a Review*; and the paper war between Taylor and Tyler in the *Spirit of the Pilgrims* beginning with Taylor's "Letter from Rev. Dr. Taylor," *SP* 5 (March 1832): 173-79, and ending with Tyler's "Dr. Tyler's Letter to the Editor of the Spirit of the Pilgrims," *SP* 6 (May 1833): 284-306.

37. Taylor, *Essays, Lectures, Etc.*, p. 199; Taylor, *Concio ad Clerum*, pp. 7, 15; and [Goodrich], "Review of Taylor and Harvey on Human Depravity," p. 377. For the source of Goodrich's second-hand, Edwardsian analogy, see Edwards, *Original Sin*, pp. 125-26. For more on the Taylorite distinction between a tendency or disposition to sin and an inherently sinful disposition, see Taylor, *Essays, Lectures, Etc.*, pp. 192-94; [Nathaniel W. Taylor], "Review of Spring on the Means of Regeneration," *QCS* 1 (September 1829): 505; and Fitch, *Two Discourses on the Nature of Sin*, pp. 20-21. It is worth pointing out here that some contemporaries felt Taylor proved too soft in his opposition to physical depravity. For example, David N. Lord, the enigmatic ex-preacher and New York merchant who anonymously authored the irregularly published journal *Views in Theology* (underwritten by the American Tract Society), devoted most of his editorial energy to the repudiation of physical depravity and argued that, while Taylor stood closer to the truth on this issue than his high Calvinist opponents, he nevertheless retained too much of their teaching and thus proferred "some inaccuracies." See esp. "Professor Taylor's Sermon on the Nature and Cause of Sin," *VT* 2 (1829): 84-104 (quotation from p. 103); "The Biblical Repertory's Review on the Calvinistic Doctrine of Depravity," *VT* 2 (November 1830): 217-69; and "The Doctrines of Physical and Voluntary Depravity," *VT* 3 (November 1832): 303-63. For brief but useful discussions of Lord (who, ironically, would ultimately become a Tylerite) and his publication of *Views in Theology*, see Crocker, *The Catastrophe of the Presbyterian Church*, pp. 230-32; and Gaylord P. Albaugh, *History and Annotated Bibliography of American Religious Periodicals and Newspapers Established from 1730 Through 1830, with Library Locations and Microform Sources*, 2 vols. (Worcester, Mass.: American Antiquarian Society, 1994), 2: 979-81.

38. Noah Porter, "Dr. Taylor and His Theology," in *The Semi-Centennial Anniversary of the Divinity School of Yale College*, p. 92. This fact belies the claims of scholars such as Wayne Conrad Tyner, "The Theology of Timothy Dwight in Historical Perspective" (Ph.D. diss., University of North Carolina at Chapel Hill, 1971), pp. 254-55, that Taylor eliminated the notion of human depravity.

39. Edwards, *Original Sin*, pp. 223-36, 380-88 (quotations from pp. 381-83); and Taylor, "Letter from Rev. Dr. Taylor," p. 174. For further evidence of Edwards's privative understanding of original sin, see also *Some Thoughts Concerning the Present Revival of Religion in New England*, in *The Great Awakening*, p. 464, where he states that "all sin is originally from a defective, privative cause"; and "Miscellanies" #290 and #1147, Edwards Papers, Beinecke. For Taylor's use of this Augustinian understanding of original sin, see also Nathaniel W. Taylor, "Letter to the Editor from the Rev. Dr. Taylor," *QCS* 5 (September 1833): 462-67, and Taylor, "Dr. Taylor's Reply to Dr. Tyler," pp. 5-12. For its source in Augustine himself, see esp. *The City of God*, 13. 13, 15, and 14. 11, 13, 27. Note, however, that while Taylor was basically Augustinian, Augustine himself tended to draw a closer connection than Taylor between deprivation and depravation (or "concupiscence," as Augustine preferred to call it), a tendency exaggerated by other Protestants who included positive depravity within their definitions of original sin itself. See, for example, Calvin's *Institutes* 2. 1. 8.

40. Harvey, *A Review of a Sermon*, pp. 28-29; Taylor, "Dr. Taylor's Reply to Dr. Tyler's Examination," p. 428; Taylor, "Dr. Taylor's Reply to Dr. Tyler," pp. 5-12 (quotation from p. 6); Taylor, *Essays, Lectures, Etc.*, pp. 195-98 (quotation from p. 195); and Taylor, "Letter to the Editor from the Rev. Dr. Taylor," pp. 462-67 (quotation from p. 465). [Chauncey Goodrich],

"Review of Taylor and Harvey on Human Depravity," QCS 1 (June 1829): esp. 365–69, also responded to Harvey's criticism and elicited two further articles in the *Quarterly Christian Spectator* regarding the dispute between Taylor and Harvey. See "Correspondence with the Editors Respecting the Review of Taylor and Harvey on Human Depravity," QCS 1 (September 1829): 536–47, and "Remarks on a Letter to the Editors, Respecting the Review of Dr. Taylor and Mr. Harvey," QCS 1 (September 1829): 547–52. For Tyler's criticisms, see Bennet Tyler, "Dr. Tyler's Examination of Dr. Taylor's Theological Views," SP 5 (June 1832): 325–36; and Bennet Tyler, "Dr. Tyler's Reply to Dr. Taylor," SP 5 (September 1832): 508–23, and (October 1832): 545–63. For further Tylerite criticism of Taylor's supposed belief that "men are born into the world without any moral character, as free from moral defilement or sinful propensity, as Adam before he fell," see the anonymous *Address, to the Congregational Churches in Connecticut, on the Present State of Their Religious Concerns* (Hartford, Conn.: Peter B. Gleason and Co., 1833), pp. 18ff.

41. See esp. Taylor's *Essays, Lectures, Etc.*, pp. 134–62, 156ff.

42. Taylor's Zwinglian doctrine of infant baptism (shared by most New England theologians) comported well with his position on infant depravity. For him, baptism did not function (as it did for some Calvinists) as a "laver of regeneration" that served (in part) to wash away the native guilt received with original sin, but only "as a seal of the covenant, exhibiting and ratifying its promises of good" concerning the children of believers. For this and the other quotations, see Taylor, *Concio ad Clerum*, pp. 24–26; Jean V. Matthews, *Toward a New Society: American Thought and Culture, 1800–1830*, Twayne's American Thought and Culture Series (Boston: Twayne, 1991), p. 34; and Lyman Beecher to Asahel Hooker, March 13, 1825, in Beecher, *Autobiography*, 2: 15. For more of Taylor's position on infant damnation and infant baptism, see his *Essays, Lectures, Etc.*, pp. 234–36, 239, and Nathaniel W. Taylor, "Dr. Taylor's Statement," August 21, 1834, Folder 38, Box 7, Divinity School Papers, SML. Interestingly, Boylan, *Sunday School*, p. 145, argues that Taylor's decision to question the doctrine of infant damnation, while not representative of a radical departure from traditional Calvinism, nevertheless "opened up the possibility that childhood training could shorten the transition from sinless child to regenerate Christian." Taylor manifested his commitment to such childhood training by serving as president of the Connecticut Sunday School Union during the 1820s. For Beecher's controversy with the *Christian Examiner* (which belies the comment of Barbara M. Cross, "Editor's Introduction," in Beecher's *Autobiography*, 1: xvii, that "throughout his career Beecher discreetly neglected the question of original sin"), see esp. "Dr. Beecher against the Calvinistic Doctrine of Infant Damnation," *The Christian Examiner* 5 (May and June 1828): 229–63, (July and August 1828): 316–40, and (November and December 1828): 506–42; and Lyman Beecher, "Dr. Beecher's Reply to the Christian Examiner," SP 3 (January 1830): 17–24, (February 1830): 72–86, and (April 1830): 181–95. For the views of Calvin, Westminster, and Edwards on the issue of infant damnation, see esp. Calvin's *Institutes* 4. 16. 17–20; *The Westminster Confession of Faith* 10. 3–4; Edwards, *Original Sin*, 134–38, 206–19, 267ff., 283; and Edwards, *Miscellanies*, vol. 13, pp. 169–70 (quotation from p. 169). On the history of the doctrine of infant damnation in New England, see Peter Gregg Slater, *Children in the New England Mind–In Death and in Life* (Hamden, Conn.: Archon Books, 1977).

43. Gardiner Spring, *A Dissertation on Native Depravity* (New York: Jonathan Leavitt, 1833). See also Gardiner Spring, *Personal Reminiscences of the Life and Times of Gardiner Spring*, 2 vols. (New York: Charles Scribner and Co., 1866), 2: 31–43; and, for a brief history of the Brick Church (which Spring served from 1810 to 1873), Theodore Fiske Savage, *The Presbyterian Church in New York City* (New York: Presbytery of New York, 1949), pp. 118–22. Spring is perhaps best known among Presbyterians as the author of the pro-Union and thus highly controversial "Spring Resolutions," presented to the Old School General Assembly in May of 1861 (just five weeks after the firing on Fort Sumter), which led to the exodus of the southerners from the Old School denomination and the formation of the Presbyterian Church of the Confederate States of America.

44. Nathaniel W. Taylor, "Spring on Native Depravity," *QCS* 5 (June 1833): 314–32 (quotation from p. 319); [Nathaniel W. Taylor], "Review of Spring on the Means of Regeneration," *QCS* 1 (September 1829): 488; and Taylor, *Essays, Lectures, Etc.*, pp. 213–33 (quotation from p. 214). For the Taylorites' claim to continuity with Edwards, Bellamy, and Dwight on this issue, see Taylor, *Essays, Lectures, Etc.*, pp. 200–201, "Review of True Religion Delineated," pp. 407–11, and [Taylor], *An Inquiry into the Nature of Sin*, pp. 12–17, respectively. For the Taylorite claim that the Tylerites themselves stood near them, see [S. R. Andrew], "What Is the Real Difference Between the New-Haven Divines and Those Who Oppose Them?" *QCS* 5 (December 1833): 657–60.

45. Leonard Woods, *An Essay on Native Depravity* (Boston: William Peirce, 1835), pp. 145–95 (quotation from p. 145); and [Harvey], *Letters*, p. 38. For the contribution of the *Evangelical Magazine*, see esp. "Review of Spring on Native Depravity," *EM* 1 (June 1833): 445–52, 2 (July 1833): 34–45, 2 (August 1833): 63–70, and 2 (September 1833): 123–29. See also "On the Import of the Phrases 'Sinful Nature,' and 'Sinners by Nature,' according to Common Theological Usage," *EM* 3 (November 1834): 209–12; and "Sentiments of Dr. Hopkins on Native Depravity," *EM* 3 (December 1834): 277–80.

46. Taylor, *Essays, Lectures, Etc.*, pp. 246–51, 255–309 (quotations from pp. 250, 171); and "Notes on the Lectures of Nathaniel William Taylor. Copied by R. C. Learned, Edward Learned, and Joshua Learned in the Years 1838–40 from the Notes of Another, Unknown Student. Vol. 2. Notes on Revealed Theology." Yale Divinity School Library, pp. 117–18. See also "Inquiries Respecting the Doctrine of Imputation," *QCS* 2 (June 1830): 339–45; "Remarks of Protestant on the Biblical Repertory," *QCS* 3 (March 1831): 156–62; "Remarks on Protestant and the Biblical Repertory, Respecting the Doctrine of Imputation," *QCS* 3 (March 1831): 162–68; and "The Biblical Repertory on the Doctrine of Imputation," *QCS* 3 (September 1831): 497–512. For just one of numerous pieces of evidence that Taylor's New England opponents denied the doctrine of imputation as well, compare the Taylor student notebook cited above with [Jacob Scales], student notebook of Leonard Woods's lectures in systematic theology, 1817–1820, pp. 130–34, owned by Wilson H. Kimnach, Woodbridge, Connecticut. It is important to note, as well, that while Taylor repudiated the doctrine of imputation with regard to original sin, he proved willing to use the word within his doctrine of justification. He never published on the classic Protestant doctrine of justification by faith alone, but he did lecture on it, describing justification per se as simply a divine declaration of pardon on behalf of rebellious sinners. As one who denied the high Calvinistic notion that the scope of Christ's atonement for sin was limited to the elect (see later discussion), Taylor did offer a somewhat innovative Reformed treatment of the doctrine of justification. But Wayne Hansen is wrong to suggest that Taylor "made justification and conversion a human work," and that therefore "Taylor's modification of justification is even more radical than his changes in the doctrine of original sin." See Taylor, *Essays, Lectures, Etc.*, pp. 310–72; and Wayne S. Hansen, "Nathaniel William Taylor's Use of Scripture in Theology" (Ph.D. diss., Drew University, 1995), p. 216. Based on the forensic discussion of sin and salvation found in the epistles of St. Paul, tied linguistically to Psalm 32:2 and Romans 4:8 (in which the Vulgate employs the Latin verb *imputo* to translate the Greek verb *logizesthai*), and developed originally throughout Augustine's anti-Pelagian writings, the doctrine of imputation gained its greatest significance in the works of the Protestant reformers. For an example of Augustine's metaphysical realism and its relation to original sin, see esp. *The City of God*, 13. 14. For a similar, though less pronounced, realism in Calvin, see the *Institutes*, 2. 1. 6–8. For a recent summary of Augustine's teaching on the oneness of all souls in Adam, see Rist, *Augustine*, pp. 126–29. Though as George Park Fisher, "The Augustinian and the Federal Theologies of Original Sin Compared," *NE* 27 (June 1868): 468–516, has noted, modern Calvinism did (for the most part) move away from this classical understanding of imputation, it did so gradually, exhibiting a spectrum of positions between what Fisher referred to aptly

as the Augustino-federalism of the early Calvinists and the more stark federalism of many later Calvinists. Cf. George Park Fisher, "Original Sin: The State of the Question," *NE* 18 (August 1860): 694–710. On the "federal theology" generally and its relation to the doctrine of imputation, consult David A. Weir, *The Origins of Federal Theology in Sixteenth-Century Reformation Thought* (New York: Oxford University Press, 1990).

47. [Archibald Alexander], "The Early History of Pelagianism," *BR*, n.s., 2 (January 1830): 112–13; "Inquiries Respecting the Doctrine of Imputation," pp. 339–45 (quotation from p. 342); and "Remarks on Protestant and the Biblical Repertory," p. 166. On this topic, see also [Archibald Alexander], "The Doctrine of Original Sin as Held by the Church, Both Before and After the Reformation," *BR*, n.s., 2 (October 1830): 481–503; "The Biblical Repertory on the Doctrine of Imputation," pp. 497–512; and "On the Early History of Theology," *QCS* 4 (June 1832): 291–311.

48. [Charles Hodge], "Inquiries Respecting the Doctrine of Imputation," *BR*, n.s., 2 (July 1830): 462, 464, 455, and passim. See also [Charles Hodge], "The Christian Spectator on the Doctrine of Imputation," *BR*, n.s., 3 (July 1831): 407–43, and Archibald Alexander, ms. on "Theories of Original Sin," n.d., Folder 17, Box 11, Archibald Alexander Papers, PSA.

49. Edwards, *Original Sin*, pp. 389–412 (quotation from p. 405). Recent engagement with Edwards's notion of humanity's oneness with Adam may be found in David Weddle, "Jonathan Edwards on Men and Trees, and the Problem of Solidarity," *Harvard Theological Review* 67 (April 1974): 155–75; and Randall E. Otto, "The Solidarity of Mankind in Jonathan Edwards' Doctrine of Original Sin," *Evangelical Quarterly* 62 (July 1990): 205–21.

50. For "Stapfer's scheme," see esp. his *Institutiones Theologiae Polemicae Universae* (Tiguri: Heideggerum and Socios, 1743–47), 1. 3. 856–57, 4. 16. 60, 61, and 4. 17. 78 (some English translation provided in Edwards's *Original Sin*, pp. 392–93, n.). For Edwards's acquaintance with Stapfer, consult also Holbrook, "Editor's Introduction," p. 83; John F. Wilson, "Jonathan Edwards' Notebooks for *A History of the Work of Redemption*," in Jonathan Edwards, *A History of the Work of Redemption*, ed. John F. Wilson, WJE, vol. 9 (Yale, 1989), p. 548; and "Note on the Manuscript of 'Images of Divine Things,'" in Edwards, *Typological Writings*, p. 46. For la Place's doctrine of mediate imputation, which like the doctrine of natural ability was condemned in the *Helvetic Consensus Formula*, see his *De Imputatione primi Peccati Adami* (Saumur, France: n.p., 1655). For Turrettini's doctrine of depravity and response to la Place, see his *Institutes of Elenctic Theology*, tran. George Musgrave Giger, ed. James T. Dennison, Jr. (Phillipsburg, N.J.: P and R Publishing, 1992–1997), IX, ix. Significantly, the Lutherans' traducian understanding of the soul's origin made it much easier for them than for the Calvinists to keep mediate and immediate imputation together. Since, for them, the soul itself was mediated to us via sexual reproduction, imputation, while occurring apart from our own hereditary depravity, had a basis in the real world. See Heinrich Schmid, *The Doctrinal Theology of the Evangelical Lutheran Church*, 3d ed., trans. Charles A. Hay and Henry E. Jacobs (Minneapolis, Minn.: Augsburg Publishing House, 1899), pp. 234–50.

51. Edwards, *Original Sin*, p. 391. Cf. Edwards's famous parallel statement regarding the relationship between the mediate and immediate aspects of justification *in Christ* in "Justification by Faith Alone," *Five Discourses on Important Subjects, Nearly Concerning the Great Affair of the Soul's Eternal Salvation*, WJE (BTT), 1: 626: "What is *real* in the union between Christ and his people, is the foundation of what is *legal*" (i.e., the forensic imputation of Christ's righteousness to our accounts). Interpretations of Edwards's doctrine of imputation have varied greatly, most scholars depicting him as a proponent of *either* mediate *or* immediate imputation. For interpretations of Edwards as a proponent of mediate imputation, see [Hodge], "Inquiries Respecting the Doctrine of Imputation," p. 453 (N.B.: Hodge felt that Edwards equivocated on this doctrine and argued in his *Systematic Theology*, 2: 207–8, that at times Edwards taught immediate imputation as well); Boardman, *A History of New England Theology*, p. 69; and Bavinck,

Gereformeerde Dogmatiek, 3: 88–89. For interpretations of Edwards as a proponent of immediate imputation, see Samuel Miller, *Life of Jonathan Edwards*, The Library of American Biography (Boston: Hilliard, Gray, and Co., 1837), p. 236; Shedd, *A History of Christian Doctrine*, 2: 163–66, n.; William G. T. Shedd, *Dogmatic Theology*, 2d ed. (Nashville, Tenn.: Thomas Nelson Publishers, 1980; 1889), 2: 171, n.; Warfield, "Edwards and the New England Theology," p. 225; John Murray, *The Imputation of Adam's Sin* (Phillipsburg, N.J.: Presbyterian and Reformed Publishing Co., 1959), pp. 52–64; and Storms, *Tragedy in Eden*, pp. 228, 231. For interpretations of Edwards as a proponent of neither mediate nor immediate imputation, but of an imputation doctrine that was sui generis, see De Jong, *The Covenant Idea in New England Theology*, pp. 138–39; Anri Morimoto, *Jonathan Edwards and the Catholic Vision of Salvation* (University Park: Pennsylvania State University Press, 1995), pp. 80–87; and Gerstner, *The Rational Biblical Theology of Jonathan Edwards*, 2: 323–35. Interestingly, Gerstner, who perhaps wrestled with Edwards's soteriological doctrines for as long as any other recent scholar, seems to have changed his mind on this issue toward the end of his life. While in the passage cited above he described Edwards's doctrine of imputation as one of a kind, as recently as 1991, in *The Rational Biblical Theology of Jonathan Edwards*, 1: 544–46, he described Edwards as an advocate of immediate imputation.

52. See [Nathaniel W. Taylor], "Application of the Principles of Common Sense to Certain Disputed Doctrines," *QCS* 3 (September 1831): 457–62; and Taylor, *Essays, Lectures, Etc.*, pp. 173–78. For Taylorite opposition to occasionalism, see "On the Nature of Providence," *CS*, n.s., 1 (April 1827): 175–77.

53. Taylor, *Essays, Lectures, Etc.*, p. 165; Samuel Hopkins, *The System of Doctrines, Contained in Divine Revelation, Explained and Defended*, 2d ed. (Boston: Lincoln and Edmands, 1811; 1793), 1: 259–61; Joyce Appleby, *Capitalism and a New Social Order: The Republican Vision of the 1790s* (New York: New York University Press, 1984), pp. 81–82 (quotation from p. 81); Fliegelman, *Prodigals and Pilgrims*, pp. 168–69; Dwight, Sermon 29, "Universality of Sin Proved from Revelation and from Facts," and Sermon 32, "Human Depravity; Derived from Adam," in *Theology Explained and Defended*, 1: 435–36, 478–79; and Park, "New England Theology," pp. 205–8 (quotation from p. 208). For an example of the vague possibility of the ontological unity of Adam and his posterity in Hopkins, see his *System of Doctrines*, 1: 245–46. For more on the Edwardsian move away from imputation, see Pope, *New England Calvinism and the Disruption of the Presbyterian Church*, pp. 23, 29, 348–49.

54. Taylor, *Essays, Lectures, Etc.*, p. 294; Fitch, *Two Discourses on the Nature of Sin*, p. 42; and [Samuel Whelpley], *The Triangle: A Series of Numbers upon Three Theological Points; Enforced from Various Pulpits in the City of New-York* (New York: Van Winkle and Wiley, 1816–1817). For the Taylorites opposition to "triangularism," see Nathaniel W. Taylor to "Brother," December 1, 1828, Folder 737, Box 19, Yale Miscellaneous Mss, SML; and Lyman Beecher to Bennett Tyler, March 1830, in Beecher's *Autobiography*, 2: 153. For further information on the Reformed doctrine of imputation primarily in middle and late nineteenth-century America, see George P. Hutchinson, *The Problem of Original Sin in American Presbyterian Theology*, International Library of Philosophy and Theology, Biblical and Theological Studies (Nutley, N.J.: Presbyterian and Reformed Publishing Co., 1972).

55. Quotation from [Goodrich], "Review of Taylor and Harvey on Human Depravity," p. 345. On this subject, see also Taylor, "Letter from Rev. Dr. Taylor," p. 175; [Goodrich], "Dr. Tyler's Remarks and Dr. Taylor's Reply," p. 456; Nathaniel W. Taylor, "Letter to the Editor from the Rev. Dr. Taylor," *QCS* 5 (September 1833): 448–69; and [Andrew], "What Is the Real Difference between the New-Haven Divines and Those Who Oppose Them?" pp. 657–60. The Taylorites always regretted the divisions between themselves and their fellow Edwardsians, the Tylerites. They thought that the Tylerites frequently misunderstood them and they hoped for reunion among the New England theologians. For further examples, see Beecher to Ebenezer Porter, June 1829, *Autobiography*, 2: 128; Chauncey A. Goodrich to Bennet Tyler, October 1,

1832, Ms. Vault File, Beinecke; and Nathaniel W. Taylor to Asahel Nettleton, 4 June 1834, Folder 2851, Box 180, Nettleton Papers, CML.

56. For an Emmonsist depiction of divine agency in the production of evil written during the Taylorite controversy, see the editorial "On Divine Agency," in *HM* 3 (March 1829): 347–52, (June 1829): 423–26, (August 1829): 463–67, (October 1829): 511–15, and (December 1829): 564–68. On Edwards's occasionalism and doctrine of continuous creation, see the sources listed in n. 34. But note also that, when comparing Edwards's occasionalism to its radicalization among the Exercisers, one must temper Fiering, "The Rationalist Foundations of Jonathan Edwards's Metaphysics," with the arguments of Lee, *The Philosophical Theology of Jonathan Edwards*, pp. 47–75, 107, Clyde A. Holbrook, *Jonathan Edwards, the Valley, and Nature: An Interpretative Essay* (Lewisburg, Pa.: Bucknell University Press, 1987), pp. 72, 88 and passim, and Sang Hyun Lee, "Edwards on God and Nature: Resources for Contemporary Theology," in Sang Hyun Lee and Allen C. Guelzo, eds., *Edwards in Our Time: Jonathan Edwards and the Shaping of American Religion* (Grand Rapids, Mich.: Eerdmans, 1999), pp. 15–44, that Edwards himself did not hold to a radical or pure occasionalism, or even a pure idealism. He carved out a significant space for secondary causes, granting "finite habits and laws . . . a relative and yet real causal function" (Lee, *The Philosophical Theology of Jonathan Edwards*, p. 107). As Edwards asserted in his "Treatise on Grace," among other places, God's covenant faithfulness conditions (and thus mollifies) the seemingly arbitrary immediacy of divine causation. See Jonathan Edwards, *Treatise on Grace and Other Posthumously Published Writings*, ed. Paul Helm (Cambridge, Mass.: James Clarke and Co. 1971), pp. 74–75. In this light, John E. Smith's contention, in *Jonathan Edwards: Puritan, Preacher, Philosopher* (Notre Dame, Ind.: University of Notre Dame Press, 1992), pp. 60, 78, 142, that the most significant element of Edwards's thought was his understanding of divine sovereignty and "vehement denial of the existence of what were called 'secondary causes,'" is exaggerated.

A substantial debate took place in the nineteenth century over the extent to which Emmons and the Exercisers radicalized Edwards's occasionalist metaphysic. In "The Theological System of Emmons," pp. 255–56, Henry Boynton Smith (a Taster himself) spoke for most observers when he said "there can be no question" that, for Emmons, "the reality is in the divine agency, and that the alleged freedom and power of the creature is an unreal and vanishing factor in the victorious and irresistible march of the divine decree." Emmons's defenders demurred, however, portraying his doctrine of divine efficiency in a much softer light. With Edwards A. Park, they contended that "the creed of Emmons is generally misapprehended" and that Emmons "did believe in the Reality of Second Causes; in the Laws, as real Forces, of Nature." See Park, *Memoir of Nathanael Emmons*, pp. 385–87, 411–30; Jacob Ide, "Additional Memoir," in *The Works of Nathaniel Emmons*, pp. lxxvi–lxxxviii; Enoch Pond, "Dr. Burton on Metaphysics," *BS* 32 (October 1875): 775; and George Park Fisher to Edwards A. Park, April 23, 1879, Edwards A. Park Papers 1835–1899, Trask. Emmons did, on rare occasions, give credance to the role of secondary causes (see his *Works*, 2: 313, 3: 408, and 6: 408). But he did so in only a very limited sense, for ultimately he viewed secondary causes as mere (albeit real) occasions for the operation of God's direct, efficient causation.

57. Nathaniel Niles, *A Letter to a Friend, Who Received His Theological Education under the Instruction of Dr. Emmons, Concerning the Doctrine Which Teaches That Impenitent Sinners Have Natural Power to Make Themselves New Hearts* (Windsor, Vt.: Alden Spooner, 1809), p. 38. It is important to note here that, like the Exercisers, the Tasters also felt that they had been misinterpreted. Asa Burton, *Essays on Some of the First Principles of Metaphysicks, Ethicks, and Theology* (Delmar, N.Y.: Scholars' Facsimiles and Reprints, 1973; 1824), pp. 366–67, vigorously denied teaching physical depravity.

58. Beecher, *Autobiography*, 1: 374–75. As Fowler, "Origin of the Theological School of Yale College," p. 7, noted, the clergy of New Haven respected Emmons enough to invite him

to preach at the town's North Church sometime during the late 1810s or early 1820s. However, they consistently rejected his occasionalism in favor of their own "mediate" view of divine providence. See [Nathaniel W. Taylor], "Application of the Principles of Common Sense to Certain Disputed Doctrines," *QCS* 3 (September 1831): 468–75; "On the Nature of Providence"; Taylor, "Essay on the Providential Government of God," in his *Lectures on the Moral Government of God*, 2: 307–20; and Taylor, *Essays, Lectures, Etc.*, pp. 180–83. The most significant Taylorite engagement with the Exercisers came in a brief paper war waged with the Emmonsist Mendon Association in the *Quarterly Christian Spectator*. In response to standard criticisms from the Taylorites, the Mendon clergy disclaimed responsibility for the more radical views of early Exercisers such as Stephen West and, in a move that caused no little surprise, professed substantial agreement with New Haven. Though the Taylorites charged them with depicting human moral capacity as merely a "passive power" to be acted upon, the Emmonsists argued that they, like Emmons himself, believed in humanity's real, "active power" to produce its own acts. See "Reed and Matheson's Visit," *QCS* 7 (December 1835): 667; "The Mendon Association," *QCS* 8 (March 1836): 170–76; "The Mendon Association and Hopkinsianism," *QCS* 8 (June 1836): 327–36; and "Correspondence," *QCS* 8 (December 1836): 671–72.

59. Beecher, *Autobiography*, 2: 118–19. On the Taylorite modification of the Exercise scheme, cf. the less charitable interpretation of Smith, "The Theological System of Emmons," pp. 243–44, 259–60.

60. "Sketch of the Life and Character of the Rev. Luther Hart," pp. 492–94 (quotation from p. 493). On the Taylorites' adoption of a modified Exercise scheme, see also [Hart], "Character and Writings of Dr. Strong." *The Spirit of the Pilgrims* (to which Beecher and other Taylorites contributed) leaned more heavily toward the Exercisers, as it was edited by the one of Emmons's former students, Enoch Pond. See, for example, "Review of Pamphlets on 'The New Divinity,'" *SP* 5 (March 1832): 169.

61. For the loose though consistent Taylorite employment of Scottish Common Sense Realism, see esp. "Review of Ernesti on Applying the Principles of Common Life to the Study of the Scriptures," *QCS* 3 (March 1831): 116–44; [Taylor], "Application of the Principles of Common Sense to Certain Disputed Doctrines," pp. 453–76; and "On the Authority of Reason in Theology," *QCS* 9 (March 1837): 151–62. For the influence of Scottish philosophy in America generally in this period, see esp. Sydney E. Ahlstrom, "The Scottish Philosophy and American Theology," *Church History* 24 (September 1955): 257–72; Theodore Dwight Bozeman, *Protestants in an Age of Science: The Baconian Ideal and Ante-bellum American Religious Thought* (Chapel Hill: University of North Carolina Press, 1977); Mark A. Noll, "Common Sense Traditions and American Evangelical Thought," *American Quarterly* 37 (Summer 1985): 216–38; and Michael Gauvreau, "The Empire of Evangelicalism: Varieties of Common Sense in Scotland, Canada, and the United States," in Mark A. Noll, David W. Bebbington, and George A. Rawlyk, eds., *Evangelicalism: Comparative Studies of Popular Protestantism in North America, the British Isles, and Beyond, 1700–1990*, Religion in America Series (New York: Oxford University Press, 1994), pp. 219–52. It is important to bear in mind here that, while Scottish philosophy did emerge from Scotland's moderate Enlightenment and was usually attached there to a liberal religious sensibility, in America Scottish thought was employed quite loosely by a wide range of thinkers. As Stanley Goodwin French, Jr., "Some Theological and Ethical Uses of Mental Philosophy in Early Nineteenth-Century America" (Ph.D. diss., University of Wisconsin, 1967), has noted, p. 268, "[B]ecause of the lack or at least the relative unimportance of substantive metaphysical theory, the Scottish Philosophy could not be substantively employed as an apologetic philosophy for any particular theological views. . . . The use of the Scottish Philosophy . . . thus did not determine theological differences between sects, but sectarian differences determined the manner in which mental philosophy was used." Taylor employed Scottish thought in support of a relatively conservative Calvinism. In fact, the Taylorites could prove quite critical of Enlighten-

ment rationalism and its liberal anthropology. See, for example, "On the Authority of Reason in Theology," pp. 157, 161–62; Taylor, "The Peculiar Power of the Gospel," p. 1; and "Brown's Philosophy of the Human Mind," CS 8 (March 1826): 141–55. For a look at the theological perspective that helped shape Common Sense Realism in Scotland, see Nicholas J. Griffin, "Possible Theological Perspectives in Thomas Reid's Common Sense Philosophy," *Journal of Ecclesiastical History* 41 (July 1990): 425–42.

62. Beecher to Ebenezer Porter, June 1829, *Autobiography*, 2: 139; Taylor, "Letter from Rev. Dr. Taylor," pp. 177–78. See also "Review of True Religion Delineated," pp. 417–20; "Memoir of James Brainerd Taylor," QCS 5 (June 1833): 311–13; "Views and Feelings Requisite to Success in the Gospel Ministry," QCS 5 (December 1833): 532; and "Causes of Unsuccessfulness in the Ministry," QCS 7 (September 1835): 355–57.

Chapter 5

1. Taylor, "The Peculiar Power of the Gospel on the Human Mind," pp. 23–24.

2. On the democratizing activities of Taylor's less traditional contemporaries, see Hatch, *The Democratization of American Christianity*.

3. Taylor, *Concio ad Clerum*, p. 36, n.; Taylor, "Essay on the Providential Government of God," in *Lectures on the Moral Government of God*, 2: 302–6; Dutton, "A Sketch of the Life and Character of Rev. Nathaniel W. Taylor," p. 260; and "The Doctrine of a Particular Providence," QCS 8 (March 1836): 2 and passim. See also [Fitch], "Fisk on Predestination and Election," p. 603, 605, and passim; Taylor, "Letter from Rev. Dr. Taylor," p. 174, and Chauncey A. Goodrich, "Prof. Goodrich's Creed," October 23, 1839, Folder 38, Box 7, Divinity School Papers, SML.

4. Taylor, "Dr. Taylor's Reply to Dr. Tyler," p. 685. Cf. [Taylor], "Application of the Principles of Common Sense to Certain Disputed Doctrines," pp. 469–70; and Taylor, *Essays, Lectures, Etc.*, p. 410.

5. Wilbur Fisk's *A Discourse on Predestination and Election* (Springfield: A. G. Tannatt, 1831), initiated this dispute. On the Methodist side, see also the other essays collected in Fisk, *Calvinistic Controversy*; "Dr. Taylor's Sermon," MQR 25 (April 1843): 205–20; and the broad-ranging analysis of Taylorism/New School theology written by the New York Methodist minister Francis Hodgson, *An Examination of the System of New Divinity; or New School Theology* (New York: George Lane, 1840), who declared that "Methodism and New School Calvinism have no affinities for each other. There is, decidedly, less agreement between them than there is between Methodism and Old School Calvinism" (p. 7). For the Taylorite response, see [Eleazar T. Fitch], "Fisk on Predestination and Election," QCS 3 (December 1831): 597–640; and [Eleazar T. Fitch], "Divine Permission of Sin," QCS 4 (December 1832): 614–60 (quotation from p. 618).

6. The Amyraldians constituted something of an exception to this rule. Though they opposed speculation on the order of the decrees, their doctrine of predestination (known as "hypothetical universalism") implied that the decree of election followed the decree of redemption (but preceded the decree to apply Christ's redemption to the elect by the power of the Holy Spirit), leading subsequent scholars to label their position "postredemptionist." On the Amyraldian doctrine of predestination, see Armstrong, *Calvinism and the Amyraut Heresy*, pp. 158–221.

7. Among the best-known proponents of supralapsarianism were Calvin's disciple Theodore Beza, the English Puritan William Perkins, the Dutchman Francis Gomarus, and the Westminster Divine William Twisse. Though not nearly as explicit with this doctrine as many of his followers, Calvin also leaned toward supralapsarianism, as became most evident during the Jerome Bolsec affair (1551). For a comprehensive (though somewhat hurried) assessment and critique of Calvin's activities during this controversy by a sympathetic, modern-day Calvinist, see Philip C. Holtrop, *The Bolsec Controversy on Predestination, from 1551 to 1555: The Statements of Jerome*

Bolsec, and the Responses of John Calvin, Theodore Beza, and Other Reformed Theologians (Lewiston, N.Y.: Edwin Mellen Press, 1993). The most significant example in English of supralapsarian doctrine is found in Perkins's *A Golden Chaine, or the Description of Theology*, in *The Work of William Perkins*, ed. Ian Breward, The Courtenay Library of Reformation Classics, vol. 3 (Appleford: Sutton Courtenay Press, 1970), pp. 169–259, which was patterned after Beza's work on predestination. The supralapsarian notion that that decree which is last in execution ought to be first in intention derives from Aristotle's analysis of the deliberations of practical reason in the realm of moral virtue. See the *Nicomachean Ethics*, 3. 3. This Aristotelian logic became common within Christendom well before the rise of high Calvinism, making an influential appearance in Aquinas's teleological theory of virtue in the *Summa Theologica*, 1–2, q. 1. Despite such logical claims by supralapsarian Calvinists, however, the infralapsarian position was adopted by many of the delegates at the Synod of Dordt (1618–19), was incorporated into the *Westminster Confession* (chapter 3), and soon became the predominant position among orthodox Calvinists. For a useful summary, see Heppe, *Reformed Dogmatics*, pp. 133–89. For important background information on the Calvinistic understanding of predestination, consult Richard A. Muller, *Christ and the Decree: Christology and Predestination in Reformed Theology from Calvin to Perkins*, Studies in Historical Theology 2 (Durham, N.C.: Labyrinth Press, 1986).

8. Edwards's theology attests to the fluidity and potential for overlap in the supra- and infralapsarian positions. While positing God's glorification and communication of divine love to the elect (i.e., in salvation) as the purpose of creation and describing redemption as the foremost of the divine decrees, Edwards sided technically with the infralapsarians. For his supralapsarian logic, see Edwards, "Concerning the Divine Decrees in General, and Election in Particular," in *Remarks on Important Theological Controversies*, WJE (BTT), 2: 525–43 (esp. pp. 528, 540–41–cf. "Miscellanies" #704, in *The "Miscellanies," 501–832*, ed. Ava Chamberlain, WJE [Yale, 2000], pp. 314–21); Edwards, *Concerning the End for Which God Created the World*, in Edwards's *Ethical Writings*; Edwards, *A History of the Work of Redemption*, ed. John F. Wilson, WJE (Yale, 1989), esp. pp. 118–19, 513–14; and "Miscellanies" #702, in Edwards, *The "Miscellanies," 501–832*, ed. Ava Chamberlain, pp. 283–309. For Edwards's explicit infralapsarianism, see "Concerning the Divine Decrees in General, and Election in Particular," p. 541. Scholars have disagreed over how best to interpret Edwards' doctrine of predestination. Fisher, "The Philosophy of Jonathan Edwards," p. 247, Foster, *Genetic History of the New England Theology*, p. 79, and now Stephen R. Holmes, *God of Grace and God of Glory: An Account of the Theology of Jonathan Edwards* (Grand Rapids, Mich.: Eerdmans, 2001; 2000), pp. 33, 126–34, have interpreted Edwards as a supralapsarian. Gerstner, *The Rational Biblical Theology of Jonathan Edwards*, 2: 142–88, interpreted him as an infralapsarian. But the most accurate summary of Edwards's position (one that takes into account both Edwards's infralapsarian commitment and supralapsarian logic) is found in David C. Brand, *Profile of the Last Puritan: Jonathan Edwards, Self-Love, and the Dawn of the Beatific*, American Academy of Religion Academy Series, No. 73 (Atlanta, Ga.: Scholars Press, 1991), pp. 149–52 (though Holmes, *God of Grace and God of Glory*, also provides a helpfully nuanced—though anachronistically Barthian—rendering of Edwards's doctrine).

9. For a rare example of an Edwardsian defending supralapsarianism per se, see Nathanael Emmons, "Purpose of Redemption," in Emmons's *Works*, 1: 130.

10. John Milton, *Paradise Lost*, 12. 468–78. On the history of the idea of the fortunate fall, see Arthur O. Lovejoy, "Milton and the Paradox of the Fortunate Fall," in Arthur O. Lovejoy, *Essays in the History of Ideas* (Baltimore, Md.: Johns Hopkins Press, 1948), pp. 277–95. For a discussion of this idea as it appeared in more secular works of American fiction, see R. W. B. Lewis, *The American Adam: Innocence, Tragedy, and Tradition in the Nineteenth Century* (Chicago: University of Chicago Press, 1955), pp. 54–73, 110–26. Despite his bias against what he calls the "Augustinian" type of theodicy, and though he does not treat the development of

Edwardsian theodicy, John Hick's *Evil and the God of Love*, rev. ed. (San Francisco: Harper San Francisco, 1977; 1966), remains the most useful general source of information on traditional Christian attempts to defend divine justice in the face of evil.

11. Gottfried Wilhelm Leibniz (1646–1716), the esteemed German philosopher who invented the infinitesimal calculus (at roughly the same time that Isaac Newton was doing the same), was also a world-renowned student of the problem of evil. In his *Essais de Théodicée sur la bonté de Dieu, la liberté de l'homme et l'origine du mal* (1710), he actually coined the term "theodicy," arguing that the existence of evil was a necessary condition for the attainment of the greatest good and that God, in infinite wisdom and goodness, has created for us "the best of all possible worlds." Leibniz's theodicy was ridiculed with devastating effect in Voltaire's much more sarcastic and pessimistic *Candide* (1759), which threw down a gauntlet toward all those who would subsequently attempt to defend the justice of God in the face of evil. Bellamy's reliance on the Leibnizians is documented in Valeri, *Law and Providence in Joseph Bellamy's New England*, pp. 110–39; and Anderson, "The Pope of Litchfield County," pp. 136–51. Though he probably never read Leibniz himself, on the advice of his Scottish friend John Erskine, Bellamy did read other Continental thinkers (such as Christian Wolff and Johann Friedrich Stapfer) who had essentially adopted Leibniz's position.

12. See Bellamy's *Sermons upon the Following Subjects, viz., The Divinity of Jesus Christ. The Millenium [sic]. The Wisdom of God, in the Permission of Sin* (Boston: Edes and Gill, and S. Kneeland, 1758), and *The Wisdom of God in the Permission of Sin, Vindicated* (Boston: S. Kneeland, 1760).

13. Bellamy, *Sermons upon the . . . Wisdom of God, in the Permission of Sin*, p. 74; and Samuel Hopkins, *Sin, thro' Divine Interposition, an Advantage to the Universe* (Boston: Daniel and John Kneeland, 1759), pp. 21, 45, 15.

14. Taylor, *Concio ad Clerum*, pp. 29–37 (quotation from p. 30). For another early example of the Taylorite theodicy, see the sermon delivered by Edward R. Tyler, pastor of the South Church, Middletown, Connecticut, to the Third Congregational Society of New Haven, October 11, 1829, *Holiness Preferable to Sin: A Sermon* (New Haven: Baldwin and Treadway, 1829). On the rise of atheism and Universalism as the occasion for the development of the Taylorite theodicy, see [Andrew], "What Is the Real Difference Between the New-Haven Divines and Those Who Oppose Them?" pp. 666–67; and see "Illustration of the Divine Government," *QCS* 8 (March 1836): 80–112 (in which the Taylorites also confirmed earlier fears that the Hopkinsians' supralapsarian logic had actually strengthened the Universalists' hand). For New Haven's retrieval of Bellamy (who, the Taylorites admitted, equivocated on this issue, sometimes appearing soundly infralapsarian and at other times appearing to espouse a supralapsarian theodicy), see [Luther Hart], "Review of Bellamy on the Permission of Sin," *QCS* 2 (September 1830): 529–40. On Taylor's continuity with the Leibnizian theodicy, see Fisher, "The 'Princeton Review' on the Theology of Dr. N.W. Taylor," pp. 319–20; and Foster, *A Genetic History of the New England Theology*, p. 484. Though Leibniz contended that God has made only "one total decree" (the decree to create the sequence of causes and effects that constitutes the best of all possible worlds), and thus avoided attributing a logical order to the traditional set of divine decrees, he strongly opposed supralapsarians and sided much more closely with the infralapsarians. See the definitive English edition of his *Theodicy*, trans. E. M. Huggard (New Haven, Conn.: Yale University Press, 1952), pp. 167–68.

15. Woods, *Letters to Rev. Nathaniel W. Taylor*, p. 440; Tyler, "Dr. Tyler's Examination of Dr. Taylor's Theological Views," p. 327; and "The Independence of God Vindicated," *EM* 2 (February 1834): 357, 363. For further Tylerite criticism of the Taylorite theodicy, see the controversy waged in the *Spirit of the Pilgrims*, beginning with the creedal "Letter from Rev. Dr. Taylor" (March 1832) and ending with "Dr. Tyler's Letter to the Editor of the Spirit of the Pilgrims" (May 1833), but also spilling over into the *Quarterly Christian Spectator* in Goodrich's

"Dr. Tyler's Remarks and Dr. Taylor's Reply" (September 1832) and Taylor's "Letter to the Editor from the Rev. Dr. Taylor" (September 1833). See also Harvey, *A Review of a Sermon*, pp. 31–38; Griffin, *The Doctrine of Divine Efficiency*, pp. 179–201; "Divine Permission of Sin," *EM* 1 (June 1833): 433–37, and 2 (July 1833): 9–22; "Divine Efficiency and Moral Agency Consistent," *EM* 2 (March 1834): 402–6; Tyler Thacher, *Taylorism Examined: Or a Review of the New Haven Theology* (North Wrentham, Mass.: Telegraph Press, 1834); and "God Able to Restrain Sin, Consistently with the Liberty of the Creature," *EM* 3 (April 1835): 463–76. David N. Lord, the anonymous author of *Views in Theology* who would eventually become one of the Tylerites' chief patrons, also proved quite critical of Taylor's theodicy. See "The Christian Spectator's Review of Bellamy on the Permission of Sin," *VT* 2 (May 1831): 343–409; "The Christian Spectator's Review of Dr. Woods' Letters," *VT* 2 (May 1831): 410–96; "Characteristics of the Theoretical and Controversial 'Plan' to Which 'Sin Is Necessarily Incidental,'" *VT* 3 (November 1831): 48–85; "The Christian Spectator's Review of Dr. Fisk," *VT* 3 (May 1832): 156–216; and "The Christian Spectator on the Permission of Evil," *VT* 3 (May 1833): 440–525. Even the Wesleyan *Methodist Quarterly Review* got in on the attack, claiming in response to an article by B. N. Martin (a former student and disciple of Taylor who taught at New York University) on Taylor's view of moral government that the Taylorite theodicy constituted little more than a restatement of John Wesley's own theodicy, albeit one tainted with a Calvinistic understanding of predestination and election. The *New Englander* answered this charge by claiming that Wesley's theodicy bore a closer resemblance to that of the Hopkinsians than that of the Taylorites. By the end of this progressively nasty paper war, neither side had scored many points for its own, purportedly superior understanding of sanctification. See B. N. Martin, "Dr. Taylor on Moral Government," *NE* 17 (November 1859): 903–67; "Synopsis of the Quarterlies," *MQR* 42 (January 1860): 146–47; "Reply to the Methodist Quarterly Review," *NE* 18 (May 1860): 473–79; "Wesleyanism and Taylorism—Reply to the New Englander," *MQR* 42 (October 1860): 656–69; "Theology of Wesley—Reply to the Methodist Quarterly Review," *NE* 19 (July 1861): 621–47; and Daniel Denison Whedon, "Wesleyanism and Taylorism—Second Reply to the New Englander," *MQR* 44 (January 1862): 129–51.

16. [Nathaniel W. Taylor and "the Editor"], "Review of Woods' Letters," *QCS* 2 (September 1830): 567.

17. Actually, Edwards himself stood closer to Bellamy than to either Taylor or the Hopkinsians and Tylerites on the issue of theodicy, contending that God could both have prevented all sin and maintained an authentically moral universe, and suggesting that God *permits* sin (by means of "negative causality") based on foreknowledge that it will provide the occasion for even greater good. See "Concerning the Divine Decrees in General and Election in Particular," in *Remarks on Important Theological Controversies, WJE* (BTT), 2: 529–32. Nevertheless, the Taylorite claim to have extended faithfully the best Edwardsian reflection on the problem of evil was ubiquitous (and not entirely wrongheaded). See especially [Hart], "Review of Bellamy on the Permission of Sin." Of the many other examples that might be cited, see [Taylor and "the Editor"], "Review of Woods' Letters," pp. 546–47, 564; and Taylor, *Lectures on the Moral Government of God*, 1: 178–79, 2: 244–45.

18. [Taylor], "Dr. Taylor's Reply to Dr. Tyler," p. 671; and Taylor, *Lectures on the Moral Government of God*, 1: 288–301 (quotations from pp. 291–92). Significantly, though Taylor moved away intentionally from the phrase "the best of all possible worlds," his own argument that this is the best of all possible universes remained very similar to the Leibnizian theodicy, which employed the term "world" to signify the "universe," or all existent things.

19. Nathaniel W. Taylor, "Essay on the Question—In What Different Respects May God Be Supposed to Purpose Different and Even Opposite Events?" Appendix 3 in Taylor, *Lectures on the Moral Government of God*, 2: 341; Taylor, *Essays, Lectures, Etc.*, pp. 382–83; and [Fitch], "Divine Permission of Sin," pp. 635–36, 660. For Fitch's support of Taylor's theodicy, see also

[Eleazar T. Fitch], "A Translation and Exposition of Romans IX. 22, 23, 24," QCS 7 (September 1835): 382–92.

20. [Taylor and "the Editor"], "Review of Woods' Letters," p. 576. For the late conciliatory posture of the Taylorites, see Taylor, "Dr. Taylor's Reply to Dr. Tyler," p. 683 n.; Taylor, "Letter to the Editor from the Rev. Dr. Taylor," pp. 448–49, 453–55, 467; and [Andrew], "What Is the Real Difference Between the New-Haven Divines and Those Who Oppose Them?" pp. 668–69.

21. Sutton, "Benevolent Calvinism and the Moral Government of God," p. 38. See also Meyer, "The American Moralists," p. 97, who offers an insightful analysis of this development despite his heavy reliance on Haroutunian.

22. Miller, Jonathan Edwards, pp. 30–32, 76–78; and Kuklick, Churchmen and Philosophers, p. 59. See also Miller's "From the Covenant to the Revival," in James Ward Smith and A. Leland Jamison, eds., Religion in American Life, vol. 1, The Shaping of American Religion (Princeton, N.J.: Princeton University Press, 1961), pp. 322–68. The literature on Puritan covenant theology is vast. For a useful summary of both this literature and the doctrine itself, see John von Rohr, The Covenant of Grace in Puritan Thought, American Academy of Religion Studies in Religion, No. 45 (Atlanta: Scholars Press, 1986).

23. Sacvan Bercovitch and Harry Stout, for example, have argued that Edwards and/or the Edwardsians retained the notion of America's national or federal covenant with God, granting a special place to America in salvation history and thus leaving a permanent mark on American national identity. See Bercovitch, The American Jeremiad (Madison: The University of Wisconsin Press, 1978), pp. 93–131; and Stout, The New England Soul, pp. 235–36. Minkema, "The Edwardses," pp. 271–310, 579, 597–603, and John Gerstner, Steps to Salvation: The Evangelistic Message of Jonathan Edwards (Philadelphia: Westminster Press, 1960), passim, and The Rational Biblical Theology of Jonathan Edwards, 2: 79–141, have found evidence of covenant theology per se, even preparationism, in Edwards and Edwards, Jr.

24. See De Jong, The Covenant Idea in New England Theology, pp. 136–85; Breitenbach, "The Consistent Calvinism of the New Divinity Movement"; Kuklick, Churchmen and Philosophers, pp. 59–63; John E. Smith, Jonathan Edwards: Puritan, Preacher, Philsopher (Notre Dame, Ind.: University of Notre Dame Press, 1992), pp. 4–5, 141–42; and Kling, A Field of Divine Wonders, p. 109. Relatedly, as Gerald R. McDermott, "Jonathan Edwards, the City on a Hill, and the Redeemer Nation: A Reappraisal," American Presbyterians: Journal of Presbyterian History 69 (Spring 1991): 33–47, has demonstrated, even the argument of scholars such as Bercovitch and Stout concerning the continued deployment of the federal or national covenant, at least as it relates to Edwards himself, is based on a misinterpretation of his millennial writings. On Edwards's ambiguous uses of the national covenant, see Grasso, A Speaking Aristocracy, pp. 128–36. The best treatment of the gradual weakening of the social force of the public covenant motif in eighteenth-century New England is also found in Grasso's A Speaking Aristocracy, pp. 24–85. For a recent, positive construction of the transition from covenant to revival in New England, see Mark A. Peterson, The Price of Redemption: The Spiritual Economy of Puritan New England (Stanford, Calif.: Stanford University Press, 1997), esp. pp. 219–39. For recent perspectives on the further decline of the covenant motif in nineteenth-century America, see Daniel J. Elazar, ed., Covenant in the Nineteenth Century: The Decline of an American Political Tradition (Lanham, Md.: Rowman and Littlefield, 1994). On the rise of federal theology proper, see Weir, The Origins of Federal Theology. Cf. the insightful recent work of Peter A. Lillback, The Binding of God: Calvin's Role in the Development of Covenant Theology, Texts and Studies in Reformation and Post-Reformation Thought (Grand Rapids, Mich.: Baker Book House, 2001).

25. Goodell, "The Triumph of Moralism in New England Piety," p. iv; Guelzo, "Jonathan Edwards and the New Divinity," p. 160; and Lawrence M. Friedman, A History of American Law, 2d ed. (New York: Simon and Schuster, 1985; 1973), pp. 155–56.

26. Taylor, *Lectures on the Moral Government of God*, 2: 1–2, 24–30, and 1: 124; and [Taylor], "Review of Spring on the Means of Regeneration," pp. 502–3.

27. See Taylor, *Lectures on the Moral Government of God*, 2: 174–84 (quotations from pp. 174, 176).

28. "An Inquiry into the True Way of Preaching on Ability," p. 228; [Taylor], "Review of Spring on the Means of Regeneration," p. 504; and Taylor, *Lectures on the Moral Government of God*, 2: 132 n. Significantly, Taylor's distinction between the rules of law and judgment represented a departure from Edwards as well, for whom the law, or covenant of works, remains God's rule of judgment. See esp. the following passage from Edwards's sermon "The Excellency of Christ," in *The Sermons of Jonathan Edwards: A Reader*, ed. Wilson H. Kimnach, Kenneth P. Minkema, and Douglas A. Sweeney (New Haven, Conn.: Yale University Press, 1999), p. 172: "[I]n his [Christ's] judging the world, he makes the covenant of works that contains those dreadful threatenings, his rule of judgment: he will see to it that it is not infringed in the least jot or tittle; he will do nothing contrary to the threatenings of the law, and their complete fulfillment. And yet in him we have many great, and precious promises, promises of perfect deliverance from the penalty of the law. And this is the promise that he hath promised us, even eternal life. And in him are all the promises of God, yea, and Amen." For Taylorite criticism of the Arminian doctrine of prevenient grace, see also Taylor, *Regeneration the Beginning of Holiness in the Human Heart*, pp. 11–13; Taylor, *Man, A Free Agent without the Aid of Divine Grace*; [Porter], "Review of the Doctrine and Discipline of the Methodist Episcopal Church," pp. 490–93; and Taylor *Lectures on the Moral Government of God*, 2: 133. For an Arminian rejoinder, see Wilbur Fisk, "Objections to Gracious Ability Answered," in *Calvinistic Controversy*, pp. 197–219.

29. Howe, *The Political Culture of the American Whigs*, p. 159; [Taylor], "Review of Spring on the Means of Regeneration," p. 493; Taylor, *Lectures on the Moral Government of God*, 1: 7–8, 337; and Bellamy, *The Wisdom of God in the Permission of Sin, Vindicated*, p. i. See also [Taylor], "Application of the Principles of Common Sense to Certain Disputed Doctrines," p. 470; and Nathaniel W. Taylor, "The Promises Designed to Make Men Holy," in *Practical Sermons*, p. 25.

30. Nathaniel W. Taylor, "On Striving to Enter in at the Strait Gate," in *Practical Sermons*, p. 308; Taylor, *A Sermon, Addressed to the Legislature of the State of Connecticut*, p. 10; Taylor, "The Rule and Test of Morality," pp. 135–36, 140; Taylor, *Lectures on the Moral Government of God*, 2: 197, 1: 19; and Nathaniel W. Taylor, "The Habitual Recognition of God," in *Practical Sermons*, pp. 71–72. For more on the radical distinction between these two affectional orientations, see Taylor, *Regeneration the Beginning of Holiness in the Human Heart*; Nathaniel W. Taylor, "The Necessity of Repentance," in *Practical Sermons*, p. 284; Nathaniel W. Taylor, "Glorifying God," a ms. sermon delivered at Yale College, October 1816, Folder 436, Box 5, Betts Autograph Collection, SML, unpaginated [pp. 8–10, 18–20]; and Taylor, *Lectures on the Moral Government of God*, 1: 18–46. On Taylor's commitment to perpetuate an Edwardsian understanding of moral agency, see also [Taylor and "the Editor"], "Review of Woods' Letters," p. 574: "Dr. Taylor has uniformly appealed in all his writings . . . to Edwards on the will, as exhibiting his theory of moral agency." And for a grudging admission by one of the Tylerites of the Taylorites' Edwardsian orthodoxy, cf. Leonard Woods's approval of Beecher's *Dependence and Free Agency. A Sermon Delivered in the Chapel of the Theological Seminary, Andover, July 16, 1832* (Boston: Perkins and Marvin, 1832), in "Dr. Woods's Third Letter to Dr. Beecher," *SP* 6 (January 1833): 19ff.

31. Cf. Edwards, *Religious Affections*, p. 95. For a helpful (though at times overworked) discussion of the difference between the New Divinity's moral voluntarism and the Old Calvinists' intellectualism, see Fiering, "Will and Intellect in the New England Mind." Cf. Breitenbach, "New Divinity Theology and the Ideal of Moral Accountability," pp. 197–214; Breitenbach, "Unregenerate Doings," pp. 484–86, 490–91; and Guelzo, *Edwards on the Will*.

32. Nathaniel W. Taylor, "Singleness of Heart," in *Practical Sermons*, p. 155 and passim; and Taylor, *Lectures on the Moral Government of God*, 1: 41, 29, and 2: 255–56, 135 (Taylor

explicates his understanding of predominant and subordinate volition throughout these lectures). See also [Goodrich], "Review of Taylor and Harvey on Human Depravity," pp. 360–62.

33. On the roots of the "Edwardsian theory" in Edwards, Bellamy, and Hopkins, see esp. Park, "The Rise of the Edwardean Theory of the Atonement," pp. ix–lxv; and Dorus Paul Rudisill, *The Doctrine of The Atonement in Jonathan Edwards and His Successors* (New York: Poseidon Books, 1971), pp. 10–68. As is clear in "Concerning the Necessity and Reasonableness of the Christian Doctrine of Satisfaction for Sin," in *Remarks on Important Theological Controversies*, pp. 565–78, Edwards himself maintained the satisfaction theory of the atonement codified in St. Anselm's *Cur Deus Homo* (1097–98) and developed further by the Protestant reformers. His general interest in moral government, however, and occasional statements regarding the necessity of God's punishing sin in order to uphold the rule of justice also adumbrated the theory of his followers. See Jonathan Edwards, "Concerning God's Moral Government, A Future State, and the Immortality of the Soul," in *Remarks on Important Theological Controversies*, pp. 511–15; Jonathan Edwards, "Great Guilt No Obstacle to the Pardon of the Returning Sinner," in *WJE* (BTT), 2: 111–12, where Edwards says that "the justice of God, as the supreme Governor and Judge of the world, requires the punishment of sin. The supreme Judge must judge the world according to a rule of justice" (p. 111); Edwards, *Miscellanies*, vol. 13, p. 391 (#306); and Edwards, "Miscellanies" #764a, #779, #864, #1127, and #1304 (toward the end), Edwards Papers, Beinecke. Cf. Holmes, *God of Grace and God of Glory*, pp. 142–59. As for the atonement theories of Bellamy and Hopkins, while neither articulated a full-fledged "Edwardsian" position, both men employed moral government language for the atonement. For example, Bellamy wrote in *True Religion Delineated*, p. 345, that if "God should come out after" this "apostate Race" and "reclaim them" without sufficient punishment, it "might seem to be going counter to the Holiness and Justice of his Nature, and to tend to expose his Law and Government . . . to Contempt." As a result of the atoning work of Christ, however, God can reclaim lost sinners in a manner "consistently with his Honor." Similarly, Hopkins employed moral government language in his *System of Doctrines*, 1: 312–15, 321–23, and concluded his lengthy manuscript "Dialogue Between Philenicos and Crito, upon the Atonement of Christ," p. 46, Samuel Hopkins Papers, Trask, by affirming in governmental terms God's "unalterable determination to punish sin" and thus "maintain his law" just "as he has threatened."

34. For the Universalism of James Relly and John Murray, see Relly's *Union: or, a Treatise of the Consanguinity and Affinity Between Christ and His Church* (Boston: White and Adams, 1779). For Chauncy's secret Universalism (referred to cryptically as "the pudding" by his liberal friends), see *The Benevolence of the Deity* (Boston: Powars and Willis, 1784); and *The Mystery Hid from Ages and Generations Made Manifest by the Gospel-Revelation: or, the Salvation of All Men the Grand Thing Aimed at in the Scheme of God* (London: n.p., 1784). On the rise of Universalism in America, see Ann Lee Bressler, *The Universalist Movement in America, 1770–1880*, Religion in America Series (New York: Oxford University Press, 2001); David Robinson, *The Unitarians and the Universalists*, Denominations in America (Westport, Conn.: Greenwood Press, 1985), pp. 47–59; and George Hunston Williams, *American Universalism: A Bicentennial Historical Essay* (Boston: Universalist Historical Society, 1971). On the role of Universalism in occasioning the Edwardsian theory of the atonement, see esp. Park, "The Rise of the Edwardean Theory of the Atonement," pp. lxxviii–lxxix; and Breitenbach, "The Consistent Calvinism of the New Divinity Movement," pp. 247–50. For the Edwardsian theory as first articulated by West, Edwards, Jr., and Smalley, see Stephen West, *The Scripture Doctrine of the Atonement, Proposed to Careful Examination* (New Haven, Conn.: Meigs, Bowen, and Dana, 1785); Edwards, Jr., *The Necessity of Atonement and the Consistency Between That and Free Grace in Forgiveness: Three Sermons*, in Park, ed., *The Atonement*, pp. 1–42; and John Smalley, *Two Sermons*, in Park, ed., *The Atonement*, pp. 43–85. On the Universalism in Edwards, Jr.'s parish, see Ferm, *Jonathan Edwards the Younger*, pp. 141–42. Cf. Colin Wells,

The Devil and Doctor Dwight: Satire and Theology in the Early American Republic (Chapel Hill: University of North Carolina Press, 2002).

35. Relly, *Union*, p. 15. For more on Murray, see John Murray, *The Life of Rev. John Murray, Preacher of Universal Salvation* (Boston: Universalist Publishing House, 1869). Significantly, as Peter Hughes has noted recently in an important revisionist article, Murray himself "preached that only those who believed in Christ while yet alive would be saved after death; others would suffer self-inflicted pain because of their continued unbelief until they became reconciled to God or until 'the restitution of all things.' Consequently, Murray disclaimed belief in universal salvation, preferring to call his eschatological outcome universal redemption." Thus, Murray may well have stood closer to Chauncy's style of Universalism than is commonly seen. Further, a more explicitly Calvinistic form of Universalism preceded Murray's arrival in America. "Calvinism improved," as it was later termed after a well-known book by that very title, simply advocated a single predestination of all to salvation. See Peter Hughes, "The Origins of New England Universalism: A Religion Without a Founder," *The Journal of Unitarian Universalist History* 24 (1997): 31–63, who argues persuasively that American Universalism proved an earlier, less theological, and more "grass-roots phenomenon" (p. 60) than is commonly recognized; and Joseph Huntington, *Calvinism Improved; or, The Gospel Illustrated as a System of Real Grace, Issuing in the Salvation of All Men* (New London, Conn.: Samuel Green, 1796).

36. Edwards, Jr., *The Necessity of Atonement*, p. 18. Of the many useful historical anlayses of the Christian doctrine of the atonement, Gustaf Aulen's *Christus Victor: An Historical Study of the Three Main Types of the Idea of Atonement*, trans. A. G. Hebert (New York: Macmillan, 1969; 1931), remains the most widely used (despite its polemical orientation). Timothy Gorringe, *God's Just Vengeance: Crime, Violence, and the Rhetoric of Salvation*, Cambridge Studies in Ideology and Religion (Cambridge: Cambridge University Press, 1996), provides a helpful analysis of the relationship between Christian atonement theories and the history of penal strategies in the West. Though Gorringe focuses on the history of the satisfaction motif, he discusses Grotius and moral government language on pp. 147–49, 156–92.

37. Rowe, "Nestor of Orthodoxy, New England Style," pp. 236–45 (quotation from p. 244). On the availability of Grotius's treatise in eighteenth-century New England, see Frank Hugh Foster, "A Brief Introductory Sketch of the History of the Grotian Theory of the Atonement," in Hugo Grotius, *A Defense of the Catholic Faith Concerning the Satisfaction of Christ, against Faustus Socinus*, trans. Frank Hugh Foster (Andover, Mass.: Warren F. Draper, 1889), pp. xliv, xlvi, who also discusses Grotius's influence on the Edwardsian theory (pp. xliv-lvi). One might also note here that Edwards himself drew heavily from Grotius's *De veritate religionis christinae* (1622) in his "Notes on Scripture." See Edwards, *Notes on Scripture*, ed. Stephen J. Stein, WJE, vol. 16 (Yale, 1998), pp. 22–23, and entry nos. 427–432. As Stein notes, this work was available to Edwards in an English edition, *The Truth of the Christian Religion in Six Books by Hugo Grotius, Corrected and Illustrated by Mr. Le Clerc. To Which Is Added a Seventh Book Concerning this Question, What Christian Church We Ought to Join Our Selves to; By the Said Mr. Le Clerc. The Second Edition with Additions. Done into English by John Clarke, D.D. and Chaplain in Ordinary to His Majesty* (London, 1719). An excellent bibliography on Grotius's theology was compiled recently by Henk J. M. Nellen and Edwin Rabbie, "Hugo Grotius as a Theologian: A Bibliography (ca. 1840-1993)," and is included in Henk J. M. Nellen and Edwin Rabbie, eds., *Hugo Grotius, Theologian: Essays in Honour of G. H. M. Posthumus Meyjes*, Studies in the History of Christian Thought (Leiden, Netherlands: E. J. Brill, 1994), pp. 219–45.

38. Taylor, "Letter from Rev. Dr. Taylor," p. 174; Nathaniel W. Taylor, "The Terror of the Lord Persuasive," in *Practical Sermons*, p. 270; Taylor, *Lectures on the Moral Government of God*, 1: 271–75; and Fisher, "A Sermon Preached in the Chapel of Yale College, March 14, 1858," pp. 34–35. For another illuminative early sermon expressing Taylor's doctrine of the atonement, see Nathaniel W. Taylor, "The Atonement a Pledge to the Christian for Every Real Good,"

in *Practical Sermons*, pp. 90–101. For further Taylorite opposition to Universalism, see "Review of Erskine on the Gospel," *QCS* 1 (June 1829): 289–306; [Eleazar T. Fitch], "Review of [Edward R.] Tyler's Lectures on Future Punishment," *QCS* 1 (December 1829): 608–12; [Leonard Bacon], "Universalism," *QCS* 5 (June 1833): 266–90; "Illustrations of the Divine Government," *QCS* 8 (March 1836): 80–112; and Taylor, *Lectures on the Moral Government of God*, 1: 365–81.

39. [Whelpley], *The Triangle*, 1st ser., p. 12; [William Giles], *Gethsemane: Or, Thoughts on the Sufferings of Christ* (Philadelphia: Anthony Finley, 1817), p. 28; and Taylor, *Lectures on the Moral Government of God*, 2: 141, 156–57. The doctrine of limited atonement was codified for many Calvinists as one of the five canons of Reformed orthodoxy at the famous Synod of Dordt. Presumably, the less generous Gethsemane doctrine received its name from Jesus' prayer to the Father in John 17 ("I pray not for the world, but for them which thou hast given me") just prior to his entrance into the garden of Gethsemane. For Ely's commitment to this doctrine, see his *Retrospective Theology, Or the Opinions of the World of Spirits* (Philadelphia: A. Finley, 1825), pp. 30–32. For general background information on the British hyper-Calvinism from which this doctrine took its rise, see Peter Toon, *The Emergence of Hyper-Calvinism in English Nonconformity, 1689–1765* (London: Olive Tree, 1967), and Alan C. Clifford, *Atonement and Justification: English Evangelical Theology, 1640–1790: An Evaluation* (Oxford, England: Clarendon Press, 1990), which treats a broader range of people with a narrower doctrinal focus. And on debates in the early Reformed tradition regarding the extent of the atonement, see the helpful recent work of G. M. Thomas, *The Extent of the Atonement: A Dilemma for Reformed Theology from Calvin to the Consensus (1536–1675)* (Carlisle, England: Paternoster, 1997). Though the Gethsemane doctrine made a notable splash for a brief period of time, Charles Hodge could report to his students in 1842 that he no longer knew anyone in the United States who maintained the Gethsemane theory. See Allen H. Brown's notes on Hodge's lectures in Didactic Theology, 1842, Folder 4, Box 33, Charles Hodge Ms. Collection, PSA, paragraph #366.

40. Benjamin Breckinridge Warfield, "Modern Theories of the Atonement," in his *Studies in Theology* (Grand Rapids, Mich.: Baker Book House, 1991; 1932), p. 289; and Goodrich, "Prof. Goodrich's Creed." Among other examples of the commitment of Taylorites and other latter-day Edwardsians to the employment of propitiationary and substitutionary themes, see esp. "An Examination of the Three Principle Schemes, Which Have Been Devised, for Explaining Away the Language of Christ and His Apostles, on the Subject of Sacrifice and Remission of Sins," *SP* 2 (October 1829): 525–32.

41. Munger, "Dr. Nathaniel W. Taylor," p. 235; Martin, "Dr. Taylor on Moral Government," p. 905; Bacon, *Leonard Bacon*, p. 114; and Dutton, "A Sketch of the Life and Character of Rev. Nathaniel W. Taylor," p. 253. For more on the importance of right reason in theology, see esp. "Cultivation of the Reasoning Powers," *QCS* 7 (June 1835): 322–30; and "On the Authority of Reason in Theology."

42. "Review of Butler's Analogy of Natural and Revealed Religion," *QCS* 2 (December 1830): 694–719, and 3 (March 1831): 85–116; "Brougham's Natural Theology," *QCS* 8 (June 1836): 179, 204; and [Nathaniel W. Taylor et al.], "Wardlaw's Christian Ethics," *QCS* 7 (September 1835): 396 and passim. Further Taylorite support for the independent study of moral science may be found in "On Moral Science, as a Branch of Academical Education," *QCS* 6 (December 1834): 561–80. For more on the significance of natural theology, see "Natural Theology," *QCS* 10 (May 1838): 319–37. For helpful background on Taylor's effort to mediate between natural and theological science, see Walter H. Conser, Jr., *God and the Natural World: Religion and Science in Antebellum America* (Columbia: University of South Carolina Press, 1993). For a brief, insightful treatment of the American tradition of "moral science," see Allen C. Guelzo, "'The Science of Duty': Moral Philosophy and the Epistemology of Science in Nineteenth-Century America," in *Evangelicals and Science in Historical Perspective*, ed. David N. Livingstone, D. G. Hart, and Mark A. Noll (New York: Oxford University Press, 1999), pp. 267–89. And on the importance of moral

science in higher education and American public life generally in the nineteenth century, see Thomas Edward Frank, *Theology, Ethics, and the Nineteenth-Century American College Ideal: Conserving a Rational World* (San Francisco: Mellen Research University Press, 1993), pp. 56–65.

43. "Review of Butler's Analogy of Natural and Revealed Religion," p. 703; "The Progress of Theological Science Since the Reformation," *QCS* 10 (August 1838): 484, 485; and Nathaniel W. Taylor to William Chauncey Fowler, November 4, 1825, in Fowler, "The Appointment," pp. 62. For more Taylorite praise of Lord Bacon and criticism of Aristotelian scholasticism, see "The Works of Lord Bacon," *QCS* 4 (December 1832): 528–57; and "Stuart on the Romans," *QCS* 4 (December 1832): 661–76. Note, however, that the Taylorites realized that theology could not proceed according to the inductive method alone. Even natural theology, they wrote, "has a much broader and surer basis than any induction of particulars can give. The universe is before it, and wherever in heaven above or in the earth beneath the traces of design, and adaptation of means to an end, are found, there are the legitimate elements of its demonstrations"(see "Brougham's Natural Theology," p. 184). Further, Taylor himself cautioned his students frequently "against falling into the common prejudice that exists against Metaphysics." In his Yale lectures on mental philosophy, he told his students: "Those who find fault with Metaphysics are in general those who know nothing about it and in this . . . as everywhere else we are not to wonder that dogs bark at strangers." Nathaniel William Taylor, "Mental Philosophy," Folder 1, Box I, Ms. 93234, CHS, unpaginated (quotations from first two paragraphs).

44. "Review of Ernesti," pp. 136, 140; Taylor, *Essays, Lectures, Etc.*, p. 180; and Taylor, "Mental Philosophy," Folder 1, Box I, Ms. 93234, CHS. For more on Common Sense Realism in America and the Taylorites' commitment to it, see the sources in ch. 4, n. 61, this volume. On the rise of Baconian inductivism generally in America, see esp. Theodore Dwight Bozeman, *Protestants in an Age of Science*; and Herbert Hovenkamp, *Science and Religion in America, 1800–1860* (Philadelphia: University of Pennsylvania Press, 1978). For useful background to the Taylorites' struggle to communicate their Calvinistic system of moral government in the language of the common people, see Kenneth Cmiel's discussion of "middling styles" of public discourse in his *Democratic Eloquence: The Fight Over Popular Speech in Nineteenth-Century America* (New York: William Morrow, 1990), pp. 55–122.

45. Dugald Stewart, *The Collected Works of Dugald Stewart*, 11 vols., ed. Sir William Hamilton (Edinburgh: Thomas Constable and Co., 1854), 1: 307; and French, Jr., "Some Theological and Ethical Uses of Mental Philosophy in Early Nineteenth Century America," p. 268. For the Scottish philosophers' critique of Edwards, see Dugald Stewart, *The Philosophy of the Active and Moral Powers of Man*, 2 vols. (Edinburgh: Adam Black, 1828), 2: 498–507. For an example of the Taylorites' commitment to empiricism and inductivism generally rather than to the Scottish Philosophy in particular, see [Jeremiah Day], "Cousin's Psychology," *QCS* 7 (March 1835): 89–127. For examples of those who view Taylor's adoption of the Scottish Philosophy as an indication of his move away from Edwardsianism (usually toward Old Calvinism), see Mead, *Nathaniel William Taylor*, p. 190; Ahlstrom, "The Scottish Philosophy and American Theology," pp. 263–64, 268–69; Guelzo, *Edwards on the Will*, p. 208, 240; and Noll, "Moses Mather (Old Calvinist) and the Evolution of Edwardseanism" (supplemented by the works of Noll cited in ch. 4, n. 52, this volume). Support for my argument that Common Sense Realism is not as useful as is usually assumed as an analytical tool for the interpretation of Taylorite theology may be found in Hansen, "Nathaniel William Taylor's Use of Scripture in Theology," pp. 1–3, 54–83. For an excellent recent introduction to the ideals of the Scottish Enlightenment and the ways in which they were manifested in British moral philosophy (especially in its use of faculty psychology), see Howe, *Making the American Self*, pp. 48–103. On the topic of Taylorism and Common Sense Realism, see also my discussion on pp. 88–90.

46. Taylor, *Lectures on the Moral Government of God*, 1: 204; "The Nature and Application of Divine Influence in the Salvation of Man," *QCS* 7 (June 1835): 309–11; Taylor, "The Pecu-

liar Power of the Gospel on the Human Mind," pp. 15, 1; "Review of Butler's Analogy of Natural and Revealed Religion," p. 701; and "Brougham's Natural Theology," p. 205. Other passages that might be overinterpreted as evidence of Taylorite rationalism include [Taylor], "Application of the Principles of Common Sense to Certain Disputed Doctrines," p. 454; Nathaniel W. Taylor, "What Is Truth?" in *Essays, Lectures, Etc.*, p. 463; and Taylor, *Lectures on the Moral Government of God*, 1: 236. On Edwards's notion of the natural "fitness" of things in God's dealings with humanity, see Fiering, *Jonathan Edwards's Moral Thought and Its British Context*, pp. 89–90. On the importance of rational (some would say rationalist) apologetics within Edwards's own theological project, see Michael J. McClymond, *Encounters with God: An Approach to the Theology of Jonathan Edwards*, Religion in America Series (New York: Oxford University Press, 1998), who reminds us aptly of the rational exigencies and inevitable mediating function of nearly all modern theology: "[A]lmost the entire course of modern theology in the West, from the deist controversy until quite recently, may be seen as a constantly shifting set of apologetic attempts to interpret the faith so as to make it understandable and credible to those who did not profess it. Consequently it is better not to separate apology from theology but to view them as interprenetrating and as mutually conditioning" (p. 84). Relatedly, Valeri, *Law and Providence in Joseph Bellamy's New England*, p. 120, notes a slight tendency toward rationalism in Joseph Bellamy that fully anticipated Taylor's own esteem for "right reason." For the Taylorites' firm commitment to the necessity and authority of revelation in the delineation of God's moral government, see also "Norton's Reasons," QCS 5 (September 1833): 437–39; "The Bible Always the Same in Its Authority and Relation to Mankind," QCS 8 (December 1836): 519–28; "On the Authority of Reason in Theology," p. 157; and Taylor, *Lectures on the Moral Government of God*, 1: 350–417.

47. [Taylor et al.], "Wardlaw's Christian Ethics," p. 397; "Review of Butler's Analogy of Natural and Revealed Religion," p. 701; "The Nature and Application of Divine Influence in the Salvation of Man," p. 302; and Taylor, *Essays, Lectures, Etc.*, p. 2. Taylor's logician-like defense of rightly stated trinitarian language did not conduce to a full-orbed doctrine of the Trinity. However, his criticism of both Unitarian detractors and fellow trinitarians whom he felt had undermined the orthodox cause does provide a fine example of his enthusiasm for the use of logic and reason in theology. See his Yale lectures on the subject in *Essays, Lectures, Etc.*, pp. 1–133; and his "Introductory Letter" to former student Alexander MacWhorter's *Yahveh Christ, or, The Memorial Name* (Boston: Gould and Lincoln, 1857), pp. ix–x. For Aquinas on the relationship between reason and revelation, see esp. his *Summa Theologica*, 1, q. 1, and q. 12, aa. 12–13.

48. Taylor, *Lectures on the Moral Government of God*, 1: 362–64; and "Review of Butler's Analogy of Natural and Revealed Religion," p. 114.

Chapter 6

1. Epigraph as quoted in David O. Mears, *Life of Edward Norris Kirk, D.D.* (Boston: D. Lothrop and Company, 1877), p. 334.

2. For a prime example of the way Taylor's commitment to saving souls gave shape to his entire theology, see his sermon on "The Peculiar Power of the Gospel on the Human Mind."

3. Nathaniel W. Taylor, "Making Excuses," in *Practical Sermons*, p. 375; Fisher, "A Sermon Preached in the Chapel of Yale College, March 14, 1858," p. 32; and Nathaniel W. Taylor, "The Harvest Past," in *Practical Sermons*, p. 442. For an example of latter-day Old Calvinist resistance to the Edwardsian notion of immediate repentance, see Ely, *A Contrast between Calvinism and Hopkinsianism*, pp. 140–55.

4. [Taylor], "Review of Spring on the Means of Regeneration," pp. 13, 16, 22, 699. Taylor's emphasis on immediate repentance and the sinful use of means proved so consistent and, at

times, extreme that it estranged him somewhat from his *Doktorvater*, Timothy Dwight. See Beecher, *Autobiography*, 1: 241.

5. [Taylor], "Review of Spring on the Means of Regeneration," p. 699.

6. See Gardiner Spring, *A Dissertation on the Means of Regeneration* (New York: John P. Haven, 1827); and [Taylor], "Review of Spring on the Means of Regeneration," pp. 14–16, 19–22. Cf. the *HM* 3 (October 1828): 229–34, for a laudatory, latter-day Hopkinsian review of Spring's *Dissertation*. But note that, while Spring did adopt a standard Hopkinsian position on the issue of the means, he did not agree with the most radical Hopkinsians that unregenerate doings proved more sinful than unregenerate inactivity. To the question, "whether it is best for unregenerated men to use the means, or neglect them?" Spring responded: "If by the question be meant, Whether unregenerated men *commit more sin* in using the means than neglecting them?—it is a question which no human being can answer. There is sin in so using them; and there is sin in neglecting them; and to know which is the more sinful we must know the heart" (pp. 40–41).

7. Bennet Tyler, *Strictures on the Review of Dr. Spring's Dissertation on the Means of Regeneration, in the Christian Spectator for 1829* (Portland, Maine: Shirley and Hyde, 1829), pp. 8, 27–30, 33–34 (N.B.: Tyler wrote these strictures before the release of the final installment of Taylor's review. Though Tyler responded to the latter in an appendix, the Taylorites were justified in feeling that he had jumped the gun and that, had he proved less precipitate, he would have gained a more accurate and less troubling understanding of the Taylorite position.). For a sampling of subsequent criticism of Taylor's doctrine of regeneration, see Bennet Tyler, *A Vindication of the Strictures on the Review of Dr. Spring's Dissertation on the Means of Regeneration, in the Christian Spectator for 1829, in Reply to the Reviewer and Evangelus Pacificus* (Portland, Maine: Shirley and Hyde, 1830); Tyler's contributions to *The Spirit of the Pilgrims*, listed in n. 27, p. 176; [David N. Lord], "The Christian Spectator's Review of the Means of Regeneration," *VT* 2 (1830): 163–210; "Dr. Taylor's Views of Regeneration," *HM* 4 (July 1832): 441–42 (extracted from the *Boston Telegraph*); "Regeneration the Exclusive Work of God," *EM* 2 (October 1833): 153–60; Hodge, *Systematic Theology*, 3: 11; and Gardiner Spring, *Personal Reminiscences of the Life and Times of Gardiner Spring*, 2 vols. (New York: Charles Scribner and Co., 1866), 2: 23–31. For the Taylorite response, see [Nathaniel W. Taylor], "Review of Dr. Tyler's Strictures on the Christian Spectator," *QCS* 2 (March 1830): 147–200; [Hubbard Winslow], *An Evangelical View of the Nature and Means of Regeneration; Comprising a Review of "Dr. Tyler's Strictures"* (Boston: Perkins and Marvin, 1830); [Chauncey Goodrich], "Brief Notice of Dr. Tyler's Vindication," *QCS* 2 (June 1830): 380–84; [Hubbard Winslow], *An Examination of Dr. Tyler's Vindication of His 'Strictures' on the Christian Spectator* (Boston: Perkins & Marvin, 1830); and the Taylorite response to Tyler's remarks in *The Spirit of the Pilgrims*: Taylor, "Dr. Taylor's Reply to Dr. Tyler's Examination"; [Goodrich], "Dr. Tyler's Remarks and Dr. Taylor's Reply"; and Taylor, "Dr. Taylor's Reply to Dr. Tyler."

8. [Taylor], "Review of Dr. Tyler's Strictures on the Christian Spectator," pp. 152–53, 197–98, 200. While Thomas Skinner's essay on "The Means of Repentance," *BR*, n.s., 2 (January 1830): 113–22, did not address all the issues germane to Taylor's scheme, it did offer general support for his doctrine of regeneration. Much like Taylor, Skinner asked, "[H]ow can the world be renounced without a deep conviction of its vanity, and how can that conviction be obtained but by reflecting on its character, and comparing it with the soul's everlasting need? The action of the mind in thus reflecting and comparing may be too quick to be discerned, but of its necessity as a means of repentance there cannot be a question." Similarly, "[I]t is not true that man is capable of no exercises before repentance which are not essentially and necessarily sinful. He is capable, and is in fact, the subject of instinctive and unavoidable exercises and operations, which, in themselves, are neither sinful nor holy" (pp. 116, 121–22). Taylor's response to Tyler's charge that he taught a progressive rather than an immediate view of conversion will be discussed later.

9. Quotation from John K. Ryan's translation of *The Confessions of St. Augustine* (Garden City, N.Y.: Image Books, 1960), 1. 1. Despite its anti-eudaemonistic polemic, Anders Nygren's *Agape and Eros*, trans. Philip S. Watson (Philadelphia: Westminster Press, 1953; 1932), remains the most comprehensive treatment of self-love and eudaemonism in the Christian tradition. On these themes in the thought of Augustine, see esp. Oliver O'Donovan, *The Problem of Self-Love in St. Augustine* (New Haven, Conn.: Yale University Press, 1980); and John Burnaby, *Amor Dei: A Study in the Religion of St. Augustine* (London: Hodder and Stoughton, 1939). Cf. St. Bernard of Clairvaux, *On the Love of God*, trans. T. L. Connally (Techny, Ill.: Mission Press, 1943). On Madame Guyon's reception in America (mainly after the period of the Taylorite controversy), see the helpful recent essay by Patricia A. Ward, "Madame Guyon and Experimental Theology in America," *Church History* 67 (Sept. 1998): 484–98.

10. Edwards, "Charity Contrary to a Selfish Spirit," pp. 254–55, 258 (emphases mine). See also Edwards's manuscript sermon on Luke 22:32, L. 10v, Edwards Papers, Beinecke, where he suggests that "when G[od] is about to Convert a sinner that never had any Grace in his soul the principle that is first wrought upon is natural Conscience & self love & that affection which first Influences them & sets them to work is fear." Other manuscripts that contain powerful evidence of Edwards's eudaemonism include his sermons on Prov. 9:12 and Prov. 19:8 (parts 1 and 2), and "Miscellanies" #530, where Edwards asserts quite clearly that "'tis impossible for any person to be willing to be perfectly and finally miserable for God's sake." All in the Edwards Papers, Beinecke. On the ethical rigorism of the New Divinity theologians, see esp. Stephen G. Post, *Christian Love and Self-Denial: An Historical and Normative Study of Jonathan Edwards, Samuel Hopkins, and American Theological Ethics* (Lanham, Md.: University Press of America, 1987); Stephen G. Post, *A Theory of Agape: On the Meaning of Christian Love* (Lewisburg, Pa.: Bucknell University Press, 1990), pp. 36–51; Peter Dan Jauhiainen, "An Enlightenment Calvinist: Samuel Hopkins and the Pursuit of Benevolence" (Ph.D. diss, University of Iowa, 1997); and Breitenbach, "Unregenerate Doings." But note that some of the leading New Divinity men, such as Jonathan Edwards, Jr., and Timothy Dwight, opposed the rigoristic extremes of the Hopkinsians. Several first-rate religious ethicists have discussed Edwards's view of self-love with much more sophistication than space permits here. Aside from the works of Stephen Post listed here, see also Roland Andre Delattre, *Beauty and Sensibility in the Thought of Jonathan Edwards: An Essay in Aesthetics and Theological Ethics* (New Haven, Conn.: Yale University Press, 1968); Roland A. Delattre, "The Theological Ethics of Jonathan Edwards: An Homage to Paul Ramsey," *Journal of Religious Ethics* 19 (Fall 1991): 83–85; Holbrook, *The Ethics of Jonathan Edwards*, pp. 149–60; Fiering, *Jonathan Edwards's Moral Thought and Its British Context*, pp. 150–99; Paul Ramsey, "Editor's Introduction," in Edwards, *Ethical Writings*, pp. 12–27; and Paula M. Cooey, "Eros and Intimacy in Edwards," *The Journal of Religion* 69 (October 1989): 484–501. On Edwards's continuity with Augustine on self-love, see also Miklós Vetö, *La Pensée de Jonathan Edwards* (Latour-Marbourg: Les Éditions du Cerf, 1987), pp. 321–24. Edwards's "Catalogue" contained references, not only to Fenelon, but to Fenelon's British disciple the Chevalier Andrew Michael Ramsay, as well. On Ramsay's possible influence on Edwards, see Fiering, *Jonathan Edwards's Moral Thought and Its British Context*, p. 173; and Douglas A. Sweeney, "Editor's Introduction" to Jonathan Edwards, The "Miscellanies" 1153–1360, WJE (Yale) vol. 23. Though such key figures as William Ames, Thomas Watson, and Samuel Willard held to an Augustinian position, ethical rigorism was also prevalent among Edwards's Puritan predecessors. See [E. H. Gillett], "Hopkinsianism before Hopkins," *The American Presbyterian Review*, n.s., 2 (October 1870): 680–99; Stephen Foster, *Their Solitary Way: The Puritan Social Ethic in the First Century of Settlement in New England*, Yale Historical Publications, Miscellany, 94 (New Haven, Conn.: Yale University Press, 1971), pp. 42–43; and Post, *Christian Love and Self-Denial*, pp. 27–33. For Calvin's opposition to ancient pagan eudaemonism especially, see his *Institues*, 2. 2. 26–27.

11. For an example of Butler's defense of self-love, see his sermon "Upon Human Nature," in *The Works of Joseph Butler*, 2 vols., ed. W. E. Gladstone (Oxford, England: Clarendon Press, 1896), 2: 38. For Taylor's reliance on Butler for his own approach to these issues, see [Nathaniel W. Taylor et al.], "Wayland's Elements of Moral Science," *QCS* 7 (December 1835): 597-629. For Taylor's appeal to Stewart on self-love, see especially his "Review of Dr. Tyler's Strictures on the Christian Spectator," p. 159. For Stewart's discussion of self-love as a morally neutral principle of action operative in the human mind, see Dugald Stewart, *The Philosophy of the Active and Moral Powers of Man*, 2 vols. (Edinburgh: Adam Black, 1828), esp. 1: 144-51, and 2: 345-48. For examples of the Taylorites' appeals to Edwards in support of their conception of self-love, see [Taylor], "Review of Spring on the Means of Regeneration," pp. 702-3; [Taylor], "Review of Dr. Tyler's Strictures on the Christian Spectator," pp. 169, 195-96; and "On Self-Love," *QCS* 7 (December 1835): 564-69. For examples of their appeals to other Edwardsians, see "Review of True Religion Delineated," p. 411, n. (Bellamy); [Taylor], "Review of Dr. Tyler's Strictures on the Christian Spectator," pp. 162, 170 (Dwight); [Hart], "Character and Writings of Dr. Strong," pp. 355-59 (Strong); "Review of True Religion Delineated," pp. 412-16 (Hopkins); and "Review of Dr. Tyler's Strictures on the Christian Spectator," pp. 169-70 (Hopkins). While Mead, *Nathaniel William Taylor*, p. 122, and others have taken Taylor's favorable view of self-love as an indication of Old Calvinist commitments, Taylor himself clearly perceived his view of self-love as an integral part of a larger Edwardsian understanding of salvation.

12. Nathaniel W. Taylor, "Holiness Alone Fits for Heaven," in *Practical Sermons*, p. 208; Taylor, *Lectures on the Moral Government of God*, 1: 20; [Taylor], "Review of Dr. Tyler's Strictures on the Christian Spectator," pp. 161, 164, 166; and "On Self-Love," pp. 568-69. For yet more on the difference between self-love and selfishness, see Taylor, *Lectures on the Moral Government of God*, 1: 153-54. It should be noted that Taylor differed from Edwards on the issue of self-love. But he did so mainly in the *degree* to which he granted self-love a foundational role in regeneration and the life of virtue. Edwards portrayed self-love as a necessary component of true religion and morality. But he also tended to believe that conversion preceded one's delight in divine things, or that "a man must first love God, or have his heart united to him, before he will esteem God's good his own, and before he will desire the glorifying and enjoying of God, as his happiness" (*Religious Affections*, p. 241). Taylor, on the other hand, proved so eudaemonistic at times as to suggest that delight in divine things must *accompany* (if not precede) conversion or, to employ Edwards's language, that one must esteem God's good one's own before one will love God, or have one's heart united to God. Taylor's understanding of the ordo of regeneration will be discussed further below.

13. Taylor, "Glorifying God," unpaginated [p. 24]. For the misleading identification of Edwardsian ethics with utilitarianism, see esp. [Archibald Alexander], "Wayland's Moral Science," *BR*, n.s., 7 (July 1835): 377-79, 382, 388-89; William K. Frankena, "Foreword" to Jonathan Edwards, *The Nature of True Virtue* (Ann Arbor: University of Michigan Press, 1960), pp. vii-viii; and David W. Haddorff, *Dependence and Freedom: The Moral Thought of Horace Bushnell* (Lanham, Md.: University Press of America, 1994), pp. 9-32. For criticism of this identification, see also Meyer, "The American Moralists," pp. 46-47; Delattre, *Beauty and Sensibility in the Thought of Jonathan Edwards*, pp. 218-19, n. 5; Holbrook, *The Ethics of Jonathan Edwards*, pp. 149-60; and Fiering, *Jonathan Edwards's Moral Thought and Its British Context*, pp. 346-53. On the use of Paley in Dwight's curriculum at Yale and throughout America during the first part of the nineteenth century, see Beecher, *Autobiography*, 1: 31; Cuningham, *Timothy Dwight*, p. 244; Leon Howard, *The Connecticut Wits* (Chicago: University of Chicago Press, 1943), pp. 235, 352, 361-65; and esp. Wilson Smith, *Professors and Public Ethics: Studies of Northern Moral Philosophers before the Civil War* (Ithaca, N.Y.: Cornell University Press, 1956), pp. 44-73. While Taylorite moral philosophy did bear certain resemblances to Paley (particularly in its emphasis on eternal sanctions in demonstrating the expediency or utility of morality), it did not

prove nearly as utilitarian as the thought of this English latitudinarian. The Taylorites could actually prove rather critical of Paley, and their combination of the utility principle with certain aspects of common sense intuitionism (which Paley opposed) attests to their eclectic use of philosophy in support of a fundamentally theological agenda. For Taylorite criticism of Paley, see [Taylor et al.], "Wayland's Elements of Moral Science," pp. 599–600. For Timothy Dwight's notion that virtue is founded in utility, see Sermon 94, "Utility the Foundation of Virtue," in Dwight's *Theology Explained and Defended*, 3: 150–62. But note, p. 159, that Dwight did *not* think, like "Godwin" and "Paley," that utility was the "measure" or "rule" of virtue. For him, "the Bible is . . . the only safe rule, by which moral beings can, in this world, direct their conduct." That Dwight's ethics, too, proved more eudaemonistic than utilitarian becomes even clearer in Sermon 25, "The Chief End of Man," *Theology Explained and Defended*, 1: 379–91; and Sermon 50, "Consistency of Benevolence with Seeking Salvation," Theology Explained and Defended, 2: 487–96. For Taylor's defense of Dwight's notion that virtue is founded in utility, see [Taylor et al.], "Wayland's Elements of Moral Science," esp. pp. 605, 606, 619; and [Taylor et al.], "Wardlaw's Christian Ethics," pp. 419–20, where Taylor refers to Dwight's sermon as "the most lucid and satisfactory discussion of this important subject, within our knowledge."

14. Taylor, *Lectures on the Moral Government of God*, 1: 240–44 (quotations from pp. 240–42); Nathaniel W. Taylor, "The Better Country," in *Practical Sermons*, p. 47; Taylor, "The Terror of the Lord Persuasive," pp. 267, 270–73; and [Eleazar T. Fitch], "Review of [Edward R.] Tyler's Lectures on Future Punishment," QCS 1 (December 1829): 616. On the importance of eternal sanctions in evangelistic preaching and for motivating true virtue here on earth, see also Nathaniel W. Taylor, "Sinners Hate the Light," in *Practical Sermons*, esp. p. 182; Taylor, "The Promises Designed to Make Men Holy," p. 26; and "Eternity Realized," QCS 6 (March 1834): 73–88. On the necessity of such sanctions in a truly moral government, and for further criticism of the Universalist position, see esp. Taylor, *Lectures on the Moral Government of God*, 1: 82–183, 251–62, and 2: 367–87.

15. Taylor, "The Terror of the Lord Persuasive," pp. 259–60; Nathaniel W. Taylor, "The Goodness of God Designed to Reclaim," in *Practical Sermons*, pp. 237–38, 231; Taylor, "The Promises Designed to Make Men Holy," p. 30; Taylor, *Essays, Lectures, Etc.*, pp. 390, 396; and Taylor, "On Striving to Enter in at the Strait Gate," p. 311. On the importance of the apprehension of gospel truth and of the motivation of self-love in regeneration, see also Nathaniel W. Taylor, "The Increase of Faith," pp. 104–5; [Hart], "Character and Writings of Dr. Strong," pp. 356–57; "An Inquiry into the True Way of Preaching on Ability," pp. 251–53; Sprague, *Memoir of Rev. Dr. Griffin*, p. 180; and Taylor, *Essays, Lectures, Etc.*, p. 421. These Taylorite emphases help to explain Taylor's tussle with Episcopalians such as Menzies Rayner, the rector of St. Paul's and St. Peter's churches in Huntington, Connecticut, over the doctrine of baptismal (i.e., infant) regeneration. For the controversy, see Taylor, *Regeneration the Beginning of Holiness*, pp. 13–18; and Menzies Rayner, *Review of the Rev. Mr. Taylor's Sermon on Regeneration, Preached and Published at New Haven, 1816* (New Haven, Conn.: Steele and Gray, 1817).

16. Edward D. Griffin, *A Series of Lectures, Delivered in Park Street Church, Boston, on Sabbath Evening*, 3d ed. (Boston: Crocker and Brewster, 1829), p. 74; and Tyler, *A Vindication of the Strictures*, pp. 19–21, 23. For Taylor's use of Griffin's statement to defend his own understanding of regeneration, see [Taylor], "Review of Dr. Tyler's Strictures on the Christian Spectator," p. 159. For a telling Taylorite interpretation of Tyler's concessions on self-love and the affectional nature of conversion, see none other than Yale's erstwhile fundraiser, Hubbard Winslow, in his anonymous *Examination of Dr. Tyler's Vindication*.

17. Tyler, *A Vindication of the Strictures*, p. 20; and Griffin, *The Doctrine of Divine Efficiency*, pp. 43, 6, 9. For more in Griffin on the limitations of unregenerate self-love, see "Natural Affections Not Holiness," in *A Series of Lectures*, pp. 49–71. For related opposition to Taylor's view of

the event of regeneration, see "Moderate Calvinists Becoming Consistent," *HM* 4 (June 1831): 121–24; and "Review of Dr. Griffin on Divine Efficiency," *EM* 4 (December 1835): 252–62.

18. Tyler, *Letters on the Origins and Progress of the New Haven Theology*, pp. 171–80. For Goodrich's assurances regarding New Haven's ongoing Edwardsian orthodoxy, see his "Brief Notice of Dr. Tyler's Vindication."

19. [Taylor], "Review of Dr. Tyler's Strictures on the Christian Spectator," p. 196; Taylor, "Letter from Rev. Dr. Taylor," pp. 177, 174–75; Saxton, "Notes of Dr. Taylor's Lectures," 2: 337 (see also 2: 343–45, in which Taylor reiterates that the "truth" is the "means" by which the Spirit elicits regeneration, but clarifies that the truth is not the "efficient" but only "the occasional cause" of this divine work); and Taylor, *Essays, Lectures, Etc.*, p. 390. It is important to point out here that, like many other of New England's orthodox trinitarians, the Taylorites emphasized the importance of the Spirit's supernatural agency, in part, as a response to its denial by Unitarians. See, for example, the Unitarian Bernard Whitman's *A Discourse on Regeneration*, 2d ed. (Boston: Bowles and Dearborn, 1828), which not only denied the supernatural agency of God's Spirit in regeneration, but also denied the Spirit's personality; and the "Review of Whitman's Discourse on Regeneration," in *SP* 1 (August 1828): 409–27. For more from the Taylorites on the Holy Spirit's supernatural role, see Taylor, *Concio ad Clerum*, pp. 18–20, 26; [Taylor], "Review of Spring on the Means of Regeneration," p. 489; "The Mendon Association and Hopkinsianism," p. 334; and Goodrich, "Prof. Goodrich's Creed." For useful background on conceptions of the Holy Spirit in this era, consult Bruce M. Stephens, "Changing Conceptions of the Holy Spirit in American Protestant Theology from Jonathan Edwards to Charles G. Finney," *Saint Luke's Journal of Theology* 33 (June 1990): 209–23.

20. Taylor, *Essays, Lectures, Etc.*, pp. 428, 374, 377–78, 417; Taylor, "Letter from Rev. Dr. Taylor," p. 175; and Fisher, "The 'Princeton Review' on the Theology of Dr. N. W. Taylor," p. 321. While Taylor's *Essays, Lectures, Etc.*, pp. 373–444, offers the most comprehensive presentation of New Haven's doctrine of election, see also [Fitch], "Fisk on Predestination and Election"; Taylor, "Letter from Rev. Dr. Taylor"; Taylor, "Dr. Taylor's Reply to Dr. Tyler," pp. 72–82; "Sprague on Revivals of Religion," *QCS* 5 (March 1833): 35–37; and Goodrich, "Prof. Goodrich's Creed." For a sampling of the criticism of this doctrine, see Fisk, *Calvinistic Controversy*, pp. 7–71; Griffin, *The Doctrine of Divine Efficiency*, pp. 13–41; Chauncey Lee, *Letters from Aristarchus to Philemon; in Which the Distinguishing Doctrines of the Gospel Are Discussed, and Objections Stated and Answered* (Hartford, Conn.: Hanmer and Comstock, 1833) passim (though Lee's criticism of the Taylorites remained tacit and indirect); and "The Converting Influence of the Spirit," *EM* 3 (November 1834): 206–8.

21. [Taylor], "Review of Spring on the Means of Regeneration" (quotation from p. 209); and Taylor, *Essays, Lectures, Etc.*, p. 392. For Taylorite opposition to the notion of physical depravity, see also [Taylor], *An Inquiry into the Nature of Sin*, pp. 8–11; Taylor, "The Peculiar Power of the Gospel on the Human Mind," pp. 4–5; and John Humphrey Noyes, *Confessions of John H. Noyes, Part I, Confession of Religious Experience: Including a History of Modern Perfectionism* (Oneida Reserve: Leonard and Company, 1849), p. 26, in which Taylor contends with his errant student that it is *physically* impossible for one to *feel* the Holy Spirit. And see the Taylorites' favorable "Review of Cox's Sermon on Regeneration," *QCS* 2 (June 1830): 345–58. Samuel H. Cox, pastor of the Laight-Street Presbyterian Church in New York, had preached a controversial sermon that criticized physical representations of depravity and regeneration at the meeting of the Synod of New York in October of 1829. The sermon drew a great deal of criticism from fellow Presbyterians (particularly at Princeton) who felt their own views of regeneration had been misrepresented. See Samuel H. Cox, *Regeneration and the Manner of Its Occurrence: A Sermon from John V. 24, Preached at the Opening of the Synod of New-York, in the Rutgers-Street Church, on Tuesday Evening, Oct. 20, 1829* (New York: Jonathan Leavitt, 1829); [Charles Hodge],

"Regeneration and the Manner of Its Occurence," *BR*, n.s., 2 (April 1830): 250–97; Samuel H. Cox, "Reply of Dr. Cox," *BR*, n.s., 3 (October 1831): 482–514; and [Charles Hodge], "Remarks on Dr. Cox's Communication," *BR*, n.s., 3 (October 1831): 514–43.

22. [Taylor], "Review of Spring on the Means of Regeneration," (quotations from pp. 22–23, 496). Even Tyler recognized that this issue of the suspension of the selfish principle represented "the turning point of the whole discussion" in New England concerning the doctrine of regeneration. See Tyler, *A Vindication of the Strictures*, p. 24.

23. [Taylor], "Review of Spring on the Means of Regeneration," pp. 16, 18–19, and passim; and [Taylor], "Review of Dr. Tyler's Strictures on the Christian Spectator," pp. 177–80 and passim.

24. [Taylor], "Review of Spring on the Means of Regeneration," pp. 695, 482, 17–18; and [Taylor], "Review of Dr. Tyler's Strictures on the Christian Spectator," pp. 183–84. On this point, see also [Taylor], *An Inquiry into the Nature of Sin*, p. 8; Taylor, "Dr. Taylor's Reply to Dr. Tyler," p. 70; and Lyman Beecher to Ebenezer Porter, June 1829, in Beecher's *Autobiography*, 2: 132–33.

25. [Taylor], "Review of Spring on the Means of Regeneration," pp. 12, 703–6; and "Man's Dependence on the Grace of God, for Holiness of Heart and Life," *QCS* 7 (March 1835): 88. On this theme, see also Taylor, "On Striving to Enter in at the Strait Gate;" [Taylor], "Review of Dr. Tyler's Strictures on the Christian Spectator," pp. 154–58; Taylor, "Letter from the Rev. Dr. Taylor," p. 176; "The Nature and Application of Divine Influence in the Salvation of Man," p. 317; and Taylor, *Essays, Lectures, Etc.*, pp. 392, 405. For Taylor's quotation of the line from Edwards, see [Taylor], "Review of Spring on the Means of Regeneration," pp. 497, and 702–3; and Taylor, *Essays, Lectures, Etc.*, p. 391. For the original in Edwards's own writings, see Jonathan Edwards, "Concerning Efficacious Grace," in *Remarks on Important Theological Controversies*, 2: 557.

26. William A. Clebsch, *American Religious Thought: A History*, Chicago History of American Religion (Chicago: University of Chicago Press, 1973), p. 64; Taylor, *Essays, Lectures, Etc.*, pp. 397, 392, 403; Taylor, "Letter from Rev. Dr. Taylor," p. 177; and Taylor, "The Peculiar Power of the Gospel on the Human Mind," p. 29. On the sinner's natural ability to convert without the aid of divine grace, see also Taylor, "Salvation Free to the Willing," in *Practical Sermons*, p. 321; [Taylor], "Review of Spring on the Means of Regeneration," pp. 223–24; "The Mendon Association and Hopkinsianism," pp. 334–35; and Taylor, *Essays, Lectures, Etc.*, pp. 376–77, 397–401.

27. "The modern question" took its name from the titles of the early tracts written on the topic, most notably *A Modern Question Modestly Answer'd* (London: James Buckland, 1737), by Matthias Maurice, a Congregationalist minister in Rothwell, Northamptonshire, and *The Modern Question Concerning Repentance and Faith, Examined with Candour in Four Dialogues* (London: Jamies Blackstone, 1742), by Abraham Taylor, a Congregationalist minister in London. While Edwards's *Freedom of the Will* incited the most controversy over this question in Great Britain, his commitment to the notion of duty faith is also evident in sermons such as that on Deut. 29:4 (Sept. 1745), where Edwards argues that "though conversion is God's gift yet it is men's duty—men's duty to turn from sin to God" (L. 20r), and in his letters to the Scottish minister and revivalist Thomas Gillespie. See Edwards to Gillespie, September 4, 1747, and April 2, 1750, in Jonathan Edwards, *Letters and Personal Writings*, ed. George S. Claghorn, WJE, vol. 16 (Yale, 1998), pp. 224–35, 326–39. Other British evangelicals who used Edwards to answer this question included John Ryland, Robert Hall, John Sutcliffe, William Carey, William Jay, and Thomas Erskine. On the history of "the modern question" and its significance for evangelical Calvinism in Great Britain, see esp. Geoffrey F. Nuttall, "Northamptonshire and *the Modern Question*: A Turning-Point in Eighteenth-Century Dissent," *Journal of Theological Studies*, n.s., 16 (April 1965): 101–23, who discusses the roots of the evangelical Calvinist position in seventeenth-century Reformed dissent (in this regard, see also Geoffrey F. Nuttall,

Richard Baxter and Philip Doddridge: A Study in a Tradition, Friends of Dr. Williams's Library, Fifth Lecture, 1951 [London: Oxford University Press, 1951]); Toon, *The Emergence of Hyper-Calvinism*, pp. 131-38, 150-52; Bebbington, *Evangelicalism in Modern Britain*, pp. 64-65, who emphasizes the role of Edwards's theology in inspiring what he sees as a uniquely modern evangelical development; Bruce Hindmarsh, *John Newton and the English Evangelical Tradition: Between the Conversions of Wesley and Wilberforce*, Oxford Theological Monographs (Oxford, England: Clarendon Press, 1996), pp. 72, 145, 157, 165; and Christopher Wayne Mitchell, "Jonathan Edwards's Scottish Connection and the Eighteenth-Century Scottish Evangelical Revival, 1735-1750" (Ph.D. diss., University of St. Andrews, 1998), who argues that Edwards helped to move evangelical Calvinism in Scotland "from its old catechising function within a godly commonwealth to a mission oriented role in which true religious faith became essentially a matter for the individual" (p. 273). Among the many other sources that treat Edwards's influence in Britain, see esp. Sir Henry Moncrieff Wellwood, *Account of the Life and Writings of John Erskine, D.D., Late One of the Ministers of Edinburgh* (Edinburgh: A. Constable and Company, 1818), pp. 196-225; J. Orr, "The Influence of Edwards," in *Exercises Commemorating the Two-Hundredth Anniversary of the Birth of Jonathan Edwards, Held at Andover Theological Seminary, October 4 and 5, 1903*, ed. J. W. Platner (Andover, Mass.: Andover Press, 1904), pp. 107-26; D. Elwyn Edwards, "The Influence of Jonathan Edwards on the Religious Life of Britain in the Eighteenth Century and the First Half of the Nineteenth Century" (B.Litt. diss., University of Oxford, 1954); A. H. Kirkby, "The Theology of Andrew Fuller and Its Relation to Calvinism" (Ph.D. diss., University of Edinburgh, 1956); G. D. Henderson, "Jonathan Edwards and Scotland," in G. D. Henderson, *The Burning Bush: Studies in Scottish Church History* (Edinburgh: Saint Andrew Press, 1957), pp. 151-62; Olin C. Robinson, "The Particular Baptists in England, 1760-1820" (D. Phil. diss., University of Oxford, 1963); Michael R. Watts, *The Dissenters*, vol. 1, *From the Reformation to the French Revolution* (Oxford, England: Clarendon Press, 1978), pp. 456-61; Harold P. Simonson, "Jonathan Edwards and His Scottish Connections," *Journal of American History* 21 (December 1987): 353-76; Roger Hayden, "Evangelical Calvinism among Eighteenth-Century British Baptists with Particular Reference to Bernard Foskett, Hugh and Caleb Evans, and the Bristol Baptist Academy, 1690-1791" (Ph.D. diss., University of Keele, 1991); and Mark A. Noll, "Thomas Chalmers (1780-1847) in North America (ca. 1830-1917)," *Church History* 66 (December 1997): 762-77. On Fuller's correspondence with Hopkins and reputation as the "American doctor," see Park, *Memoir*, 1: 222-27. I have found Fuller-Hopkins correspondence in Box 7, Case 11, Gratz Collection, HSP, and in Ms. Case No. 3, Rare Book Room Cage, CL; and have found correspondence between Hopkins and Fuller's colleague John Ryland in the Samuel Hopkins Papers, Trask. Interestingly, Jonathan Edwards, Jr., preached a sermon on the duty of faith in June of 1788, just three years after Fuller's *The Gospel Worthy of All Acceptation*. See his ms. sermon on Luke 13:24, first preached on June 8, 1788, Jonathan Edwards, Jr., Papers, Trask. Further, *The Hopkinsian Magazine* was still appropriating Fuller's writings more than 10 years after his death. See "Mankind Under Obligation to Love God, " *HM* 2 (March 1826): 59; "The Right of Private Judgment in Matters of Religion," *HM* 2 (July 1826): 163-65; "How to Address Sinners under Conviction," *HM* 2 (August 1826): 187-89; and "Benefit of Self-Examination," *HM* 2 (February 1827): 333-34. On the development of Fuller's Edwardsian Calvinism in Britain, see also E. F. Clipsham, "Andrew Fuller and Fullerism: A Study in Evangelical Calvinism," *The Baptist Quarterly* 20 (January 1964): 214-25.

28. Nathaniel W. Taylor, ms. sermon on Romans 10: 9-10, PHS (quotation from p. 4); Taylor, "The Peculiar Power of the Gospel on the Human Mind" (quotation from p. 38); Taylor, "Immediate Repentance Practicable," pp. 288, 299; and Taylor, "The Sinner's Duty to Make Himself a New Heart" (quotation from p. 402). Cf. Taylor, "Letter from Rev. Dr. Taylor," p. 177. For Taylorite appreciation of Fuller and his British cohorts, see "Review of the Life and Writings of the Rev. Andrew Fuller," *QCS* 2 (December 1830): 577-98; and "Review of the Works

of the Rev. Robert Hall" (son of the Robert Hall who was a colleague of Fuller), QCS 3 (June 1831): 202–27. Note also that an eight-volume edition of *The Works of the Rev. Andrew Fuller* was published in New Haven at the Converse press in 1824–25. For evidence of Tylerite appreciation, see "Extracts from the Experience of the Late Rev. Andrew Fuller," *EM* 2 (November 1833): 234–39.

29. [Taylor], "Review of Spring on the Means of Regeneration," pp. 706–10 (quotations from pp. 706, 707).

Chapter 7

1. Beecher, *Autobiography*, 2: 117. Beecher might have added that even Princeton proved friendly to the Taylorites before the end of the 1820s, as evidenced in Samuel Miller's urgent plea to Beecher to settle in a recently vacated Philadelphia pulpit. See Miller to Beecher, April 2, 1828, The Stowe-Day Foundation, Hartford.

2. Asahel Nettleton to Lyman Beecher, April 2, 1824, in Beecher's *Autobiography*, 1: 409–10. The Unitarian criticism referred to here is found in "Beecher's Sermon at Worcester," *Christian Examiner* 1 (January and February 1824): 48–81, which was a review of Beecher's *The Faith Once Delivered to the Saints: A Sermon, Delivered at Worcester, Mass., Oct. 15, 1823, at the Ordination of the Rev. Loammi Ives Hoadly* (Boston: Crocker and Brewster, 1823).

3. On Finney, the Finneyites and the so-called new measures, see esp. Hambrick-Stowe, *Charles G. Finney and the Spirit of American Evangelicalism*; Keith J. Hardman, *Charles Grandison Finney, 1792–1875: Revivalist and Reformer* (Syracuse, N.Y.: Syracuse University Press, 1987); and the helpful bibliography in Garth M. Rosell and Richard A. G. Dupuis, eds., *The Memoirs of Charles G. Finney: The Complete Restored Text* (Grand Rapids, Mich.: Zondervan, 1989), pp. 671–701.

4. Lyman Beecher to Asahel Nettleton, January 30, 1827, Folder 63, Box 2, Beecher-Scoville Family Papers, SML; Lyman Beecher, *To the Congregational Ministers and Churches of Connecticut. Copy of a Letter from the Rev. Dr. Beecher, to the Editor of the Christian Spectator, Boston, December 18th, 1827* (Boston: n.p., 1827), p. 2; and *Letters of the Rev. Dr. Beecher and Rev. Mr. Nettleton on the "New Measures" in Conducting Revivals of Religion. With a Review of a Sermon, by Novanglus* (New York: G. and C. Carvill, 1828). On the historic New Lebanon Conference, which met July 18–26, 1827, see Beecher's *Autobiography*, 2: 89–108; Rosell and Dupuis, eds., *The Memoirs of Charles G. Finney*, pp. 216–25 (quotation from p. 224); Mead, *Nathaniel William Taylor*, pp. 200–210; Hambrick-Stowe, *Charles G. Finney and the Spirit of American Evangelicalism*, pp. 46–73; George Hugh Birney, Jr., "The Life and Letters of Asahel Nettleton, 1783–1844" (Ph.D. diss., Hartford Theological Seminary, 1943), pp. 114–54; and the published minutes of the Conference in the Unitarian *Christian Examiner and Theological Review* 4 (July and August 1827): 357–70. The difficult question of Finney's dependence on New Haven Theology will be discussed later.

5. Hambrick-Stowe, *Charles G. Finney and the Spirit of American Evangelicalism*, p. 67. The best evidence of Nettleton's more uniformly negative reaction to Finney is found in his letters regarding Finney. In addition to the letters cited earlier, see esp. those collected in Birney, Jr., "The Life and Letters of Asahel Nettleton," pp. 269–78, 279–95, 307–20, 408–15.

6. Lyman Beecher to Chauncey Goodrich, May 28, and June 10, 1828, Folder 62, Box 2, Beecher-Scoville Family Papers, SML; and Rosell and Dupuis, eds., *The Memoirs of Charles G. Finney*, p. 349 n. 89. In April of 1831, Leonard Bacon invited Finney to preach in New Haven as well. And though Finney declined in part "on account of the prejudices of your people," he dismissed "the noise about '*Taylorism*' & '*Finneyism*,'" expressed a desire to meet with Taylor, and suggested that "the time is fast going by when the idle prattle about *isms* can frighten people. After all in this country people will finally think for themselves." The following spring, Taylor

himself invited Finney to preach in New Haven, though I have yet to find any evidence that Finney did so. In a letter written on June 11, 1832, Taylor wrote to Finney: "The sooner you come, the better. The students are now assembled. The senior class will as usual disperse early in July. You will be received with universal [and] entire cordiality; there is, I think a state of feeling in the congregation to which I preach, in some degree auspicious; [and] God I trust [and] expect will greatly bless your labours. Come if you can, so as to begin early next week, [and] so as to preach for several successive evenings, that the impression may *at once* be strong [and] be felt." See C. G. Finney to Leonard Bacon et al., April 22, 1831, Folder 31, Box 2, Ser. 1, Bacon Family Papers, SML; and Nathaniel W. Taylor to Charles G. Finney, June 11, 1832, Folder "May-June 1832," Box 3, Ser. "Letters and Papers," Finney Papers, Oberlin College Archives.

7. In recounting these events to his children long after the end of the Taylorite controversy, Beecher suggested that Nathaniel Hewit "was the chief agent in inflaming the opposition [against New Haven]. Then, when Nettleton wanted us to break fellowship with the New-Measure men, and we would not, he became dissatisfied, and availed himself of what Hewitt [sic] had begun, and they began to work on Porter of Andover, and Tyler of Portland, and others. Nettleton never did much good after he got crazy on that subject." See Beecher's *Autobiography*, 2: 117.

8. May, "Asahel Nettleton," p. 323, an excellent source on Nettleton's opposition to Taylor and Yale.

9. Asahel Nettleton to Leonard Woods, May 6, 1829, and Nettleton to Woods, December 16, 1830, both in Birney, Jr., "The Life and Letters of Asahel Nettleton," p. 335, 353. Cf. Nettleton's other letters against Taylor collected in Birney, Jr., "The Life and Letters of Asahel Nettleton," pp. 330–46, 353–55, 366–69; and Tyler, *Memoir of the Life and Character of Rev. Asahel Nettleton*, pp. 291–94, 297–301.

10. Ebenezer Porter to Lyman Beecher, May 22, 1829, printed in *The Presbyterian* (of Philadelphia) 6 (December 24, 1836): 202. Tyler, *Letters on the Origin and Progress of the New Haven Theology*, p. 24, quoted Porter as saying in a subsequent letter to an unnamed colleague that Taylor's views were "virtually Arminian; at least, they will be so understood as to bring up a race of young preachers thoroughly anti-Calvinistic." For more on Porter's opposition to Taylorism, see Lyman Matthews, *Memoir of the Life and Character of Ebenezer Porter, D.D.* (Boston: Perkins and Marvin, 1837), pp. 219–25; and Tyler, *Letters on the Origin and Progress of the New Haven Theology*, pp. 33–34. The most helpful treatment of Woods's views is Harold Young Vanderpool, "The Andover Conservatives: Apologetics, Biblical Criticism, and Theological Change at the Andover Theological Seminary, 1808–1880" (Ph.D. diss., Harvard University, 1971), esp. pp. 163–203. Andover's former professor of pulpit eloquence, Edward Dorr Griffin (now president of Williams College), also began to have doubts about Taylor at this time, as evidenced most clearly in a letter he wrote to Taylor on divine efficiency. See Edward Dorr Griffin to Nathaniel W. Taylor, March 6, 1832, Box 8, Case 9, Gratz Collection, HSP.

11. Woods, "Letters to Rev. Nathaniel W. Taylor," in The Works of Leonard Woods, D.D., vol. 4 (Andover, Mass.: John D. Flagg, 1850), pp. 343–459. On the meeting in Porter's study, see Tyler, *Letters on the Origin and Progress of the New Haven Theology*, pp. 24ff.; and Birney, Jr., "The Life and Letters of Asahel Nettleton," pp. 155–94. See also Asahel Nettleton to Charles Hodge, December 7, 1837, Folder 2, Box 18, Ser. 14, Charles Hodge Papers, PUL, who noted that Beecher "was the great apologist [and] advocate of Dr. Taylor" at this meeting, "as will be recollected by all present."

12. Lyman Beecher to Ebenezer Porter, June 1829, and Lyman Beecher to Nathaniel W. Taylor, September 6, 1830, both in Beecher's *Autobiography*, 2: 128, 171–72. As will be discussed later, Beecher, though an ardent and impetuous defender of Taylor, would not always remain so militaristic. In fact, though deeply offended by Woods's *Letters*, he was soon working to mend the breach with Andover. See his *Autobiography*, 2: 172–76.

13. Nettleton had asked for this meeting, Beecher obliging him reluctantly. For after the meeting in Porter's study the previous month (September of 1829), Nettleton had determined to head south again, taking Porter with him this time. And before he did, he wanted to make crystal clear his opposition to Taylor. As Nettleton would relate to Charles Hodge several years later, Beecher called the Boston clergy back to his study in 1832 (on the eve of his move to Lane Seminary in Cincinnati), telling them, "'Do not mind what Nettleton says. Hold on to N. Haven. Taylor is right, [and] Nettleton is wrong.'—or words to that effect." See Asahel Nettleton to Charles Hodge, December 7, 1837, Folder 2, Box 18, Ser. 14, Charles Hodge Papers, PUL.

14. On this incident, see both Beecher's *Autobiography*, 2: 287-88; and Asahel Nettleton to Charles Hodge, December 7, 1837, Folder 2, Box 18, Ser. 14, Charles Hodge Papers, PUL.

15. The exchange between Hawes and Taylor (including Taylor's 11-point creed) was published in Hartford's *Connecticut Observer* (February 20, 1832): 1-8; New Haven's *Religious Intelligencer* 16 (February 25, 1832): 614-16; Boston's *Spirit of the Pilgrims* 5 (March 1832): 173-79; and New Haven's *Quarterly Christian Spectator* 4 (March 1832): 171-76. The publication led to a major paper war between Taylor and Tyler over Taylor's annotations in the *Spirit of the Pilgrims* 5-6 (1832-33), after which an anonymous Taylorite, exhausted, wrote in New Haven's *Religious Intelligencer* 18 (November 16, 1833): 392, "[T]here are no doubt wolves in sheep's clothing, but we have seen with pain, a growing disposition among Christians of the present day, to dress every sheep that they can catch out of their own fold, in wolve's clothing, and set the dogs upon them." Harvey's comments are found in his *Letters, on the Present State and Probable Results of Theological Speculations in Connecticut*, quotation from p. 6. They were echoed by Bennet Tyler, not only in the *Spirit of the Pilgrims* but also *Letters on the Origin and Progress of the New Haven Theology*, pp. 46-47. Cf. David N. Lord's commentary on this exchange in his "A Letter to Rev. Joel Haws, D.D. on Dr. Taylor's Theological Views," *VT* 3 (May 1832): 217-63. And note that Hawes's role in this affair was not soon forgotten by Taylor's opponents, as evidenced in the representative claim made years later by the staunch Old School Presbyterian Samuel Baird, that the Hawes-Taylor exchange "was a device to hoodwink the public." See Samuel J. Baird, *A History of the New School, and of Questions Involved in the Disruption of the Presbyterian Church in 1838* (Philadelphia: Claxton, Remsen, and Haffelfinger, 1868), p. 203. For all their vitriol, the Tylerites were right to suggest that the *Connecticut Observer*, as well as the *Religious Intelligencer*, were now siding clearly with the Taylorites. The *Intelligencer*, especially, had supported Taylor ever since the emergence of the Taylorite controversy. See, for example, "Harvey's Review of Dr. Taylor's Concio ad Clerum," *RI* 13 (April 25, 1829): 762-63; as well as the later support offered in articles such as "Taylor and Tyler's Letters," *RI* 18 (November 16, 1833): 392. Cf. Albaugh, *History and Annotated Bibliography of American Religious Periodicals and Newspapers*, 2: 827-29.

16. The Beecher-Woods exchange was published in *SP* 5-6, beginning in July of 1832 and ending in January of 1833. For Beecher's creed, see *SP* 5 (September 1832): 496-501. For Woods's response, see *SP* 5 (September 1832): 503-8 (quotation from p. 505).

17. With regard to the major themes of Christian theology, the Saybrook Platform was based largely on the Savoy Declaration of 1658 (adopted in Massachusetts in 1680) and, in turn, on the Westminster Confession of 1646 (its presbyterian predecessor). For more on the Saybrook Platform and its history, see Williston Walker, *The Creeds and Platforms of Congregationalism* (New York: Pilgrim Press, 1991; 1893), pp. 463-523.

18. See Nathaniel W. Taylor, "Dr. Taylor's Statement" and "Dr. Taylor's Explanation," August 21, 1834, Folder 38, Box 7, Divinity School Papers, SML (quotation from the latter document); as well as Taylor's original "Declaration of Assent to Saybrook," December 31, 1822, in the same folder at the SML, which includes a creed submitted by Taylor verifying that he did subscribe originally to the Saybrook Platform only "for substance of doctrine."

19. Noah Porter et al., "Report on Articles of Faith," August 1, 1834, Folder 38, Box 7, Divinity School Papers, SML. Significantly, the Tylerites began now to profess a literal adher-

ence to the Saybrook Platform, much as the Old School Presbyterians would affirm that the Westminster Confession of Faith contained the "system of doctrine," rather than the "substance of doctrine," taught in the Bible. Illuminating early assessments of this controversy at Yale may be found all over the contemporary periodical literature, but also in Daniel Dow (who left the Yale Corporation to become a board member at the Tylerites' Theological Institute of Connecticut, discussed later), *New Haven Theology, Alias Taylorism, Alias Neology; In Its Own Language* (Thompson, Conn.: George Roberts, 1834), pp. 52–56 and passim; Tyler, *Letters on the Origin and Progress of the New Haven Theology*, pp. 78–85; and Crocker, *The Catastrophe of the Presbyterian Church*, pp. 244–50. For Tylerite commentary in the press, see also "An Appeal to the Public in Behalf of the Theological Institute of Connecticut," *EM* 3 (November 1834): 232–40 (which was also published in the *Connecticut Courant*); David N. Lord's extremist "Letter to the Corporation of Yale College, on the Doctrines of the Theological Professors in That Institution," and "The Statement and Remarks of the Professors in the Theological Department of Yale College," both in *VT* 4 (May 1835): 291–341, and 342–401; and note that Dow offered a shorter version of his *New Haven Theology* in the pages of the *Connecticut Observer*. See also the Taylorite response to the Tylerite expose, "Remarks on a Late Appeal from the Trustees of the East Windsor Theological Institute by the Professors of the Theological Department of Yale College," published in the *New York Observer* (November 29, 1834), edited by Sidney E. and Richard C. Morse (both sons of Jedidiah Morse and tacit sympathizers with Taylor), in which it was argued that the Tylerites' scare tactics were confusing and manipulating the laity, and that the founders of the Theological Institute of Connecticut were not the literal adherents to the Saybrook Platform they claimed to be.

20. "Who Are the True Conservatives?" *QCS* 10 (November 1838): 616.

21. Chauncey A. Goodrich to Charles Hodge, March 9, 1831, Folder 9, Box 16, Charles Hodge Papers, PUL.

22. Bacon, "A Sermon at the Funeral of Nathaniel W. Taylor," p. 8. Nettleton, who had suffered from poor health throughout his life, did not actually die until May 16, 1844. Tyler, *Memoir of the Life and Character of Rev. Asahel Nettleton*, pp. 300–301, confirmed that the "interview" described by Bacon "was tender and affectionate," and that "nothing was said in regard to theological differences." He went on to add, however, that two days later Nettleton wrote Taylor a final warning about the evil tendencies of his doctrine. Tyler printed the letter (dated January 19, 1843) in full. "I would cherish the hope," wrote Nettleton, "that your own religious experience is at variance with some things which you have published; particularly on the subject of self-love, and the great doctrine of regeneration. It does seem to me, I experienced all which you make essential to regeneration, while, as I now fully believe, my heart was unreconciled to God. And this is the reason which leads me to fear that what you have written, will be the means of deceiving and destroying souls." Nettleton closed the letter in an ominous tone: "Farewell, my brother. We shall soon meet at the judgment seat of Christ. God grant that we may meet in heaven."

23. Taylor, "Letter to the Editor from the Rev. Dr. Taylor," p. 448. On the Taylorites' Edwardsian ecumenism, see also Chauncey A. Goodrich to Bennet Tyler, October 1, 1832, Ms Vault File, Beinecke, in which Goodrich laments that "no opportunities have been afforded us of comparing our views in *conversation*, where misapprehensions can be removed and objections obviated in a moment"; Nathaniel W. Taylor to Asahel Nettleton, June 4, 1834, Folder 2851, Box 180, Nettleton papers, CML; "On Christian Union," *QCS* 9 (March 1837): 65–93, and (June 1837): 289–313; and "On Dissensions Among Christian Brethren," *QCS* 9 (December 1837): 554–69.

24. Fisher, "Historical Address," p. 21. Throughout the Taylorite controversy, enrollments increased at Yale's Theological Department, and always outnumbered those at the Tylerite's Theological Institute of Connecticut (discussed later). By 1840, there were 72 students enrolled

in Yale's Department, making it the second largest divinity school in New England (behind the older and more established Andover Seminary). Well after Taylor's death, an anonymous reviewer for *The New Englander* would characterize Taylor's resilience by noting that "the attempt to proscribe men for sympathizing with Dr. Taylor's theology is [now] almost as obsolete in New England as the custom of hanging witches." See Wayland, *The Theological Department in Yale College*, p. 123 and passim; Miller, *Piety and Intellect*, pp. 201–2; and "The Princeton Review for January," *The New Englander* 28 (April 1869): 408.

25. Tyler, by comparison, served as preacher only in 1837, and never served as moderator. And Nettleton never served in either capacity. See *Contributions to the Ecclesiastical History of Connecticut*, pp. 145–46.

26. Fearing Beecher's removal to Cincinnati, where he would not only serve as president of Lane but also as pastor of the city's Second Presbyterian Church, Taylor wrote him on November 8, 1830, arguing: "I can not think that the cause of Christ calls you to Cincinnati. . . . Suppose, now, that the man in New York [Arthur Tappan, who was paying $20,000 for Beecher's appointment at Lane] could be induced to give his $20,000 to found a professorship for you at Yale, would it not be better? . . . Now, if you say it would be better for you to come here, Goodrich and I will go and see Tappan, to persuade him if we can."

27. Anon., *An Address, to the Congregational Churches in Connecticut, on the Present State of Their Religious Concerns* (Hartford, Conn.: Peter B. Gleason, 1833), pp. 50, 54, 58. Significantly, Tyler himself believed that the writer of this anonymous pamphlet had gone too far in referring to Taylorism as "fundamentally" heretical and calling for such a strict separation from it. See Bennet Tyler to Asahel Nettleton, October 10, 1833, Folder 856, Box 49, Bennet Tyler Papers, CML; and Bennet Tyler to John C. Smith, November 16, 1833, Folder 3584, Box 259, Bennet Tyler Papers, CML.

28. The Tylerites' monthly *Evangelical Magazine*, which represented a resuscitation of the earlier *Connecticut Evangelical Magazine*, was published out of Hartford beginning in July of 1832. Though always a Tylerite publication, it was not assumed as property by the Pastoral Union until May 13, 1834. It never sold very well, and on May 4, 1836 the Pastoral Union voted to shut it down after only four volumes. In the last issue of the magazine, its editors gave notice of its folding and recommended to their readers "as a good substitute for the Evangelical Magazine, The Watchman, a weekly religious paper, published in Hartford, and edited by Rev. Joseph Harvey, D.D., former editor of this work," and a staunch critic, as we have seen, of Nathaniel Taylor. See "To Our Readers, Subscribers, and Agents," *EM* 4 (June 1836): 576. Harvey's *Hartford Watchman* (later the *Northern Watchman*) began in 1836 after the Tylerites failed to gain control of the *Connecticut Observer*. It, too, had a short life, and merged with *The Congregationalist* in 1839.

29. These Articles of Agreement, which together comprise a 20-point Tylerite doctrinal statement, are printed in Curtis Manning Geer, *The Hartford Theological Seminary, 1834–1934* (Hartford, Conn.: Case, Lockwood, and Brainard, 1934), pp. 33–35.

30. On these and subsequent institutional developments, see esp. Crocker, *The Catastrophe of the Presbyterian Church*, pp. 234–68; George A. Calhoun, *Letters to the Rev. Leonard Bacon, in Reply to His Attack on the Pastoral Union and Theological Institute of Connecticut* (Hartford, Conn.: Robins and Folger, 1840), pp. 72–79; Charles Hyde, "Theological Institute of Connecticut," in *Contributions to the Ecclesiastical History of Connecticut*, pp. 185–89; Geer, *The Hartford Theological Seminary*, pp. 26–67; and May, "Asahel Nettleton," pp. 368ff.

31. In founding a manual labor school, the Tylerites were riding a wave of pedagogical experimentation that crested in the early years of the 1830s. Like the students in a growing number of other schools during this period, the young men of the Theological Institute of Connecticut (TIC) engaged in regular farming and shop work both to keep their bodies in shape and to help defray tuition expenses. The Tylerites patterned their emphasis on manual labor in part

after that at Lane Seminary, which had been run as a manual labor school since 1830. They also benefited from the advancement efforts of The Society for the Promotion of Manual Labor in Literary Institutions, founded in 1831, whose first agent was none other than the indomitable Theodore Dwight Weld. But whereas Lane required three to four hours of manual labor per day of its students, the TIC organized its program on a voluntary basis and its labor experiment began to peter out by the late 1830s. On the manual labor school movement, see Abzug, *Cosmos Crumbling*, pp. 116–24; and Laura Graham, "From Patriarchy to Paternalism: Disestablished Clergymen and the Manual Labor School Movement in Antebellum America" (Ph.D. diss., University of Rochester, 1993). For Tylerite support of manual labor schools, see "Weld's Report on Manual Labor in Literary Institutions," *EM* 2 (October 1833): 161–68, which is a review of the *First Annual Report of the Society for Promoting Manual Labor in Literary Institutions; Including the Report of Their General Agent, Theodore D. Weld, January 28, 1833* (New York: S. W. Benedict and Co., 1833); and "An Appeal to the Public in Behalf of the Theological Institute of Connecticut," pp. 239–40. Cf. Princeton's slightly more cautious view of manual labor schools, "Manual Labor Schools," *BR*, n.s., 3 (January 1831): 22–37.

32. At Andover, we know that Moses Stuart and Ralph Emerson opposed the founding of a new school, while Leonard Woods, who was apprehensive initially, eventually came around and supported it fully. See Bennet Tyler to Asahel Nettleton?, November 9, 1833, Folder 3584, Box 259, Bennet Tyler Papers, CML; Leonard Woods to Asahel Nettleton, June 26, 1834, Folder 2851, Box 180, Asahel Nettleton Papers, CML; and Leonard Woods to Bennet Tyler, n.d., Folder 3583, Box 259, Bennet Tyler Papers, CML.

33. Bennet Tyler, *An Address to the Alumni of the Theological Institute of Connecticut, Delivered July 15, 1857, on the Occasion of the Author's Resigning His Office of President and Professor of Christian Theology* (Hartford, Conn.: Case, Lockwood, and Company, 1857), p. 7 (the $20,000 were not actually subscribed until the following January, still only an impressive four months after the subscription was initiated).

34. See *Inaugural Address of Rev. Bennet Tyler, D.D.; and Addresses of Rev. Dr. Perkins and Rev. Mr. Riddel, on Laying the Corner Stone of the Theological Institute of Connecticut, Delivered at East Windsor, May 14, 1834* (Hartford, Conn.: P. B. Gleason and Co., 1834), pp. 8–9, 12, 21.

35. The TIC pleaded with Nettleton to join its faculty as well. But citing his poor health and the desire to maintain an itinerant preaching ministry, Nettleton only taught from time to time on an adjunct basis. In addition to the works cited above that pertain to the history of the Tylerite Institute, see "Theological Institute of Connecticut," *EM* 2 (December 1833): 289–94, which offers a public rationale for the founding of the Institute based on comments made by Pastoral Union members at their founding meeting. On the details of Tyler's subsequent life and ministry at TIC, see esp. Nahum Gale's *Memoir* in Tyler, *Lectures on Theology*, pp. 13–149; and E. A. Lawrence, "Dr. Tyler and His Theology," *NE* 17 (August 1859): 746–70.

36. There will be more on this later. For now, suffice it to say that the skirmish began with a letter to the editor of the *New Haven Record* (August 31, 1839), in which Calhoun opposed the *Record*'s recent coverage of the annual meeting of Connecticut's General Association. It culminated in a lengthy exchange concerning a wide range of ecclesiastical developments that had to be published in pamphlet form after the *Record* was criticized for encouraging controversy. See Bacon, *Seven Letters to the Rev. George A. Calhoun, Concerning the Pastoral Union of Connecticut, and Its Charges against the Ministers and Churches* (New Haven, Conn.: B. L. Hamlen, 1840); Calhoun, *Letters to the Rev. Leonard Bacon*; and Bacon, *An Appeal to the Congregational Ministers of Connecticut against a Division. With an Appendix, Containing Short Notes on Mr. Calhoun's Letters* (New Haven, Conn.: B. L. Hamlen, 1840). Bacon's pamphlets also carried the serial title *Views and Reviews*. His first pamphlet comprised *Views and Reviews* No. 1 (January 1840). His second pamphlet comprised *Views and Reviews* No. 2 (May 1840). The anonymous editor of *Views and Reviews* hoped to continue the pamphlet series with a third installment, a reprinting

of Ezra Stiles's famous *Discourse on the Christian Union* . . . (orig. Boston: Edes and Gill, 1761), preached originally before the convention of Congregational clergy in Rhode Island on April 23, 1760–but he never did. On Bacon's role in the Taylorite controversy, see also the recent book by Hugh Davis, *Leonard Bacon: New England Reformer and Antislavery Moderate* (Baton Rouge: Louisiana State University Press, 1998), pp. 102–6.

37. In 1854–1855, Bennet Tyler and Joseph Harvey debated the now-classic Edwardsian question concerning the ability of the unregenerate to turn to God in faith. Tyler argued in typical Edwardsian terms for the sinner's "natural" (though not moral) ability to repent and believe the gospel, while Harvey concluded in more traditional Calvinist language that "the *entire* impotence and hopelessness of man in himself is a vital truth in the economy of redemption" (emphasis mine). See Bennet Tyler, *Discourse on Human Ability and Inability* (Hartford, Conn.: Case, Tiffany, and Company, 1854); Joseph Harvey, *A Letter to the Rev. Dr. Tyler in Reply to His Discourse on Human Ability and Inability* (Springfield, Mass.: S. Bowles, Printers, 1855); Bennet Tyler, *A Letter to the Rev. Joseph Harvey, D.D., in Reply to His Strictures on a Sermon of the Author, Entitled "A Discourse on Human Ability and Ability [sic]"* (Hartford, Conn: Case, Tiffany, and Company, 1855); and [Joseph Harvey], *A Review of Recent Publications on Human Ability and Inability* (Hartford: Calhoun Steam Printing Company, 1855), quotation from p. 29. This debate attracted comment from others as well, including the editors of major religious periodicals such as *The New Englander* and *The Presbyterian*. See esp. Ira Case, *A Letter to the Rev. Dr. Tyler, Respecting His Discourse on Human Ability and Inability, and His Letter to the Rev. Dr. Harvey* (Hanover, N.H.: Dartmouth Press, 1855); and "Natural and Moral Ability and Inability," *NE* 13 (August 1855): 387–96.

38. May, "Asahel Nettleton," pp. 390–97; and Miller to Nettleton, March 14, 1834, Folder 6, Box 3, Ser. 2, Samuel Miller Papers, PUL. A good number of the letters between the Tylerites and moderate Old School Presbyterians remain and are housed primarily in collections such as the Simon Gratz Autograph Collection of the HSP, and the Ashbel Green and Charles Hodge Papers at the PUL.

39. Taylor's role in the Presbyterian schism is discussed later.

40. On this debate, see the reports reprinted at the beginning of Bacon, *Seven Letters to the Rev. George A. Calhoun*, pp. 9–42. And note that at the General Association meeting of 1837 (held in New Milford), the clergy had already decided after much debate not to take sides with regard to the Presbyterian schism and not to speak out regarding the Old School abrogation of its "Plan of Union" with Congregationalists, even though most in the association clearly favored the New School (both the Presbyterian schism and the Plan of Union are discussed at greater length later). Further, at the General Association meeting of 1838 (held in Norwalk, and at which Taylor served as moderator), it had been decided that delegates from both parties in the now-divided Presbyterian church would be seated at Connecticut's General Association meetings.

41. Lyman Beecher to Nathaniel W. Taylor, March 17, 1846, in Beecher's *Autobiography*, 2: 377–78. The enrollment statistics cited come from Hyde, "Theological Institute of Connecticut," p. 188; Wayland, *The Theological Department in Yale College*, pp. 120–24; and Miller, *Piety and Intellect*, pp. 201–2, who notes that the five largest seminaries in the country in 1840 (ranked by the number of their enrollments) were Andover (153), Princeton (110), Union, NY (90), General (74), and Yale (72). Goodrich, "Obituary Notice," p. 43, provides a somewhat lower estimate of the total number of Taylor's students, stating that "nearly seven hundred young men have enjoyed the benefit of his instructions."

42. As Goodrich exclaimed to Beecher in March of 1840: "The whole length of the Connecticut River, on one side or the other, from its mouth to the borders of Massachusetts, is lined with revivals. Saybrook, Westbrook, Essex, Chester, Deep River, Haddam, Wethersfield, Rocky Hill, Glastonbury, East Hartford, Windsor, Ellington, and, I believe, Suffield, together with New Britain, Worthington, and part of Woodbridge, are at this moment visited. . . . You will not

misunderstand my feelings when I remind you that in all the places above-mentioned, except one or two, the pastors and laborers in the work are New School men, or at least men who have no hostility to New Haven sentiments. We can not be too thankful that God, notwithstanding our weakness and deficiency, does not leave us without witnesses." See Beecher's *Autobiography*, 2: 338.

43. Edward A. Smith, "As a Theological Teacher," in Merriam, ed. *Noah Porter*, p. 107; and Fisher, "Historical Address," pp. 21-22. On the decline of Yale's divinity program at the end of Taylor's life, see also Wayland, *The Theological Department in Yale College*, pp. 120-24, 160-70, 409, who notes that during the last five years of Taylor's life, the Department's average enrollment was only 23.4 students; Gerald Everett Knoff, "The Yale Divinity School, 1858-1899" (Ph.D. diss., Yale University, 1936), pp. 14-26; Bainton, *Yale and the Ministry*, p. 161; and Fisher, "Historical Address," pp. 21-22. And note that as Donald Scott has shown in *From Office to Profession*, the period after the height of the Taylorite controversy was one of socioeconomic decline for New England clergy generally. Many poor and rural students entering the ministry could not afford to attend schools like Yale, and so often did most of their preparation at smaller, regional colleges. On the institutional history of Yale generally during this period, see Brooks Mather Kelley, *Yale: A History* (New Haven, Conn.: Yale University Press, 1974), pp. 140-231.

44. On the merger proposal of 1855, see Knoff, "The Yale Divinity School," pp. 45-57; Geer, *The Hartford Theological Seminary*, pp. 99-100; Wayland, *The Theological Department in Yale College*, pp. 414-16; "Meeting of Alumni of Yale Theological Seminary," *The Independent* (August 7, 1856): 256; Leonard Bacon to Noah Porter, January 15, 1856, Folder 29, Box 5, Divinity School Papers, SML; and Noah Porter to ?, March 1, 1856, Folder 29, Box 5, Divinity School Papers, SML, who expressed concern that the faculty of the TIC would use the proposed merger as a means to enforce a literal adherence to their own doctrine of original sin, which included the notion that unregenerate infants will be damned.

45. "Meeting of the Alumni of Yale Theological Seminary," p. 256.

46. In 1864, six years after Taylor's death and while still struggling financially, the Yale faculty extended a merger proposal of their own to the TIC. This proposal failed for many of the same reasons as before. And by 1872, when Leonard Bacon made a third proposal, the TIC had removed to Hartford and was loath to move again. See Knoff, "The Yale Divinity School," pp. 45-57; Bacon, *Leonard Bacon*, pp. 515-16; and Davis, *Leonard Bacon*, pp. 227-28.

47. On the life of Delia Bacon, see Vivian C. Hopkins, *Prodigal Puritan: A Life of Delia Bacon* (Cambridge, Mass.: Belknap Press of Harvard University Press, 1959), whose title indicates that Bacon did not always remain an adherent of the Edwardsian tradition; and Theodore Bacon, *Delia Bacon: A Biographical Sketch* (Boston: Houghton, Mifflin, 1888). For more on her view of the Baconian provenance of Shakespeare's plays, see esp. Nina Baym, "Delia Bacon, History's Odd Woman Out," *New England Quarterly* 69 (June 1996): 223-49.

48. MacWhorter, *Yahveh Christ, or, The Memorial Name*. As noted in chapter 3, MacWhorter's lecture notes survive on Taylor's course in revealed theology. See Alexander MacWhorter, "Notes on a Course of Lectures in Revealed Theology by Nathaniel W. Taylor, D.D.," 1844, Folder 147A, Box 30, Yale Lectures, SML.

49. On the affair, see Catharine E. Beecher, *Truth Stanger Than Fiction: A Narrative of Recent Transactions, Involving Inquiries in Regard to the Principles of Honor, Truth, and Justice, Which Obtain in a Distinguished American University* (Boston: Phillips, Sampson, and Co., 1850); Bacon, *Leonard Bacon*, pp. 281-83; Hopkins, *Prodigal Puritan*, pp. 71-130; Kathryn Kish Sklar, *Catharine Beecher: A Study in American Domesticity* (New Haven, Conn.: Yale University Press, 1973), pp. 187-92; and Davis, *Leonard Bacon*, pp. 122-25, 179-80. Illuminating commentary on this affair by a classmate of MacWhorter and regular fixture at Yale College may be found in Moseley, ed., *Diary (1843-1852) of James Hadley*, esp. pp. 11-12, 61, 97, 289, 313 n. 1.

50. After considering Leonard Bacon's charges against MacWhorter, the New Haven West Association adopted the following resolution by a vote of 12 to 11: "Resolved, 1ˢᵗ, That action in this case by this body is deemed unnecessary; by which we do not intend to imply that what the aforesaid licentiate [MacWhorter] has reported of the relative [Delia Bacon] of the complainant [Leonard Bacon] is true. Resolved, 2dly, That as, in the view of some members of this Association, the aforesaid licentiate [MacWhorter] has been in a greater or a less degree imprudent, that a committee of three . . . give, with Christian and paternal kindness, such admonition to him, as in their view the case may require." Though MacWhorter seems to have escaped this scandal with relatively little damage, however, his new father-in-law, among others, appears have treated him with contempt for years to come. Mr. Blake, for example, was said "never to have addressed remarks directly to his son-in-law even at the family table." See Moseley, ed., *Diary of James Hadley*, p. 313 n.1.

51. Moseley, ed., *Diary of James Hadley*, p. 289.

52. Catharine Beecher to Lyman Beecher, January 1, 1823, in Lyman Beecher's *Autobiography*, 1: 368–74. On Catharine Beecher's life and ministry, see esp. Sklar, *Catharine Beecher*; and Mae Elizabeth Harveson, *Catharine Esther Beecher: Pioneer Educator* (Philadelphia: University of Pennsylvania Press, 1932). Cf. Caskey, *Chariot of Fire*; and Milton Rugoff, *The Beechers: An American Family in the Nineteenth Century* (New York: Harper and Row, 1981). Compounding Beecher's grief and confusion over the loss of her fiancé was the fact that Fisher, a young adjunct professor of natural history and philosophy at Yale, had never testified to a conversion experience—and Beecher feared that she would not see him again in heaven.

53. Catharine E. Beecher, *Letters on the Difficulties of Religion* (Hartford, Conn.: Belknap & Hammersly, 1836); QCS 8 (December 1836): 671, where the Taylorites refer to Beecher's *Letters* as "a volume well worthy of attentive perusal," "deserving of all praise,"and suggest that "even those who are not willing to admit all her conclusions, will not, we think, say, that she is unfair in her statements, or wanting in ingenuity in her mode of meeting the difficulties which she aims to remove"; and Catharine E. Beecher, ed., *The Biographical Remains of Rev. George Beecher, Late Pastor of a Church in Chillicothe, Ohio, and Former Pastor of a Church in Rochester, New-York* (New York: Leavitt, Trow, and Co., 1844). On the main contours of Catharine Beecher's theology, which has never been interpreted well, see Mark David Hall, "Catharine Beecher: America's First Female Philosopher and Theologian," *Fides et Historia* 32 (Winter/Spring 2000): 65–80; Sklar, *Catharine Beecher*; and Caskey, *Chariot of Fire*, pp. 71–100.

54. Nathaniel W. Taylor to Lyman Beecher, October 12, 1850, Beecher Collection, Stowe-Day Foundation, Hartford.

55. Sklar, *Catharine Beecher*, p. 189; and Catharine E. Beecher, *Common Sense Applied to Religion, or, The Bible and the People* (New York: Harper and Brothers, 1857).

56. Beecher, *Common Sense Applied to Religion*, pp. 297, 306–8. Cf. Beecher's next major work of theology, *An Appeal to the People in Behalf of Their Rights as Authorized Interpreters of the Bible* (New York: Harper and Bros., 1860), in which, amazingly, she claimed continuity with Edwards himself, stating that her views comported with those in his *Dissertation Concerning the End for Which God Created the World* (p. 204). Note, too, that, as Hedrick, *Harriet Beecher Stowe*, p. 278, has shown, Beecher solicited Taylor's counsel regarding *Common Sense* before it was published, wanting to know if she had represented his views fairly. Taylor replied that she had not and suggested some revisions. But though she later claimed to have incorporated his suggested revisions verbatim, Beecher still managed to misconstrue his views. Significantly, Hedrick fails to recognize the theological confusion that Beecher generated, and so suggests that "in all likelihood the real issue was Catharine's usurpation of the male ministerial role by writing a volume of systematic theology."

57. Lyman Beecher to Nathaniel W. Taylor, December 1850, in Beecher's *Autobiography*, 2: 407.

58. On Taylor's final months, see esp. Dutton, "A Sketch of the Life and Character of Rev. Nathaniel W. Taylor," pp. 252, 265 (quotation from p. 265); Goodrich, "Obituary Notice," pp. 41–43 (first printed in the *New Haven Daily Palladium*, March 10, 1858); and Bacon, "A Sermon at the Funeral of Nathaniel W. Taylor, D.D.," p. 10. For Taylor's resignation from Yale, see Nathaniel W. Taylor to the Rev. President and Fellows of Yale College, July 13, 1857, Folder 29, Box 5, Divinity School Papers, SML.

59. Dutton, "A Sketch of the Life and Character of Rev. Nathaniel W. Taylor," pp. 265–66; and Fisher, "A Sermon Preached in the Chapel of Yale College, March 14, 1858," pp. 15, 37.

60. Bacon, "A Sermon at the Funeral of Nathaniel W. Taylor, D.D.," p. 3. Subsequent funeral orations were preached at the North Church and the College Chapel.

61. Examples of Park's historical reclamation efforts include Park, "The New England Theology"; Park's *Memoir* of Samuel Hopkins in *The Works of Samuel Hopkins, D.D.*; Park, ed., *The Atonement*; Park, *Memoir of Nathanael Emmons*; and Edwards A. Park, *The Life and Character of Leonard Woods, D.D, LL.D.* (Andover, Mass.: W. F. Draper, 1880). On Park's attempt to paper over the internal dissensions within the Edwardsian tradition, see also Conforti, "Edwards A. Park and the Creation of the New England Theology"; and Anthony C. Cecil, Jr., *The Theological Development of Edwards Amasa Park: Last of the "Consistent Calvinists"* (Missoula, Mont.: Scholars' Press, 1974). On the rise of "progressive orthodoxy," consult Daniel Day Williams, *The Andover Liberals: A Study in American Theology* (Morningside Heights, N.Y.: King's Crown Press, 1941); Frank Hugh Foster, *The Modern Movement in American Theology: Sketches in the History of American Protestant Thought from the Civil War to the World War* (New York: Fleming H. Revell Company, 1939); William R. Hutchison, *The Modernist Impulse in American Protestantism* (Cambridge, Mass: Harvard University Press, 1976); and Gary Dorrien, *The Making of American Liberal Theology: Imagining Progressive Religion* (Louisville, Ky.: Westminster John Knox Press, 2001).

62. On this period of transition at Yale, see esp. Foster's chapter "The Later New Haven Theology," in *A Genetic History of the New England Theology*, pp. 401–29; and Louise L. Stevenson, *Scholarly Means to Evangelical Ends: The New Haven Scholars and the Transformation of Higher Learning in America, 1830–1890* (Baltimore, Md.: Johns Hopkins University Press, 1986).

63. Munger, "Dr. Nathaniel W. Taylor—Master Theologian," p. 240. On this theme, much else could be cited. But see esp. the insightful comments of Taylor's younger colleagues at Yale: Fisher, "Historical Address," pp. 21–24; Porter, "Dr. Taylor and His Theology," p. 98; and George P. Fisher, *History of Christian Doctrine* (Edinburgh: T. and T. Clark, 1949; 1896), p. 437.

64. See Bruce Kuklick, *The Rise of American Philosophy: Cambridge, Massachusetts 1860–1930* (New Haven, Conn.: Yale University Press, 1977), pp. 24–25; and Bruce Kuklick, *Churchmen and Philosophers: From Jonathan Edwards to John Dewey* (New Haven, Conn.: Yale University Press, 1985), p. 223.

65. For only the most recent example, see Nicholas Wolterstorff, *Thomas Reid and the Story of Epistemology* (Cambridge: Cambridge University Press, 2001).

66. The naive nonchalance of Edwards A. Park was rather typical. In a letter to New England liberal George A. Gordon at century's end, Park wrote: "I have no great fear of theistic evolution; but I do not believe that when the advocates of it are agreed among themselves they will regard it as justifying any great revolution in theology." Edwards A. Park to George Angier Gordon, March 30, 1897, Edwards Amasa Park Papers, Trask. Park never accepted evolutionary theory. But he was not threatened by it either. Believing that all truth is God's truth, he contended casually that whatever truths Darwinism might contain could be reconciled easily with theology.

Chapter 8

1. First epigraph taken from Thomas E. Buckley, S.J., ed., *"If You Love That Lady Don't Marry Her": The Courtship Letters of Sally McDowell and John Miller, 1854–1856* (Columbia: University of Missouri Press, 2000).

2. On this theme, see esp. David W. Kling and Douglas A. Sweeney, eds., *Jonathan Edwards in Historical Memory* (Columbia: University of South Carolina Press, 2003); and Conforti, *Jonathan Edwards, Religious Tradition, and American Culture.*

3. Shils, *Tradition*, p. 258.

4. Conkin, *Uneasy Center*, p. 220.

5. In a chapter entitled "The Later New Haven Theology," in *A Genetic History of the New England Theology*, pp. 401–29, Frank Hugh Foster discussed Taylor's influence at Yale during the remainder of the nineteenth century. Stevenson, *Scholarly Means to Evangelical Ends*, offers an expert account of the secularization at Yale after Taylor, an account expanded upon in a spate of recent literature on the secularization of the academy in America, esp. George M. Marsden and B. J. Longfield, eds., *The Secularization of the Academy* (New York: Oxford University Press, 1992); George M. Marsden, *The Soul of the American University: From Protestant Establishment to Established Non-Belief* (New York: Oxford University Press, 1994); and Jon H. Roberts and James Turner, *The Sacred and the Secular University* (Princeton, N.J.: Princeton University Press, 2000).

6. Fisher, "Historical Address," p. 28.

7. On Porter, see esp. George P. Fisher, "Theological Opinions," Edward A. Smith, "As a Theological Teacher," and W. W. Andrews, "Student at Yale," all in Merriam, ed., *Noah Porter*, pp. 102–6, 110–111, 17–22; and Stevenson, *Scholarly Means to Evangelical Ends*, p. 172, n. 10. And on Bacon's Taylorism, see Bacon, *Leonard Bacon*, pp. 122–41, 153–55 (quotation from p. 123); and George B. Stevens, *The Life, Letters, and Journals of the Rev. and Hon. Peter Parker, M.D.* (Boston: Congregational Sunday-School and Publishing Society, 1896), p. 51.

8. Perry Miller, "The New England Conscience," in John Crowell and Stanford J. Searl, Jr., eds., *The Responsibility of Mind in a Civilization of Machines: Essays by Perry Miller* (Amherst: University of Massachusetts Press, 1979), p. 185. Cf. William T. Dwight's discussion of the role of the New England Theology in the development of "the New England character," in his *Characteristics of New England Theology: A Discourse, Delivered at the First Public Anniversary of the Congregational Board of Publication, at the Tremont Temple, Boston* (Boston: Congregational Board of Publication, 1855), pp. 28–32. I will survey the highlights of the Taylorite exportation of this conscience or character below. An excellent recent evocation of this export not tied directly to the Taylorites may be found in Robert M. Crunden, *Ministers of Reform: The Progressives' Achievement in American Civilization, 1889–1920* (New York: Basic Books, 1982), esp. pp. 3–15.

9. John H. Giltner, *Moses Stuart: The Father of Biblical Science in America*, Biblical Scholarship in North America (Atlanta, Ga.: Scholars Press, 1988), pp. 111–15 (quotation from pp. 112–13). For more on Stuart and his views, consult Edwards A. Park, "Moses Stuart," in Park's *Memorial Collection of Sermons*, compiled by Agnes Park (Boston: Pilgrim Press, 1902), pp. 177–217; and William Adams, *A Discourse on the Life and Services of Professor Moses Stuart; Delivered in the City of New-York: Sabbath Evening, January 25, 1852* (New York: John F. Trow, 1852).

10. Though this claim will strike some as revisionary, I am not the first to suggest that Park was largely a follower of the Taylorites. See also Kuklick, *Churchmen and Philosophers*, pp. 211–14; Cecil, Jr., *The Theological Development of Edwards Amasa Park*, esp. pp. 268–69; and Foster, *Genetic History of the New England Theology*, pp. 473ff.

11. Significantly, Hatch, *Personal Reminiscences and Memorials*, p. 41, noted that Park was a regular preacher at Yale's College Church. And as is evident in correspondence received by Park from his father (the Rev. Calvin Park of Stoughton, Massachusetts, formerly a professor of languages, moral philosophy, and metaphysics at Brown University, and a student, friend, and

admirer of Nathanael Emmons), both father and son took an early interest in Taylor's *Concio.* See Calvin Park to Edwards A. Park, January 30, 1829 and March 31, 1829, Park Family Papers, C. R. Park family, Nashville. On Park's dissatisfaction with Woods and appreciation for Taylor, see Cecil, pp. 33–35; and Foster, *A Genetic History of the New England Theology,* p. 473. On the resistance offered by Andover's old guard (including Woods, trustee Daniel Dana, and at times even Moses Stuart) to Park's theological agenda, see Foster, *The Life of Edwards Amasa Park,* p. 118; and Cecil, pp. 52–53. Park's adoption of essentially Taylorite views becomes most clear upon the inspection of the extant student notebooks of his theological lectures. (Though he never published a systematic presentation of his views, in his lectures, year in and year out, Park dealt with the main loci of evangelical theology.) While it would take too much space to cite all the instances of Taylorism in Park's lectures, the following is a list of some of the instances found in two of the notebooks held at Andover and one notebook held at the Essex Institute: on the doctrine of original sin, see Gabriel H. DeBevoise's student notebook, class of 1864, 2 vols., Student Notebooks—E. A. Park, Trask (hereafter GHD), 2: 272, 298–99, and Park's Lectures, Trask (hereafter PL), vol. 4, unpaginated; on predestination and theodicy, see GHD, 2: 33, and Cha[rle]s H. Trask, ms., "An Abstract of Lectures by Prof. E. A. Park, Andover Theological Seminary 1846-1848, Ms. Sermons, EI, pp. 111-15; on predominant and subordinate volition, see GHD, 2: 87–88; on the atonement and on regeneration, see PL, vol. 6, unpaginated (significantly, however, while Park agrees with Taylor that, in regeneration, "the change of nature [and] of the will are both included in one complex state of mind," he does not echo Taylor's teaching on the suspension of the selfish principle).

12. On Parks's habit of employing the methodological and hermeneutical principles discussed in his famous essay "The Theology of the Intellect and That of the Feelings," *BS* 7 (July 1850): 533–69 to paper over disagreements among Edwardsians, see Cecil, pp. 214–15, 222–23, 232–33. Cf. my "Edwards and His Mantle," pp. 97–100. As alluded to earlier, Park did invent a certain seamlessness for *his* Edwardsian tradition that his critics found misleading and naive, but he did not invent the tradition of the New England Theology per se, at least not any more so than Edwards's improvers had always done. On the significance of the invention of tradition in the modern west, see Eric Hobsbawm and Terence Ranger, eds., *The Invention of Tradition* (Cambridge: Cambridge University Press, 1983).

13. Tylerite fears were not unfounded. Such attempts to accommodate the evangelistic pragmatism of clergy west of the Appalachians led to the deletion of the word "Calvinism" from the Congregationalist "Statement of Faith" at the National Council of Congregational Churches held in Boston in 1865. See the *Debates and Proceedings of the National Council of Congregational Churches, Held at Boston, Mass., June 14–24, 1865. From the Phonographic Report by J. M. W. Yerrinton and Henry M. Parkhurst* (Boston: American Congregatinal Association, 1866).

14. On the Albany Convention, which Taylor himself did not attend (but at which Leonard Bacon played a leading role), see esp. *Proceedings of the General Convention of Congregational Ministers and Delegates in the United States, Held at Albany, N.Y., on the 5th, 6th, 7th and 8th of October, 1852. Together with the Sermon Preached on the Occasion, by Rev. Joel Hawes, D.D.* (New York: S. W. Benedict, 1852). The cooperative spirit pervading the Convention was occasioned in part by fears that Congregationalist home missions were being co-opted by Presbyterians under the terms of the Plan of Union (1801), which is discussed more fully later. In fact, these fears led to the virtual abrogation of the Plan of Union by the Congregationalists in a set of resolutions passed in Albany (see the *Proceedings,* pp. 19–20, 69–76). Delegate Edward Lawrence (a minister in Marblehead, Massachusetts) represented the fears of most: "Here, then, we have a Plan of Union, but substantially in its elements, and in its original workings, a Presbyterian institution. I would not speak of it in any way to disparage our Presbyterian brethren. I love them. They have often come from the West to our New England, and ranged over our fat pastures, and borne away the fleeces from our flocks; they have milked our Congregational cows,

but they have made nothing but Presbyterian butter and cheese. (Laughter.) Of this I do not complain. . . . but when they insist on a monopoly, when they would allow no other denomination to bring the brick and the shingles and the nails from New England, to put them into a Congregational edifice, we think they go too far" (p. 71).

15. As documented in Wayland, *The Theological Department in Yale College*, pp. 119–48, the vast majority of Taylor's 815 students became ministers, one-fourth of these ministers settling west of Pennsylvania (mostly in Ohio and Illinois). Significantly, Wayland also notes that 40 of Taylor's students became businessmen, 29 became foreign missionaries, 26 became teachers, 22 entered government service (18 of these 22 were also ministers), and 18 became doctors or lawyers.

16. Blake, *Chronicles of New Haven Green*, pp. 103–4. On the Edwardsian/Taylorite missions to the Hawaiian Islands, see also Rufus Anderson, *The Hawaiian Islands: Their Progress and Condition under Missionary Labors* (Boston: Gould and Lincoln, 1864); Rufus Anderson, *History of the Sandwich Islands Missions* (Boston: Congregational Publishing, 1870); Sylvester K. Stevens, *American Expansion in Hawaii, 1842–1898* (Harrisburg, Penn.: Archives Publishing, 1945); Bradford Smith, *Yankees in Paradise: The New England Impact on Hawaii* (Philadelphia: J. B. Lippincott, 1956); Charles De Varigny, *Fourteen Years in the Sandwich Islands, 1855–1868*, trans. Alfons L. Korn (Honolulu: University Press of Hawaii, 1981); and Mary Zwiep, *Pilgrim Path: The First Company of Women Missionaries to Hawaii* (Madison: University of Wisconsin Press, 1991).

17. On Sturtevant and other Taylorites/Edwardsians in the Mississippi Valley, see Sturtevant, *An Autobiography*; C. Ephraim Adams, *The Iowa Band*, rev. ed. (Boston: Pilgrim Press, [1868]), which focuses primarily on Andover Seminary's contributions in the region; as well as the works cited in chapter 3, n. 84. On Sturtevant's heresy trial, see Timothy David Whelan, "Julian M. Sturtevant (1805–1886)," in George H. Shriver, ed., *Dictionary of Heresy Trials in American Christianity* (Westport, Conn.: Greenwood Press, 1997), pp. 402–10.

18. On Barnes, see Gabriel, *Religion and Learning at Yale*, pp. 144–45.

19. Notably, 121 of the 275 ships that made it to San Francisco in 1849 had sailed from New England ports. On Joseph Benton and the religious culture of early California, see Kenneth L. Janzen, "The Transformation of the New England Religious Tradition in California, 1849–1869" (Ph.D. diss., Claremont Graduate School and University Center, 1964), who emphasizes Taylor's influence in California on pp. 103–31; as well as John Wright Buckham and Charles Sumner Nash, eds., *Religion on the Pacific Slope* (Boston: Pilgrim Press, 1917); William Ferrier, *Pioneer Church Beginnings and Educational Movements in California* (Berkeley, Calif.: n.p., 1927); Kevin Starr, *Americans and the California Dream, 1850–1915* (New York: Oxford University Press, 1973), esp. chapter 3, "City on a Hill," pp. 69–109; and Laurie F. Maffly-Kipp, *Religion and Society in Frontier California* (New Haven, Conn.: Yale University Press, 1994).

20. The literature on the exportation of New England culture is vast. See esp. Lois Kimball Mathews, *The Expansion of New England: The Spread of New England Settlements and Institutions to the Mississippi River, 1620–1865* (Boston: Houghton Mifflin, 1909); William Warren Sweet, *Religion on the American Frontier: The Congregationalists* (Chicago: University of Chicago Press, 1939); Stewart H. Holbrook, *The Yankee Exodus: An Account of Migration from New England* (New York: Macmillan, 1950); Whitney R. Cross, *The Burned-Over District: The Social and Intellectual History of Enthusiastic Religion in Western New York, 1800–1850* (Ithaca, N.Y.: Cornell University Press, 1950); Susan E. Gray, *The Yankee West: Community Life on the Michigan Frontier* (Chapel Hill: University of North Carolina Press, 1996); and John T. Foster, Jr., and Sarah Whitmer Foster, *Beechers, Stowes, and Yankee Strangers: The Transformation of Florida*, The Florida History and Culture Series (Gainesville: University Press of Florida, 1999), which discusses the exportation of New England culture to Reconstruction-era Florida. On the notion that the exportation of New England culture was always contested, negotiated, and never represented a simple transplantation or imposition of New England values on these "frontiers," see esp. Amy

DeRogatis, "Moral Geography: The Plan of Union Mission to the Western Reserve, 1787–1833" (Ph.D. diss., University of North Carolina at Chapel Hill, 1998).

21. Wayland, *The Theological Department in Yale College*, pp. 119–48.

22. Crocker (who served as a delegate from the General Association of Connecticut to the infamous Presbyterian General Assembly of 1837), *The Catastrophe of the Presbyterian Church*, pp. 6–46, has also provided the best source available on the history of the Plan of Union. Cf. William S. Kennedy, *The Plan of Union* (Hudson, Ohio: Pentagon Steam Press, 1856); and Walker, *The Creeds and Platforms of Congregationalism*, pp. 524–41 (Walker provides a helpful, though now rather dated, bibliography on the Plan of Union on p. 524). For the Old School abrogation of the Plan of Union at the 1837 General Assembly, see *Minutes of the General Assembly of the Presbyterian Church in the United States of America, From A.D. 1821 to A.D. 1837 Inclusive* (Philadelphia: Presbyterian Board of Publication and Sabbath-School Work, n.d.), esp. pp. 604–14. While New School Presbyterianism was not entirely a Northern phenomenon (indeed, through the ministry of Hopkinsians such as Hezekiah Balch and Charles Coffin of Greenville/Tusculum College, Indian missionary Gideon Blackburn, and Isaac Anderson of Southern and Western Theological Seminary/Maryville College, it permeated even the young Synod of Tennessee), it was imbued with the New Haven Theology. Of the many useful sources on the role of the New England Theology generally and Taylorism in particular on the Old School–New School Presbyterian divide, see esp. Pope, *New England Calvinism and the Disruption of the Presbyterian Church*; and Marsden, *The Evangelical Mind and the New School Presbyterian Experience*. On Balch, see AAP, 3: 308–19; Leah M. Brown, *Rev. Hezekiah Balch, D.D., 1741–1810: A Biography* (Milwaukie, Or.: privately published, 1988); Thompson, *Presbyterians in the South, Volume One: 1607–1861*, 352–54, 409; Marsden, *The Evangelical Mind and the New School Presbyterian Experience*, pp. 40–41; and Guelzo, *Edwards on the will* pp. 197–98. On Coffin, Blackburn, and Anderson, see esp. AAP, 4: 43–58, 246–56, and the sources cited in chapter 2, n. 71. On New School Presbyterianism in the South, see also Thompson, *Presbyterians in the South, Volume One: 1607–1861*, pp. 269–72, 353–55, 410–11; Smith, "The Doctrine of Imputation and the Presbyterian Schism of 1837–1838," pp. 129–51; and the related documents in William Warren Sweet, *Religion on the American Frontier, 1783–1840, Vol. 2, The Presbyterians* (New York: Cooper Square Publishers, 1964; 1936), pp. 862–85.

23. On the heresy trials of Beecher and Barnes, see esp. Daryl Fisher-Ogden, "Albert Barnes (1798–1870)," and Bernard H. Cochran, "Lyman Beecher (1775–1863)," in Shriver, ed., *Dictionary of Heresy Trials in American Christianity*, pp. 11–20, 27–37. For Taylorite support of Barnes's Edwardsianism, see "Case of the Rev. Mr. Barnes," QCS 3 (June 1831): 292–336. On the New School/New England proclivities of the early faculty members at Union Seminary, see esp. George Lewis Prentiss, *The Union Theological Seminary in the City of New York: Historical and Biogaphical Sketches of Its First Fifty Years* (New York: Anson D. F. Randolph and Co., 1889), pp. 34–44; and G. L. Prentiss, *The Union Theological Seminary in the City of New York: Its Design and Another Decade of Its History. With a Sketch of the Life and Public Services of Charles Butler, LL.D.* (Asbury Park, N.J.: M., W., and C. Pennypacker, 1899), pp. 7–12.

24. The classic presentation of the former view is C. Bruce Staiger, "Abolitionism and the Presbyterian Church Schism, 1837–1838," *The Mississippi Valley Historical Review* 36 (December 1949), who argues (pp. 391ff.) that "if it had not been for the developments concerning slavery in the Assemblies of 1835 and 1836, the break would never have occurred." But see also the less strident argument of C. C. Goen, *Broken Churches, Broken Nation: Denominational Schisms and the Coming of the Civil War* (Macon, Ga.: Mercer University Press, 1985), pp. 68–78. The best exposition of the latter view is found in Marsden, *The Evangelical Mind and the New School Presbyterian Experience*, pp. 98–99, 250–51. Cf. Elwyn A. Smith, "The Role of the South in the Presbyterian Schism of 1837–38," *Church History* 29 (March 1960): 44–63; and Thompson, *Presbyterians in the South*, 1: 411, 394–99. On the broader history of Edwardsian influence on the Presbyterian Church,

see also Pope, *New England Calvinism and the Disruption of the Presbyterian Church*; and Guelzo, *Edwards on the Will*, pp. 176–207.

25. By 1834, Old School promoters of the "Western Memorial" and "Act and Testimony" had begun to speak out publicly and explicitly against New England at General Assembly. Though the New School defended its orthodoxy in the largely Taylorite "Auburn Declaration" (Auburn Seminary's Edwardsian theologian, James Richards, was president of the Auburn Convention of 1837 at which the "Declaration" was drafted), Old School opponents continued to press for the abrogation of the Plan of Union, as well as the theological culture of the Edwardsians that it had advanced. A written record of the many debates that yielded schism in 1837 may be found in the *Minutes of the General Assembly . . . , From A.D. 1821 to A.D. 1837 Inclusive*, esp. pp. 604–58. The text of the Auburn Declaration remains easily accessible in Philip Schaff, ed., *The Creeds of Christendom, with a History and Critical Notes*, 3 vols. (Grand Rapids, Mich.: Baker Books, 1983; 1931), 3: 777–80. Old School commentators who attributed the schism largely to New England–influenced doctrinal laxity include James Wood, *Old and New Theology; or an Exhibition of Those Differences with Regard to Scripture Doctrines, Which Have Recently Agitated and Now Divided the Presbyterian Church* (Philadelphia: William S. Martien, 1838); Lewis Cheeseman, *Differences between Old and New School Presbyterians* (Rochester, N.Y.: Erastus Darrow, 1848); Baird, *A History of the New School* [1868]; Samuel Miller, ms. "Lecture on [the] Disruption in 1837," n.d., Folder 24, Box 4, Samuel Miller Papers, PSA; and countless essayists in the *Christian Advocate* and *Presbyterian*. New School/New England commentators include Crocker, *The Catastrophe of the Presbyterian Church*; "The Revolution in the Presbyterian Church," *QCS* 9 (December 1837): 597–646; "The Troubles in the Presbyterian Church," *QCS* 10 (May 1838): 337–47, a favorable review of Crocker's book; and E. H. Gillett, *History of the Presbyterian Church in the United States of America* (Philadelphia: Presbyterian Publication Committee, 1864). For an illuminating New England critique of Baird's *History of the New School*, see Leonard Bacon's "The Presbyterian Disruption of 1838," *NE* 28 (January 1869): 137–82.

26. Nathaniel W. Taylor to Lyman Beecher, March 3, 1837, in Beecher's *Autobiography*, 2: 315.

27. Dr. James P. Wilson had asked Taylor to succeed him at Philadelphia's First Presbyterian Church in 1830, moving on to ask Albert Barnes only after Taylor declined. See Bacon, "The Presbyterian Disruption of 1838," pp. 173–74. Of the seven New England Congregationalists sent as delegates to General Assembly in 1838, three (Taylor, as well as the delegates from New Hampshire and Rhode Island) aligned themselves with the New School, while the other four (including the other delegate from Connecticut, the Rev. Peter H. Shaw) refused to align themselves with either Presbyterian body.

28. Bacon, *Seven Letters*, p. 80. For the New School reception of Taylor's speech, see *Minutes of the General Assembly of the Presbyterian Church in the United States of America [New School]. From A.D. 1838 to A.D. 1858, Inclusive. Vol. 1* (Philadelphia: Presbyterian Board of Publication and Sabbath-School Work, 1894), p. 41. For the Old School and Tylerite reaction, see esp. "Dr. Taylor and the Pastoral Union," *The Presbyterian*, August 25, 1838, p. 134, which was reprinted in the Tylerite *Hartford Watchman* (in August 1838), as well as in Bacon's *Seven Letters*, pp. 85–87 (for the purpose of refutation).

29. Pope, *New England Calvinism and the Disruption of the Presbyterian Church*, p. 359. Cf. Douglas M. Strong, *Perfectionist Politics: Abolitionism and the Religious Tensions of American Democracy*, Religion and Politics (Syracuse, N.Y.: Syracuse University Press, 1999), p. 50.

30. The best-known representative of this view is Timothy L. Smith, who associated Finney with Wesleyanism and its Arminianization of American Calvinism. See his "The Doctrine of the Sanctifying Spirit: Charles G. Finney's Synthesis of Wesleyan and Covenant Theology," *Wesleyan Theological Journal* 13 (Spring 1978): 92–113, as well as his *Revivalism and Social Reform*, pp. 108–13.

31. See, for example, Foster, *A Genetic History of the New England Theology*, p. 453; Wayland, *The Theological Department in Yale College*, pp. 343–44; and, more recently, Harold K. Bush,

Jr., *American Declarations: Rebellion and Repentance in American Cultural History* (Urbana: University of Illinois Press, 1999), p. 113.

32. This via media is represented in one form or another by Walker, *A History of the Congregational Churches in the United States*, p. 364; Boardman, *A History of New England Theology*, pp. 275–76; Cross, *The Burned-Over District*, pp. 159–60, 250; Leonard I. Sweet, "The View of Man Inherent in New Measures Revivalism," *Church History* 45 (June 1976): 206–21; Glenn A. Hewitt, *Regeneration and Morality: A Study of Charles Finney, Charles Hodge, John W. Nevin, and Horace Bushnell* (Brooklyn, N.Y.: Carlson 1991), pp. 22–23; Hambrick-Stowe, *Charles G. Finney and the Spirit of American Evangelicalism*, pp. 24, 32–33, 60, 72, 80, 223; Guelzo, "Oberlin Perfectionism and Its Edwardsian Origins, 1835–1870"; and Allen C. Guelzo, "An Heir or a Rebel? Charles Grandison Finney and the New England Theology," *Journal of the Early Republic* 17 (Spring 1997): 61–94, the best overall assessment of the significance of Finney's thought. On the relationship between these interpretaions of Finney and the Wesleyan/Arminian views of his thought, see also "Are There Two Roads to Holiness? Charles G. Finney and the Reinterpretation of Wesleyan/Holiness Origins: A Conversation between Allen Guelzo and Douglas A. Sweeney," *Wesleyan/Holiness Studies Center Bulletin* 6 (Spring 1998): 1–3.

33. As Taylor wrote to Finney in November of 1833, "I have lately heard a report respecting a conversation between you [and] me, the truth of which I wish to investigate. I am directly informed, that Mr. Nettleton has made the following statement, viz.–that you and I had a conversation on the subject of regeneration, special grace, divine moral suasion &c, in which opinions were expressed diverse from those which I have published to the world–that at the close of the conversation I said, 'I believe, brother Finney, that I perfectly agree with you on this subject'–and that you replied, 'why don't you come out [and] say so to the world'–that I answered–'the time hasn't come, the public will not bear it,' or something of like import, meaning that I practiced concealment respecting my theological system. . . . Now, Brother, I have no recollection that any thing ever passed between us out of which such a story could be made, even by any possible perversion. You will be aware, that such a charge of studied concealment of my views of theological doctrine must be deeply injurious to my character, [and] I am sure that you have said nothing to authorize it. I request you therefore, to inform me whether you have ever made to Mr. Nettleton, or to any other person such a statement as the above; or whether you recollect any thing which you have said, which could be perverted into such a representation of what has passed between us. . . . I shall hope to hear from you in reply as soon as possible." Nathaniel W. Taylor to Charles G. Finney, November 3, 1833, Folder "September-December 1833," Box 4, Ser. "Letters and Papers," Finney Papers, Oberlin College Archives.

34. See Beecher's *Autobiography*, 2: 226–27; as well as Asa Rand, *The New Divinity Tried, Being an Examination of a Sermon Delivered by the Rev. C. G. Finney, On Making a New Heart* (Boston: Light and Harris, 1832); *Review of "The New Divinity Tried": Or an Examination of Rev. Mr. Rand's Strictures on a Sermon Delivered by Rev. C. G. Finney, on Making a New Heart* (Boston: Peirce and Parker, 1832); [Benjamin B. Wisner], "Review of Pamphlets on 'The New Divinity,'" *SP* 5 (March 1832): 161–69; Asa Rand, *A Vindication of "The New Divinity Tried," in Reply to a "Review" of the Same. From the "Volunteer"* (Boston: Peirce and Parker, 1832); and [Asa Rand], *Letter to the Rev. Dr. Beecher, on the Influence of His Ministry in Boston* (Lowell, Mass.: Rand and Southmaid, 1833). Much of this material was also printed in Rand's periodical *The Volunteer, Devoted to the Promotion of Revivals, Evangelical Doctrines, and Congregationalism* (Boston: William Hyde and Co., 1832–1833). For another tepid Taylorite defense of Finney's new measures, see "Sprague on Revivals of Religion," *QCS* 5 (March 1833): 41–45, a review of William B. Sprague, *Lectures on Revivals of Religion* (Albany: Packard and Van Benthuysen, 1832).

35. James H. Fairchild, "President Finney–The Preacher, the Teacher, and the Man," in *Reminiscences of Rev. Charles G. Finney. Speeches and Sketches at the Gathering of His Friends and Pupils, in Oberlin, July 28th, 1876, Together with President Fairchild's Memorial Sermon, Delivered*

Before the Graduating Class, July 30, 1876 (Oberlin: E. J. Goodrich, 1876), p. 89. For more of Fairchild's interpretation of Finney's connection to New Haven and Edwards, see James Harris Fairchild, "Oberlin Theology," Box 29, J. H. Fairchild Papers, Oberlin College Archives. Cf. George F. Wright, "President Finney's Theological System and Its General Influence," in *Reminiscences of Rev. Charles G. Finney*, pp. 68–76; and George Clark, "Remarks of Rev. George Clark, of Oberlin," in Reminiscences of Rev. Charles G. Finney, p. 49, who noted that he had "first met Mr. Finney at the house of Dr. Taylor, in New Haven" (c. 1836).

36. On Finney's evangelical feminism, see Nancy A. Hardesty, *Your Daughters Shall Prophesy: Revivalism and Feminism in the Age of Finney*, Chicago Studies in the History of American Religion (Brooklyn, N.Y.: Carlson 1991); and Donald W. Dayton, *Discovering an Evangelical Heritage* (Peabody, Mass.: Hendrickson 1976), pp. 85–98. On the importance of Finneyite/Taylorite theology for evangelical abolitionism, see esp. Lawrence Thomas Lesick, *The Lane Rebels: Evangelicalism and Antislavery in Antebellum America*, Studies in Evangelicalism, No. 2 (Metuchen, N.J.: Scarecrow Press, 1980), pp. 84–88; Robert H. Abzug, *Passionate Liberator: Theodore Dwight Weld and the Dilema of Reform* (New York: Oxford University Press, 1980); and Sloan, *Perfectionist Politics*, pp. 27–29, 71–72, who also discusses Taylor's connection, through Finney, to Liberty Party politics. Cf. *A Statement of the Reasons Which Induced the Students of Lane Theological Seminary to Dissolve Their Connection with That Institution* (Cincinnati, Ohio: n.p., 1834).

37. On Taylorite/evangelical influence on immediate abolitionism generally and on Garrison in particular, see Anne C. Loveland, "Evangelicalism and 'Immediate Emancipation' in American Antislavery Thought," *Journal of Southern History* 32 (May 1966): 172–88; John L. Thomas, *The Liberator: William Lloyd Garrison* (Boston: Little, Brown, 1963), pp. 56–59, 163–64, 227–35; and Henry Mayer, *All on Fire: William Lloyd Garrison and the Abolition of Slavery* (New York: St. Martin's Press, 1998), pp. xix–xx, 213–39. On Garrison's later move away from evangelicalism, see esp. William L. Van Deburg, "William Lloyd Garrison and the 'Pro-Slavery Priesthood': The Changing Beliefs of an Evangelical Reformer, 1830–1840," *Journal of the American Academy of Religion* 43 (June 1975): 224–37. On a similar transition at Oberlin toward the end of the nineteenth century, see also John Barnard, *From Evangelicalism to Progressivism at Oberlin College, 1866–1917* (Columbus: Ohio State University Press, 1969). Cf. Lewis Perry, *Radical Abolitionism: Anarchy and the Government of God in Antislavery Thought* (Ithaca, N.Y.: Cornell University Press, 1973), on the relationship between moral government theory and antislavery reform.

38. For Noyes's reliance on Taylor's thought, see the *Confessions of John H. Noyes, Part I, Confession of Religious Experience: Including a History of Modern Perfectionism* (Oneida Reserve: Leonard and Company, Printers, 1849), esp. pp. 12, 19, 26. And consult Robert David Thomas, *The Man Who Would Be Perfect: John Humphrey Noyes and the Utopian Impulse* (Philadelphia: University of Pennsylvania Press, 1977), pp. 13–49; and Robert Allerton Parker, *A Yankee Saint: John Humphrey Noyes and the Oneida Community* (New York: G. P. Putnam's Sons, 1935), pp. 21–30.

39. On the Edwardsian roots of the liberal theology of the later nineteenth century, see esp. the works of Frank Hugh Foster, and Williams, *The Andover Liberals*. Among several fine works that discuss Pragmatism's roots in Congregational New England, see Paul K. Conkin, *Puritans and Pragmatists: Eight Eminent American Thinkers* (New York: Dodd, Mead, and Company, 1968); Kuklick, *Churchmen and Philosophers*; and many of the writings of John E. Smith, most recently, *Jonathan Edwards: Puritan, Preacher, Philosopher* (Notre Dame, Ind.: University of Notre Dame Press, 1992). For a discussion of the progressives that is most sensitive to their religious roots (often in Edwardsian New England), see Crunden, *Ministers of Reform*.

40. Munger, "Dr. Nathaniel W. Taylor—Master Theologian," p. 236. Munger went on to make clear his mentor's repudation of Taylor's doctrine: "Bushnell learned much from Dr. Taylor,

but it was chiefly a mass of theological material from which he dissented, or which he reinterpreted into such form and meaning as to be almost another gospel. The two men had little in common except native gifts of character. . . . When it came to thought, they lived in different worlds" (pp. 239–40). Cf. Theodore T. Munger, *Horace Bushnell: Preacher and Theologian* (Boston: Houghton, Mifflin, and Company, 1899), pp. 40–43, where we read that the relationship between Taylor and Bushnell "was close, but it was not sympathetic. . . . From the first [Bushnell] had been an alien to the school of Edwards," even that Taylor and Bushnell "were not within hailing distance, hardly on the same side of the planet." Apparently, Taylor himself would have agreed with this assessment. According to a "Review of Current Literature," *Christian Examiner* 80 (March 1866): 277, "Dr. Taylor used to say, in the rough fashion which was gladly tolerated in him, 'Bushnell don't know any thing.'"

41. Stokes, *Memorials of Eminent Yale Men*, 1: 67.

42. On this theme, see, for example, Taylor, *Concio ad Clerum*, pp. 37–39; and Fitch, *Two Discourses on the Nature of Sin*, pp. 32–34. Mead, *The Lively Experiment: The Shaping of Christianity in America* (New York: Harper and Row, 1963), p. 124, contended (exaggeratedly) that Taylor "almost made 'preachableness' in revivals normative for doctrines."

43. See esp. Kling and Sweeney, eds., *Jonathan Edwards in Historical Memory*.

44. [Stowe], "New England Ministers," p. 487. For more on the widespread reception and appropriation of Edwardsianism throughout American culture in the nineteenth and twentieth centuries, see Joseph A. Conforti, *Jonathan Edwards, Religious Tradition, and American Culture: From the Second Great Awakening to the Twentieth Century* (Chapel Hill: University of North Carolina Press, 1995). For the vivid and recurring image of Edwards in modern American intellectual and literary history, see the following works by Donald Weber: "The Image of Jonathan Edwards in American Culture" (Ph.D. diss., Columbia University, 1978); "Perry Miller and the Recovery of Jonathan Edwards," in Perry Miller, *Jonathan Edwards* (Amherst: University of Massachusetts Press, 1981), pp. v–xxv; "The Figure of Jonathan Edwards," *American Quarterly* 35 (Winter 1983): 556–64; and "The Recovery of Jonathan Edwards," in Hatch and Stout, eds., *Jonathan Edwards and the American Experience*, pp. 50–70. See also Daniel B. Shea, "Jonathan Edwards: The First Two Hundred Years," *Journal of American Studies* 14 (August 1980): 181–97; and esp. M. X. Lesser, "Jonathan Edwards in Praise and Verse," a paper delivered at the conference on "The Writings of Jonathan Edwards: Text and Context, Text and Interpretation," Bloomington, Indiana, 1994.

45. See esp. Marsden's *The Soul of the American University: From Protestant Establishment to Established Non-Belief*.

46. George M. Marsden, "The New School Heritage and Presbyterian Fundamentalism," *Westminster Theological Journal* 32 (May 1970): 129–47.

47. The definitive history of this revival is Long's *The Revival of 1857–58*.

48. Between 1776 and 1850, Congregationalists declined in number from 20.4 percent of all religious adherents in the United States to 4.0 percent of these adherents. See Finke and Stark, *The Churching of America*, p. 55.

49. "Meeting of Alumni of Yale Theological Seminary," *The Independent* (August 7, 1856): 256. On the role of the Methodists in this transformation of evangelical spirituality and cultural authority, see esp. Hatch, *The Democratization of American Christianity*; and Wigger, *Taking Heaven by Storm*.

50. Wright, "Professor Goodrich and the Growth and Outcome of the Revival Movement," pp. 93–94. The day of prayer for colleges was an annual event held on the last Thursday in February, which in 1858 fell on February 25. Many thanks to Kathryn Long for this piece of information.

51. Mitchell, *The Great Awakening*, p. 51.

Index